W9-BGF-503

SOCIAL SECURITY

The Unfinished Work

The Hoover Institution gratefully acknowledges
Paul H. and Elisabeth E. Bauer
for their significant support of this publication.

SOCIAL SECURITY

The Unfinished Work

Charles Blahous

HOOVER INSTITUTION PRESS
Stanford University | Stanford, California

Hoover Institution Press Publication No. 595

Hoover Institution at Leland Stanford Junior University,
Stanford, California, 94305-6010

First printing 2010
16 15 14 13 12 11 10   9 8 7 6 5 4 3 2 1

Manufactured in the United States of America

The paper used in this publication meets the minimum
Requirements of the American National Standard for
Information Sciences—Permanence of Paper for Printed
Library Materials, ANSI/NISO Z39.48-1992. ∞

Cataloging-in-Publication Data is available from
the Library of Congress
ISBN 978-0-8179-1194-2 (cloth)
ISBN 978-0-8179-1196-6 (e-book)

CONTENTS

LIST OF FIGURES AND TABLES

Figures

Tables

ACKNOWLEDGMENTS

THIS BOOK WAS MADE POSSIBLE by a grant from the Smith Richardson Foundation. I am greatly indebted to Mark Steinmeyer of the Foundation for his helpful guidance in turning my rough initial proposal into a final form worthy of support.

Thanks as well to John Raisian and the Hoover Institution for their efforts in seeing this book through to publication. Hoover dedicated the work of an extremely talented team of professionals to the effort, including Barbara Arellano, Marshall Blanchard, Tess Evans, Sarah Farber, Shana Farley, Stephen Langlois, LaNor Maune, Jennifer Navarrette, Christie Parell, Jennifer Presley, Julie Ruggiero, Eryn Witcher, and Ann Wood. Especial thanks go to Barbara Egbert, whose exceptional editing talents were indispensable in improving upon my original draft.

I greatly appreciate the many helpful suggestions on the text provided by (alphabetically) Andrew Biggs, Keith Hennessey, Donald Marron, Dick Parsons, Korok Ray, and Syl Schieber.

Many thanks to my beloved wife, Jill Hauser, whose unfailing love, support, and patience were well supplemented by her astute and objective counsel.

Thanks also to the Hudson Institute and, in particular, to its CEO, Ken Weinstein, for providing me with institutional and moral support during the writing of the book.

Throughout my professional career, I have been blessed by wonderful bosses who treated me with unfailing generosity and served as inspiring examples. I am deeply grateful first and foremost to President George W. Bush, U.S. Senator Judd Gregg, and U.S. Senator Alan Simpson. Within the White House, I was extremely fortunate to serve four remarkable directors of the National Economic Council—Larry Lindsey, Steve Friedman, Al Hubbard, and Keith Hennessey—whose dedication to the public good, knowledge, faith, and support enabled me to learn much of what is presented here.

The list of colleagues to whom I owe a great professional or personal debt is too long to summon here and I ask their forgiveness for my failure to name them. The faults and flaws of the text that follows derive from me alone, while any wisdom in it has been amassed from the contributions of countless individuals.

INTRODUCTION

I F YOU ATTEND A SUFFICIENT NUMBER of fiscal policy roundtable discussions in Washington, D.C., you'll eventually hear one of the participating experts say, "I think that everything on this subject has been said, just not by me"—after which he or she will repeat (while visibly straining to rephrase) everything the others have been saying for the last hour.

This is an inevitable ritual. After all, facts are facts; even experts of opposing philosophies are often bound to acknowledge those same facts and thus to repeat one another. And so, too, experts are experts; even if he's the last one to speak, the typical Washington analyst just can't resist putting his two cents into every discussion.

On Social Security, it sometimes seems as though everything has been said dozens of times. Over the past two decades, there have been countless books, articles, and advisory panel reports, all purporting to explain the program's operations and finances. Many of these argue for (and against) specific measures to ensure adequate program financing. More than a few of them portray Social Security as being under threat from the designs of others with wrongheaded or malicious ideas.

Based on more than fifteen years of work on Social Security policy, first in the U.S. Senate and later in the White House, I have reached the opposite conclusion: everything has *not* been said—far from it. I believe that there *is* a dire need for another Social Security book, and in particular for a fundamentally different kind of book than those published to date.

Perhaps the best way to explain what makes this Social Security book different from others is to describe what it is *not*:

This book is not a general history of the Social Security program.

This is not a book that argues why one philosophical approach to Social Security policy is correct, nor why different approaches are sinister and destructive.

This is not a book that tabulates different possible ways to resolve the Social Security shortfall without examining whether the scorekeeping underpinning each solution is appropriate, widely supported, or even sensible.

This is not a "tell-all" book. I have had the great privilege of spending eight years advising a U.S. president on Social Security, as well as eleven years advising two U.S. senators. Although I explain the rationales behind important policy decisions, I'm not going to tell you who said what during internal meetings and discussions.

This book instead is premised upon the conviction that our national Social Security debate is more polarized than it needs to be, even given the depth of legitimate differences over the program's appropriate future direction. Our Social Security disagreements often devolve into mutually uncomprehending shouting matches, founded upon unexamined analytical differences. Unless we identify and understand our respective initial assumptions, we will not be able to fathom the conflicting policy initiatives that they drive.

Many of these conflicting initial assumptions are in turn fostered by the confusing program accounting that is an enduring legacy of the 1983 Social Security reforms. Those 1983 reforms created an additional layer of confusion over program finances, and thus a further tendency toward gridlock in what was already an intensely polarizing issue.

Before 1983, there existed profound disagreements about Social Security policy choices but general agreement on the state of Social Security finances. Increasingly after 1983, there was widespread disagreement on both. This has had a paralyzing effect on our capacity to agree upon adjustments to Social Security policy and has perpetuated confusion that will fatally undercut any future legislative discussions until it is untangled.

Accordingly, this book begins with a review of the events of 1983, focusing on the substance, intent, and scorekeeping of that year's Social Security reforms. To understand where we are today, we must understand what happened then, why, and how it has led to sharply divergent views of program finances today.

The book then reviews the competing value judgments to be made in Social Security policy going forward. Some of this material is indeed covered elsewhere, but I will delve fairly deeply into the rationales behind those competing value judgments, without (as is too often done) attributing these differing views to malicious intent.

This book also will review various analytical and scorekeeping controversies in the Social Security debate. This is absolutely vital to an understanding of competing policy positions. To a great extent, Social Security policy ideas are driven by initial analytical assumptions and scorekeeping. One person's policy choice is incomprehensible to another person if the latter is trying to solve a different problem and analyzing it in a different way. Until there is broader understanding of how these analytical differences drive opposing policy conclusions, we will continue to talk past and over each other, with little allowance for negotiation and compromise.

This is intended to be a book about *ideas*, not about personalities. I will on occasion critique a Social Security policy argument while mentioning the names of its key proponents only in the endnotes. It is my intention to pay these proponents the compliment of treating their arguments seriously and as being worthy of dissection, without appearing to be criticizing the individuals themselves.

Finally, this book provides a brief history of President George W. Bush's Social Security reform initiative, as well as the rationales for some of the policy decisions made during that initiative. I had originally intended to treat this subject lightly, wanting this book to be comparably useful to individuals from a broad array of policy perspectives. I was, however, surprised to learn from fellow Social Security experts of an opposing perspective that they were desirous of more explanatory information about the Bush administration's decision-making process, and so I have included it.

This material serves the book's theme that policy choices flowing naturally from a given set of starting assumptions may seem mysterious to others working from different starting assumptions. Without further explanation of those competing assumptions, we will all continue to be like the workers in the tower of Babel, speaking ever more passionately and urgently, but being less and less understood.

Social Security is by no means the only area of such mutual perplexity in our national political discussion. From health care to energy, different individuals' prescriptions are shaped by profoundly different underlying philosophical goals.

Social Security, as I attempt to show on these pages, is nevertheless distinct. In Social Security, individuals with the *same* philosophical viewpoint will reach different policy conclusions if they happen to look at different numbers. Just as readily, individuals can be confused by the program's complex accounting into taking positions whose substantive effects would run *counter to* their own philosophical inclinations. Without better understanding Social Security's relevant recent history as well as a bit about its scorekeeping, we will be confused not only about others' positions, but even about our own.

Although I am proud to have worked in President Bush's White House and to have supported his Social Security reform efforts, I have addressed the following pages to the current president and Congress. I have done so for a number of reasons.

One is that, to be faithful to history, a man has "got to know his limitations," as Harry Callahan said in *Magnum Force.* To write copiously about President Bush's decision-making process would, I fear, aggrandize my own importance to that process. I am confident that if my former White House colleagues were polled as to who knew the most about Social Security policy, my name would be spoken. I am equally confident that if my former colleagues were polled as to who possessed the best insights into the mind of the president, my name would not be. Though I was a committed member of the team, I must leave that story to others better qualified to tell it.

Second, this book is about the future, not the past. Throughout the final months of the Bush White House, an ethic was persistently transmitted from the top down: all staff members were to do everything possible to help the incoming officeholders solve the many challenges facing the nation. I have tried to write this book in a manner that honors that ethic.

The pages that follow are therefore offered in the hope that they will help readers not only to develop their own informed opinions about Social Security policy, but also to better understand and to appreciate the merit of competing opinions as well.

PART ONE

ORIGINS OF
A PROBLEM

CHAPTER 1

A Memorandum to the President and Congress

MEMORANDUM
TO: PRESIDENT OBAMA AND CONGRESS
FROM: CHUCK BLAHOUS
RE: SOCIAL SECURITY

AS YOU WELL KNOW, you have assumed great public responsibilities at a time of dire challenges to our nation's economy and to the individual well-being of millions of Americans. Our citizens have looked to you for solutions to long-intractable national challenges, many of which have absorbed your energies during your first several months in office. To move us beyond years of political gridlock and policy paralysis in these and other areas, your most creative and inclusive thinking will be required.

One of the most profound responsibilities you have accepted is for the financial sustainability and effective functioning of Social Security, the federal government's largest and arguably its most important domestic program.

Meeting this responsibility will not be easy. Social Security faces substantial challenges in the decades ahead. Moreover, Americans care deeply about Social Security while holding a wide variety of conflicting, impassioned views about how to render the program strong and beneficial going forward.

Compounding these challenges is that, in the Internet age, Americans are turning increasingly to disparate sources for the basic factual predicates of the Social Security discussion. It is forbiddingly difficult to foster a policy agreement among those making different value judgments when they cannot even agree on the facts and on the problem to be solved.

Despite enormous efforts over the years—by bipartisan advisory councils, congressional bodies, and Presidents George W. Bush (whom I served) and Bill Clinton—to objectively define and quantify Social Security's challenges, agreement even on these factual predicates remains elusive. An equitable Social Security solution will be unattainable unless you bring stakeholders together around a common understanding of the facts and of the need to take action to address them.

This challenge, though difficult, must be met if Social Security is to serve future generations as it has served us. Toward this end, the following memorandum presents some basic factual background about Social Security—about how it affects program participants and about the demographic, economic, and political factors that threaten its future efficacy. These issues will be probed in greater depth in the chapters that follow.

What Americans Pay for Social Security

Social Security's official name is the "Old-Age, Survivors, and Disability Insurance" program. Most working Americans (and their employers) are required to pay into it, and after ten years[1] of such contributions are eligible for an array of benefits.

Social Security's primary source of revenue is a 12.4 percent tax levied on workers' wages. Unlike the federal income tax, the Social Security payroll tax admits of no exemptions and no deductions. It is levied on the first dollar of earnings. Ostensibly, the worker pays 6.2 percent and the employer pays 6.2 percent, but economists generally agree that both ends of the payroll tax come from workers' wages and that we can best think of the Social Security payroll tax as a full

12.4 percent tax on the worker.[2] In effect, one out of every eight dollars workers earn is provided to the government to operate Social Security.

The 12.4 percent tax is actually split into two pieces: a 10.6 percent assessment to fund retirement and survivors' benefits and a 1.8 percent assessment for Social Security's disability insurance program.[3]

There is a limit to the application of the payroll tax to wage income. It is currently levied on the first $106,800 of a worker's wages[4] and not beyond. This reflects Social Security's design as a contributory entitlement program: the more you pay in, the more benefits you receive. This ethic has long distinguished Social Security in the public's mind from welfare programs.

In a welfare program, higher-income individuals may pay in while receiving nothing out, while poorer Americans may receive something out while paying nothing in. Social Security does not function this way.[5] Accordingly, exposing more income to the Social Security payroll tax would result in additional benefits for those who need them least, unless deliberate action is taken to deny benefits based on these additional contributions.

The payroll tax is the largest—but not the only—source of Social Security revenue. Social Security benefits are also subject to the income tax. Part of the resulting revenue is provided to the Social Security program.[6]

Together, these revenues currently add up to more than $700 billion paid annually into Social Security: $677 billion in payroll taxes and another $24 billion in benefit taxation.[7] These figures give a sense of how heavily invested are Americans in Social Security and how great a role it plays in their economic lives. In 2006, an Urban Institute study found that for two-thirds of Americans, their payroll tax payments (including both Social Security and Medicare) exceeded their income tax payments.[8]

The large annual contributions made by Americans to Social Security have in recent decades been more than enough to fund payments to the program's beneficiaries. This is, however, starting to change, as the following information will detail. But first, let us examine what Americans receive for these payments into Social Security.

Social Security Benefits

Americans tend to think first of retirement benefits when thinking of Social Security. Indeed, Social Security pays more retirement (technically "old-age") benefits than any other kind. But Social Security provides many other categories of benefits as well.

In its 2009 report, Social Security's Board of Trustees estimated that the program would spend $683 billion for the year.[9] Out of all benefits paid, roughly 62 percent would be worker retirement benefits.[10]

The Social Security retirement benefit formula is complex, but the basics are as follows. The Social Security Administration keeps track of each worker's wages subject to the Social Security payroll tax each year. These past earnings years are then indexed into today's terms, using a method that reflects how national wages have grown in the interim. This wage growth adjustment enables a determination as to which years were effectively the worker's highest thirty-five years of earnings. These thirty-five years are then averaged to produce an average indexed monthly earnings (the AIME) for the worker, in today's terms.[11]

Once each worker has an average earnings profile, this number is converted into a Social Security benefit. The benefit formula is progressive, meaning that it delivers higher returns on the first dollars each worker earns than on the last dollars earned by the highest-wage workers. As one example, the first $100 of a worker's average monthly earnings will produce $90 in monthly benefits in retirement, whereas the last $100 of taxable earnings of a high-wage worker will only produce $15 in monthly benefits.[12]

All of this calculating determines the benefit that a worker receives if he or she claims benefits at the Normal Retirement Age (NRA). The NRA is currently sixty-six and is scheduled to gradually rise to sixty-seven for people born in 1960 or later.[13] A worker can claim benefits earlier, as early as age sixty-two, but by doing so he or she receives a lower annual benefit to adjust for the longer period of time that benefits will be collected. Similarly, the worker can delay a benefit claim for up to three years after NRA and thereby receive a higher annual benefit via the Delayed Retirement Credit (DRC).[14] No matter at what age a worker retires, the benefits are adjusted each year thereafter for price inflation through a Cost-of-Living Adjustment (COLA) based on that year's change in the Consumer Price Index.[15]

Whether or not one masters all of these technical elements, there are three aspects of Social Security benefits that can and should be borne in mind.

One is, again, that the benefit formula is *progressive*. Lower-wage workers (all other things being equal) receive a higher return on their investment than higher-wage workers.[16] Thus, while both high-wage and low-wage workers earn credits for their contributions, Social Security generally redistributes income from high wage to low. There is some tension and opacity in a system that has the dual features of redistributing income while maintaining a contribution-benefit connection for high earners. Policymakers continually debate how much income redistribution the system should impose to protect low earners, as well as what is a sufficient return to higher-income workers to ensure their continued political support.

Another important factor is that benefit earnings stop where tax assessments stop. *Workers earn benefits only on their wages that were subject to the Social Security tax.* They do not earn benefits on wages that were not so taxed. Again, this reflects the program's design to provide a floor of income protection based on taxpaying work.

Thus, the system literally cannot "see" most of the earnings of a Bill Gates, nor does he earn any benefits based on most of his earnings. As a result of such earnings being invisible to the system, a worker with a calculated AIME equivalent to $62,000 annually is actually in the top 19 percent of all workers.[17] Such counterintuitive figures sometimes create great confusion as to how many people would be affected by a proposed benefit change.

The third factor of note is that the initial benefit formula (in addition to the worker's wage history, which we've already discussed) is *wage-indexed*. I will explain this in depth later, but essentially what this means is that each class of retirees is provided with initial benefits higher than those paid to those retiring the previous year, assuming that national wages have increased in the meantime, as they usually do. This feature of Social Security was not included in the system originally implemented by President Franklin D. Roosevelt and the Congress of 1935. It was enacted in its current form in 1977. If it did not exist—if, for example, initial benefits simply grew with price inflation—Social Security would not now face a projected shortfall at all.

If 62 percent of Social Security payments are to retired workers, what about the other 38 percent? The largest shares of the remainder are paid to disabled workers (16 percent) and surviving spouses (aged widows and widowers, 13 percent).[18] In addition to these, there are a number of other beneficiaries: non-working spouses, child survivors, and children of retired and disabled workers, among others.

These auxiliary benefits are all generally linked to the basic retirement benefit in some fashion. A surviving spouse, for example, will generally get the higher of the two benefits received by each half of the couple when alive. A disabled worker's benefit is also based on the retirement benefit formula, with the wrinkle that the number of years used to determine his or her average earnings is determined by the age of disability rather than the age of retirement.[19] The overriding principle to recognize is that the retirement benefit formula generally drives benefit levels for other beneficiaries, such as the disabled and survivors, as well.

The Problem

Social Security is fully able to meet today's benefit payments. Even with our current economic difficulties, no one is seriously worried about whether the federal government can meet its Social Security obligations next year.

That, however, will soon change. The first symptoms of the change are already starting to be felt, and will intensify in the coming years.

Social Security's challenge is one of the easiest issues to grasp, once shorn of superfluous detail, in all areas of federal policy. One remarkable aspect of the public Social Security debate is how such arcane concepts as "solvency," "actuarial balance," and Social Security Trust Fund accounting can obscure simple realities and make a truly straightforward issue seem very complex.

It is not at all complex. The simple reality is this: more people are now heading into retirement than ever before and will under current law be collecting higher benefits for a longer period of time. This means that higher costs will face our children and grandchildren than we have ever been asked to shoulder.

On October 15, 2007, Kathleen Casey-Kirchling, born on New Year's Day, 1946, became the first baby boomer to claim Social Security benefits.[20] With Ms. Casey-Kirchling in the lead, the enormous baby boom generation began to head into retirement. Thereupon began a surge of benefit claims that will swell Social Security costs steadily and dramatically over the next couple of decades.

In 2009, roughly 52 million people were drawing Social Security benefits of one kind or another.[21] It is expected that over the next twenty-five years this number will grow to over 88 million, an increase of more than 70 percent. As a result, the cost of paying Social Security benefits is expected to roughly double, even after adjusting for inflation, over that same time span: from just over $680 billion to over $1.4 trillion—for one program alone.[22]

This cost surge is not a faraway phenomenon. It is already starting to happen. In 2008, the number of new retired worker beneficiaries shot upward by more than 11 percent relative to 2007, itself a record-setting year.[23] In both of the first two quarters of 2009, there was a further 20 percent rise in new retiree beneficiaries relative to the same quarters of 2008.[24]

Over this and the next presidential term, the total number of retirees on Social Security is projected to grow by roughly 24 percent while the number of workers contributing taxes grows by only 7 percent.[25] The long-anticipated tidal wave of Social Security beneficiaries has finally reached the shore.

One reason for the surge in the number of retirees is, among other factors, that Americans are living longer than ever before.[26] What causes it to play out so rapidly, however, is that the generation just now heading into retirement is the enormous baby boom generation born between 1946 and 1964. Those baby boomers, in turn, had fewer children than their parents did.

All of these factors combine to produce a situation in which there will soon be far fewer workers paying Social Security taxes to support each beneficiary. Today there are roughly 3.1 workers paying taxes to support each person receiving Social Security benefits. By 2030, that ratio will be 2.2 per recipient.[27]

Let's put these figures another way. Today, one hundred workers must pay enough in taxes to support thirty-two Social Security beneficiaries. One hundred workers in 2030, however, will need to support forty-six beneficiaries (figure 1.1).

FIGURE 1.1 A Rising Number of Beneficiaries for Workers to Support

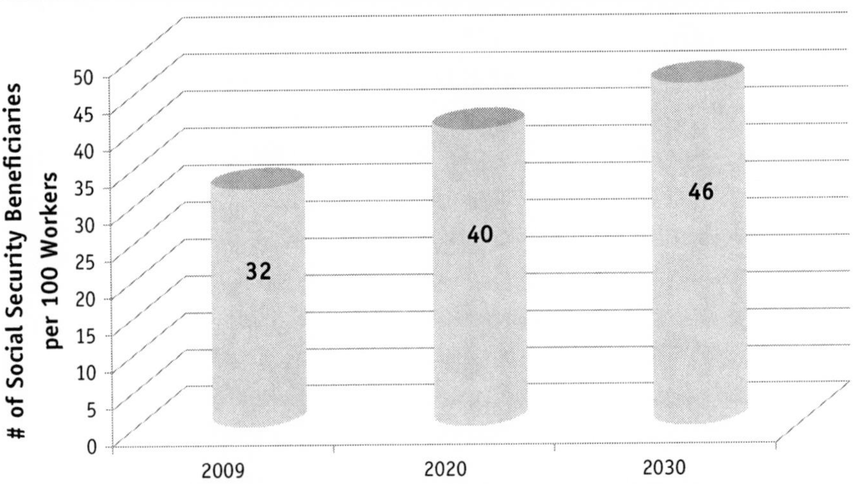

Source: Based on data from the 2009 Social Security and Medicare Trustees' report.

The principal manifestation of this rise in the number of beneficiaries is that, as Social Security is currently constructed, the cost of paying benefits will absorb a sharply increasing share of each taxpaying worker's wages.

In 2008, benefit costs equaled a little bit more than eleven cents of each taxable dollar earned by workers.[28] The leftover portion of the 12.4 percent payroll tax was provided to the federal government to otherwise spend, in exchange for bonds issued to the Social Security Trust Fund. More on this later.

In 2009, due in part to a struggling economy, the cost of paying benefits rose to more than 12 percent of each worker's taxable earnings.[29] Within the next twenty years, under current law, the cost of Social Security will rise to more than 16.5 percent of each worker's taxable earnings, as shown in figure 1.2.

Meanwhile, workers will simultaneously be asked to pay for similarly sharp increases in the cost of Medicare.[30] All told, the next genera-

FIGURE 1.2   The Rising Cost of Social Security

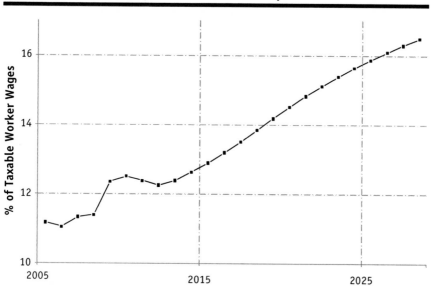

Source: Based on data from the 2009 Social Security and Medicare Trustees' report.

tion of workers will be asked to part with the equivalent of roughly one-third of their taxable wages to support these two programs alone.[31] Everything else that the various levels of government tax workers to support—from national defense, roads and bridges, and state education expenses to the massive federal health care expansion enacted in early 2010—would be levied on top of these unprecedented individual program costs.

The combination of these trends would result in enormous adverse implications for the economic experience of future generations, or—to put it more starkly—whether our children and grandchildren will be permitted an after-tax standard of living comparable to what we have enjoyed.[32]

By 2016, under 2009 projections, annual Social Security costs will exceed the tax revenue the program generates.[33] This date is likely to appear even sooner when the 2010 trustees' report is released. This means that our already cash-strapped federal government will need to find additional revenues to fully pay benefit obligations. Though the deficits will start small, they will exceed $100 billion (in today's dollars) by 2021 and $200 billion by 2026 under the 2009 projections that I will continue to cite here. It bears repeating that these are not total Social Security costs, but just the annual *deficits* that must be financed beyond the 12.4 percent payroll tax.

Technically, the program will still be solvent and will maintain a positive Trust Fund balance well after 2016, not becoming insolvent until 2037. There is a fierce ongoing debate about the meaning of "solvency" and the significance of the Trust Fund, which the following chapters will examine in greater detail. This debate is very important, as policy agreements are unlikely except between those with a shared understanding of solvency and of the Trust Fund. But all sides of the Social Security debate agree on one thing: the Trust Fund consists of debt issued by the federal government. It indicates the extent to which the Social Security system has accrued a right to call upon the rest of the federal government for support, but it is not an external means of financial support for the government as a whole. The government will need to find actual cash to service Trust Fund debt and to keep full benefits flowing, starting (under current projections) in 2016.[34]

The Mounting Cost of Delay

Another notable aspect of the Social Security challenge is the cost of continued delay in repairing program finances. The longer that we put off dealing with Social Security, the less fair the solution will be.

We could, hypothetically, make the system permanently sustainable today without raising Social Security taxes in any way, without changing benefits for those now in retirement, and while still allowing future retirees to receive benefits that are higher than those paid today even after adjusting for inflation. That is, benefits could grow smoothly on a path that rises consistently in real terms, without raising taxes.

Within just a few years, however, that will no longer be true. Within about a decade, a Social Security solution would require a choice among raising taxes, reducing benefits for those already in retirement, and/or forcing future retirees to receive lower benefits than previous retirees received. Either we'd need to tell young Americans that their taxes are going up or we'd need to start telling retirees that their standards of living are going down.[35]

If we run this thought experiment all the way out to 2037, we see that we would then face a choice of suddenly reducing benefits by 24 percent, increasing taxes by 31 percent, or some equally disagreeable point between those poles. Moreover, even this array of choices assumes that we'd be willing to suddenly cut a retiree's benefit from $2,000 in one month to $1,520 the next—hardly likely. If instead we wanted to shield then-current retirees from sudden cuts, we could only get a comparable amount of savings by cutting the *entirety* of benefits for new retirees.

Whether we define the "problem" as occurring in 2016 or 2037 thus matters little to the question of whether we should act soon. Either way, a solution enacted today will be far fairer across generations, and involve far less concentrated pain, than one enacted ten or even five years from now. As we delay for reasons of political expediency, the ironic consequence is that the political difficulties of reforming Social Security only mount.

Why is delay so costly? There are a number of reasons, one of which I just touched upon: the bipartisan political consensus that we shouldn't cut benefits for those now in retirement or about to retire. Thus, every year that passes, another class of retirees joins the rolls with benefit obligations locked in as politically inviolate.

Moreover, due to the wage-indexing[36] of the benefit formula, each year's delay means that we're also locking in a greater base benefit level. This makes it less and less possible to avoid future declines in real benefit levels without raising tax burdens. In practical effect, delay inevitably exacerbates the tax increases that we will oblige young Americans to accept.

Perhaps the easiest way to understand the consequences of delay is to note that each year that we fail to act, we take another cohort of Americans—specifically, a historically large class of baby boomer retirees—out of the solution process. This means that the burden of filling the Social Security shortfall must be borne by a shrinking fraction of the population. Further concentrating the sacrifice on younger Americans is particularly unfair given that these generations already stand to lose money, net, through Social Security as it is.

A very valuable table in the Social Security trustees' report illuminates the cost of delay for young Americans.[37] This table shows that the present value of the Trust Fund was $2.4 trillion in 2009. This basically meant that, so far, all of those who had entered the Social Security system had contributed $2.4 trillion more than they had received in benefits.

The table also shows, however, that those already in Social Security will, in the future, get back *$18.7 trillion* (in present-value dollars) more than they will contribute henceforth. In short, their past excess contributions, even if they had been saved, are nowhere near the amount needed to pay for their future benefits.

This is where young and future generations come in. Social Security is a pay-as-you-go system: each generation's benefits are paid primarily by taxing those that follow (this is true even if we adopt the controversial viewpoint that the $2.4 trillion Trust Fund is effective pre-funding). Were we to exclude current program participants from the solution, those just entering Social Security now will effectively be asked to put an additional $16.3 trillion into the system beyond what they will ever receive.

Figure 1.3 depicts the enormous $18.7 trillion difference between future benefit payments and tax contributions for those already in the Social Security system. As the picture dramatizes, even if the $2.4 trillion Trust Fund were a cost-free source of financing future benefits, younger generations would still have a $16.3 trillion hole to fill.

Some analysts will object that the use of such enormous figures exaggerates the actual shortfall that must be filled in by younger generations. After all, this $16.3 trillion gap would be spread out over all eternity. They would note that this figure amounts to "only" 3.7 percent of workers' taxable wages, or 1.2 percent of the economy (GDP).[38]

FIGURE 1.3 The Social Security Hole Being Left by Current/Past Generations for Future Generations (Trillions of $PV)

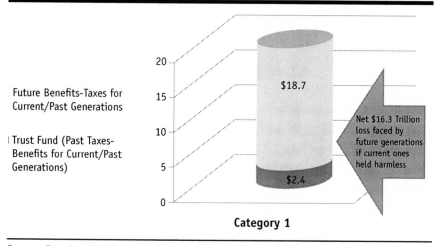

SOURCE: Based on data from the 2009 Social Security and Medicare Trustees' report.

That is true, but remember that 3.7 percent of wages is not the *total* amount that future workers would contribute to Social Security. It is, rather, the amount of their net *loss*—the amount by which their benefits will fall short of their contributions. In other words, the Social Security program, on balance, would subtract nearly 4 percent from their lifetime taxable income under current law.

This is not, therefore, simply a talking point, nor an abstract or ideological concern. It means concretely that the longer we delay, the more that future generations will lose through Social Security and the poorer they will all be. Both the program's effective functioning and its political support would be severely jeopardized.

To sum up the problem and the consequences of delay:

- Social Security's costs are now beginning to rise dramatically—not in the distant future, but right now, today.
- By 2016 (under the 2009 projections), these costs will exceed incoming program taxes and will continue to rise from there.
- Assuming that we don't want to cut benefits for those in retirement, and that any benefit changes will be gradually phased in, our window of opportunity for a salable and fair Social Security solution is closing fast.
- The longer we wait, the more we threaten both the program's efficacy and its long-term political viability.

The Divisions

Brokering a solution to this challenge will require your sound and creative policy thinking, as well as your political skills and your gifts for persuasion. If it were easy, it would have been done already. The Social Security problem has overwhelmed many attempts at resolution over the last decade and a half. Moreover, time is not on your side. As delay worsens the policy trade-offs, the politics will become more difficult as well.

You are already well aware that there exist starkly conflicting views of what constitutes a desirable Social Security solution. The following paragraphs will grossly simplify these divisions, failing to do justice to the intricacies of the thinking of the various actors in the Social Security policy debate. This is merely an introduction to the existing policy and political divisions. The nuances of these disparate positions will be explored in greater detail in subsequent chapters.

We do not now enjoy, across the political spectrum, a common understanding of the scope of the Social Security problem. Even if such a common understanding existed, however, there would still be stark policy differences to bridge.

On the right, there is resistance to raising taxes to fund Social Security (or anything else). On the left, there is resistance to slowing Social Security cost growth to the extent required to render a tax increase unnecessary.

On the right, there is a fear of "going first" and a belief that the politics of Social Security will always be used to their disadvantage. On the left, there is suspicion of the motives of the right and a concern that changes to Social Security will undermine rather than strengthen the program.

On the questions of progressivity and income redistribution, patterns are less clear than one might at first assume. Proposals from the right are often more progressive and would thus redistribute more income than substantive positions often taken by the left. There are, nevertheless, some predictable patterns.

Both right and left tend to agree that the benefits of poorer Americans should be largely held harmless in any Social Security fix, with slight exceptions that I will later discuss in detail. The disagreements tend to come with respect to the treatment of middle-income to high-income Americans; grossly generalizing, the right would tend to constrain the growing cost of benefits to these groups while the left would require them to pay higher taxes.

There are differences between right and left over how to allocate risk. Neither proposals from the right nor from the left can eliminate the risks associated with funding Social Security, but they differ as to who should bear the risk, and how. The left generally prefers that 100 percent of the risk be borne by taxpayers, though their preference for government-provided defined benefits means that beneficiaries would remain subject to the political risk of benefit changes. The further one travels to the right, the more one finds a willingness to share a portion of the funding risk between taxpayers and those beneficiaries who choose to accept it (in exchange for receiving the higher potential benefits that accompany such risk).

Perhaps most fundamentally of all, there remain stubborn differences as to how to define the problem to be solved. At the extremes of the political spectrum, even the necessity of system solvency is not a given. For some on the left, continued drift toward insolvency is perfectly acceptable, as they know that no solution other than raising taxes will be possible at the last minute. Some of these actors realize that they can avoid difficult politics today by downplaying the problem and delaying action until a tax-increase scenario unfolds as a virtual inevitability. Some on the right see the pay-as-you-go financing of traditional Social Security as a fatally flawed design, and will thus be skeptical of any compromise to "prop it up," especially if it involves tax increases.

These are the extreme poles. But even when we move away from these poles, we still find fundamental differences as to goals. Such an agreement on goals is an essential predicate for constructive Social Security policy negotiations. Unless you can induce participants to speak a common language about what we are together trying to do, we will continue to talk past one another and to accomplish nothing.

Perhaps the most salient example of such a divide is in the definition of the program's financial health. For some, mostly left of center, the standard of "seventy-five-year solvency" is more than sufficient. A "seventy-five-year balance" was how the Greenspan Commission defined long-range solvency back in 1983. The AARP today, for example, routinely publishes tables of policy measures, defining the fraction of the "shortfall" that each measure would solve solely in terms of the seventy-five-year imbalance. From this perspective, restoring Social Security to financial health seems fairly innocuous; it merely involves the enactment of measures sufficient to close what appears to be a surmountable deficit in the seventy-five-year actuarial imbalance.

To the naïve ear, the label of "seventy-five-year solvency" is bound to sound more than sufficient. Social Security itself hasn't even been around for seventy-five years. How are we possibly to know what our economy will be like seventy-five years from now? If we're fine for the next seventy-five years, isn't that more than enough time to make any further adjustments we need?

This all goes to show how misleading terminology can sometimes be. Many analysts have found the metric of seventy-five-year solvency to be somewhere between insufficient and counterproductive. Since the 1983 reforms, numerous advisory councils have taken pains to explain why the metric fails to direct the program toward a sustainable path.[39] Several people—including former participants in the 1983 Greenspan Commission itself—have cited the reliance on this figure as the principal reason that the 1983 reforms created more of an appearance than a reality of sustainable finances.

There is not space in this introductory memorandum to list all of the problems discovered with the metric of seventy-five-year balance, which will be elaborated upon later. The short list that follows is provided to convey a sense of why a discussion predicated on such scorekeeping is unlikely to lead anywhere.

For one thing, the measure is susceptible to gimmicks: we could achieve seventy-five-year balance today without actually solving anything, simply by issuing $5.3 trillion in bonds to the Social Security Trust Fund.

Second, the metric's definition of "balance" allows for the averaging of enormous annual *imbalances* as well as the heavy discounting of future deficits. For example, if we run a $250 billion surplus today and plan a $1 trillion deficit in fifty years, our calculation will say that we are "balanced" even if we spend all of today's $250 billion surplus on a massive government program to buy hula hoops and party hats.

Third, the measure ignores the Social Security benefits promised to millions of Americans even as it counts those same Americans' payroll taxes, severely underestimating the program's structural deficit.

Fourth, commonly suggested measures to achieve seventy-five-year solvency[40] would only delay the onset of permanent cash deficits by eight years, while actually adding to the system's projected cost explosion.

Fifth, the metric counts the Social Security Trust Fund as an asset, without regard for whether it is saved or whether the government has a means to redeem it.

And sixth, but by no means last, a solution that aims only at a "seventy-five-year balance" will likely be out of balance by that very same criterion only one year after enactment, furthering public cynicism and causing embarrassment to negotiators.

This is but one example of a fundamental analytical difference that can prevent individuals of good faith from bridging their policy differences. Sometimes these analytical disagreements are but a surface manifestation of deeper disagreements in value judgments.

For example, seventy-five-year solvency may be a sufficient metric for success for an individual who is focused mainly on whether Social Security is provided with resources adequate to meet its benefit obligations, and is less concerned with where those resources come from. For an individual who is instead concerned about the total cost of Social Security to taxpayers, who wants to evaluate pre-funded and pay-as-you-go solutions on a level playing field, or who is concerned about whether Social Security is truly operating as the self-financing program it is represented as being, the metric will be deemed insufficient, as it does not satisfactorily address any of those questions.

The moral of all this is that discussions cannot be fruitful if they are pursuant to outcomes that many, if not most, stakeholders will see as illegitimate. To bring Americans together behind a solution for Social Security, therefore, you will not only need to bridge many strongly held policy differences, but you will first need to forge agreement on just what we are trying to accomplish.

The Confusion

As we have seen, barriers to constructive action on Social Security include fully informed disagreements about policy, often deriving from fully informed disagreements about the problem to be solved.

There is, however, another layer of barriers to bipartisan action, consisting of pockets of confusion in the public discussion. Sometimes expert commentary about Social Security takes an unfortunate tone of, "We all understand what the problem is . . . we just need to put aside our petty partisan bickering and agree on what to do about it." But then the subsequent policy discussion sometimes devolves into a shouting match, often because one or both sides have internalized erroneous presumptions about Social Security finances that have in turn closed minds to one policy response while overrating the efficacy of another.

There are multiple examples of how such confusion can arise.

Is a person earning $85,000 "middle class" or not? The answer depends on whether we are talking about annual wage income or Social Security's average-earnings calculation. It is counterintuitive to many to contemplate that a benefit change affecting someone with an AIME of $62,000 actually affects fewer middle-income workers than raising the $106,800 cap on taxable wages. But the confounding of *annual* income with *average-lifetime-indexed-taxable-wage* income can cause great confusion in press accounts of how individuals would be affected by policy proposals.[41]

To take another: Isn't it true that the transition cost for a proposal to establish personal accounts would have been as much as $5 trillion over twenty years, at a time when the shortfall under the current system was only $4 trillion?[42] The answer, if one uses self-consistent terminology, is a resounding no. These separate statements conflate the very different metrics of present-value dollars and current dollars. The persistent substitution of present value, constant dollars, and current dollars (sometimes by learned analysts who know better) has caused enormous confusion in the public debate.

How accurate have the Social Security trustees' projections been in the past? Have they tended to be too conservative or too aggressive in their assumptions? How likely is it that Social Security's future finances might differ markedly from what is now projected? This is one of the most persistent sources of confusion in the entire debate, to which I will return.

Is it true that establishing personal accounts would increase federal debt? Some would immediately answer "yes," but the right answer is: it depends on several things. It depends on how the personal accounts are financed. It depends on whether we count the saving within the accounts. It depends on whether the government spends just as much money as before, even once it can no longer spend Social Security revenue. And it depends on whether we consider Trust Fund debt as "real" debt or not. Both advocates and opponents of personal accounts—even many experts—persistently fall prey to inconsistent measurements of federal indebtedness when discussing this question, as we shall see.

A particularly great source of confusion in the Social Security debate is the nature and meaning of the Social Security Trust Fund. One's view of the Trust Fund plays a great role in whether one sees a problem arising in 2009, 2016, or not until 2037.[43] The Social Security debate will always have plenty of fire, and these fundamental analytical differences only add fuel.

It will be hard enough for you, our elected leaders, to broker a Social Security solution even if everyone comes to the table with the same clear understanding of program finances. But not only will many points of confusion inevitably exist, some on both sides of the aisle will deliberately perpetuate these points of confusion for political purposes. You will need to overcome these hurdles to have a fair chance to succeed.

The story on the following pages represents a good faith attempt to lay out the factual predicates of the Social Security debate. First I will review some key events in the program's history that have given rise to the analytical disputes that currently paralyze prospects for bipartisan action. I will then lay out the spectrum of policy choices that now face us all.

You and I may be at different positions on these various policy spectra, but we need to conduct a civil discussion about why we occupy our respective positions and respectfully express our concerns about one another's. The interests of younger American generations depend greatly on our mutual willingness to do so.

Much of the analytical confusion that now paralyzes good-faith efforts at bipartisan compromise derives specifically from the nature of the 1983 legislation to shore up Social Security. To put it even more strongly: it is impossible to fully disentangle the current policy discussion without understanding what happened then, as well as why it happened that way. In the next chapter, therefore, I will shift our narrative back to the 1983 Social Security amendments in an effort to better explain how we got here, and how we can together move forward.

CHAPTER 2

1983

A Temporary Rescue

A PRIL 20, 1983 dawned a chilly, blustery day in Washington, D.C. Amid unseasonable cold, a throng of dignitaries gathered on the South Lawn of the White House. They were there to observe the ceremonial signing by President Ronald Reagan of the 1983 Social Security amendments, legislation designed to ensure the soundness of America's most treasured domestic program for decades to come.

Presidential ceremonies always involve an extended setup period, during which attendees flow in sporadically to their assigned places, then wait for several minutes during which nothing happens that most in the audience can see. The spell of seeming inactivity is then suddenly broken when the president's arrival is announced and the ceremony startlingly commences at full speed.

On this day, at the designated moment, President Reagan strode jauntily onto the stage to the triumphal strains of *Hail to the Chief*.[1] Though others onstage, such as House Speaker Tip O'Neill, were bundled in heavy coats in deference to the chill, President Reagan was coatless. His upbeat demeanor conveyed to all who watched the satisfaction and optimism of the occasion, even as gusting winds intermittently distorted his miked voice.

"I want to extend to all of you a very warm welcome," the president said, quipping, "*Something* ought to be warm!"

25

President Reagan then spoke in praise of the Social Security legislation he was about to sign. His speech was followed by remarks, respectively, from the Speaker of the House, Massachusetts Democrat Tip O'Neill, and the Senate Majority Leader, Tennessee Republican Howard Baker.

Common sentiments ran through the words of each of the three men. Each, as would be expected, extolled the Social Security program as well as the specific amendments about to become law. But each of the speakers laid at least as great an emphasis on the bipartisan spirit and process that had brought about this day. Palpable throughout the ceremony was a feeling of relief, a sense of honorable compromise, a sense that politics had been subordinated to the public good, and an awareness that Social Security's healthful continuation might just as easily not have happened.

The president concluded his remarks with another reference to the weather, indicating that he would sign the twelve letters of his name with twelve separate pens. "They're too cold . . . they can only sign one letter, each pen."

President Reagan then walked across the stage to take his seat at the small signing table. As so often throughout his public appearances, the president's demeanor was that of a man in relaxed command, smiling and joking even as disruptive breezes messily flapped the pages before him and as cold thickened the ink of the signing pens.

As the president signed, a microphone picked up the sound of O'Neill's deep voice, making small talk from behind.[2] "What's the W stand for, Mr. President?" asked the Speaker, noting President Reagan's middle initial. "Wilson," replied the president over his shoulder. "Wilson? I didn't know that," said O'Neill, then turning to Congressman Claude Pepper standing beside him, "The W stands for Wilson. He was a Woodrow Wilson baby!"[3]

The pleasant banter typified the relationship between President Reagan and Speaker O'Neill. Each represented a starkly different viewpoint with respect to the optimal construction of public policy, and each would advocate relentlessly on behalf of his own philosophy while

President Reagan signs the 1983 Social Security amendments[4]

sternly critiquing the other's. But these strongly held differences didn't prevent these two men from working together, in a fashion, or from interacting collegially time and again. Indeed, this day was only possible because many influential individuals of starkly different policy views had chosen similarly to cooperate despite their differences.

The law that President Reagan signed on that day was a significant bipartisan achievement and among the most important pieces of legislation in Social Security's history. Over a quarter-century having passed since its enactment, we now have some historical perspective on the event and on three aspects of it in particular.

Three Legacies of the 1983 Reforms

The first of these three key aspects of the 1983 Social Security legislation is as a *process* model. This aspect of the 1983 reforms drew the most positive reviews at the time of their enactment, and that judgment has largely been borne out by history. A fair measure of the success of the process model is that both Congress and the president faced daunting substantive and political challenges which the 1981–83 process enabled them to overcome. The fact that afterward neither party felt compelled to make a priority of revisiting the agreement is further testimony to its procedural success.

The second facet of the reforms warranting our review is as a *substantive policy* model. Here it is fair to say that many analysts would give a passing grade to the 1983 reforms, even though in many respects the substantive verdict is mixed. Substantively, the 1983 reforms achieved much that is praiseworthy. The reforms averted the projected near-term insolvency of Social Security. They built in a margin for error, in case their projections were wrong (some of this cushion, it turned out, was in fact needed). They ensured the financially sound operation of Social Security for decades to come.

Given the size of the challenge faced down in 1983, these achievements should be sufficient to warrant our commendation for a substantive job well done. Having said that, the substantive result of the 1983 reforms was not perfect. They failed to place Social Security on a permanently sustainable course and, indeed, the long-term trend line they produced could be seen as unsustainable as soon as the law was signed. They achieved long-term balance only in the sense of averaging out large annual *imbalances*, with no safeguards to ensure that saving was built in surplus years to meet the expenses of deficit years. They missed a chance for genuine pre-funding of Social Security's mounting future obligations, left in place a trend of perpetually worsening treatment of each succeeding generation, and put the interests of beneficiaries and taxpayers in the 2020s and beyond on a collision course.

These critiques, however, could be regarded as 20/20 hindsight. The negotiators of 1983 transformed an imminent insolvency into roughly thirty years of program surpluses. For this alone, our gratitude should take precedence over our faultfinding. The substantive model may not suit each of our respective policy preferences, but its successes warrant our recognition and respect.

This brings us to the third aspect of the 1983 reforms, one that has been too little appreciated over the last several decades but which is now becoming, with the perspective of history, starkly apparent.

This aspect is the *political legacy* of the 1983 reforms. Closely related to their substantive content, this constitutes the effect of the 1983 reforms upon future efforts to strengthen Social Security. This is the 1983 legislation's great failure. Its damaging effects are now being felt so acutely that on balance it is yet possible that the 1983 legislation may ultimately prove to pose more of a threat to, than a safeguard of, Social Security's long-term future.

Specifically, certain aspects of the 1983 reforms have had a polarizing, even paralyzing, effect on subsequent efforts to shore up Social Security. Indeed, much of the confusion that attends the current Social Security debate, and many of the reasons that policy advocates now talk past each other, are directly traceable to decisions made in 1983. We will not be able to place Social Security on an equitable and sustainable course unless we understand what happened then, why it happened that way, and how the resultant product fosters confusion today.

From 1981 through the enactment of the 1983 reforms, both Republicans and Democrats knew there was a problem and that it was coming fast. The 1981 trustees' report warned that Social Security "will be unable to make benefit payments on time beginning in the latter half of 1982."[5] The 1982 report repeated this warning, although a few months of additional time had been bought by a patchwork of legislative tinkering late in 1981.[6] The key players on both sides of the aisle all understood that prompt action was needed to save Social Security. Even with that understanding, it nearly didn't happen.

This essential clarity was fostered in part by a shared understanding of how Social Security worked. Everyone, Republicans and Democrats alike, understood that benefits were paid by taxing current workers. If annual taxes collected were insufficient to fund benefits, a problem very obviously arose. There was indeed a Trust Fund then, but its balances were deliberately kept small and it was not designed to carry the program through extended periods of significant cash shortfalls.

As the 1981 trustees' report stated:

There is general agreement that the OASDI system should be financed on the basis of a "current-cost" method, under which total income each year is intended to be approximately equal to total outgo during the year, plus an additional amount needed to maintain the trust funds at appropriate contingency-reserve levels. Under this financing method, the trust funds should not become too large (through continued annual surpluses) nor too small (through continued annual deficits).[7]

The trustees' statement was not mere lip service. Up through that time, annual program income and outgo had been persistently balanced or close to it, with the Social Security Trust Fund balance never rising or falling by more than $6 billion in any single year.[8] Not since 1960 had the Trust Fund commanded assets sufficient even to fund two years' worth of benefits. This was a result of a long-shared bipartisan understanding that Social Security benefits were paid from Social Security tax revenues as they came in, and in no other way.

Indeed, so little credence was then given to the idea that the Trust Fund was a meaningful source of pre-funding for future benefits that the assets of the Trust Fund were not even included in measurements of Social Security's future balance. The actuarial method relied upon by 1983's negotiators thus "did not take into account the trust fund balances at the start of the valuation period."[9]

Many now wrongly assume that the crafters of the 1983 legislation deliberately intended to depart from this historic practice, that they intended to run decades of annual surpluses and thereby build up a significant Social Security Trust Fund that would pre-fund a portion of benefits of the baby boom generation. Given the substantive consequences of the 1983 reforms, this is an understandable misperception.

The historical record is clear, however, that there was no such intent. Today's large Trust Fund, the meaning of which is so hotly contested, was actually an unwitting byproduct of the 1983 reforms—and an equally unwitting destruction of the analytical clarity that had enabled the 1983 reforms themselves to be possible.

This unintended consequence of the 1983 legislation severely undercuts our ability today to understand each other, to work together, and thereby to ensure that Social Security is sound for the future. To fully understand this legacy of the 1983 reforms, we will examine the events that led to them in greater detail.

Origins of the Crisis of 1981–83

This book is not intended to be a detailed history of the Social Security program. For those who wish such a history, a number of excellent texts are available, including *The Real Deal* by Sylvester J. Schieber and John B. Shoven. Here we will concentrate on those aspects of Social Security's history that bear most directly upon the problems that arose in 1981–83 and which remain to a great extent before us today.

The first such element is the decision implemented in the 1939 amendments to have, not a fully funded system, but a pay-as-you-go system. When Ida May Fuller became the first recipient of Social Security benefits,[10] the system didn't limit her benefits only to the amount of her own contributions. In fact, she had paid only $24.75 into the system over three years before collecting decades of benefits far in excess of that amount, starting with a monthly $22.54 retirement check in January 1940, on up through her death at the age of 100 in 1975.[11]

In other words, Social Security was not set up like an IRA or a 401(k) account, in which an individual's benefits are determined by and limited to the amounts that same individual had previously contributed, plus the earnings on those contributions. Instead, the first generation's benefits were paid primarily by the working generation that followed, that generation's benefits were paid primarily by the generation that followed it, and so forth.

This financing structure inevitably brings about comparisons to a "pyramid scheme" or "Ponzi scheme." Social Security's strongest advocates are understandably offended by such characterizations, particularly as the name of Ponzi is synonymous with intent to defraud. One needn't intend to denigrate Social Security, however, to recognize that there are inevitable mathematical consequences of funding each generation's benefits primarily with the tax dollars of the following generation. Such a system's financial health cannot help but be highly dependent upon the growth of the population paying into the system.

Two specific consequences flowed from the pay-as-you-go financing method. One is that in the early years of the program, robust growth in the number of contributing workers enabled Congress to repeatedly increase Social Security benefits, and their own political benefits along with them. A second is that in the later years, with the ratio of workers to collectors dropping significantly, the chain can't be kept going in the same way unless late entrants to the system agree to contribute a lot more (in present value) than they later receive. This is a problematic reality that we have inherited.

Another key aspect of Social Security's history is that, at its inception, it did not include many of the benefit features that it does now. There was, originally, no annual COLA, the current automatic adjustment to benefits for each year's inflation. There was originally no wage-indexing, the system's current feature that causes the growth of initial benefit levels to *exceed* inflation. There were no disability or spousal benefits. There was no early retirement option; retirees had to wait until age sixty-five, instead of claiming benefits at sixty-two as they can now. These and other features of Social Security were added over the following decades.

These limitations on the original benefit package carried various consequences. Because Social Security benefits were not indexed, they automatically became more affordable whenever the workforce and the economy grew. (This is exactly the opposite of our current situation, in which the program extracts higher costs from the economy even if economic growth accelerates.) As a result, politicians were repeatedly presented with the pleasant opportunity to enact ad hoc Social Security benefit increases, which they repeatedly did, typically in even-numbered years.[12]

One of the ironies of the current debate is that had Social Security's benefits simply remained as designed by FDR and the Congress of

1935, the program would be more than adequately financed now. Our contemporary debate about Social Security thus has little to do with undoing the promises of the original Social Security Act and everything to do with confronting the ongoing consequences of benefit expansions enacted far later.

In 1972, there occurred a historic benefit expansion that made inevitable a systemic financing shortfall that had to be addressed in 1977, again in 1983, and which we will need to address again. On its surface, 1972 was simply another case of Congress and the president seizing an opportunity to increase Social Security benefits in an election year. But the implications were vast. First, Social Security benefits were increased a whopping 20 percent across the board. In addition, a new feature was added: annual COLAs, giving retirees protection from each year's price inflation.[13] But the most consequential change was to the formula that determined a retiree's initial benefit level—a botched adjustment, it turned out, that rapidly brought Social Security to the brink of insolvency.

The 1972 amendments erroneously double-indexed the initial Social Security benefits paid to new retirees. These benefits were effectively indexed (meaning adjusted each year) both for wage growth *and* for price inflation. As a result, benefit levels began to grow so drastically that had this continued, retirees on Social Security would ultimately have received more money for not working than they had ever been paid for working. This rate of benefit growth vastly exceeded congressional intent as well as what was reasonably affordable. This forced the enactment of new amendments to Social Security in 1977, but with an important difference from past legislation: this time, Congress would need to scale back benefit promises rather than to increase them, ending one era of Social Security and ushering in the next.

To fix the system in 1977 required that, for the first time, Congress had to tell a generation of new retirees that it was not going to get what had recently been promised in law. The erroneous benefit formula had to be phased out and a new, corrected one phased in. The birth classes (1917–21) included in the transition period between the two formulas became known as the "notch babies," who promptly formed various organizations to demand the restoration of the previously (and erroneously) enacted benefit formula.

In reality, the "notch babies" had little cause for complaint. They would, as a group, receive far more from Social Security than they contributed, certainly a far higher return on their investment than any subsequent generation will get. But they represented the vanguard of a political class that will now forever be with us: individuals who will get less than they were, at one time, promised by Social Security.

The adjustments in 1977 had to be drastic because the 1972 errors had been so severe. Our ongoing Social Security debate today is often marred by exaggerated claims about the size of proposed "benefit cuts." Nothing on the table today would affect future benefit promises to anything close to the extent of the 1977 reforms. Specifically, no one today is proposing changes in future benefits that would reduce them by more than 2 percent of workers' taxable wages over the next seventy-five years.[14] The amendments of 1977, by contrast, shaved more than 6 percent of projected taxable payroll off of the ensuing seventy-five-year deficit.

Though politically difficult, this was the right and necessary thing to do. In dealing with Social Security in 1977, Congress correctly understood that the policy goal was not to uphold untenable benefit promises made in prior law, but to arrive at a more sensible path for cost growth going forward and at a sensible means of financing that growth. Our current Social Security debate would benefit enormously from a similar approach.

The shared understanding that the 1972 indexing method was wrong did not by itself establish what benefit formula would be right. The 1977 amendments reflected the response of legislators to this accompanying question. They implemented a method of benefit indexation that remains essentially in use today—the method of *wage-indexation*. This method pays each class of retirees a level of initial benefits higher than the previous one's by the amount that national wages have grown in the meantime.

Why was this wage-indexing formula chosen? The essential goal of wage-indexation is to maintain "wage replacement"; that is, for Social Security benefits to provide a consistent percentage of what each generation earns before retirement. The idea is that, for example, if one generation gets a Social Security benefit equal to 40 percent of its typical working wages, the next generation should get a benefit equal to 40 percent of its working wages, too.

If the worker-collector ratio never changed, then such wage replacement would be financially sustainable even in a pay-as-you-go system. The benefits paid by Social Security would rise with wages as dictated by formula. At the same time, taxes paid by workers would also naturally rise with wages, because the payroll tax, after all, is paid as a percentage of wages. Financing would be stable and each generation would get a comparably fair deal.

A problem with this method arises, however, when society ages and the worker-collector ratio drops. If that happens, then wage-indexation imposes a higher cost rate on each succeeding generation as there are more elderly to support. One generation might pay a 10 percent lifetime wage tax to get that 40 percent replacement rate—but a later generation, supporting more retirees during its working years, may have to pay a 15 percent lifetime wage tax rate to get that same 40 percent replacement rate. Consequently, each generation receives a worse deal than the one before, with the youngest generations losing money outright.[15]

The 1977 amendments, therefore, corrected the 1972 indexing mistake, but also bequeathed a system that would impose perpetually rising tax burdens as far as the eye could see.

It should be recognized, however, that this punitive treatment of the young isn't the result of wage-indexation per se. Wage indexation is just a particular way to impose the adverse outcome. The combination of demographic change and pay-as-you-go financing is what causes younger generations to face a net benefit loss.

Wage-indexation reflects a policy choice to provide consistent wage replacement at the cost of perpetually rising tax burdens. This choice can certainly be defended, though it is occasionally defended with fallacious reasoning. One such fallacy is the oft-repeated argument that "since Social Security contributions rise with worker wages, Social Security benefits should rise with wages, too."

This argument misses a key point. When the worker-collector ratio drops, no such correspondent relationship between individual tax and benefit levels can be maintained. If individual Social Security benefits rise with wages, then worker tax burdens must rise by *more* than wages; and if tax burdens rise proportionately with wages, then individual Social Security benefits must rise by *less* than wage growth. This is the inevitable math of a declining ratio of workers to collectors in a pay-as-you-go system.

$$\frac{\text{(Per-capita benefits as a \% of worker wages)}}{\text{(Ratio of Workers to Beneficiaries)}} = \text{(Worker tax burden, as a \% of wages)}$$

As can be seen in the equation above, benefits can remain a constant percentage of wages without imposing a higher tax rate, if the worker-beneficiary ratio never declines. If our society were not aging, wage-indexation would be fiscally sustainable. But if the worker-collector ratio declines—as it does in an aging society—then one of two things must happen: either benefits must grow more slowly than wages, or tax burdens must rise.

The value choice embodied in wage indexation was questioned by many experts at the time that it was made. Foremost among those expressing concerns was a consultant panel hired by the Congressional Research Service to prepare a report to the Senate Committee on Finance and the House Committee on Ways and Means.

The Consultant Panel on Social Security, known as the Hsiao Panel after its chairman, William Hsiao, put it presciently:

> The wage-indexing method proposed by President Ford may require a future generation of workers to pay a payroll tax that is 70 percent higher than the present level. This panel gravely doubts the fairness and wisdom of now promising benefits at such a level that we must commit

our sons and daughters to a higher tax rate than we ourselves are willing to pay.[16]

The Hsiao panel recommended that initial benefits be indexed instead by price inflation. Price-indexed benefits would not rise as rapidly as wage-indexed benefits, but they would fully maintain the purchasing power of subsequent generations of retirees without imposing perpetually rising tax burdens.

In agreement with this view were a number of other experts, including Henry Aaron, who chaired the 1979 Social Security Advisory Council:

> Future Congresses will be better equipped than today's Congress to determine the appropriate level and composition of benefits for future generations . . . Congress might elect to give more to certain groups of beneficiaries than to others, or to provide protection against new risks that now are uncovered. But precisely because we cannot forecast what form those desirable adjustments might take, we feel the commitment to large increases in benefits and taxes implied under current law will deprive subsequent Congresses, who will be better informed about future needs and preferences, of needed flexibility to tailor Social Security to the needs and tastes of generations to come.[17]

To put it another way: if we establish an affordable benefit formula, then future generations will have the option of increasing benefits if they so choose. But if we put in place a benefit formula that is unaffordable without imposing higher tax burdens, we leave future generations with far less flexibility as to how to meet the needs of their times.

Fundamentally, we face a value choice about how much of our children's tax dollars we should pre-commit to pay benefits to ourselves. Wage-indexation of benefits, by requiring perpetually rising tax burdens to support it, represents an aggressive claim by current generations upon the resources of future generations.

Some have speculated that the decision to adopt wage-indexation in 1977 was affected by the debate's taking place during an atypical period.

Specifically, real wages declined during 1970, 1974, and 1975, and would again in 1979 and 1980.[18] In such an environment, perhaps wage-indexation did not seem to legislators like such an expensive proposition for the long term. Regardless of the rationale, however, the new wage-indexed system soon found itself careening toward insolvency again in the early 1980s.

By the time the Greenspan Commission was convened in 1981, these various features of Social Security had quickly become entrenched: automatic benefit indexation, cost growth in excess of the underlying tax base, and a growing gap between future benefit promises and projected revenues. These elements necessitated legislation in both 1977 and 1983 to increase taxes and to reduce benefit growth, and will require further corrective measures for as long as they remain in existence.

The Greenspan Commission

Despite the painful corrective action of the 1977 amendments, Social Security thereafter still remained on a collision course with insolvency. The first trustees' reports of the 1980s warned Congress that insolvency—and the benefit disruptions that would accompany it—was imminent. The bipartisan Greenspan Commission was appointed in 1981 to make recommendations to avert this failure. After many false starts, twists, and turns, the commission's final report ultimately laid the foundation for the law signed by President Reagan on that blustery day in April, 1983.

Rather than provide a detailed history of the 1981–83 Greenspan Commission and the subsequent legislation, let us instead focus on a few salient features of the rescue most relevant to the story that continues through today.

A first important feature of the Greenspan Commission's story was the demonstrated failure of one party (or, at least, the Republicans) to fix the problem without the other. Soon after entering office, the Reagan administration proposed various measures to roll back some of the recent benefit increases that had led Social Security to financial extremity.

Despite the obvious need for some corrective measures, the administration was slapped hard for these proposals, not only by Democrats but by Republican allies as well. A 96–0 vote of a Republican-controlled Senate[19] condemned the essence of benefit changes that President Reagan had put on the table.

After this defeat, it was clear that President Reagan would get nowhere without bipartisan cooperation. He then turned to the bipartisan process of the Greenspan Commission and congressional Democrats agreed to participate in it.

A second important feature was the Greenspan Commission's composition, which arose from a noteworthy selection process. The commission consisted of fifteen members: five were appointed by President Reagan, five by the House Speaker, Democrat Tip O'Neill, and five by the Senate Majority Leader, Republican Howard Baker.

The method of appointing the commission contributed greatly to its efficacy. Each appointing individual was limited to selecting no more than three of his five choices from his own political party.[20] President Reagan thus appointed two Democrats, as did Baker, while O'Neill appointed two Republicans. This contrasts with many other commissions, to which Republicans have appointed only Republicans, and Democrats have appointed only Democrats.[21] The Greenspan Commission consequently included several individuals who could work cooperatively across the aisle, in contrast with other commissions that were collections of the most intransigent members of the respective party caucuses.

The Greenspan Commission also struck a fine balance between members within and outside of Congress. It included enough members of Congress (Senator Pat Moynihan, Senator Bob Dole, and Congressman Claude Pepper, among others) to ensure congressional buy-in, but enough from outside of Congress (notably Chairman Alan Greenspan and former Social Security Commissioner Robert Ball) to provide the prestigious cover of acknowledged experts. Other more recent commissions lacking such a balance have failed to see their recommendations enacted into law. Those composed primarily of members of Congress have failed to reach agreement, while those altogether lacking elected

The Greenspan Commission[22]

members have seen their recommendations ignored by Congress.[23] These are among the reasons why the Greenspan Commission model endures as a favorable process model. It successfully engaged both parties and facilitated the subsequent passage of legislation.

A third important feature of this story, as we have seen, is that there was bipartisan understanding that the Social Security system was in deep and immediate trouble. The annual trustees' reports had made this abundantly clear. Negotiators understood and implicitly agreed on how the system was financed, and further understood that the program's income wasn't sufficient to meet its obligations. The system's accounting practices reflected this shared understanding.

It is sobering to realize in retrospect how close the process came to failure, though this would have meant that Social Security benefit checks would soon be delayed or possibly missed altogether. Much of the commission's deliberative time was frittered away amid avoidance and delay. Each party ducked tough choices until the 1982 elections had passed. After the elections, when the commission finally got down to serious work, it bogged down in disagreement and disarray. The commission's December 31, 1982 deadline came and went without any conclusive action other than a temporary extension of its charter.

Only after Dole and Moynihan together started a final last-ditch effort, facilitating negotiations between a working subgroup of commission members and representatives of the Reagan White House, was a compromise agreement reached and the situation saved.

Thus, another moral of the commission story is that success was a close-run thing even in an atmosphere of imminent crisis and even with a widely shared understanding of system finances.

A fourth important feature with enduring consequences was the result of a prudent discretionary choice by the commission. There was concern at the time that legislators had previously been burned by the trustees' overly rosy projections, and that the system had returned so soon to the crisis point despite earlier assurances of stability. The commission was determined to avoid a repeat of this adverse outcome.

Accordingly, members evaluated their policy options not only with an eye toward averting near-term insolvency under the trustees' intermediate projections, but also toward averting insolvency if the intermediate projections proved too optimistic.

Accordingly, the Greenspan Commission's staff memoranda generally presented three columns of projections for each policy option:

- Its short-term effect under intermediate (best-guess) assumptions
- Its short-term effect under another, more pessimistic scenario
- Its long-term effect under intermediate (best-guess) assumptions[24]

Each provision's effects were evaluated by all three yardsticks.

Taking this cautious approach had a number of ancillary effects. It turned out that, indeed, the trustees' intermediate projections were once again too optimistic, at least over the period extending through today. The prudent inclusion of a cushion against such over-optimism is a principal reason that no further rescues were necessitated for decades. This prudence is another important lesson for today's policymakers.

Though some of the margin for error was in fact needed, not all of it was. Finances turned out somewhat better than the worst-case projections. As a result, the program thereafter began to build up sizable annual surpluses, with significant consequences that we will later discuss.

The fifth important aspect of the Greenspan Commission process is the way that it defined fiscal success. As we have noted, the members established goals of averting near-term insolvency even in a worst-case scenario, and averting long-term insolvency in a best-available-guess scenario. Specifically, they defined long-term solvency as actuarial balance over seventy-five years.

Equally important is what they did *not* seek to do. They did not build in the same margin for error in their long-term solution that they did in the short term. If their intermediate long-term projections proved to be too rosy—as indeed turned out to be the case—then their solution would not hold.

Nor did they aim at long-term financial balance except on *average* over seventy-five years. They did not observe and enforce the earlier-cited tradition of ensuring that the program remained roughly in balance *each year.* This means that their solution could consist of huge annual *imbalances*—huge surpluses in some years, huge deficits in others. This is, in fact, what resulted.

The implications of the goals they set—and the goals they did not set—were profound, as we shall see.

The sixth important aspect of the Greenspan Commission's work is that, even after the last-minute negotiations that produced an agreement, the commission itself was unable to agree on a complete solution for long-term solvency. Instead, it produced roughly two-thirds of an agreement, and left it to Congress to fill in the remaining third.[25]

Numerous other texts review the details of the 1983 Social Security amendments, which are not central to our story here. It is relevant to remember, however, that the Greenspan Commission did not issue a report of thoroughly analyzed recommendations for keeping the system in balance for the next seventy-five years. Instead, it provided a package of recommendations to get part of the way, while also outlining separate options for Congress to close the remainder of the gap—again, on average. The Greenspan Commission did not present to Congress a fully fleshed-out analysis of a single plan for long-term solvency.

The limitations upon the analysis performed by the Greenspan Commission have had a great impact on the historical memory of the 1983 amendments. Many contemporary commenters assume that certain aspects of the 1983 reforms were intended, when in reality the Greenspan Commission simply had not performed a detailed analysis that showed those consequences coming about.

A seventh critical aspect of the story is that, in the end, Congress enacted a package of politically difficult measures, overcoming the concentrated opposition of seniors' advocacy groups, most notably the American Association of Retired Persons (AARP). It is now conventional Washington wisdom that Social Security can only be stabilized for the long term with the cooperation and support of this powerful elderly lobby. History shows the opposite: that a long-term solution was only possible because legislators were willing to buck AARP's pressure.

AARP's opposition to the 1983 reforms is rich in ironies. One is that AARP now speaks of the 1983 reforms as a model for bipartisan Social Security reform.[26] AARP generally declines to mention that it fought against those efforts when they occurred, just as it has continued to oppose every recent congressional proposal to render Social Security financially sustainable.[27] AARP also now represents itself as believing that "any changes to the program should maintain the link between benefits and contributions."[28] But in 1983 (and at other subsequent times), AARP supported a severance of the contribution-benefit connection. Its counterproposal to the Greenspan Commission was to increase a compendium of unrelated taxes and to transfer these revenues to Social Security, without crediting these contributions toward Social Security benefits.[29]

From 1983 through today, AARP has consistently opposed specific measures to render the system financially sustainable, while offering lip service in support of the goal of a financially healthy system. What distinguishes the 1983 experience is only that legislators on both sides of the aisle were then willing to stand up to the obstructionist posture of the lobbying behemoth.

The seven elements we have described here embody, if not a detailed summary, a synopsis of the key features of the 1983 process and reforms. Below are listed these seven features of the 1983 reforms once more:

1) The initial failure of unilateral presidential leadership
2) An unusual appointment process in which a commission, composed of members both inside and outside of Congress, included appointments of Democrats by Republicans and vice versa
3) Shared bipartisan understanding of the size, scope, and immediacy of the program's financing shortfall
4) Prudent fiscal goals that included withstanding a worst-case scenario in the near-term, but—
5) Which analyzed the long-term only on *average*, only under intermediate assumptions, and *not* on a year-by-year basis
6) No in-depth analysis by the commission of a full comprehensive plan, and
7) Bipartisan willingness within Congress to withstand lobbying pressure from AARP

Components that contributed to the success of the rescue included the fact that both party's leaders provided their blessing, that the negotiators themselves were willing to compromise, that there was shared analytical clarity on the problem, that overly rosy near-term assumptions were not relied upon, and that Congress defied pressure from AARP.

On the downside, the 1983 projections for the long term proved too optimistic and certain key questions about the long-term solution were not adequately analyzed and answered.

As a result, the 1983 solution began to unravel almost immediately after enactment.[30] Worse yet, future discussions about an even-larger Social Security shortfall would take place in an environment where the formerly shared analytical clarity had been destroyed—ironically, by the 1983 reforms themselves.

After the Greenspan Commission: The Re-emergence of the Shortfall

Many of the issues that divide Social Security policy experts today derive from the particulars of the 1983 Social Security rescue. To make sense of it all, let us start with the basic facts in agreement concerning the reemerging shortfall and then proceed to the areas where disagreement and confusion reign.

The 1983 amendments successfully resolved Social Security's near-term funding crisis. Starting in 1984, Social Security once again collected more tax revenue than was needed to pay benefits.[31] These surpluses were small at first but quickly grew, as a previously scheduled payroll tax increase was accelerated by the recent law.

The surpluses continued nearly through the present day, and are just now starting to disappear as the baby boomers head into retirement. In their 2009 report, the trustees predicted the arrival of deficits in 2016, the first year since 1983 that incoming tax revenue would be less than the cost of paying benefits.[32]

Adding up all of Social Security's past surpluses (mostly accumulated since 1984) and compounding the sum with interest produces a total of $2.4 trillion, the reported 2009 balance of the Social Security Trust Fund.[33] We'll turn later to arguments about the Trust Fund's true significance. Here we will simply note that the Trust Fund represents the interest-compounded value of the Social Security taxes previously collected that have not already been spent on benefits.[34]

Going forward, we see that the recent age of annual surpluses is transforming rapidly into a future age of large annual deficits. Starting in 2016 (according to the 2009 projections), the cost of paying benefits will exceed the amount of incoming tax revenue (figure 2.1). These deficits will start small but quickly grow large, exceeding $200 billion in today's dollars by 2026. In fact, by 2019, these annual deficits will be larger, even relative to today's larger tax base, than those experienced in the crisis years of 1977 and 1982.[35] This picture will likely look still worse in the 2010 trustees' report.

FIGURE 2.1   Social Security's Looming Shortfalls

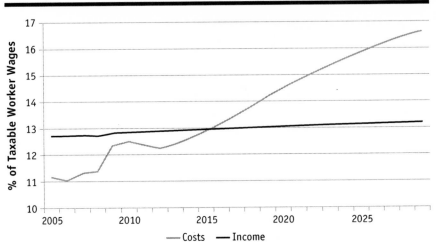

SOURCE: Based on data from the 2009 Social Security and Medicare Trustees' report.

When incoming tax revenue is insufficient to pay full benefits, the Trust Fund, under current law, comes into the picture in a new way.[36]

Experts argue endlessly about the economic significance of the Trust Fund. They agree, however, on its mechanics. The Trust Fund consists of bonds issued by the federal treasury. When Social Security runs a surplus, that surplus money is used to finance other federal spending. In return for the use of this money, the government provides a bond to Social Security, which earns interest.

If Social Security later faces a cash deficit and needs more money to pay benefits, the flow is reversed: the rest of the federal government must pony up money to redeem some bonds, money which provides the extra cash to pay full benefits. This happens until the Trust Fund bonds are all gone, at which point Social Security's authority to pay full benefits expires.[37]

The trustees recently projected that this point of insolvency will be reached in 2037. Economically, however, little changes in 2037. Social Security's annual imbalance of obligations and tax income will be nearly the same in 2038 as in 2036 (it's actually *larger* as a percentage of taxable wages in 2036).[38] In either year, approximately the same level of revenue increase must be generated in order to pay full benefits.

The significant difference between the post-insolvency date of 2038 and the pre-insolvency date of 2036 is that in 2036, the Social Security Trust Fund would hold bonds that *oblige* the government to find the additional money to fund benefit obligations. Whether there is a problem in 2037 or before depends in large part on whether one is discussing the *obligation* or the *means* of paying benefits. The obligation—or at least the full obligation—only expires in 2037, but this is separate from the question of determining the appropriate *means,* which is a policy problem well before then.

What does all of this have to do with the 1983 reforms? It was those reforms that put the pattern in motion: significant surpluses for three decades, perpetually growing cash deficits thereafter. It's this pattern that causes so many arguments and so much confusion today.

This pattern was publicly visible, not during the Greenspan Commission deliberations, but soon after the 1983 legislation was signed. We can see it in figure 2.2, based on data from the 1983 trustees' report issued in June, a few months after the legislation.[39]

This picture, which was publicly available soon after the 1983 fix, showed already that the solution wouldn't hold forever and that a future rescue would eventually be needed. As we can see, it shows that by the early twenty-first century program costs would be growing significantly faster than income and would exceed revenues by the early 2020s.

One could also see, at least by June 1983, that the advertised seventy-five-year "balance" was actually an averaging out of offsetting large annual *imbalances:* of large annual surpluses followed by large annual deficits.

We now know that the 1983 scorekeepers significantly overestimated those surpluses and likely underestimated the deficits. The system's shortfalls are now arriving more quickly than they anticipated because their assumptions were too optimistic. The basic pattern of large annual

FIGURE 2.2   Social Security's Annual Income and Cost as Projected after the 1983 Amendments (June 1983)

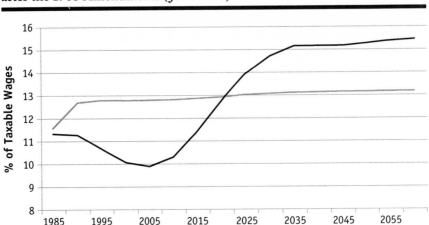

SOURCE: Based on data from the 1983 Trustees' report.

imbalances, however, was clearly visible by June 1983, even with these over-optimistic assumptions.

With this background, let us turn to some of the critical questions about which policymakers argue today, and understand how they are fueled by the 1983 reforms.

One of the foremost questions is: when does the Social Security shortfall arise, and when do we need to do something about it? Does the problem arrive in 2016, or in 2037? One's answer influences how soon one believes there is a need to act, as well as how large a shortfall there is to fill.

At one pole of possible answers is that the problem arrived two years ago in 2008. This is the answer one gets if one defines the problem as arriving when our situation starts to markedly change. The surge of baby boomer retirements has already begun and, with it, costs and pressure on the federal budget are rising. Aggregate payments will skyrocket in the years immediately to come, and these more expensive payments can't arrive in bank accounts and mailboxes around the country unless someone pays for them.

Hence, in this view, we have a problem to budget for already. It is only made more dire by the fact that the ongoing recession is simultaneously depressing payroll tax revenues.

Another view is that the problem really arises when costs are projected to exceed tax income, recently projected for 2016. As we have seen, the trend line has already shifted direction before then, but there is a further significance when annual operations go from the black to the red.

This viewpoint is premised on the observation that when costs exceed income, we must find more money from somewhere, so we need to determine how that will be done. Moreover, the deficits that begin small rise sharply thereafter, so it will be difficult to make significant headway in reducing these deficits unless we start phasing in a solution now. Indeed, we should have done so well before today.

Although this viewpoint is usually accompanied by calls to prompt action, it does not technically define the problem as *arriving* until 2016 (in last year's projections), because tax revenue will exceed program costs until that year.

Note that a focus on 2016 does *not* assert, as some have sensationally suggested, that the government would or should "default" on the bonds held in the Trust Fund. One typical version of this sensationalized attack is exemplified in the following quote by economist Dean Baker, here preemptively warning President Obama:

> If Mr. Obama plans to cut Social Security in the near future, then this effectively amounts to a default on the bonds held by the trust fund which were purchased with workers' Social Security taxes.[40]

This assertion, however, conflates two different concepts: statutory benefit formulas, on the one hand, and the amount of debt held by the Social Security Trust Fund on the other. They are two fundamentally different things.

Social Security's Trust Fund balance and one's individual benefit entitlement are concepts that do not mutually correspond. For example,

Social Security's benefit formula promises a persistent increase in benefits through 2036, through 2037, through 2038, and beyond. The limitation on the bonds in the Social Security Trust Fund, by contrast, would mandate a sudden cut in benefits in 2037.

The balance of the Social Security Trust Fund simply reflects the excess of taxes collected over benefits paid to this point. The Social Security benefit formula, on the other hand, represents a set of benefit promises made *irrespective* of the amount of bonds in the fund. It has nothing to do with the amount of benefits that the Trust Fund can sustainably pay nor with the amount of benefits "prepaid" by past contributions.

Even if we accepted the controversial view that the Trust Fund represents an effective, pre-funded entitlement to benefits, never in any year would the amount of benefits "pre-funded" in this way exceed even one quarter of the total amount scheduled.[41] The Trust Fund is never projected to have enough assets to pay even for four years' worth of total benefits, let alone all scheduled benefits from 2016–2037. The vast majority of benefit payments, even in the years of the biggest Trust Fund drawdown, would be funded by taxing the *next* generation of workers.

Just as tomorrow's workers' taxes will be the primary source of today's workers' benefits, today's workers' taxes are used primarily not to pre-fund *future* benefits but to pay for *today's* beneficiaries. The $2.4 trillion in excess taxes that system participants to date have paid into Social Security wouldn't, even if saved, come close to pre-funding the $18.7 trillion in excess future benefits now scheduled for system participants to date.[42]

Thus, when experts focus on 2016 as a year in which a financing problem arises, this has nothing whatever to do with any intent to "default" on the bonds in the Trust Fund. Instead, it's just a recognition that we must find real money to pay for benefits in any year when there is a cash deficit.

In the end, there probably is no single magic date at which the problem arrives. As long as Social Security's trend line is unsustainable, a problem exists. Our goal shouldn't be to limp along to a predictable crash point, waiting only until the last possible moment and thus hitting future generations with the most severe possible combination of tax increases and benefit reductions.

Such an irresponsible approach would fall well short of the requisite honesty with future generations about how they will be treated by Social Security. It leaves unspecified the rather substantial further sacrifices that we know must yet be required. Regardless of when we view the date of extremity to be, we do younger generations no favors by selfishly exempting ourselves from the solution and leaving trends in place that our best information shows are wholly unsustainable.

The Trust Fund and the Intent of the 1983 Reforms

In 1981–83, as we have seen, negotiators agreed on the immediacy of the Social Security problem. Today, not everyone sees the same problem, in immediacy or in size. The reasons for this have much to do with the nature of the 1983 reforms themselves.

According to the 2009 trustees' report, Social Security's permanent annual cash deficits will arrive in 2016. They will start small but will rapidly grow. By 2019, they will actually be significantly larger, even relative to our larger tax base today, than the annual deficits experienced in the crisis years of 1977 and 1982. Yet many believe that there is no real problem until decades hence, in 2037. Why?

The answer lies in the Social Security Trust Fund, whose large current balance was facilitated by the 1983 reforms. A prototypical example of the viewpoint that there is no problem for decades is embodied in a *NewsHour* interview with a prominent U.S. senator:

> What we're saying is there is no crisis. This is a manufactured crisis. Social Security, if we don't do anything, it's safe for approximately the next 50 years. When I mean safe, people will draw 100 percent of their benefits.[43]

Let us put aside for a moment a principle established in chapter 1: namely, that even if there is no shortfall for decades, continued delay in legislating is still inadvisable because of the time needed to phase in a tolerably fair solution. Let us instead focus solely on the question of how to measure the size and immediacy of the problem.

The 1983 negotiators disregarded the balance of the (admittedly small) Trust Fund when assessing the extent of Social Security's future shortfalls. Today, many advocates rely upon the balance in the Trust Fund to argue that the Social Security shortfall is decades away.

The opinion that Social Security's financing problem only emerges decades from now when Trust Fund insolvency is threatened is generally supported by arguments that fall into four categories. As we shall see, many of these arguments are premised on particular interpretations—indeed, misinterpretations—of what happened in 1983.

The four categories of arguments are these:

- The "full faith and credit" argument
- The "storehouse of saving" argument
- The "social justice" argument
- The "1983 intent" argument

We will examine each of them in turn.

The full faith and credit argument.   This argument is a simple one, and is basically limited to extolling the safety and soundness of the Trust Fund's investment in Treasury bonds. The Trust Fund is invested in Treasury bonds, and Treasury bonds are the most secure investments in the world, so what problem could there be? A typical example of the argument is sounded by AARP:

These [Trust Fund] bonds aren't only safe; they're earning approximately 7 percent in annual interest. Last year, about 13 percent of Social Security's total income—that's nearly $80 billion—was just interest alone. There you have it. For over two hundred years, in good times and in bad, these government bonds have paid off.[44]

This line of argument is probably the weakest of the four. If the matter were as simple as this, then solving the Social Security shortfall would be a trivial exercise: we could simply issue $5.3 trillion of bonds to the Trust Fund and declare it solvent for the next seventy-five years. Going further, we could issue $15.1 trillion (the size of the infinite-horizon shortfall) and declare the problem solved forever.

One needn't think very deeply to realize, however, that issuing these bonds sidesteps the critical question of where the money will come from to pay them off when due. This argument, therefore, is unresponsive to the fundamental question of how we will finance Social Security in the future.

The relevant factor here is not whether U.S. Treasury bonds are a sound investment. To understand why, consider the example of an individual with a pristine credit record. That individual cannot raise the money to buy a new car, no matter how sterling his credit, by issuing debt to himself. Similarly, the government cannot create the resources to finance future Social Security obligations *solely* by exchanging debt between its own accounts—no matter how solid its credit.

We can choose to issue more bonds to Social Security at any time. Doing so doesn't create the resources to pay Social Security benefits. That happens only when we develop a plan for paying off the bonds.

The storehouse of saving argument. Experts agree on what the Social Security Trust Fund literally *is:* it consists of bonds issued from the general fund of the Treasury. It is an asset to the Social Security system to the same degree that it is a debt to the other government accounts. It is thus not a *net* asset of the government as a whole. It is an asset held by one part, a debt held by another.

On this, experts agree. Where experts disagree is on the economic reality behind these debt issuances.

Some believe that the Social Security system, by running surpluses for several years, has been a storehouse of saving. Because the federal government was able to borrow and spend Social Security money for the past few decades, so this viewpoint holds, it was able to reduce the amount of borrowing that it would otherwise have done to finance its spending. By reducing federal debt held by the public, the Social Security system has improved the government's overall fiscal position and, in a sense, built savings to finance the system's post-2016 deficits.

For much of Social Security's history, Trust Fund balances remained so small as to prevent a definitive resolution of an ongoing debate as to whether the Trust Fund embodied real saving. Since the appearance of large surpluses in the 1980s, however, it has generally been understood that the Social Security surplus has not been used to reduce federal debt. Explanations of Trust Fund financing from the late 1980s through the 1990s generally found that the federal government was spending surplus Social Security money, and specifically doing a lot of spending that it would not otherwise be doing. A typical passage explaining the situation is from 1988 by Henry J. Aaron, Gary Burtless, and Barry P. Bosworth:

If OASDHI revenues exceed expenditures, the resulting surpluses may be used to pay for current public or private consumption . . . As the OASDHI surpluses increase, so would deficits elsewhere in the federal budget. Although this policy may seem peculiar, it closely resembles the course on which the United States has embarked today. Under this policy, the reserve does not add to national saving (because it does not reduce the overall government budget deficit) and thus it does not add to future productive capacity. . . . Although such a policy might hold down future payroll tax rates, it does not protect future taxpayers from shouldering the expense of rising benefit costs. When and if the Trust Funds are drawn down to pay for future benefits, other federal taxes will have to be increased to finance the repurchase of government debt previously bought by the OASDI Trust

Funds. In addition, the incomes against which those taxes will be imposed will be no larger than if those reserves never existed.[45]

This type of explanation was standard from the late 1980s, when the large surpluses began to be noted, throughout the 1990s and up through 2001. Similar explanations appeared in publications of the Social Security Public Trustees, the Congressional Budget Office,[46] the General Accounting Office,[47] the Congressional Research Service,[48] the Concord Coalition, and even President Clinton's annual submitted budgets[49] during those years. In 2001, President Bush's Social Security Commission cited these various sources and described the Trust Funds in similar language in its Interim Report:

> Revenue must be raised from taxpayers to redeem these bonds. Social Security has run payroll tax surpluses since the mid-1980s and will continue to do so until 2016. . . . The problem is that when Social Security begins running cash deficits in 2016, the nation will face very difficult choices. This situation arose because past payroll taxes were not truly saved, but were used to finance other government spending. As a result, future repayment of Trust Fund bonds will not be any less difficult.[50]

However, 2001 marked a shift in how the meaning of the Trust Fund was publicly debated.[51] President Bush having made reform a priority and appointed a commission to make recommendations, Social Security policy entered a more contested realm. Greater controversy began to attend not only policy disagreements but also basic factual analyses. Some policy advocates began again to argue that the Social Security Trust Fund actually *did* embody a storehouse of saving. In one example, it was asserted:

> The Commission asserts that in the future, "the nation will face the same difficult choices as if there had been no Trust Fund at all." This assertion ignores the economic contributions of the Trust Fund.

The accumulation of Trust Fund reserves raises national saving, reduces
the public debt and thereby reduces the annual cost of paying interest
on the debt, and promotes economic growth.[52]

After the Commission's Interim Report, nonpartisan scorekeeping
agencies continued to publish explanations of the lack of saving embodied in Trust Funds, similar to the commission's description.[53] But
the new critiques had reopened a debate. The schism created a fresh
set of reasons for some to resist the idea that Social Security faced financing issues well before the insolvency date, which was still decades
away.

The joining of this debate prompted new academic reviews of the
empirical evidence as to whether the Social Security surpluses have over
the years been a meaningful storehouse of saving. The results of these
analyses have returned us to a reinforced appreciation that they have not
been. Kent Smetters of the University of Pennsylvania's Wharton School
found that the presence of Trust Fund surpluses actually *reduced* saving
by inducing legislators to spend additionally in amounts *greater* than
the Social Security surplus.[54] Shoven and Sita Nataraj reported similar
results.[55]

Though the precise quantification varies from paper to paper, the
generally consistent finding has been that the Trust Fund has not been
an effective storehouse of saving, and thus there is little empirical basis
for the claim that it has postponed the problem of financing Social Security benefits from 2016 to 2037.

This does not necessarily mean that all participants will agree with
these analyses if and when Social Security reform re-enters the realm of
political negotiation. But generally speaking, the view that the Social
Security Trust Fund embodies real saving and that we have effectively
pre-funded full benefit payments through 2037 is inconsistent with the
best empirical evidence that has been gathered.

The social justice argument.   The empirical finding that Social Security surpluses since the mid-1980s have not been saved has moved some

to embrace a different rationale for declining to see a problem in 2016. Its essence is to argue that it really doesn't matter whether Social Security surpluses were saved or not. Basically, this argument is a version of the following: "If the Social Security surplus for decades subsidized the rest of the federal government, then it's only right and proper that the rest of the government subsidize Social Security for decades after that, with whatever general revenue payments it needs to make."

This viewpoint is sometimes expressed from the vantage point of distributional politics. Those who pay the payroll tax generally have a lower income profile than those who pay the income tax. If workers pay more in payroll taxes than is needed to pay for benefits, and if that overpayment allows the federal government to hold down income taxes, shouldn't the government later do the fair thing and raise future income taxes in order to pay these workers' benefits when those bills come due?

A typical example of this argument comes from Paul Krugman:

> If the trust fund is meaningless, by the way, that Greenspan-sponsored tax increase in the 1980's was nothing but an exercise in class warfare: taxes on working-class Americans went up, taxes on the affluent went down, and the workers have nothing to show for their sacrifice. But never mind: the same people who claim that Social Security isn't an independent entity when it runs surpluses also insist that late next decade, when the benefit payments start to exceed the payroll tax receipts, this will represent a crisis—you see, Social Security has its own dedicated financing, and therefore must stand on its own.[56]

This may sound reasonable at first until one thinks it through. The fatal flaw in the logic above is that the issue is not as simple as one fixed body or group borrowing from another, and then paying it back later on.

The more complex reality is that different generations pay taxes and receive benefits at different times. When this is considered, the "social justice" argument not only falls apart, it bears contrary implications altogether.

The working generations of the 1980s and 1990s paid more in payroll taxes than was then needed to pay Social Security benefits.

That surplus money was consumed—whether through direct spending or by allowing lower income taxes—by those same generations. As that money was spent, bonds were issued to the Social Security Trust Fund.

Current law obliges future workers in the 2020s and 2030s to commit higher general revenues, beyond their payroll taxes, to redeem trillions in bonds of the Social Security Trust Fund. These higher cost burdens would be imposed to pay Social Security benefits—mostly to the same generations that earlier consumed the Social Security surplus.

The problem with the "social justice" argument thus becomes apparent: the generations who spent the Social Security money on themselves aren't the same generations who are being asked to foot the bill later on for its repayment.

To better understand this, consider a simple analogy of a family that has set up a retirement fund. Everyone in the family agrees to put a certain amount of money into the fund while working, and each is told that he or she can withdraw money in retirement.

Now let's assume that the family father dips into the fund during his working years. He spends the money on himself in other ways—perhaps on a few golf trips, perhaps a new den, maybe a sailboat. Each time he does so, he puts a note in the fund and promises to pay it back in the future.

When it is time for the father to retire, it turns out that there is no money in the fund—only his notes promising that the fund will be paid back. On that date, the father approaches his son and says, "Son, it's time for me to retire. By the way, I withdrew the money from the retirement fund, to pay for some other things I wanted. But now I am ready to claim my retirement benefits, so it's time to pay back that money. Fair is fair: this family borrowed money from the fund all these years, and now this family has got to pay it back. So in addition to the retirement fund payments we previously agreed that you would make, you'll need to come up with additional contributions to pay back all of the money that I spent."

Obviously, the son would not be too excited about this arrangement. It would not escape his notice that the person who borrowed and spent the money (the father) is not the same person who is being asked to pay it back (the son).

This is the basic flaw in the "social justice" argument. It assumes two separate and fixed groups—modest-income workers under Social Security versus upper-income people who pay income taxes—without accounting for generational differences. It confuses what is essentially an intergenerational transaction with an inter-class transaction (see table 2.1).

What's ironic about the "social justice" argument is that there *is* available a mechanism for requiring the repayment of Social Security

TABLE 2.1 The Social Justice Argument

The Flawed "Social Justice" Argument	
1980s–2000s	*2010s–2030s*
Joe Sixpack Payroll Taxpayer subsidizes government for high-income taxpayers	High-income taxpayers need to pay back Joe Sixpack Payroll Taxpayer via higher income taxes to pay his Soc. Sec. benefits.

The Neglected Generational Aspect of the "Social Justice" Argument	
1980s–2000s	*2010s–2030s*
Surplus Soc. Sec. taxes were used to subsidize government for working generations of 1980s-2000s.	Workers of 2010s–2030s to pay higher income taxes to provide Soc. Sec. benefits to workers of the 1980s–2000s.

If We Buy the "Social Justice" Argument, What Is the Solution?	
Wrong	*Right*
Not by raising taxes on workers of the 2010s–2030s, who did not participate in the spending of 1980s–2000s Soc. Sec money.	If "social justice" finds that high-income Americans benefited in the 1980s–2000s and this money needs to be paid back, this would need to come from *seniors* in the 2010s–2030s—not young taxpayers.

money by the same generations and income levels who spent it. If we accept the depiction that the excess payroll tax collections of the 1980s and 1990s were a form of class warfare benefiting affluent income tax payers in those years, then the appropriate place to turn to have the money paid back would *not* be to the young taxpayers of the 2020s and 2030s.

Instead, it would mean getting the money back from the affluent income taxpayers of the 1980s and 1990s, who of course are far more likely to be retirees in the 2020s and the 2030s. This would be straight-forwardly accomplished by reducing benefits for those with higher wage histories, not by raising general revenues to pay off the Trust Fund.

In summary, because it neglects issues of income redistribution across generations, the "social justice" argument for the meaning of the Trust Fund collapses upon inspection. Carried through to its logical conclusion, the argument actually supports a reduction in the growth of Social Security benefits well before 2037.

The 1983 intent argument

By far, the most widely held misinterpretation of the Trust Fund has to do with the intentions of the negotiators who crafted the 1983 reforms that built it up. Indeed, the pervasiveness of this misconception is the chief reason we have included this detailed Trust Fund discussion within this historical chapter on the 1983 reforms.

The essence of the argument is this: "Maybe it's true that Social Se-curity Trust Fund surpluses weren't saved. Maybe it's unfair to young generations to hand them the bill for redeeming the Trust Fund. But fair or not, there was a societal compact in 1983. We all agreed that baby boomers would overpay their payroll taxes beyond what was then needed, to pre-fund their own future retirement benefits. Maybe it didn't work out as we planned. But that was the deal. Like it or not, to be fair, we have to carry through on the common understanding. It wouldn't be right to appreciably change the benefit structure for the baby boomers when for so many years we collected surplus Social Security payroll taxes with the understanding that they would go toward funding future benefits."

This belief is widely held—by the press, by public figures, and even by many widely cited Social Security experts.

It's also completely false.

A typical example of this portrait of Social Security's history comes from this paper from the National Bureau of Economic Research:

> [T]he Greenspan Commission's plan was for Social Security to depart from pay-as-you-go financing and to partially pre-fund the retirement costs of the baby boom generation. The idea was to offer some relief to the workers in the 2015 to 2050 period in supporting the enormous population forecast for that period. By forcing workers in 1984–2015 to pay higher payroll taxes than required to finance current retirement benefits, the hope was that workers in the 2016–2050 era could pay lower than PAYGO taxes. The trust fund buildup and subsequent drawdown would spread the burden of the retirements of the baby boomers over 65 years, rather than 30 years, and to some degree even out the tax burden faced by different generations of workers.[57]

One can find any number of nearly identical quotes from different sources. This view is held without regard to politics or ideology; sources for it range from advocates of action, to defenders of the status quo, to opponents of personal accounts, to proponents of personal accounts. Some, like a recent paper from the National Academy of Social Insurance, even approach an implication that the onrushing post-2016 deficits are not a bug but a benign feature of 1983's far-seeing plan. ("This is not a crisis. In fact, this is precisely what the 1983 reforms intended to happen.")[58]

It's unsurprising that so many analysts should reach a similar conclusion. After all, the singular feature of the 1983 reforms is the remarkable pattern of surpluses and subsequent deficits that they engendered. Surely, it is assumed, such an enormously consequential outcome must have been intentional. Why else would the 1983 negotiators have done this, unless they believed that the surpluses in the near-term could be banked in the Trust Fund to finance the deficits in the long term?

The documentary evidence, however, instead shows that not only has the Trust Fund *not* been saved, but the framers of the 1983 amendments were laboring under no misconceptions that it would or could be. Neither the Greenspan Commission nor members of Congress realized during their deliberations that the proposed reforms would produce decades of Social Security surpluses, and would not have regarded such a result as desirable or effective pre-funding even if they had known.

First, there is the documentary evidence of the statements of those involved with the Greenspan Commission's work. Commission Executive Director Robert Myers, in a 1995 interview, asserted that there had been no plan or expectation of building up large Trust Fund surpluses:

> MYERS: It just developed. It wasn't planned. Nobody said let's do it this way. It was just the natural result of saying we'll fix up the long-range situation in 75 years on the average. We'll fix it up and we'll do this in part by having a high tax rate beginning in 1990. When you have a level tax rate and increasing benefit costs, then averaging out higher benefits later you're bound to build up a fund and you're bound to use it up.
>
> Q: *As we look at it today, some people rationalize the financing basis by saying that it's a way of partially having the baby boomers pay for their own retirement in advance. You're telling me now this was not the rationale. Nobody made that argument or adopted that rationale?*
>
> MYERS: That's correct. The statement you made is widely quoted, it is widely used, but it just isn't true. It didn't happen that way, it was mostly happenstance that the Commission adopted this approach to financing Social Security. The way they thought about it was that in order to achieve long-range balance we have to have this high tax rate in 1990, instead of putting it in steps. We could have fixed it up with a series of steps, lower in 1990, about the same in 2010, higher in 2015, that could have fixed it up just as easily, but there wasn't time. It was not intentional.[59]

Myers in the same interview goes so far as to describe the Trust Fund buildup essentially as an accidental flaw of the 1983 reforms, and suggests that had the commission had the time and opportunity, it would have fixed the solution to do away with it.

> But the Commission never really looked at the long range situation except wanting to be able to say we recognized it. We've raised the retirement age to help solve this problem and so forth. So in hindsight critics can say, "Hey, why didn't you guys do a more thorough job?" When a house is burning down you can't always take care of every problem. That was the situation. Obviously in an ideal world we would have done a better job. I would have done a better job, but it would have been silly for me to get up before the Commission in the closing days and say, "Hey look guys. Sure you fixed up the short-range. Sure you recognized the long-range problem but you didn't really thoroughly study the long-range problem." They couldn't be bothered with that.[60]

These were not mere recollections well after the fact. Myers's own appendix to the Greenspan Commission report itself states clearly that the intention of policymakers for several years had been, and remained, to fund Social Security on a pay-as-you-go basis.

> Over the years, the original emphasis on building up and maintaining a large fund was reduced. Gradually, the funding basis shifted, in practice, to what might be called a current-cost or pay-as-you-go basis. The intent under such a basis is that income and outgo should be approximately equal each year and that a fund balance should be maintained which will be only large enough to meet cyclical fluctuations both within the year and also over economic cycles which have durations of several years. There is no established rule as to the desirable size of a contingency fund, although the general view is that it should be an amount equal to between 6 and 12 months' outgo.[61]

The subsequent behavior of key players on the commission is further evidence in support of Myers's interpretation. A few years later, when

Social Security's mounting annual surpluses had been publicly noted, former Greenspan Commission member Senator Daniel Patrick Moynihan recognized that the attainment of "seventy-five-year solvency" had been to a great degree illusory, predicated as it was on the near-term buildup of annual surpluses that would never be saved. Moynihan thus led a legislative effort to cut the payroll tax in the near term and allow it to rise in the long term, to prevent the federal government from spending the near-term surplus money and thus render solvency a fiction.

The floor debate on the Moynihan bill reflects contemporary views of the situation. Notably, he describes the surpluses even in 1990 as having caught them "unawares."

> MOYNIHAN: The trust funds are now rising at approximately $1.5 billion a week, and will shortly be rising at $2 billion, soon $3 billion, then $4 billion a week. They will, in sum, accumulate a surplus of some $3 trillion in the next 30 years. Three trillion dollars is a sizable sum. The stocks of all the companies listed on the New York Stock Exchange would sell for about $3 trillion. This money is coming in. It is the largest revenue stream in the history of public finance. One of the extraordinary facts is that *it has come upon us almost unawares, and we have yet to make a decision about how to treat these moneys.*[62] (Italics added.)

During this floor debate, Moynihan offered his recollections of the evolving awareness of the surpluses and of his conviction of what to do with them:

> MOYNIHAN: In any event, a commission on Social Security reform was established in 1982 and in 1983, again Senator Dole being very active. I was a member of the commission. We put together the Social Security amendments of that year. We proposed them; they were enacted almost without change, very brief . . . for all of the attention, all we did was accelerate rate increases already in place. Then, Mr. President, we began to notice the surplus. When did we notice the surplus? Well, I do not know that I can say for certain. I think

that by 1988 it was getting to be pretty clear, that not only was there a surplus, but also an opportunity. On August 8, 1988, I asked the General Accounting Office for a study of the subject. I might say that prior to that, in the spring, in May 1988, so that some people will understand we are not coming here with some sudden proposition that nobody has heard about, we held hearings in the Subcommittee on Social Security and Family Policy . . . Robert J. Myers, a man of great distinction, who was chief actuary of the Social Security system, and National Commission on Social Security Reform in 1982—came before us a sad, but truthful man. He said, "Gentlemen, go back to pay-as-you-go financing. Because, gentlemen, you are never going to save the surplus. The old Presbyterian belief, you might say, that temptation is never overcome. The flesh is weak, the spirit notwithstanding. Give it back before it becomes a habit you cannot break."[63]

Future Senate Majority Leader Harry Reid took Moynihan's side in that 1990 debate. They together mocked the idea that the Social Security Trust Fund was building a meaningful accumulation of reserves, at variance with the Democratic leadership's later posture that the Trust Fund ensured Social Security's vitality for several decades into the future:

MR. MOYNIHAN: There are no reserves. They have all been embezzled. They have been spent.

MR. REID. Will the Senator yield?

MR. MOYNIHAN. Yes.

MR. REID. Maybe what we should do in conjunction with the President to really carry this conspiracy to its appropriate end, is rather than having it called the Social Security trust fund, why do we not change it and call it the "Social Security slush fund?"

MR. MOYNIHAN. Our policy staff, honestly, somehow believe there are reserves. What there are in IOU's from the Treasury. This money has been spent as general revenue, as the Senator from South Carolina says. I prayed for them with the Democratic Party and I hope the Republicans pray for us as well.

Not only commission members and staff, but the legislators who later crafted the bill to implement the 1983 reforms, shared Myers's and Moynihan's understanding. In a May 17, 1983 letter to the Wall Street Journal—notably, *after* the Social Security amendments had been signed into law—Texas Democrat Jake Pickle, chair of the Social Security Subcommittee of the House Ways and Means Committee, wrote:

> [W]e would not want to fund our national retirement program other than on a pay-as-you-go basis. To accumulate now funds to pay all future benefits would require a government reserve in the trillions of dollars—a build up of government investments not likely to be tolerated by the public.[64]

These and other statements document that the crafters of the 1983 reforms not only did not intend to build up a large Trust Fund, but in many cases opposed such an outcome, and believed the public did so as well.

Of course, the memories and perspectives of individuals are fallible. But the other documentary evidence tells the same story.

The Greenspan Commission did not report a single complete plan to Congress, and thus could not have analyzed the annual cash flows for any such plan. Instead, the commission provided to Congress recommendations for provisions that would close roughly two-thirds of the seventy-five-year solvency gap *on average*, and left it for Congress to choose among options to fill in the remaining third.[65] Nowhere in the Greenspan Commission report is there a comprehensive plan that is analyzed for its effect on the flow of Trust Fund balances over time.

In its internal deliberations over different policy options, the commission reviewed memoranda describing each provision's near-term effects under both intermediate *and* high-cost scenarios and its long-term effects *on average* under intermediate projections.[66] The annual flows of long-term effects are not presented on those memoranda. (Indeed, one of the reasons that the Social Security Office of the Actuary now analyzes individual provisions much more thoroughly, showing annual flows as well as those averaged over time, is precisely to enable legislators to avoid some of the shortcomings of the 1983 analysis.)[67]

The commission's prudence in ensuring that insolvency would be averted in a worst-case scenario is one of the chief reasons for the subsequent Trust Fund buildup. Reality has arrived at a point somewhere in between their intermediate and worst-case scenarios, which meant that a good deal of the margin for error was later realized in the form of mounting program surpluses. The Congressional Research Service, in an excellent and comprehensive 1997 paper, explained well the consequences of this prudence:

> Various misperceptions of their intent have developed over the years, among them being that Congress wanted to create surpluses to "advance fund" the benefits of post World War II baby boomers. . . . There is, however, little evidence to support the view that the surpluses were intended to pay for the baby boomers' retirement. The record suggests that the goal was to assure that the system was not threatened by insolvency again, not to advance fund future benefits.[68]

The CRS report goes on to explain that the focus on avoiding insolvency even under the pessimistic scenario continued to guide deliberations of the Senate Finance and House Ways and Means committees when they had assembled final completed packages to evaluate. Like the Greenspan Commission, the committees reviewed estimates for both the intermediate and pessimistic scenarios, and evaluated their work to ensure it would survive the worst-case possibilities in the near term. Again, quoting from CRS:

> To suggest that these balances were intended to finance or to "advance fund" the benefits of the baby boomers and subsequent retirees presumes that the authorizing committees (and the Congress generally) designed the measures specifically to create significant excess income and believed this income would be isolated from the financial operations of the rest of the government such that it would have accumulated as a "nest egg." Neither of the reports from the House Ways and Means

and Senate Finance Committees made any reference to such "advance funding."[69]

CRS also goes on to document the failure to analyze the annual flows of the 1983 reforms, relying upon "averaged" effects on the seventy-five-year balance:

> The discussion in Committee markups revolved around the average 75-year deficit and how much the various options would affect that figure. Hence, there was very little understanding that a period of surpluses would be followed by a period of deficits—or that "actuarial balance" was not achieved on a pay-as-you-go basis.[70]

If this evidence seems overwhelming, none of it is actually the evidence that most firmly clinches the issue. But there is another piece of evidence that irrefutably demonstrates that the crafters of the 1983 amendments never intended to build up a large Trust Fund.

That piece of evidence is this: *The crafters of the 1983 reforms did not use an actuarial method that is consistent with solvency as defined using Trust Fund accounting.* To the contrary, there is a mathematical inconsistency between the accounting of a large accumulated Trust Fund and the method used in 1983 to calculate actuarial balance.

Today, the Trustees employ a method for determining actuarial balance known as the "level financing" method. This method, in effect, averages out the program's future surpluses and deficits in a particular way: specifically, it discounts the size of future imbalances by a rate of interest—the rate of interest the Trust Fund is projected to earn.

Using this method ensures consistency between our measures of "actuarial balance" and the size of the Trust Fund. The point at which the actuarial balance goes negative is the point at which the Trust Fund reserves are depleted. These two methods are internally consistent: we project that the Trust Fund will earn a certain rate of interest, and we also discount future deficits by that rate of interest. This method tells us both that the Trust Fund will be positive through 2037 and that the system is in actuarial balance through 2037. This method was not adopted until 1988.[71]

In effect, this method implicitly assumes that the Trust Fund is "real." It treats the Trust Fund as saving that is pre-funding future deficits, without regard for whether it is actually saved. Many analysts, such as this author, thus find fault with the method. Further, it significantly discounts the size of future deficits relative to other federal budgetary conventions. For example, a deficit that would require the workers of 2080 to contribute a further 5 percent of their wages to make up could well be treated, by this method, as a smaller deficit than one that would require a 3 percent payroll tax hike on the workers of 2050.[72] Such a method can tend to distort our picture of the relative tax burdens faced by different generations.

Putting aside these analytical concerns, however, the method adopted in 1988 reflects a critical analytical decision not reached until that year: to align the measure of the Trust Fund balance with the measure of the actuarial balance. By 1988, at the latest, the trustees realized that Trust Fund accounting methodology and the actuarial balance calculation were yielding different results.[73]

This is not, however, the method that the Greenspan Commission used.

The Greenspan Commission used a different method known as the "average cost" method. This method simply averaged out the future surpluses and deficits of Social Security expressed as a percentage of worker wages. This method implicitly assumes that Social Security benefits are paid by taxing the wages of workers at the time those benefits are paid—and *not* by drawing down the accumulated reserves of a Trust Fund.

There is a mathematical conflict between Trust Fund accounting and the method the Greenspan Commission used. If the Greenspan Commission had compared its projection for actuarial balance over seventy-five years, with the result that would arise from Trust Fund accounting, they would have produced two different answers.

Moreover, as we have previously mentioned, the actuarial calculations of 1983 "did not take into account the trust fund balances at the start of the valuation period."[74] No commission that believed that the Trust Fund was an effective source of advance funding would perform its calculations in disregard of the Trust Fund balance to date.

It is abundantly clear, based on all of this documentary evidence, that neither the Greenspan Commission, nor the Congress as a whole in 1983, intended that the 1983 reforms build up a large Trust Fund, nor did they believe that it was possible to pre-fund future benefits by doing so.

Summary and Conclusions

What lessons should we remember from the 1983 reforms?

One is that reforming Social Security is a daunting political task. The 1983 reform effort was narrowly rescued from failure, despite broad bipartisan agreement on the scope and immediacy of Social Security's problems.

The analytical understanding widely shared in 1983 also contains detailed lessons for us. Reformers in 1983 did not rely on Trust Fund balances to reduce the apparent size of Social Security's projected future shortfalls. They looked squarely at the coming deficits and fully recognized the relative burden they would place on future worker wages.

The crafters of the 1983 reforms did not intend to build up a large Trust Fund, nor would they have believed that so doing would pre-fund future benefits. They would not have agreed with the statements made by some today that Social Security faces no problems between 2016 and 2037.

It is also worth remembering that the crafters of the 1983 reforms were determined by an unusual bipartisan process in which participants were often selected by others from across the aisle.

The crafters of the 1983 reforms, indeed Congress as a whole, enabled reform via bipartisan resistance to the lobbying pressure of seniors' advocacy organizations such as AARP. Similar fortitude is required today.

These are among the positive lessons of 1983, but there are cautionary lessons as well. Not everything was done perfectly. The biggest mistake then made was to take only an "averaged" view of the program's future balance, neglecting to account for the practicability of Social Security's projected annual operations.

To successfully address Social Security today, we will need to get right what they got right in 1983 (bipartisanship, courage in the face of lobbying pressure, and honest recognition of Social Security's shortfalls) while avoiding their mistakes. A process today that does any less is unlikely to bear fruit.

CHAPTER 3

The Warning Bell Tolls . . . and Tolls

F ROM THE LATE 1980S THROUGH the turn of the twenty-first century, the story of Social Security's finances was one of fairly steady deterioration and of a dawning sense among close observers that not all had turned out well with the 1983 reforms.

As early as 1985, the trustees were reporting that Social Security was out of long-range balance again.[1] Every year from 1984 through 1997 Social Security's long-range imbalance was reported as worse than the year before.[2] By 1992, less than one decade after the fix, the projected long-range deficit was again already larger than the one supposedly repaired in 1983.[3] What had gone wrong?

The biggest problem, it was soon discerned, was that the 1983 reforms had not placed Social Security on a sustainable course. As was detailed in the last chapter, the "balance" achieved in the reforms was actually a composite of large annual *imbalances:* decades of surpluses followed by decades of deficits. Thus, with each passing year, a surplus year faded into the past while a large new annual deficit appeared over the horizon. This meant that even under the 1983 projections, time alone would ensure that insolvency would occur in the absence of further tax increases or cost restraints.

This, however, wasn't the only problem. Another involved simple mistakes in the 1983 computations. Perhaps the most serious one had to do with the treatment of immigrants. As I described this in a 2007 presentation, "[P]reviously, immigrants had been treated as though younger than the general population, thereby overestimating their amount of future tax payments, and postponing the date at which their benefit claims would be counted. Correcting this error alone worsened the seventy-five-year actuarial imbalance by more than 10 percent of its currently projected size."[4]

Another problem was that the trustees' intermediate assumptions had been too optimistic with respect to program finances.[5] Recall as reviewed in the last chapter that legislators had ensured that the system would remain in balance *in the near term*, no matter whether the trustees' intermediate or worst-case projections came to pass. But they didn't build in a similar cushion for the long term. If the intermediate projections were too rosy—as indeed they turned out to be—the system would not even remain in balance under the incomplete solvency definition that the 1983 negotiators had relied upon.

One of today's most persistent myths about Social Security finances is that the trustees' projections have a track record of being too conservative. This is indeed a myth, as we will review in some detail later; the vast majority of trustees' reports over the past several decades have used assumptions that proved to be too *aggressive*. The 1983 economic assumptions were a prime example of over-optimism (figure 3.1). It was assumed then that worker wages would grow henceforth by 1.5 percent above inflation.[6] This was an overestimate, considered in the context of real wage growth that has averaged 0.8 percent over the last forty years.[7]

Social Security finances are not as sensitive to wage growth as many often wrongly assume, because both taxes and benefits grow proportionally with wages under current law. But slower real wage growth does hurt Social Security finances in the near term because it reduces near-term revenue. The trustees' overly aggressive 1983 predictions for real wage growth thus meant that the system's deficits would arrive sooner than projected.

All of these factors—an inherently unsustainable financial path coupled with overly rosy assumptions and simple methodological mistakes—

FIGURE 3.1 The 1983 Real Wage Growth Assumptions: Projections
That Exceeded Reality

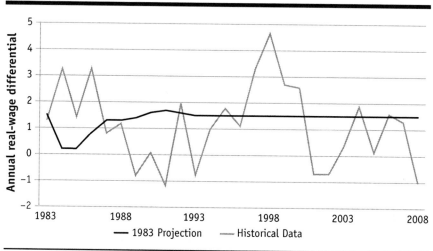

SOURCE: Based on data from the 1983 and 2009 Trustees' reports.

meant that Social Security was soon once again drifting into trouble.
Despite just having been the object of major bipartisan exertions, Social
Security's problems quickly returned to the national agenda.

1988: The Trustees Shrink the Deficit—On Paper

As indicated previously, this book is not intended to provide a detailed
history of the Social Security program. Our goal in reviewing specific
episodes of program history is to highlight those aspects that bear most
directly upon today's policy debate. Several such turning points took
place during the period from 1983 to 2000.

One especially critical event was a technical change that took effect
in 1988 with virtually no public awareness. Indeed, to this day, even
many Social Security experts remain unaware of it.

The event was a change in the 1988 Social Security trustees' report
that made the Social Security shortfall appear smaller. It was not a
finding that the shortfall was smaller; the deficit itself had grown

during that year. Instead, it was merely a decision to measure the deficit in a different way—one that shrank its apparent size by roughly one-third.

Because of the 1988 accounting change, many now wrongly believe that today we face a long-range Social Security deficit that is no larger than was seen in 1981–83. This is not true. The long-range (seventy-five-year) deficit we face today is *much* bigger. We simply make it appear smaller by the way we now keep our books. The 1988 change is one of the reasons today that many believe that the program can be fixed by a "nip and a tuck"—minor adjustments that in reality would be far inadequate to put the program on a sustainable course.

Figure 3.2 shows that in the 1982 trustees' report, Social Security's seventy-five-year imbalance was projected to equal 1.8 percent of all taxable wages. Today, the seventy-five-year deficit is defined to be only slightly larger: 2 percent of all taxable wages. But this is not an apples-to-apples comparison. Using the same methods employed in 1982, today's deficit is much larger: 3 percent of taxable wages. We already have a lift facing us that is over 50 percent heavier than the one that was so difficult to manage in 1983.

FIGURE 3.2   Social Security's Projected 75-Year Imbalance: Pre-1988 and Post-1988 Methods

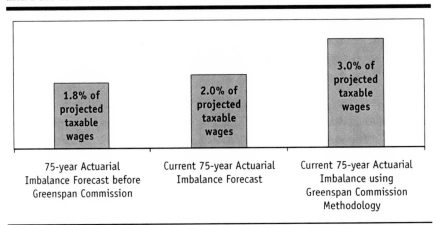

The 1988 change pertained to how future Social Security deficits are discounted into today's terms. Discounting is a method used to reflect the changing value of money over time. It's an imperfect art. How many dollars in 2075 are comparable to a dollar today? The answer depends on the discount rate one uses.

In 1983, the trustees measured future deficits as a percentage of taxable wages in every year evaluated. This reflected a recognition that future benefits would be paid by taxing future workers. As the tax base grew over time, it was understood, so did our ability to finance future benefit payments.

This method was simple and straightforward. If it cost 10 percent of worker wages to pay benefits today, but 15 percent of worker wages to pay benefits in some future year, then we'd treat the cost in that future year as 50 percent larger. In the 1983 method, a deficit in one year of 2 percent of worker wages would require a surplus in another year—also of 2 percent of worker wages—to balance it.

The new method adopted in 1988, however, discounted future benefits much more aggressively, by the rate of interest "earned" by the Social Security Trust Fund.[8] Drawing upon the example in the last paragraph, the new method might instead say that the system is perfectly "balanced" if a surplus of 2 percent of wages today is followed in the future by a deficit of 4 percent, or 5 percent, or 6 percent—or even more, depending on the span of time. One can easily see how this second method makes future deficits appear far smaller.

This type of discounting would be fully appropriate if we had a different kind of Social Security system. If the Social Security surplus were saved and used to reduce federal debt, then the savings to the government would equal not only the amount of that surplus, but also the interest payments avoided. In such a system, discounting by the Trust Fund interest rate would produce an accurate proxy for the government's ability to finance future deficits.

As we saw in the last chapter, however, this is not how Social Security has been operated. The Trust Fund was not saved, and indeed there was no original intent to save it. Despite this reality, we shifted in 1988 to a new methodology that implicitly *assumed* it was being saved, and thereby made the future shortfall appear much smaller.

Shrinking the apparent size of the Social Security deficit wasn't the only effect of the 1988 accounting change. A side effect was to bias the comparative evaluation of different policies.

In particular, the accounting switch tilted the playing field in any future policy discussions in favor of tax increases and against advance funding. An example may be helpful in fully understanding why.

Suppose, for example, that we contemplated raising the cap on taxable wages. To evaluate the effects of this under the 1983 methods, we would simply measure how much revenue this would raise as a percentage of worker wages. We would also determine how much in additional future benefits would be paid, again as a percentage of worker wages. Altogether, the policy would be tested by how much it would shrink the future shortfall—always as a percentage of future worker wages.

The new post-1988 method, however, overstates how much of the fiscal gap would be closed by raising taxes in this way. It does so by implicitly assuming that the government will save any additional tax money provided today, and that the savings would result in interest payments that compound enormously over time. Thus, over the very long term, it appears as though the near-term tax increase has greatly improved our ability to finance future benefits—even though this assumption doesn't conform to the empirical reality that the government spends rather than saves the money.

The method also heavily biases the policy discussion against advance funding. Suppose hypothetically that we moved *2 percent of worker wages* today into a savings vehicle, and further that by so pre-funding some future benefits, we reduce worker tax burdens by *3 percent of worker wages* at some future date. In the 1983 methodology, we would perceive that we had improved the system's balance sheet. But in the new 1988 methodology, we could shrink that savings of 3 percent of future worker wages down via discounting so that it appears smaller than 2 percent of worker wages today. Thus, it appears as though we have actually *wors-*

ened system finances—even though we have reduced the deficits future workers must finance.

The 1988 actuarial change thus had several adverse consequences. One is that it shrank the apparent deficit, such that many today do not realize we face a much bigger problem than was faced in 1983.

Another is that it built in, within the actuarial methodology, the *assumption* that we were already effectively pre-funding through the Trust Fund. This inherently biases the policy discussion against efforts to move toward true pre-funding and in favor of measures, such as tax increases, that are now scored as adding to our pre-funding even if in practice they would not.

The 1988 changes thus injected a significant amount of confusion into our Social Security debate. Today, one often reads pronouncements about the size of the future Social Security shortfall or of the supposed fiscal effects of various policy proposals. One only rarely, however, encounters recognition of how the 1988 accounting changes shape these evaluations both of the current-law shortfall and of proposals to address it.

To sensibly chart our course going forward, we need to recognize the assumptions built into the 1988 accounting changes and to adjust our thinking for where they deviate from empirical reality. A general failure to do so has, unfortunately, undercut the policy debate through the present time.

Senator Moynihan and the 1989–90 Effort to Return to Pay-as-you-go

Perhaps the first significant event in Social Security politics after the 1983 reforms followed the dawning realization that the reforms had created large annual imbalances—decades of surpluses followed by decades of deficits. This meant that one of two things would have to happen: either the government would have to find a way to ensure that these near-term surpluses would be saved or else it must be recognized that the so-called seventy-five-year balance just advertised was actually an illusion.

As we demonstrated in the last chapter, the 1983 negotiators did not intend to create this situation. They did not intend to build up annual surpluses or a large Trust Fund. Nor did they believe that doing so would effectively pre-fund future Social Security benefits. As Senator Daniel Patrick Moynihan expressed it a few years later, the large surpluses came upon policymakers "unawares."

Intended or not, by the late 1980s Social Security's large surpluses were a reality that had to be recognized and dealt with. So too was the accompanying reality, recognized by a broad spectrum of experts, that the Social Security surpluses were not being saved but instead were being used by the government to finance its ongoing spending.[9]

For Moynihan, the answer was clear and simple: cut the payroll tax in the near term, when the surplus money was simply being spent, and raise it later, when additional money was actually needed to pay benefits. As Moynihan put it in his inimitable way on the Senate floor:

> On August 8, 1988, I asked the General Accounting Office for a study of the subject. I might say that prior to that, in the spring, in May 1988, so that some people will understand we are not coming here with some sudden proposition that nobody has heard about, we held hearings in the Subcommittee on Social Security and Family Policy . . . Robert J. Myers, a man of great distinction, who was chief actuary of the Social Security system and National Commission on Social Security Reform in 1982—came before us a sad, but truthful man. He said, "Gentlemen, go back to pay-as-you-go financing. Because, gentlemen, you are never going to save the surplus. The old Presbyterian belief, you might say, that temptation is never overcome. The flesh is weak, the spirit notwithstanding. Give it back before it becomes a habit you cannot break."[10]

The subject had seized the attention of policy experts at about the same time it had seized the senator (unsurprisingly, because Moynihan should himself be regarded as an expert). Carolyn Weaver of the American Enterprise Institute edited a volume entitled "Social Security's Looming Surpluses," published in 1990, presenting the discussion that took place at a conference held in March 1989. The conference asked a range of experts on both sides of the aisle their opinions as to what should be done about the emerging surpluses.

What is striking about this discussion in retrospect is the high degree of agreement across ideological lines that the Social Security surpluses, under current practices, were never going to be saved. Nobel Prize-winning economist James Buchanan described the recognized phenomenon, first in somewhat hypothetical terms:

> [T]o the extent that the trust fund surpluses are offset by expansions in other federal spending, there will be no induced increase in the rate of private capital formation in the economy. There will be no direct or indirect "funding" of the future pension obligations. The social security account, treated as an administratively separate unit, will accumulate claims against the Treasury, and hence the general taxpayer, but there will be no increase in future income that will allow such claims to be more easily financed, either through taxation or debt issue.[11]

Later, however, Buchanan dropped the posture of agnosticism and indicated that, indeed, the path Social Security had been placed upon was one of illusory solvency, of shifting unrecognized costs to future generations:

> Current nonpayroll taxpayers and non-social-security program beneficiaries gain in an opportunity cost sense. They are not required to reduce the benefits they get from the spending flows that generate the current deficit. Future taxpayers generally (payroll and other) along with future beneficiaries of other government programs lose . . . The result seems clear. The pattern of gains and losses . . . is not what motivated the 1983 legislation. The National Commission on Social Security Reform (the Greenspan Commission) and its advocates may have produced a fiscal chain of events that was no part of their intention. Would they have been so enthusiastic in support of the changes and so self-satisfied with their apparent accomplishments if they had looked more realistically on the working of modern democratic politics?[12]

By the "working of modern democratic politics," Buchanan referred to the irresistible temptation for the government to spend the surplus Social Security money that the 1983 reforms had inadvertently left sitting on the federal ledger.

As quoted in the same volume, Barry Bosworth—like many of the conference participants—asserted that the Social Security surpluses, if indeed they could be saved, could in theory be a boon to efforts to prepare for the coming retirement of the baby boomers:

> [S]etting aside the surplus to add to national saving has enormous appeal from an economic point of view. It provides a means of responding to the inadequate national saving and to the excessive trade deficit. Adding the surplus to national saving would recognize the increased saving required for an aging future population.

But then Bosworth also recognized that this just isn't going to happen:

> We can take some time in debating this . . . because it is not a realistic option in the next several years . . . In view of the political difficulties of dealing with the budget financing issue within the context of the current ideological battle over taxes and expenditures, we may have to consider seriously the third option: . . . move back toward a pay-as-you-go system by cutting the payroll tax now and raising it in future decades to keep income in line with outgo. While I much prefer the . . . option of saving the surplus, I strongly agree that this third option is better than the current decision to use the social security reserve to finance other government consumption programs.[13]

This is, of course, exactly what Moynihan had proposed.

Senator Moynihan was defeated in his efforts to cut the payroll tax and to return the system explicitly to pay-as-you-go financing. Because the federal government continued to spend Social Security surpluses, we now have the worst of both worlds: the full challenge of funding the rising Social Security costs as they materialize—that is, in 2016 under the

2009 projections—coupled with the accounting misrepresentation that a portion of these future benefits have been pre-funded through the Trust Fund (through 2037).

The Kerrey-Danforth Commission

By the time the Clinton administration entered office, the entirety of the 1983 reforms' apparent improvement of the long-term outlook had been wiped out. The 1992 trustees' report showed a system out of long-range balance by even more than the long-range balance projected in 1982.[14] As we have discussed, the worsening had been somewhat obscured by the 1988 change in actuarial methodology. Still, policymakers soon recognized that the Social Security problem was back with a vengeance. The debate reawakened over what to do about it.

Throughout the 1990s, a number of important commissions, advisory councils, and technical panels convened and reported on Social Security's finances. Some of them had the charge of producing recommendations to render Social Security financially stable and effective in the future. Others simply offered technical recommendations on how to better estimate and present various facets of program finances.

One of the first such important commissions was the so-called Kerrey-Danforth Commission of 1994. The commission was appointed by executive order of President Clinton, largely pursuant to pledges made to Senator Bob Kerrey when the Nebraska Democrat agreed to vote in favor of the president's budget proposal. Kerrey had been concerned that the president's budget ignored the nation's pressing long-term fiscal problems. The entitlement commission was convened to address those issues.

The Kerrey-Danforth Commission was co-chaired by Kerrey and Senator John Danforth (R-MO) and consisted of thirty-two members: in addition to the two co-chairs, ten members of the House (five from each side of the aisle), ten from the Senate, and ten from the private sector.

Like many subsequent commissions, the Kerrey-Danforth Commission found it easier to diagnose the problem than to agree upon solutions. By a 30-1 vote, its interim report of August 1994 concluded, among other things, that "[c]urrent trends are not sustainable," "[t]he Nation cannot continue to allow entitlement programs to consume a rapidly increasing share of the Federal budget," that health care cost growth and demographic changes were driving these problems, and that Medicare and Social Security had to be fixed.

But when it came time to offer solutions in the final report issued in January 1995, only eight of the thirty-two commissioners did so, in five separate submissions. These submissions contained various proposals to reform Social Security.

The Kerrey-Danforth Commission sounded an important alarm, but the work of developing a policy consensus remained.

The 1994–96 SSAC: Policy Disagreements, Philosophical Agreements

In 1994–96, another important commission examined Social Security in somewhat closer detail. This was the Social Security Advisory Council (SSAC) appointed by the Clinton administration's Health and Human Services secretary, Donna Shalala.[15] This was the last of several similar advisory councils, required every four years under the Social Security Act, which examined the program's long-term finances.

By 1994, Social Security's long-range imbalance had grown to exceed that prior to 1983, even under the new actuarial methods that shrank the reported shortfall. Despite the growing urgency, the SSAC (like the Kerrey-Danforth Commission) could not come to agreement on recommendations, splitting into three camps backing three different plans.

For our purposes, more notable than the points of disagreement are those matters on which the SSAC agreed. The SSAC adopted a number of unanimous recommendations, some of which are directly relevant to today's Social Security policy debate. These principles united council members spanning the full spectrum from left to right, including such noted experts as former Social Security Commissioner Robert Ball, economist Ned Gramlich, Carolyn Weaver and Syl Schieber. Their unanimous recommendations are reflective of the extent of conceptual agreement upon which future bipartisan reform efforts could be built.

Advance funding.   One such principle was that "The Council favors partial advance funding for Social Security."[16] As we have reviewed, the 1983 Greenspan Commission did not explicitly advocate building up saving reserves to pre-fund the future benefits of baby boomers. In contrast, the 1994–96 SSAC did unanimously advocate such partial advance funding.

Equally of note, however, is that none of the three plans put forward by SSAC members reflected a belief that genuine advance funding could be accomplished via existing Trust Fund mechanisms. Two of the three proposals advocated building the saving through personal accounts. The third suggested exploring the investment of a portion of the Trust Fund in the stock market. None of the three camps adopted a view that future benefits could best be pre-funded by continuing to provide surplus payroll taxes to the government in a form that it could spend.

Sustainable solvency.   Another unanimous finding of the SSAC was, "The long-term actuarial balance of Social Security should not be adversely affected solely by the passage of time." They backed up this view by offering proposals, not just for solvency, but for *sustainable* solvency.

This finding of the SSAC was implicitly a critique of the 1983 reforms' reliance on the flawed metric of "long-range balance" without adequately examining whether the program was actually being put on a sustainable path.

Most serious Social Security proposals offered from the 1990s through today have been premised on the SSAC's goal of sustainable solvency. Occasionally, we continue to see proposals that aspire only to the standard of "seventy-five-year solvency" that the SSAC and other advisory councils found to be inadequate and sometimes misleading. But for the most part, there is agreement that sustainable solvency is the appropriate goal.

A focus on sustainable solvency does not imply, as some mistakenly believe, that we claim to see accurately for seventy-five years out, one hundred years out, or longer periods of time. It simply says that to the extent we *do* project future finances, we owe it to future generations not to further trends that our best information tells us are unsustainable.

Fair money's worth.   The SSAC also unanimously opined that "Social Security should provide benefits to each generation of workers that bear a reasonable relationship to total taxes paid, plus interest." In detailing this opinion, the SSAC indicated:

> [I]t is important that young workers perceive that the system is fair. This perception in turn suggests that the younger generation should be well treated in terms of the issue of money's worth, taking into account the fact that within each generation there will be a redistribution toward the lower paid.

As we briefly discussed in chapter 1, continued delay renders this principle of intergenerational equity more difficult to achieve. If we continue with our pay-as-you-go system, the declining worker-collector ratio will inflict a steadily worsening deal upon young workers. As things currently stand, future generations will contribute far more to the system than they receive, especially if they must shoulder the entire cost of putting the system back into balance.

Beyond intergenerational implications, there is another message behind this principle: everyone should get something back for the contributions they make to Social Security. Social Security has long been distinguished from welfare by the fact that every contribution to Social Security earns a benefit. High-wage workers get lower returns than low-wage workers, but all wages that have been taxed count toward benefits in some way. In this way, Social Security escapes the stigma of welfare, in which high-income taxpayers may pay for benefits without receiving them, while low-income Americans receive benefits they haven't paid for.

Recently, some have proposed severing this contribution-benefit link for some individuals, thereby abandoning this long-held principle. We will review some of these proposals in subsequent chapters.

A separate self-financed system.   The SSAC also unanimously opined that "Social Security should be financed by taxes on workers' earnings, along with taxes paid by employers, earmarked taxes on benefits, and interest earnings on accumulated reserves, without other payments from the general revenue of the Treasury." The SSAC went on to detail the importance of maintaining Social Security's historical self-financing structure:

> The fiscal discipline in Social Security arises from the need to ensure that income earmarked for Social Security is sufficient to meet the entire cost of the program, both in the short run and long run, rather than from competition with other programs in the general budget. Unless a program is especially protected as, for instance, by dedicated taxes, the Federal budget results are inevitably determined by competition in allocating spending during the budget cycle, depending on the revenue generally available. Social Security, on the other hand, is a very long-range program—people pay dedicated taxes today toward benefits that may not be received for 30 or 40 years—and should not be part of an annual budgetary allocation process.

This (again unanimous) finding is also experiencing renewed challenges today. For decades, the ethic of Social Security has been to consider it separately from the rest of the federal budget. It was to be kept in balance on its own, neither providing benefits in excess of taxes the program itself generates, nor providing excess revenues to permanently subsidize other federal spending.

In more recent years, there has been an increasing number of proposals to tap other revenues to prop up Social Security—and thus to implicitly break the contribution-benefit link. Robert Ball, coauthor of the passage above, later espoused using estate tax revenues to shore up Social Security before his recent passing. The Diamond-Orszag plan would impose a new "legacy surcharge"—separate from any benefit credits—to pump tax revenue into the program. Others have proposed cutting the payroll tax and replacing the lost revenue with an increased tax on gasoline consumption. The Clinton administration also proposed transfers of general revenues, with no specifically identified source, to extend program solvency. All of these proposals would end the program's self-financing ethic, sever the contribution-benefit link in some way, or both.

These proposals reflect the thinking of individual plan authors; it is not yet clear how much broader support they would receive. They have not been fully debated by bipartisan panels of experts, as were the unanimous principles of the Social Security Advisory Council. It remains to be seen whether these new proposals represent an enduring shift away from Social Security's historic ethic, or whether they will lose favor while Social Security's longstanding principles are reasserted. If they do indeed gain momentum, Social Security will in the future become more like other welfare programs, its finances intermingled with the rest of the budget.

The 1999 SSAB Technical Panel

Whereas the SSAC was charged with making policy recommendations, other advisory panels were convened with a narrower mission of reviewing technical issues. These panels also reinforced the strengthening viewpoint that Social Security's worsening financial instability was fed in part by previous analytical shortcomings. One such panel was the 1999 Technical Panel on Assumptions and Methods convened by the Social Security Advisory Board.[17]

By 1999, the Social Security debate was in full swing. President Clinton had led a year of national discussion in 1998, and his and other proposals were being vigorously debated. The 1999 Technical Panel issued its findings in this context.

The panel's analysis of the inadequacy of the seventy-five-year solvency metric echoed that of previous panels:

> The Panel would like to reinforce concerns about the overemphasis on 75-year actuarial balance raised by previous panels and addressed in part by the procedures adopted by the 1994–96 Advisory Council on Social Security. . . . When reformers aim only for 75-year balance . . . they usually end up in a situation where their reforms only last a year before being shown out of 75-year balance again. The 1994–96 Advisory Council wisely tried to accept only reforms that produced sustainability over the longer term—sustainability defined in a way that would ensure that taxes and benefits were more or less in line after the 75th year.[18]

Once again, a bipartisan panel had seen a glaring flaw in the analytical approach employed in 1983. In simple terms, it wasn't enough to be in balance "on average" over seventy-five years if some years had huge surpluses, others huge deficits, and nothing was being done to save the surpluses. The Technical Panel specifically recommended that reform efforts ensure that annual "taxes and benefits were more or less in line" through the end of the valuation period, to avoid repeating this mistake.

By this time, the Office of the Social Security Actuary had clearly internalized the message. No longer would analyses of reform plans show only averages over seventy-five years. Starting in the 1990s, the Actuary's Office produced projections showing how plans would affect Social Security's income and outflow in *each* year of the valuation period. The Actuary's Office continues this practice through the present day, with most serious reform proposals[19] endeavoring to achieve the Technical Panel's standard for sustainable solvency.

The 1999 Technical Panel made other recommendations that influence our ongoing debate. One was to add a "closed-group" analysis to the trustees' report, which had previously only included "open-group" analyses.

Putting this recommendation in such terms smacks of technical jargon. The concept behind a "closed group" analysis, however, is really quite straightforward. The basic idea is simply to count all taxes *and* benefits for any person represented in the analysis. If we only look forward for ten years, for example, we'll see the taxes that I pay into Social Security but not the benefits I'm earning with those contributions. We'd thus get an incomplete picture of my overall net contribution to Social Security finances. To see the whole picture, we need to look at *both* sides of the equation—taxes and benefits—for any person or group that we include.

This addition to the trustees' report is useful for a number of reasons. One is that by showing both taxes *and* benefit promises, we get a fuller picture of overall system finances. Another is that it's helpful in understanding the program's expected net treatment of different generations. It also more accurately illuminates the fiscal implications of proposals to shift from our current pay-as-you-go system to a partially funded system.

Today, the "closed group" analysis is but one of an expanded compendium of analyses in the Trustees' Report, all of them showing different aspects of program finances. With more metrics in the report than ever before, the report reflects more perspectives than ever before. None of these metrics is perfect; each has shortcomings. As we will see, policy advocates have a tendency to emphasize some metrics while ignoring others, as serves their policy preferences.

Another focus of the 1999 Technical Panel was the need to better quantify the degree of uncertainty in the trustees' projections. The trustees had had a long practice of showing alternative "high-cost," and "low-cost" scenarios alongside the standard "intermediate" projection. The Technical Panel found fault with this presentation as not giving a clear sense of the relative likelihood of each outcome:

> The current system of presenting low- and high-cost alternatives to the intermediate projections is inadequate . . . without any model of the probabilities of the underlying parameters taking on the alternative

values, there is no way to use the alternatives to form a distribution of possible outcomes. It is inadequate to show any forecast without an indication of the uncertainty that surrounds it.[20]

In part to address this, the panel recommended the inclusion of a "stochastic" analysis—in short, an analysis that shows the probability of different outcomes.

[S]tochastic modeling has two primary roles to play in the Trustees' Report. First, it is far superior to the current presentation of Alternatives I and III in displaying the range of uncertainty in the actuaries' forecasts . . . second, it is a useful tool to understand the interaction among variables.

This recommendation was ultimately accepted and the trustees' report now contains such an analysis. Basically, what this means is that the trustees' standard intermediate projection is accompanied by an analysis showing the degree of confidence and precision in the forecast. For example, in 2009 the trustees projected that the system would enter permanent cash deficits in 2016. The stochastic analysis conveyed the potential margin of error in this prediction, showing an 80 percent chance that the permanent deficits would arrive between 2010 and 2017 and a 95 percent chance that they would arrive between 2009 and 2019.[21]

The trustees' stochastic analysis is an extremely useful tool. It is remarkable, however, how underutilized it is in the public debate. Reading it each year, one is struck by how incredibly improbable are the respective "low-cost" and "high-cost" scenarios presented by the trustees.

For example, the 95 percent confidence range of the projections—stretching from the 2.5th percentile to the 97.5th percentile of possible outcomes—includes *neither* the "low-cost" nor the "high-cost" scenario. That is to say, each of these illustrative scenarios is so improbable that it has a less than 2.5 percent chance of coming to pass. This is because each of these scenarios depends upon not only one variable breaking, but a long string of variables breaking, all in the same direction. Sometimes these extreme scenarios require two inversely correlated variables to break in the same direction. This defies considerable odds.

Despite this publicly available analysis, there remained a persistent misperception in some quarters that the highly unrealistic "low-cost" scenario was just as likely to come to pass as the trustees' intermediate projection.[22] The stochastic analysis in the trustees' report clearly shows how wildly improbable such an outcome would be. Greater public and press attention to this analysis would pay enormous dividends, enabling individuals to debate their different policy views while drawing upon a well-grounded, common understanding of the likely factual situation.

In sum, the 1990s were a fertile period for bipartisan expert analysis of Social Security. Much of this work took place outside of the hot glare of political debate and exemplified the common understandings that could be reached between serious people of opposing perspectives.

The various commissions and advisory panels who reported on Social Security in the 1990s recognized not only the fact of deteriorating system finances, but the reasons for this deterioration after the 1983 reforms. A significant culprit, it was found, was inadequate scorekeeping methodology. Clear warnings were issued not to repeat these mistakes.

By exposing the flaws of the "seventy-five-year actuarial balance" method viewed in isolation, by highlighting the importance of attending to the system's *annual* operations, by making the case for *sustainable* solvency, and by better explaining the degree of precision in existing projections, these panels pointed the way forward to practicable solutions. Now it was up to policymakers, acting within the political system, to build upon this foundation.

Legislative Proposals of the 1990s: Pain Caucusers and Free Lunchers

The warnings of these advisory panels did not fall on deaf ears. Throughout the 1990s, legislators responded by drafting proposals to secure Social Security's future. We will not here cover all of the provisions of these plans, but certain features of them are nevertheless relevant to our story.

The 1990s featured close cooperation within bipartisan teams of Social Security plan authors. From the vantage point of 2009, it is striking how, throughout the 1990s, Democrats and Republicans stepped forward in roughly equal numbers. Authors on the Democratic side included senators such as Bob Kerrey, Pat Moynihan, and John Breaux, and House members such as Charlie Stenholm, who recruited several of his Democratic colleagues to his bills. These Democrats worked closely with Republicans such as Judd Gregg, Al Simpson, Jim Kolbe, and Fred Thompson.

Though these plans differed in their details, they tended to have certain features in common. Among them:

1) Provisions to achieve sustainable solvency, mostly by constraining cost growth
2) Personal accounts
3) Added protections for low-income workers

All three characteristics tended to reappear for consistent, substantive reasons.

First, the plans attempted to fix the problem that Social Security was no longer in long-term balance (even "on average"). Some of these plans would have raised tax revenues; others would not. But the general consensus among plan authors was that the problem was primarily one of unsustainable system cost growth. Thus, these plans tended to concentrate on cost containment, achieved through changes to the benefit formula or to the retirement age. These changes were developed to be sufficient to attain not only seventy-five-year solvency, but sustainable solvency.

Second, the plans were based on the longstanding recognition that "average" balance was not enough, if the program's annual cash flows were badly out of whack. At the time these proposals were developed, Social Security was generating near-term surpluses equal to roughly 2 percent of worker wages, while facing large future deficits. Knowing that the government would not save that 2 percent of worker wages, many of these plans proposed to move roughly that amount into personal accounts. This would have pre-funded a portion of future benefit obligations while ensuring that some near-term spending would have been converted into near-term saving.

It is important to recognize the rationale behind these personal account proposals. Many today incorrectly believe that the case for personal accounts was premised solely upon a particular investment choice (stock investments) and/or a representation that higher returns could be achieved without investment risk. Indeed, there have been several proposals—both with and without personal accounts—that sought to tap higher stock market returns as a way of avoiding tough choices on Social Security, as we shall see.

But these bipartisan plans were not among them. These plans would have balanced Social Security's finances irrespective of market returns and would have created the personal accounts primarily to prevent the government from spending Social Security money. These plans thus sought to prevent the adverse outcome of 1983, in which claims of long-standing solvency had been based on a faulty premise.

The third feature often appearing in these proposals was increased income protections for low-income workers. Authors of the proposals were concerned that Social Security would provide inadequate retirement income security for low-wage workers, especially when implementing the measures necessary to repair system finances. They thus often built provisions into their plans to ensure that low-wage workers would not retire into poverty.

About the time that these various bipartisan plans were being developed, a family of plans was also developed that sought to avoid tough choices on Social Security (such as raising taxes or cutting benefit growth) by tapping returns on stock market investment.

Some such proposals were offered by opponents of personal accounts, some by proponents. Robert Ball's contingent on the 1994–96 Advisory

Council explored investing the Trust Fund collectively in the stock market, banking on the assumption of higher returns to avoid significant changes in promised benefits. The Clinton administration later offered a specific proposal to invest the Trust Fund in the stock market. AARP also voiced support for the idea of investing a portion of the Trust Fund in stocks.

These proposals had their echo among some supporters of personal accounts. Senator Phil Gramm offered a proposal, and the House Republican team of Bill Archer and Clay Shaw another, to use stock investments *within* personal accounts to solve the Social Security shortfall—without cutting the growth of benefits or raising the payroll tax.

With or without personal accounts, the principle behind all of these proposals was the same: Social Security contributions would be invested in the stock market. The government, not the Social Security beneficiary, would accept the downside risks of these investments. If the return was higher than the return on government bonds—and the calculations assumed that it would be—these higher returns would be used to close the Social Security shortfall without raising taxes or slowing benefit growth.

In the Clinton and Ball proposals, this would have been achieved through collective investment, while the Republican proposals would have achieved it through personal accounts. But in neither set of proposals would the individual truly "own" the risk and reward of investment decisions. In both approaches, the assumed higher returns would be used to enable the government to resolve its financing problem.[23]

Thus, in the 1990s there developed two families of plans. The family of bipartisan congressional plans (sometimes nicknamed the "Pain Caucus") made explicit choices—changes to benefits, taxes, or both—to achieve sustainable solvency. These plans often included personal accounts, not as a means of avoiding these tough choices but as a means of ensuring that some Social Security contributions would be saved rather than spent. By reducing both near-term surpluses and long-term deficits, these plans sought to move Social Security toward more transparent, honest accounting.

The second family of plans sought to tap the promise of higher returns on stock investments as a means of avoiding tough choices to change benefits or taxes. Some of these plans were offered by Republican supporters of personal accounts, others by Democratic opponents.

The philosophical schism between these two basic viewpoints was perhaps the defining policy split of the 1990s. As we shall later discuss, there are many decision spectra that can and do divide policymakers: raising revenues versus containing costs, advance funding versus continuing with pay-as-you-go, and others. But throughout the 1990s, there may have been no more fundamental philosophical divide than this one: could stock investment returns save Social Security without tough choices to change benefits or taxes?

Fascinatingly, answers to this question did not fall along party lines. The "pain caucus" contingent included centrists from both sides of the political aisle. The "free lunch" contingent encompassed the left section of the Democrats and the right section of the Republicans.

This counterintuitive overlap between the positions of left and right—specifically, the desire to tap stock investments to avoid politically tough choices—is what made it nearly possible for a deal to be struck between the Clinton White House and Speaker of the House Newt Gingrich in 1998. But before we can understand the nature of this potential deal, we need to describe a new "free lunch" temptation that had arisen by the late 1990s: the rise of unified budget surpluses.

The Clinton Administration's "Save the Surplus" Proposal

In the late 1990s, a surge in economic growth raised revenues to the federal coffers beyond all previous forecasts. Before this surge, President Clinton and the Republican Congress had been at loggerheads over budget and fiscal policy. But with so much additional revenue on the table it became possible for the two sides to bridge their differences and to agree to the 1997 Balanced Budget Act, to their mutual credit and advantage.

With the arrival of budget surpluses, President Clinton saw a historic opportunity to deal with Social Security. He called for 1998 to be a year of discussion, scheduling a series of forums in which reform options were debated. He called upon Congress to "Save Social Security First." This was a succinct way of saying, in effect, "Republican Congress: Don't dissipate the newfound surplus with a big tax cut. Let's tap it first to shore up Social Security solvency." The president displayed an open policy mind throughout the 1998 forums, conveying a willingness to consider a wide range of ideas.

The following year, at his 1999 State of the Union Address, President Clinton put forward a proposal to "save the surplus for Social Security." On the surface, his proposal was to transfer the newfound budget surplus to Social Security, thereby extending program solvency. Another element of the announced proposal was to invest a portion of the Trust Fund in the stock market, as previously discussed.

By this point in the debate, many Social Security proposals had been put forward, some of them quite complex. President Clinton's proposal may have been the most confusing of all. To this day, it causes great confusion. Here we will attempt a simplified explanation of the issues it raised.

The logic of the president's proposal was roughly as follows: Instead of exploiting the surplus as an occasion to cut taxes or to raise spending, we would use the surplus to retire government debt. By retiring government debt, the government's fiscal position would be improved. The government would thus be in a better position to pay future Social Security benefits.

Thus, a simple set of core principles: Save the Social Security surplus. Pay down debt now. Make the payment of benefits more affordable later. This was the idea of the "lockbox" later so frequently invoked by Vice President Al Gore.

Put so simply, it sounds reasonable. Unfortunately, it wasn't that simple. The administration wanted not only to make it easier to finance benefits when Social Security entered its cash deficit period; it also sought credit for *extending* the system's solvency. And that's where the significant troubles with the administration proposal began.

The root of the problem was this: the Social Security Trust Fund is *already* credited for the surplus it runs, and interest on that surplus is also already credited to the Trust Fund. In other words, government accounting before President Clinton's proposal already credited Social Security as though its surpluses were being saved.

Remember what we reviewed about the 1983 reforms: how negotiators then never believed that the Trust Fund could be an effective mechanism for pre-funding. President Clinton's proposal sought to turn it into one.

If the Trust Fund wasn't ever saved, then we face a problem when incoming taxes are short of benefit obligations (2016 in the trustees' latest projections). If *every* surplus had been saved, on the other hand, then one could argue that all is well until 2037.

Thus, if President Clinton had had a magic wand and could go back in time to 1983, saving every penny of every Social Security surplus accumulated since then, making the Trust Fund a truly effective way to pre-fund, then he could have rightly claimed that the system was in good shape up through 2037. Clearly, however, he could not do that.

Unfortunately, the Clinton administration wanted to claim much more: that solvency had been extended *beyond* 2037.[24] And making that claim required some accounting gimmicks.

The administration essentially had two options for claiming an extension of the system's solvency:

1) Double-credit Social Security for its role in buying down federal debt.
2) Credit Social Security for the role of *other* government accounts in buying down debt—that is, start funneling revenues unrelated to Social Security into the Trust Fund and thereby end the program's historic self-financing ethic.

These were the only two choices available to the Clinton administration once it decided to seek credit for extending solvency without changing anything about Social Security itself. Seeking this new form of "free lunch" required either that it engage in some double-crediting or that it begin to finance Social Security with unrelated taxes—or both.

This had the unfortunate effect of turning a constructive national conversation about how best to fix Social Security into a public dissection of the accounting techniques used by the administration to claim a solvency extension. As Government Accountability Office Comptroller General David Walker testified about the administration proposal:

> . . . (I)t is important to note that the President's proposal does not alter the projected cash flows imbalances in the Social Security program. Benefit costs and revenues currently associated with the program will not be affected by even 1 cent . . . The changes to the Social Security program will thus be more perceived than real.[25]

Of the accounting issue itself, Walker had this to say:

> While there are many benefits to reducing publicly held debt, it is important to recognize that under the current law baseline—i.e., with no changes in tax or spending policy—this would happen without crediting additional securities to the trust funds. The administration has defended this approach as a way of assuring both a reduction in debt held by the public and giving Social Security first claim on what they call the 'debt reduction dividend' to pay future benefits. However, issuing these additional securities to the SSTF is a discretionary act with major legal and economic consequences for the future. Some could view this as double counting.[26]

Why double-counting? Because Social Security would receive two doses of credits for its contribution to the government's bottom line. Clinton administration economists were aware of these issues, as evidenced by a paper later released by three prominent former economic advisors of the administration:

> One important disadvantage of these plans was their vulnerability to the charge of "double counting" the Social Security surplus. Much of the

projected unified budget surpluses originated in Social Security and therefore were already credited to the Social Security trust fund under current law. Thus, according to the critics, transferring unified surpluses to Social Security caused the same dollars of revenue in effect to be counted twice to the benefit of Social Security. Yet, the status quo involved precisely the same approach to budgeting: as long as the budget process was focused on balancing the unified budget, dollars that were credited to the Social Security trust fund were still perceived to be available for new spending or tax cuts. The administration's economic team believed that a dollar of the unified budget surplus could therefore be legitimately transferred to Social Security and credited to the trust fund, provided that the dollar would take the dollar off the table and prevent it from being used for other purposes. In that case, the transfer would result in an extra dollar's worth of public debt being paid down relative to the status quo, and therefore an extra dollar of government saving. Nevertheless, the administration was well aware that the approach had "bad optics" and internally a number of economists argued vigorously against adopting a plan that would be subject to this criticism.[27]

This is a fascinating passage, showing that the Clinton administration was cognizant that its proposal would double-count the Social Security surplus. The perceived justification for this double-counting was that there was also double-counting under the status quo via the persistent spending of Social Security surplus money. But instead of proposing to end this double-counting, the Clinton administration proposed to replace one form of double-counting with another.

This embrace of double-counting as a deliberate policy offended many of the sponsors of congressional Social Security plans from both parties. These legislators had accepted substantial political risks. They had offered concrete, difficult policy choices to bring the program's benefit outflows and revenue intake into line. They also had expended considerable effort to craft a more transparent, honest basis for Social Security accounting.

These various plan authors detected an abdication of leadership, even cynicism, in the administration proposal to effectively formalize and extend the problematic double-counting of Social Security revenue. This

proposal thus effectively marked the beginning of the end of serious efforts to address Social Security until the arrival of a new century and a
new president.

At this point, it is necessary to zoom out and to recognize that none
of this was happening in a vacuum. All of this happened at a time when
President Clinton was under growing threat (later the reality) of impeachment by Congress. Congressional reformers at the time suspected
that the administration's new policy position reflected a decision to tack
to its political left to shore up support among Democrats during impeachment proceedings.

These suspicions were later supported by a number of sources, including Steven Gillon's recent book *The Pact*. Gillon's book asserts that it
was the Monica Lewinsky scandal, specifically, that derailed the progress of promising Social Security discussions between President Clinton
and Speaker Gingrich.

The administration's own economists, writing after the fact, couldn't
help but wonder if the threat of impeachment had guided the policy:

> The President proposed transferring general revenue into the trust fund
> and investing a portion of the transferred amounts in equities . . . The
> decision may have been influenced by the changing political dynamic by
> late 1998, as the possibility that the President would be impeached came
> clearly into view. Whether the President would have pursued a different
> approach in the absence of impeachment will never be known.[28]

From the vantage point of today, these events appear as a tragic missed
opportunity. Many stars were then in alignment. There was a newly generated surplus, making it easier for Republicans and Democrats to bridge
their policy differences. The White House was occupied by a Democrat,
the party historically more trusted by the public on Social Security.

Moreover, President Clinton was not a traditional ideologue, but instead was willing to consider departures from traditional party orthodoxy
to strengthen Social Security for the future. The congressional Republican leadership for its part was willing to work with him.

All of these conditions existed at a time when there had recently been substantial work by bipartisan legislative teams of Republicans and Democrats and by advisory councils and technical panels who had equipped policymakers with better tools to understand policy ramifications. It is difficult to imagine a more promising environment for Social Security reform.

It didn't happen. From that high point of promise, it seemed as though one event after another conspired to undermine future prospects for reform.

Steven Gillon writes that the Clinton-Lewinsky scandal was a pivotal moment after which nothing was the same. Serious Social Security discussions collapsed. Partisan divides intensified as the impeachment process continued. Vice President Gore, a Democrat far less willing to address Social Security, was nominated for the presidency in 2000.

The economy turned south in late 2000, and with it the previous rosy budget projections, thus destroying the remainder of the fragile argument that Social Security could be shored up by "saving the surplus" alone.

Then came the bitterly contested 2000 election, fought all the way to the Supreme Court. The contest ended with the inauguration of a new president, eager and willing to reform Social Security. But George W. Bush, a Republican, came to office with a profoundly polarized electorate and with a congressional minority in little mood to work collaboratively on Social Security.

Other trends further undermined prospects for a bipartisan reform deal. One by one, moderate reformers on both sides left Congress, via retirement and defeat: Breaux, Kerrey, Simpson, Stenholm, Moynihan. Discipline within each party increased and compromise with the other party decreased—on all issues.

Meanwhile, the explosion of information sources via the Internet made it increasingly possible for individuals across the political spectrum not only to choose their own opinions but to repeatedly consult their own prejudice-reinforcing facts and to filter out data inconsistent with those views. Shared understanding of even the Social Security problem itself began to break down.

Then, too, there was the terrible ordeal of 9/11 and its aftermath.

But we are getting ahead of ourselves. Before discussing President Bush's substantive approach to Social Security, and the environment in which he tried to reform it, let's review the basic policy value judgments that he faced and which continue to face us all.

PART TWO

THE SOCIAL SECURITY
POLICY CHALLENGE

Implementing Value Judgments
Through Social Security Policy

S TRIPPED TO ITS ESSENCE, Social Security policy comes down to a series of value judgments. We must together decide what kind of Social Security system we *want*, and then determine how to make that vision a reality.

If you're reading this book, then you probably care more than the average citizen about the details of those decisions. Other Americans, though less interested in the details than you, may nevertheless feel strongly about certain fundamental Social Security policy values. Together, we must determine a future course for the system that fairly reflects our respective priorities.

The process is not all that different from designing one's dream home. You must decide what you want as well as how much you're willing to pay for it. Perhaps you're the sort of person who cares only about your home fulfilling certain basic needs; you might be content to allow another member of your family to arrange the furniture and decide the color of the walls. But maybe you're a second type of person who cares profoundly about how every individual room is structured and organized.

In that case, you might expend great amounts of time directing details ranging from plumbing fixtures to bathroom tile. And, even with the most particular homebuyers, there's usually a level of detail at which a third group, the professionals, have to take over.

As with home-buying, Social Security policy involves many decisions from large to small. Some are fundamental value choices for society at large; others are details of technical implementation to be resolved by legislative and administrative staff. This book is aimed at those of you in between: the person who isn't a Social Security policy professional, but who does care to develop and express opinions about a number of important policy questions. The following chapters will lay out a few of these questions to assist you in deciding where your own views land.

This section of the book is *not* about advocating a particular policy viewpoint. Still less is it about explaining why one policy viewpoint is noble while another is immoral. There are already countless books, papers, and blogs written about Social Security, many of them serving the primary purpose of exalting one viewpoint over another. Far too frequently in these forums, issues are characterized as though there is only one viewpoint that seeks to honorably protect and defend Social Security, while others are dismissed as being based on nefarious motives, ignorance, or deliberate obfuscation.[1]

Such self-serving portrayals do not well serve the public interest. Certainly there *is* slanting and outright misrepresentation from various sides of the Social Security debate. It's certainly appropriate to expose misleading or false statements where they occur. But we do not, as a practical matter, face decisions between good and evil, in which instance our choices would be trivially easy. Instead, we face decisions about which the most well-intentioned individuals may fundamentally and honorably disagree. To persistently attribute such disagreement to sinister motives is no more a way to constructive sound decision-making by policymakers than it is by married couples. To get anywhere worth getting, we each need to identify and explain our own value judgments, to listen openly and respectfully to those of others, and to determine where we can agree.

Two additional points on our debate ethics are worth making. First, the reasons that we need this respectful airing of different proposals go beyond mere considerations of courtesy. When we caricature one another's views, the damage isn't limited to irritating one another and inhibiting our willingness to cooperate. It also blurs important policy issues that warrant greater understanding. "I'm good, the other guy is bad" is usually little more than a cheaply evasive means of avoiding an illuminating, substantive exchange. As soon as you hear someone say, "Let's ignore the substance of this person's argument because he's a social-ist" or "because he's a rightwing nut trying to destroy Social Security," your BS antennae should be activated.

The second point is that each decision comes with trade-offs, and the public needs to understand them to make informed judgments. If Person A charges Person B with wanting to "cut benefits by 33 percent," then Person A must also admit that his own preferred policy would have taxes that are "higher by 50 percent." He should also be willing to clearly ex-plain, of these so-called benefit cuts, "relative to what?" Are we talking about benefit cuts relative to today's levels, or relative to a far higher level of benefits promised in the distant future? Again, public understanding suffers when these details are obscured or omitted altogether.

Each policy choice has an upside. Each has a downside. If you want the system to pay higher benefits than I do, then you'll have to impose higher taxes than I would. Acknowledge that and make the case for it. Our responsibility as policy advocates is to equip the public to decide the future of Social Security knowingly, with its eyes fully open.

The following chapters review some of the spectra of Social Security policy decisions that face us. It is by no means an exhaustive list, but it covers the most significant issues that require resolution going forward.

CHAPTER 4

Decision Spectrum No. 1

Slowing Benefit Growth Versus Raising Taxes

PERHAPS THE MOST FUNDAMENTAL ISSUE of the Social Security debate is whether we should close the projected shortfall by raising revenues (taxes) or by slowing the growth of system costs (benefits). First, let's examine the policy spectrum before us, and then examine the case from both angles.[1]

Today, there are 3.1 workers paying taxes to support each Social Security beneficiary.[2] A career medium-wage worker retiring today at the Normal Retirement Age (NRA) (sixty-six) receives a benefit of $17,600 per year.[3] The cost of paying these benefits now absorbs roughly 12.4 cents of each taxable dollar earned by workers (figure 4.1).[4]

By 2035, there will be only 2.1 workers to support each Social Security beneficiary.[5] Each medium-wage beneficiary retiring in 2035 at the Normal Retirement Age (then sixty-seven) is being promised a benefit of $22,500 in today's dollars.[6] The cost of paying these higher benefits to a larger number of retirees would absorb a far higher *17.1 cents of each taxable dollar* earned by workers.[7]

So we see: costs will rise dramatically under current law. Why? Mainly for three reasons:

- *Population aging*: More people will be collecting benefits.
- *Pay-as-you-go financing*: We don't have a pre-funded system, but rather one in which benefits for current beneficiaries are paid primarily by taxing current workers.

FIGURE 4.1 Projected Social Security Cost Growth as a Share of
Worker Wages

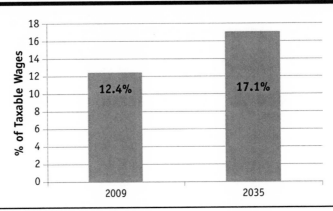

SOURCE: Based on data from the 2009 Trustees' report.

- *Wage-indexing*: The amount we pay to each year's new group of beneficiaries is generally higher (even after inflation) than the amount
  paid to individuals who began to receive benefits in the previous year.

Let's explore each of these a bit further.

Population aging we have already discussed: when there are more
people collecting benefits, then naturally it costs more money to pay all
of them.

We will discuss pay-as-you-go financing in detail later in the next
chapter. Here we'll simply note that we do not have a pre-funded system. The money that is paid to today's beneficiaries comes from taxing
today's workers. So, as costs go up, worker tax burdens rise.

Wage-indexation is the other component of cost increases that must
be understood. Each year, the Social Security benefit formula is adjusted
automatically according to law.[8] This adjustment causes benefits to rise
along with national average wage growth. Historically, wage growth is
generally faster than inflation over significant periods of time.[9] So benefits generally grow faster than inflation as well.

What this means is that retirees in one year generally get benefits that start out a little bit higher than those initially paid to the previous year's retirees. And it means that those who retire decades later are promised benefits that are a *lot* higher, as figure 4.2 shows.

There are arguments both for and against this method of indexing benefits, which we will cover later. For now, we'll simply note that the benefit formula does cause benefits to rise faster than inflation, and provide a brief reminder of the history of how this came to be.

Wage-indexation of the benefit formula is the main reason that we can't grow our way out of the Social Security problem. If our economy grows faster, then wages grow faster, and the system's tax revenues increase. But, along with these higher wages and contributions, the system's benefit cost obligations also increase, roughly proportionally. Basically, as the economy gets bigger, everything about Social Security gets bigger, too—including both its taxes and its benefits.

In a faster-growth scenario, the higher tax revenues come in the door before the higher benefits are paid out, so faster growth can postpone

FIGURE 4.2 Real Benefit Value Rises Across Generations

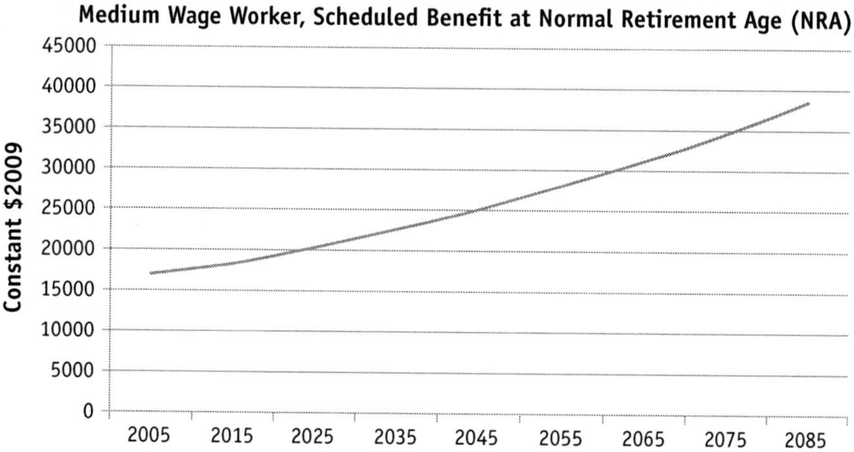

Medium Wage Worker, Scheduled Benefit at Normal Retirement Age (NRA)

SOURCE: Based on data from the 2009 Trustees' report.

the insolvency date by a few years. This is largely an illusory improvement, however, because of the later effect of higher benefit payments. In fact, an important paper by Jagadeesh Gokhale and Andrew Biggs has found that faster growth won't shrink the dollar amount of the *total* Social Security deficit at all.[10]

As discussed in chapter 2, wage-indexing was not an original feature of Social Security. Multiple experts at the time of its implementation, including the Hsiao Consultant Panel and the Social Security Advisory Council, warned that wage-indexing would impose costs upon future generations far higher than those that previous generations had been willing to bear. For better or for worse, Congress did not heed these warnings and so we today have a Social Security benefit formula that causes system costs to rise significantly faster than its supporting tax base.

Thus, as a result of the three factors of population aging, pay-as-you-go financing, and wage-indexing, Social Security costs would under current law hit our children and grandchildren much harder than they hit us. By 2035, they would have to pay roughly one-sixth of their total taxable wages to support this one federal program alone, compared to about one-eighth today. At the same time, Medicare costs are growing even more rapidly, meaning that our children and grandchildren may need to give up roughly *one-third* of their wages to support just these two federal programs—even before they are taxed to fund the other obligations of federal, state, and local governments, from national security and education to highways and everything else.

The Case for Cost Restraint

For many policy analysts, constraining cost growth is the essence of the solution because cost growth is the essence of the problem. The taxable wage base is already indexed to grow so that revenues automatically grow with wage growth in the larger economy. As we have seen, this rate of growth is generally faster than inflation. The problem is that costs are growing even *faster*. In this perspective, it makes most sense to focus on cost containment because that's where the problem lies.

Advocates of constraining cost growth often argue that current law is heavily biased in favor of higher tax costs and a more expensive system. The benefit formula, as we have seen, grows faster with inflation. So does the cap on taxable wages. Even if we fixed system finances entirely by constraining the growth in benefits, cost burdens facing our children would *still* rise markedly—for example, to over 15 percent of wages by 2025—before ultimately trending down toward today's levels.[11] Thus, even with a solution consisting *solely* of benefit restraints, most of the system's bias in the direction of increasing cost and tax burdens would still remain in place for several decades.

The Hsiao Commission's argument against wage-indexing, cited in chapter 2, is really a precursor of today's leading argument for fixing Social Security by constraining cost growth. That is, if we focus on raising taxes, we'll simply be perpetuating an inequity in which we force the next generation to carry tax burdens that we ourselves have never tolerated, to pay benefits to *us* that are higher (even after inflation) than anyone before us received. This violates many Americans' sense of the appropriate legacy to leave to our children.

Advocates of a cost-restraint solution also note that we *can* quite easily, and relatively painlessly, avoid imposing a tax increase on younger workers. Were we to reform Social Security today, we could attain sustainable solvency without cutting benefits for those in or near retirement, and without causing the real (inflation-adjusted) level of benefits to shrink from one class of retirees to the next. The purchasing power of America's seniors would continue to increase. Since we can get the job done without a tax increase (assuming we act soon), shouldn't we do so?

At the same time, let's remember that while we can fix Social Security without a tax increase, no one seems to know how to fix Medicare without one. Since we *can* fix Social Security without raising taxes, in this line of argument, we ought to. It would be irresponsible to leave Social Security on a course requiring tax increases, given that most analysts believe that it would be imposed on top of further tax increases for Medicare as well.

Of course, the general case that is always made against raising taxes is also made specifically against raising Social Security taxes. Social Security represents a substantial drag on wages, imposing a 12.4 percent cost upon the first $106,800 of wages earned by all workers. Raising this cost further, it is argued, would harm job creation, wage growth, and general economic growth. In our current economic environment, this concern is especially strong.

Another argument against raising Social Security taxes is that there may not be an acceptable way to do it. Raising the payroll tax *rate* is very unattractive, because this tax hits the poorest of poor workers as well as those better off. Presidents Clinton and Bush both ruled out raising the payroll tax rate when presenting their frameworks for acceptable Social Security solutions. But significantly raising the *cap* on taxable wages is also potentially problematic. If the contribution-benefit link is retained, then raising the cap obligates additional benefit payments to higher-income individuals who least need them, with the inefficient result that most (though not all) of the additional money collected would be paid back out. The only alternative to this (severing the contribution-benefit link) would be a significant break with the historic distinction between Social Security and welfare programs. That's certainly a choice we could make, but there exists on both sides of the political aisle strong philo-sophical resistance to turning Social Security into a welfare program.

The case for fixing the system with cost restraint is also made from the standpoint of generational equity. Under current law, the younger you are, the worse your treatment under Social Security—even without considering your share of the cost of paying off the Social Security Trust Fund.[12] Generally speaking, tax increases have a greater effect on younger Americans relative to benefit changes.

Thus, raising taxes would further shift the burden of fixing Social Security onto the shoulders of those generations already receiving the worst net treatment. In the latest trustees' report, it was found that those now entering the Social Security program will experience a net benefit loss of $16.3 trillion unless current system participants are required to share some of the burden of restoring solvency.[13] To fairly spread the burdens of restoring Social Security to solvency, we should be spreading the burdens around as widely as possible—which means restraining cost growth as rapidly as possible.

A further argument for constraining cost growth is rooted in projection uncertainty. We cannot know the future course of the American economy nor the challenges that our children will face. If we are going to err in our projections, it is better to err on the side of lower costs than higher costs. If we set benefits "too low" and thus create budget surpluses, it is easier for future generations to adjust by increasing benefit levels than it is for them to adjust if we err in the opposite direction and commit future budgetary resources that fail to materialize.

Finally, there is a case for restraining traditional system cost growth that is largely linked to decision spectrum no. 2 (pay-as-you-go financing versus pre-funding), a value choice that we will later review in greater detail. This argument begins with the observation that, at least for the pay-as-you-go portion of the system, higher benefit promises can only be paid by imposing higher tax costs on the next generation. Because the system engages in no saving, it does not increase the net resources available to generate retirement income. In such a system, one generation can only increase its retirement security at the expense of another's.

Given these realities, this viewpoint holds that our own desire for higher benefits should instead be met by increasing our *own* saving, rather than allowing the pay-as-you-go obligations of the current system to mount upon younger generations as is now projected.

The Case for Raising Taxes

There are plenty of arguments made on the other side as well. Let's examine some of them.

Perhaps the central argument against slowing benefit growth, and in favor of raising revenues, is based on *replacement rates*. The "replacement rate" is, loosely speaking, the percentage of one's pre-retirement earnings that one receives as retirement income. If, after you retire, your income is 70 percent of what it was before you retired, then you have a 70 percent "replacement rate." (For a typical person, Social Security alone provides a lower percentage than this, with individuals relying on other sources for the rest of their income.)

The fact that benefit levels are rising faster than inflation is not, to many policy advocates, a persuasive reason to slow benefit growth. For later generations to receive the same replacement rates as earlier generations, they note, benefits must remain linked to wages. If wages rise at one rate, while Social Security benefits rise at a slower rate, then Social Security benefits will replace a lower percentage of pre-retirement wages. Since individuals should plan for retirement in terms of receiving an adequate replacement rate, these policy advocates believe that maintaining Social Security replacement rates (which is what wage-indexing aims to achieve) is the appropriate policy.

Earlier, we noted that there seems to be no good way to raise taxes. In the eyes of some policy advocates, a similar problem exists on the benefit side. If benefits for middle- or low-income persons grow more slowly, then their replacement rates will be lower and retirement income adequacy will be threatened. If, on the other hand, slower benefit growth is confined only to higher-income persons, they will feel less of a commitment to the Social Security program and may withdraw their crucial political support for it.

Another reason sometimes given for raising Social Security revenues is the fact that, over the last few decades, the share of total wage income subject to the Social Security tax has declined and is projected to decline further in the future. In 1983, the year of the last major Social Security reforms, the ratio of taxable payroll to GDP was placed at a relative high—42.2 percent. It has steadily declined since then, to less than 39 percent today. The trustees project that it will further decline in the future, to roughly 33 percent by 2085.[14]

One reason for this decline is that income above the cap (not subject to the Social Security tax) has grown faster than income below the cap (subject to the Social Security tax). Some policy advocates believe that the cap should thus be raised so that the share of total national income subject to the Social Security tax is closer to what it was in 1983.

A related rationale for raising Social Security revenues is so that the program's income does not decline as a percentage of our overall economy. Today, we collect roughly 5 percent of GDP for Social Security. That is projected to decline to roughly 4.4 percent by 2085.[15] Many experts believe it would not make sense for the nation to commit a declining percentage of its resources to Social Security when there are more elderly than ever to support.

One caveat should be issued with respect to both of the last two paragraphs: maintaining revenues as a constant percentage of GDP, or raising the cap so that taxable payroll remains a constant percentage of GDP, will not by itself accomplish more than a small fraction of the objective of restoring the system to sustainable solvency. Benefit constraints or further revenue increases would still be necessary.

Some policy advocates believe that revenues should be raised by taxing other forms of compensation than wages. Currently, Social Security taxes are levied on wage income. Individuals are not taxed on certain other benefits that they receive, such as employer-provided health care premiums. This creates inequities. A person who must buy his own health coverage must pay payroll taxes on the money spent on health care premiums. But a person whose employer pays his health care premiums doesn't pay taxes (nor does he earn benefits) based on those premiums.

Some have suggested exposing employer-provided health benefits to taxation, to level the playing field between those who buy their own health care and those who receive it through their employers. In some of these proposals, a "standard exclusion" would be created—a basic amount of everyone's health care premiums not subject to the payroll tax—so that people's payroll tax burdens don't skyrocket as a result of the policy change. Depending on where this exclusion is set, and how it is indexed to grow in the future, these proposals could result in more revenue for Social Security.[16]

Some have advocated raising taxes for Social Security primarily for political reasons; they are skeptical that sufficient support can be found among legislators to fix the system solely by restraining the growth of benefits. Even some of those who believe that the best policy would be to restrain the growth of benefits alone believe that tax increases have to be on the table to achieve a bipartisan accord.

Some Common Points of Confusion

Widely varying views on the appropriate balance between restraining costs and raising revenues are held by a broad diversity of responsible experts. At the same time, some more specious rationales for policy positions are occasionally offered.

One such point of confusion is the argument that Social Security benefits should rise with wages because taxes rise with wages. Whenever your wages grow, then your Social Security contributions grow, too, so shouldn't your benefits grow proportionally? That sounds reasonable on the surface. The problem is that maintaining this type of correspondence isn't mathematically possible in a pay-as-you-go system facing our demographics.

If the worker-collector ratio never changed, then wage-indexing *would* be sustainable without perpetually rising tax rates. Taxes would rise with wages, so would total benefits, and all would be well.

But when the number of beneficiaries grows faster than the number of workers, then something has to give: either we would have to raise the tax rate to maintain wage-indexed benefits, or else we would have to pay a rate of benefit growth that is less than wage-indexation.

Suppose, for example, that you wanted to pay every beneficiary a benefit equal to 40 percent of a typical worker's wage. If you had four workers to support each beneficiary, and you always had four workers over time, then you could forever maintain a tax rate of 10 percent (40/10). But if the number of beneficiaries grew so that you only had two workers to support each one beneficiary, then you'd need a tax rate of 20 percent.

That's the problem. In an aging society, you can't have both taxes and benefits rise proportionally—at least, not in a pay-as-you-go system. If benefits rise with wages, then tax burdens must rise by *more* than wages.

So, one way or the other, younger generations are going to get a worse deal, as long as we maintain our pay-as-you-go system and as long as our society keeps aging. Wage-indexing doesn't create benefit equity: by contrast, it simply requires each succeeding generation to pay a *higher* tax burden to get the *same* replacement rate.

Another specious attack involves the use of misleading terminology to create the misimpression of the infliction of unnecessary pain. One typical example is a Century Foundation paper which stated, "If full price indexing was implemented beginning in 2009, guaranteed benefits would be reduced 46 percent by 2075."[17]

There are multiple reasons why this statement is highly misleading. One is that to a typical listener, the term "reduced" sounds as though levels are going *down*. But under the concept being criticized here, benefits would not be 46 percent *lower* in 2075 than today; they would be 46 percent lower than another figure that is far *higher* than today's benefit levels, and which far exceeds what the current system can deliver without a significant tax increase.

Which leads us to the second point: the criticism that "benefits would be reduced 46 percent" necessarily implies that the speaker favors an alternative in which tax burdens are 85 percent *higher*. Again, if we're going to attack others for proposing slower benefit growth, then we must acknowledge the far higher tax burdens that the alternative would impose on our children and grandchildren.

There remains the fundamental point that it can often be confusing to assert that something is being "reduced" only in comparison to a *rising* point of comparison. Look at the blue line depicting benefits under a reformed system for year 2085 in figure 4.3 below. Does it depict a 25 percent benefit cut or a 60 percent benefit increase for beneficiaries in 2085? The answer depends on whether we compare to today's benefit levels or to a steadily rising baseline of scheduled (but unfinanced) benefits.

FIGURE 4.3   A 25% Benefit Cut or a 60% Benefit Increase?

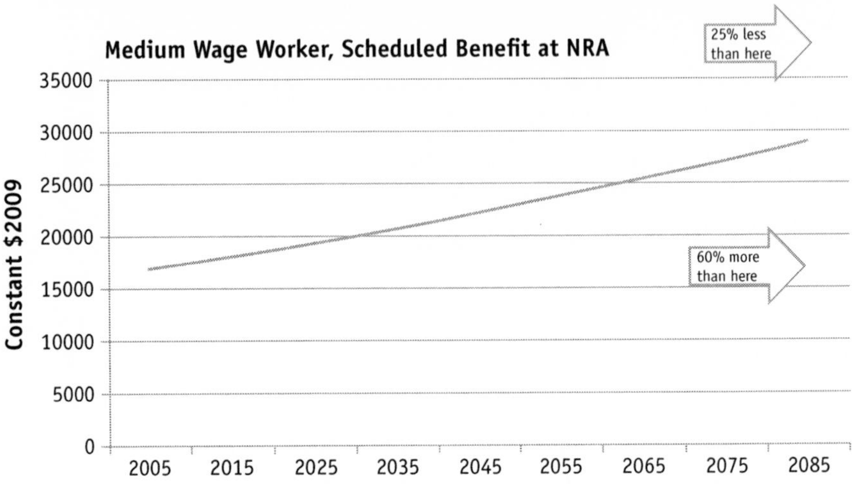

Medium Wage Worker, Scheduled Benefit at NRA

25% less than here

60% more than here

SOURCE: Based on data from the 2009 Trustees' report.

Without clarity on this point, we risk misleading Americans about the consequences of different paths.

Another specious argument is that no changes are necessary during the period of Trust Fund solvency—that is, not until 2037. So long as Social Security is solvent, it is argued, how can one justify either reducing benefits or raising taxes? Only at the point that 2037 approaches, so says this line of argument, should any changes be made.

As a practical matter, this vantage point would produce highly undesirable results. Suddenly in 2037, after decades of benefits rising at an unsustainable rate, both new *and* previous retirees would face the risk of sudden benefit cuts of 24 percent. Assuming that we don't want to suddenly reduce benefits for those already receiving them, we would need to *completely* eliminate benefits for the new retiree class to avoid a tax increase. Since it's unlikely we'd want to do that, the likely outcome of this course would be to raise the tax rate suddenly to 17.1 percent of taxable wages.

We thus see a fatal flaw in this line of argument: the duration of the Trust Fund solvency period has nothing to do with the reforms that are desirable or equitable. Basing our benefit payments on Trust Fund solvency alone would mean that we'd pay benefits in 2037 that are 24 percent higher than we pay in 2038. This would make no policy sense.

Policy sense would require a smooth and fair rate of growth in benefits, and a comparably smooth and fair rate of growth in tax burdens. We can maximize this smoothness by acting *soonest*—by spreading the burdens of attaining solvency among the *largest* number of birth cohorts—not by delaying, exempting ourselves, and thrusting the full adverse effects of programmatic imbalance upon one particularly unlucky generation.

Thus we see that there are both compelling and specious arguments for and against raising taxes and slowing benefit growth. To close this section, we will simply reiterate the question: how much, if at all, should we attempt to constrain benefit cost growth, relative to the current projection in which worker cost burdens grow from 12.4 percent today to 17.1 percent in 2035? How much, if at all, should we attempt to constrain real benefit growth for typical workers, which sits at $17,600 today, but will be $22,500 (in today's dollars) by 2035?

Once we come to agreement on how big and expensive the system should be in the aggregate, then we can decide on other matters, including how and when we will fund these benefits. We will turn next to this subject.

CHAPTER 5

Decision Spectrum No. 2
Pay-as-you-go Versus Advance Funding

Once we have decided what level of benefits to pay, and thus what level of costs to impose, we must decide who will pay for these costs, and when. These questions require fundamental value judgments about the importance of younger generations' interests relative to our own.

Pay-as-you-go Versus Advance Funding: Some History

At one extreme of the possibilities is a fully "pay-as-you-go" system. In a "pay-as-you-go" system, the government produces the revenue to pay benefits only as needed (figure 5.1). This is essentially how Social Security works now.

When Ida May Fuller became the first American to collect Social Security benefits in 1940, we did not require that she, or other members of her generation, had paid in sufficient money to fund the benefits she and they would receive. Instead, her generation's benefits were paid primarily by taxing the following generation. Later, when that younger generation was also eligible for benefits, these were paid in turn by taxing the working generation following it. And so on.

At the opposite side of the spectrum of possibilities would be a *funded* system. In a funded system, each generation builds saving—spending less than it earns—sufficiently to fund its own eventual retirement benefits in advance. An Individual Retirement Account (IRA) or a 401(k)

FIGURE 5.1   Pay-as-you-go vs. Funded System

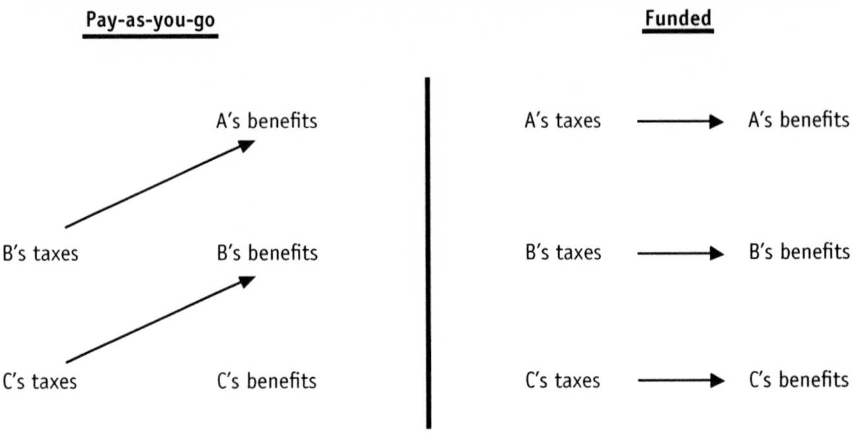

account is an example of a funded account. When a person with a 401(k) account retires, her benefits are limited to the amount that previous contributions, and the earnings on those contributions, can pay for.

A funded system is less directly sensitive to changes in the worker-collector ratio than is a pay-as-you-go system. If you're in a funded system, your benefits depend on what you (or someone on your behalf) previously contributed—not on what the following generation is able and willing to pay through its tax contributions when you are in retirement.

This chapter will necessarily simplify the issue of "pre-funding" somewhat. Even in a pre-funded system, your benefit dollars needn't literally be the same physical dollars, and earnings thereupon, that you yourself contributed. Funding can be more indirect, in the sense that your contributions are saved, this saving fuels economic growth, and the resulting higher future economic output is later tapped to pay for your benefits. The key to a funded system, however, is still very simple: it's a system in which consumption is restrained and savings built to finance future benefits.

Whether Social Security should be a pay-as-you-go system, a funded system, or a partially funded system is a debate that has raged almost from Social Security's inception. Again, here we are not attempting a general history of Social Security, which can be gleaned from other texts.[1] Here we will simply note the arguments made on both sides.

Generally, advocates of a funded system have long stressed generational equity: that is, the unfairness of leaving the cost of one generation's retirement benefits for the next generation to pay. Advocates of a pay-as-you-go system have often expressed opposition, on the one hand, to amassing vast saving reserves under government control and direction, and on the other to the risks associated with individual control.

During Social Security's infancy, this was an intense debate. But in due course, a consensus was reached to have a *pay-as-you-go* system. This consensus remained in force for many decades. In chapter 2, we cited a typical passage from the 1981 trustees' report, summarizing this longstanding agreement: incoming system taxes and outgoing benefit costs should be roughly balanced in each year.

We also explained how even after the 1983 reforms, the system effectively still remained a pay-as-you-go system, in the sense that no saving was being amassed to pre-fund future retirement benefits. As a result, substantial additional budgetary pressure will build starting in the year that the current-law 12.4 percent payroll tax plus benefit tax revenue are together no longer adequate to cover benefit costs (most recently projected to be 2016). For decades after that date, the costs facing workers will continue to rise sharply (figure 5.2).

As also discussed in chapter 2, it is less well understood that there was no intent in 1983 to depart from pay-as-you-go financing. The evidence for this is vast: in the accounts of Congressman Jake Pickle and Greenspan Commission Executive Director Bob Myers, in the memoranda of the Greenspan Commission itself, and elsewhere.

Thus, we currently have a system that is pay-as-you-go both in *fact* and in *intent*. Unfortunately, the system's accounting practices (specifically the large positive Trust Fund balance) disguise this reality. This creates in many minds the misimpression of partial pre-funding and understates the true size of the coming shortfall.

FIGURE 5.2 The Rising Cost of Pay-as-you-go Financing

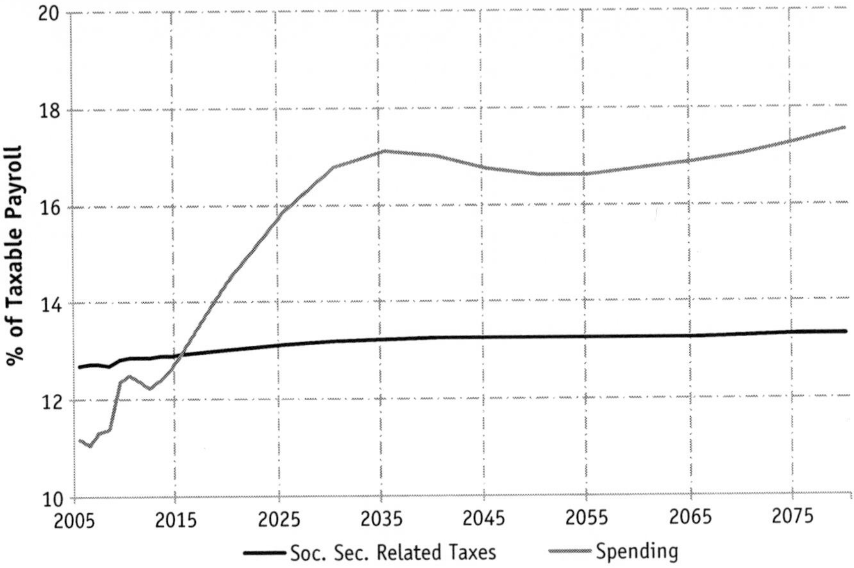

SOURCE: Based on data from the 2009 Trustees' report.

Reasons for Shifting to Partial or Full Funding

Since the 1983 reforms, a debate has swirled as to whether we should shift from a pay-as-you-go to a funded or partially funded system. As we saw in chapter 3, the 1994–96 Advisory Council unanimously recommended partial advance funding for Social Security. The members disagreed on the best *means* of pre-funding (two groups favoring personal accounts, one favoring collective investment of the Trust Fund), but they agreed that it was desirable. They also agreed that it would not be accomplished through the existing Trust Fund system.

Perhaps the central element of the case for pre-funding is *intergenerational fairness.* As we discussed on the previous pages, a pay-as-you-go system cannot maintain a proportional relationship between taxes and benefits as the worker-collector ratio drops. This is because a pay-as-you-go system is inevitably governed by the simple equation earlier cited:

$$\frac{\text{(Benefits as a \% of worker wages)}}{\text{(Worker-collector ratio)}} = \text{(Tax burden as a \% of worker wages)}$$

In a pay-as-you-go system, every time the worker-collector ratio drops, the treatment of participants becomes less favorable. If you want to pay each beneficiary $20,000, and you have four workers to tax per beneficiary, then you must tax each worker $5,000. But if you have only two workers to tax, then you must tax each worker $10,000.

One of two things must happen in a pay-as-you-go system whenever the worker-collector ratio declines. If we want to maintain constant replacement rates, then worker tax burdens must rise. If we don't want worker tax burdens to rise, then replacement rates must diminish. No matter which occurs, younger generations get less value for their money.

We see these adverse results in our current system, which will generally impose net benefit losses upon younger generations.[2] A program that imposes net losses upon whole generations will be far less effective in reducing elderly poverty among them.

As an example of these effects, compare a scaled medium-wage worker in 2005 with a scaled medium-wage worker in 2035.[3] To keep things simple, we'll assume that each is sixty years old in these respective years and that each plans to retire at sixty-five.[4]

Figure 5.3 shows that under pay-as-you-go, the worker working in 2035 is being asked to foot a bill that is *much* higher—defined as a percentage of his annual wages—even though his benefit will actually be slightly *lower*, if we also define that benefit as a percentage of his wages.

As we discussed in the last section of this chapter, whether we should think of Social Security in terms of real benefit levels, replacement rates, tax burdens, or measures relating both sides of the question is a value judgment. But no matter which value we uphold, the system will offer

FIGURE 5.3   Pay-as-you-go Imposes Lower Returns on Younger
Generations

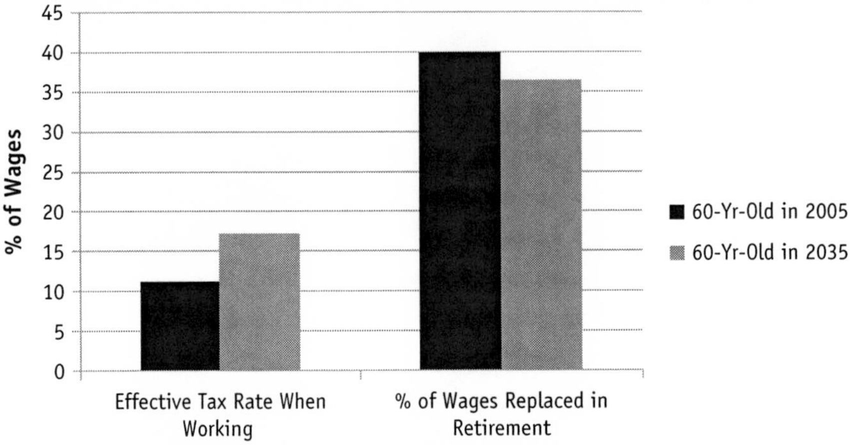

SOURCE: Based on data from the 2009 Trustees' report.

worsening treatment to younger generations as long as our aging society
continues with pay-as-you-go.

This inevitably introduces the policy question: do we *want* to have a
Social Security system that treats each generation worse than the one
before? Or, should we instead change the financing structure to ensure
that tomorrow's workers are treated as well by the system as we will be?
Are we willing to save today to improve their situation tomorrow?

This national choice is not so different from choices that face individual Americans. If you want to have a certain amount of money in
retirement, you can choose to put aside a little bit of saving today, restraining your spending. This makes life a little less comfortable today,
but it is likely to make life more comfortable later when your income
sources are scarcer.

The alternative is to spend everything you've got today—but then
you have the whole income problem waiting for you when you retire.
People thus often choose to smooth their consumption over their

lifetimes—to spend a little bit less than they could spend today, so that they have some money available in the future when they no longer have earned income.

Nationally, our choices are similar. We either restrain our spending appetite today and build saving for tomorrow, or else we leave the full problem of funding future benefits to be met in the future. There is one critical difference with the individual analogy, however: nationally, if we stick with pay-as-you-go, the adverse consequences aren't solely or even primarily ours. Instead, we're leaving the problem for someone *else*—namely, our kids—to face.

Thus, the decision to fund, or not to fund, is largely a decision as to *who* should pay. Pay-as-you-go is the easiest course for today's generation. It also sticks our kids with the biggest bill. Alternatively, our own generation can agree to pick up part of our own tab. Depending on how much saving we're willing to do, we might still face a smaller relative burden than the one we're leaving for our kids.

It's interesting to observe how self-interested considerations influence these decisions. Individual Americans often make the choice to save for their own retirement, knowing that they personally should ultimately benefit from this decision. We have thus far been unwilling to do the same, however, with our national retirement system. This may be, sadly, in part because our generation won't suffer the primary adverse consequences of our failure to save, whereas the next generation will.

In debating the question of whether we should begin to advance-fund, certain additional considerations need to be understood.

One is that future generations will get a lower return from the system than past generations, no matter *what* we do. Early participants got very high returns, because they contributed very little before receiving benefits. No matter what, young generations today face the burden of paying for the benefits of those already in retirement. Peter A. Diamond and Peter R. Orszag coined this phenomenon the "legacy debt." As they once explained it,

The benefits paid to almost all current and past cohorts of beneficiaries exceeded what could have been financed with the revenue they contributed, including interest. This history imposes a "legacy debt" on the Social Security system. . . . A reasonable estimate of the program's legacy that needs to be financed by those younger than 55 years old is $11.5 trillion.[5]

To put it simply: it's too late to pre-fund the benefits of those already in retirement. We're already stuck with that bill. What we have yet to decide is whether to pre-fund benefits that are not yet accrued—the only benefits that we can still pre-fund.

Although younger workers will have lower returns than previous generations no matter what we do, this does not mean we cannot improve intergenerational equity. If we continue with pay-as-you-go, for example, then returns will keep worsening as long as the worker-collector ratio keeps dropping. If we shift to a partial prefunding of these obligations, however, we could arrest or even somewhat reverse the trend. Some economists would also note further that if Social Security serves to increase national saving, the result would be higher economic growth over the long term, which could be translated into either higher Social Security benefits or other societal wants.

What does pre-funding mean for taxpaying workers today and tomorrow? The particulars vary from plan to plan, but the basics can be understood by looking at some deliberately extreme examples.

On the left in figure 5.4 we see the consequences for future generations of paying full scheduled benefits under pay-as-you-go financing. This is the path of least resistance today—but it imposes a harsh treatment upon future generations.

At the other extreme, we see the results of a hypothetical plan to immediately convert to a system in which future benefits are fully funded by personal accounts equal to 11.8 percent of worker wages.[6] This would have the highest cost today: current workers would need to fund the entirety of today's benefit costs (roughly 12.4 percent of their wages) while also contributing another 11.8 percent to personal accounts.

FIGURE 5.4   Effective Tax Rates under Pay-as-you-go vs. Hypothetical
Funded Plan

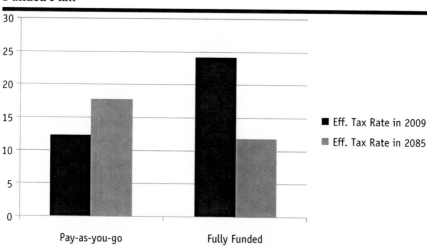

SOURCE: Based on data from the 2009 Trustees' report with additional calculations by the author.

But for workers in the distant future, a fully funded system would be by far the *best* outcome: they would be completely excused from legacy debt obligations, while also receiving the entire benefits funded through their accounts. Even if the funded accounts remained invested entirely in low-yield Treasury bonds, returns to future workers would on average be far higher than under current law, simply because they would be freed of the entirety of the legacy debt.[7]

In sum, pay-as-you-go minimizes the costs today and maximizes them for future generations. Full funding, on the other hand, maximizes the costs today and minimizes them for future generations. Partial pre-funding (for example, a combination of funded accounts with a scaled back pay-as-you-go system) would be somewhere in the middle between these extremes.

As an example of partial pre-funding, imagine that young workers were given the opportunity to contribute some of their payroll taxes to a personal account. Those young workers are already obliged to contribute 12.4 percent of their wages to pay for current benefits. To also contribute

2 percent or 3 percent of wages to a personal account would increase their total effective system contributions to 14.4 percent or 15.4 percent of wages. These total effective contributions would be more than workers are now facing, but would be significantly lower than the 17.1 percent of wages the workers of 2035 now face under current law.

Thus, the comparative burden of financing a transition to a funded system depends on one's point of view: it is *more today* than pay-as-you-go requires of us now—while also being *less* than what the current-law path requires of future generations. How we weigh these competing interests depends in turn on our attitude toward the differential treatment of different generations under current law.

How quickly would an investment in pre-funding "pay off" in the form of lower system costs? The answer depends on the details. If a sixty-year-old worker prefunds some of his future benefit this year, then the saving of that pre-funding would begin to be realized almost immediately, when he starts collecting benefits. By contrast, a younger worker has much more time to contribute genuine funding to the system, but it will also be longer before the saving from that pre-funding is realized in the form of lower future tax burdens. How it all adds up depends on the plan.

Some Arguments for Continuing Pay-as-you-go

Pay-as-you-go financing continues to have advocates. For decades, pay-as-you-go was indeed the ascendant Social Security philosophy, and many still believe it best.

One argument for continuing with pay-as-you-go is that worsening returns over time are merely an expression of an affirmative policy choice to transfer resources from young generations to older ones. In some eyes, this is a *desirable* policy result, given that we have long expected younger generations to have higher real incomes than those before them.

In recent years, however, this particular argument has been increasingly questioned, as it is no longer so clear that younger generations will continue to enjoy rising real after-tax incomes, if pay-as-you-go financing of Social Security and health care entitlements are continued. In a May 2008 paper, Syl Schieber found that ". . . continuing down our current path in regard to retirement policy has the potential to reduce standards of living for large segments of the population."[8] A more recent study by Steven A. Nyce and Schieber found that proposed legislation (later enacted) to expand federal health care commitments would likely cause wages for lower-wage workers to actually shrink.[9]

Other rationales exist for continuing with pay-as-you-go. Some advocates oppose allowing any part of Social Security to be under individual ownership and direction. This stance would rule out pre-funding through personal accounts. Some of these advocates, at the same time, would not trust the government to responsibly save and invest any portion of Social Security assets.

The late Congressman Pickle, former chairman of the Social Security Subcommittee, was strongly committed to a pay-as-you-go system. The late Senator Moynihan felt that, whatever was decided on the question of personal accounts, the traditional defined benefit portion of Social Security should be funded on a pay-as-you-go basis. Many pay-as-you-go advocates simply believe that there is no practicable or desirable way to build saving through traditional Social Security.

Some analysts also believe that it is now effectively too late to partially pre-fund Social Security, with the baby boomers heading into retirement. Some of these analysts concede that it would have been better to shelter the Social Security surpluses amassed since the 1980s in personal accounts rather than to allow them to be dissipated.

These advocates believe, however, that a transition to a fully funded system cannot be adequately financed at this point given the impending benefit claims of baby boomers. They also do not see the intergenerational equity gains of partial advance funding as sufficient to justify taking on the other policy challenges associated with it. In this viewpoint, continuing pay-as-you-go may not be optimal from an equity perspective, but it bypasses having to answer the difficult policy questions associated with pre-funding.

This argument for pay-as-you-go may gain strength with the recent disappearance of the projected Social Security surplus. Personal account advocates may argue that the surpluses might in the past have been saved had they been deposited in personal accounts. But if there are no significant surpluses to speak of going forward, then there is no longer a real opportunity to use such surpluses for pre-funding.

One specious reason given against pre-funding (often raised specifically in regard to personal accounts) is that the cost of transition would lead to an explosion of debt. This is incorrect. Shifting to a pre-funded system—whether through personal accounts or otherwise—would indeed impose a near-term transition cost, as workers today must save more and spend less. If, while devoting federal resources to a new saving vehicle, our generation failed to restrain other spending, it is true that publicly held debt[10] would increase.

This, however, would not be a consequence of pre-funding but rather of a *failure* to pre-fund. That is, if we were to increase saving in one vehicle, while increasing dis-saving elsewhere, we would simply remain in the same boat of our current pay-as-you-go system. In this worst-case outcome, we would be no worse off than we are now.

To explain via a simple analogy: Today we are doing $0 in saving to meet tomorrow's Social Security obligations. We face a policy choice: should we continue to save $0? Or should we, instead, save $1?

If we put aside $1 and reduce our spending by $1 as a result, then we've succeeded in building saving. No additional debt has accrued.

If, on the other hand, we put $1 into a savings vehicle and then borrow $1 to replace it, then we are right back where we started. We have $1 of saving we didn't have before, but we also have $1 of debt that we didn't have before. That constitutes a *failure* to pre-fund. Economically, we are no better off than under pay-as-you-go, but we are no worse off either.

Some critics of personal accounts have a tendency to stress the additional $1 in debt that *might* accrue while downplaying the additional $1 in savings that *would* accrue.

Of course, the decision as to whether we should shoulder the transition cost of pre-funding is also influenced by what is deemed affordable in the political and economic moment. As these words are being written, the United States (like the world) is undergoing severe economic turbulence, including unprecedented deficits. In this context, many would feel relieved that we do not simultaneously face additional near-term fiscal pressures arising from an effort to transition to a partially-funded Social Security system.

Of course, this argument cuts both ways. The size of our current fiscal imbalance is so large, as are recent expansions of federal spending commitments, that they make the cost of transition to personal accounts appear relatively small by comparison. The Bush administration proposed investing roughly $675 billion in personal accounts over ten years.[11] This is less than the amount of the $862 billion stimulus package enacted in 2009, and significantly less than the nearly $1 trillion for additional federal health care coverage enacted in 2010, each of which embodies new spending rather than saving.

More important, whereas the cost of the recently enacted stimulus package was simply added to previous spending—and the net cost of health care legislation was as well—the $675 billion in proposed personal account investments would instead have been primarily a means of pre-funding *existing* Social Security obligations, rather than an addition to our financial commitments.

While personal accounts are the hot-button issue in the pre-funding discussion, pre-funding isn't solely about accounts. Some have proposed pre-funding, not through personal accounts, but by saving and investing the Social Security Trust Fund in the stock market.

Whether the pre-funding is accomplished through collective investment or through personal accounts, the economic issues are the same: the same need to finance a transition, the same need to reduce near-term spending, and the same threatened result of increased borrowing from the public if transition costs are not paid for. These questions accompany *all* proposals for pre-funding, not just personal account proposals.

In the end, the decision as to whether we should have real pre-funding in Social Security is a value judgment: given the rising cost of paying benefits, and the projected burdens on the next generation, do we want to fund any of those costs in advance?

If the answer is, "no," then we continue with pay-as-you-go and leave the rising bill for our kids.

If the answer is "yes," then we need to determine how we want to accomplish that pre-funding and how we will finance the transition investments.

If the answer is "partially," then we'll relieve our children and grand-children from *some* of the projected cost explosion, meaning we'll need to put aside enough saving in the near term to fund a *portion* of future benefits.

This middle ground of "partial advance funding" is where many reform plan authors have ended up, including both proponents and opponents of personal accounts.

CHAPTER 6

Decision Spectrum No. 3

How Much Should Social Security Redistribute Income?

Framing the Progressivity Question

A NOTHER FUNDAMENTAL question in the Social Security debate is the degree to which a person's Social Security benefits should reflect her *own* contributions to the system and how much they should reflect *other people's* contributions.

Understanding this policy spectrum may be accomplished most easily by outlining the extremes of the available possibilities:

Perspective no. 1: A person's Social Security benefit should reflect only what he or she contributed to the system.

Perspective no. 2: A person's Social Security benefit need have nothing to do with what he or she personally contributed. It is acceptable for one person to contribute taxes without receiving benefits and also acceptable for another person to receive benefits without contributing any taxes.

Perspective no. 2 is closer to what most people think of as a "welfare" program. In a welfare program, we don't keep track of individuals' contributions. A poor person might receive benefits from a welfare program despite never having contributed any taxes to it. A wealthy person might contribute taxes to it, but never receive benefits. This separation of contributions and benefits is embedded in a welfare program's ethic. It is

137

deliberately designed to redistribute income from those who don't need it to those who do.

Social Security has never operated that way. Rich and poor alike contribute to Social Security, and rich and poor receive benefits from it. Moreover, *every* wage dollar that it taxes—even the last dollar contributed by a high-income taxpayer—earns benefits.

Still, as we have seen, Social Security benefits are not determined solely by one's own contributions. Social Security does redistribute substantial income from some participants to others.

Thus, Social Security lies in a policy realm somewhere between model 1 and model 2. There is a link between individual contributions and benefits, but there is also significant income redistribution as well.

We thus face the policy question: how much income redistribution (if any) *should* there be in Social Security? And once we decide how much there should be, how should we achieve it?

It is unsurprising that policy experts endlessly debate these questions. There is no clear "right" amount of income redistribution. Some advocates who believe that the purpose of Social Security is to protect people from falling into poverty will argue for more income redistribution. Others are more concerned that the program remain distinct from welfare in the public's mind, to preserve the political support Social Security has long received and which welfare programs lack. These experts sometimes say that "a program for the poor is a poor program"[1] and resist efforts to increase Social Security's income redistribution (progressivity).

One intriguing feature of this aspect of the Social Security debate is how little it conforms to the stereotypes of political party positioning. On other Social Security issues, the stereotypes seem to hold: conservative Republicans are far less willing than liberal Democrats to raise taxes, while Democrats are generally less willing to slow benefit growth; conservative Republicans are more receptive than liberal Democrats to the concept of personal accounts.

But on progressivity/redistribution questions, patterns are difficult to find. It's often the case that conservative Republicans argue for a *more* progressive system and liberal Democrats a comparatively *less* progressive one.[2] There are also counterexamples. Overall, there is no distinct pattern across the political spectrum with respect to how progressive Social Security should be.

To develop informed views on how Social Security income redistribution might perhaps be redirected going forward, we must understand the various ways in which the program *currently* redistributes income.

First, a word about the figures that I will cite here to measure income redistribution. In this section I will make ample use of the Social Security Administration's rate-of-return calculations. This is not done to prejudge another policy debate among experts: namely, whether it makes policy sense to think of Social Security's utility in terms of rates of return. This is by no means a settled question.

I use rates of return here, however, because we cannot understand income redistribution without addressing *both* sides of the equation: contributions in and benefits out. Some measures (like benefit replacement rates or payroll tax burdens) measure one side but not the other, giving an incomplete and sometimes misleading picture of overall income redistribution.

Some analysts argue compellingly for other measures that capture both sides, such as "net benefits" or "net benefit rates." Rather than enter into the debate over the best metric, I will use SSA's rate-of-return information here largely because it is readily understood, publicly accessible, widely regarded as objective, encompasses disability/survivor benefits as well as retirement benefits, and adequately illuminates the redistributive trends.

Let us now turn to some of the ways that Social Security redistributes income.

Redistribution by Wage Income Level

All other things being equal, you get a better deal from Social Security if you are a low-wage earner than a high-wage earner. (All other things are rarely equal, but I will turn to those other things later.)

Redistribution by wage income is accomplished primarily via the benefit formula. The Social Security benefit formula has different "brackets" which determine that the lower your career wage income, the higher your return.[3] For the first $744 in average monthly wage income earned over your career, you accrued a monthly Social Security benefit of *90 percent* of that amount. If you were on balance a high-wage earner, any of your wages taxed near the maximum-taxable wage income earned a Social Security benefit of only *15 percent* of those amounts.

Thus, generally speaking, the less you earned while working, the better the return on your Social Security contributions. This can be seen in the rate of return calculations of the Social Security Actuary's Office. A typical low-wage, two-earner couple born in 1949 will receive a 3.44 percent return (above inflation) on their Social Security contributions, while a typical high-wage couple born in the same year will get a 1.71 percent return.[4]

Longevity

Once you are old enough to claim retirement benefits, Social Security will pay you such benefits for as long as you live. Naturally, then, the longer you live, the greater the total return you receive on your contributions. This means that groups that tend to have longer lives get generally better returns. Women live longer than men, so they get more of their contributions back as benefits than men do. African American males do not tend to live as long as their Caucasian counterparts, so they tend to get lower returns than others with the same wage income (from the retirement portion of Social Security).

The degree to which these trends offset the progressivity of the benefit formula is a subject of intense debate among analysts, a subject to which I will return later in this chapter. Generally speaking, here we will note that because higher-income groups tend to live longer than lower-income groups, redistribution according to longevity tends to work against the progressivity created by the benefit formula. Because this counter-trend is a function of life length, its effects are more pronounced in the retirement portion of the program than in the disability component.

Marital Status

Social Security tends to redistribute income according to marital status, paying higher returns to traditional one-earner married couples than to single unmarried earners or to two-earner couples. This is due primarily to the non-working spouse benefit, which is equal to 50 percent of the primary household earner's benefit. This benefit is paid for any spouse who either didn't work in paid employment at all or who while working only earned a benefit of less than 50 percent of the primary earner's benefit.

The non-working spouse benefit is intended to recognize the value of work performed by stay-at-home spouses, including the income sacrifice made when one parent stays home to care for a child. The benefit, however, cuts sharply against the progressivity of the Social Security program. The 50 percent benefit paid to the spouse of a high-income worker might well be greater, despite that spouse contributing no tax dollars, than a spouse working for minimum wage might earn over many years of Social Security contributions.

As a result, Social Security offers lower returns to singles (and to two-earner couples) than to traditional one-earner couples. A medium-wage one-earner couple born in 1949 would expect a 4.38 percent return (above inflation) on their contributions, whereas a single male would expect only a 1.97 percent return. In fact, despite the progressive benefit formula, a *low*-income single female born in 1949 would expect a lower return (3.42 percent) than a high-income one-earner couple (3.72 percent).[5]

Generally, the closer the amounts of income received by two halves of a married couple, the worse their returns from Social Security. If the primary earner in a one-earner couple born in 1949 is of medium wage, the expected return is 4.41 percent. If instead both spouses earn a medium wage, the expected return drops to 2.39 percent. As a result of this regressive distributional component, low-income two-earner couples tend to fare worse than *high*-income one-earner couples.

Birth Year

As discussed in the previous chapter, maintaining a pay-as-you-go system in a society with our demographics imposes lower returns on younger generations. A typical medium-wage two-earner couple, both born in 1920, received a 3.63 percent return (above inflation). The typical medium-wage couple born in 2004 will expect a 1.71 percent return (above inflation). These figures actually likely *overstate* the 2004 birth cohort's true returns, as it neglects their income tax cost of redeeming debt held by the Trust Fund up through 2037.[6] In other words, this calculation pretends that some pre-funding is lessening the burden on young workers, even though empirically no pre-funding is taking place.

As a general rule, the younger the individual, the worse his return from Social Security. This redistribution of income from younger Americans to older Americans is an implicit consequence of continuing a pay-as-you-go system as the worker-collector ratio drops.

The Payroll Tax

The payroll tax is not really a source of redistribution separate from the factors described above. The returns previously presented take into account both taxes contributed and benefits received.

I provide here, however, a separate discussion of the payroll tax because it is sometimes a source of confusion. To understand Social Security redistribution, one cannot talk either in terms of benefits alone or in terms of taxes alone. One has to look at both sides of the equation to understand the total picture.

The Social Security payroll tax is 12.4 percent: 6.2 percent ostensibly paid by workers, 6.2 percent paid by their employers. In effect, the entire 12.4 percent payroll tax is paid from worker wages. The tax is levied up to $106,800 of annual wage income (this cap is normally adjusted upward each year automatically[7]). Above the wage cap, no further payroll taxes are paid. Also, above the wage cap, no further benefits are earned.

Our political system often evinces a schizophrenic, inconsistent attitude toward the payroll tax. If we think of the payroll tax purely as part of the burden of funding the government as a whole, apart from any benefit entitlement, then it is regressive. That is, if we just look at the payroll tax alone while ignoring benefits, it seems to hit low earners harder than high earners due to the presence of the wage cap.

If, on the other hand, we look at both sides of the equation and think of the payroll tax as creating an entitlement to benefits, then it is *not* regressive. To the contrary, the payroll tax contributions of low earners buy benefits at a higher rate than the contributions of high earners.

Political advocates have a tendency to speak inconsistently about the payroll tax. They often describe the payroll tax as "regressive," a burden from which low-income taxpayers warrant relief.[8] But at the same time, Social Security benefits are often spoken of as though they have been "earned" by payroll taxes.

These two perspectives are in conflict. If paying the payroll tax establishes a claim to a monetary benefit, then it is *not* a regressive tax burden because those benefits are paid out in a progressive fashion. Politicians, nevertheless, are fond of discussing the payroll tax simultaneously as a burden to be *relieved* (through refundable tax credits) but also as creating an entitlement to benefits to be *protected*. It can't really be both.[9]

It needs to be noted that projected payroll tax collections are inadequate to fund future Social Security benefits under current law. It thus cannot be the case that payroll tax contributions have truly "earned" the full amount of future benefits now scheduled. Still, even if projected benefit growth were reduced to affordable levels, the benefit formula would remain a progressive one under existing Social Security proposals.

The key point in discussing payroll taxes is that no accurate picture of systemic income redistribution can be gleaned by looking solely at either the benefit side or the tax side. As long as Social Security benefits remain linked to contributions, a view of only one side of the equation is a misleading picture.

Putting It All Together:
Aggregate Trends in Redistribution

There is an ample body of literature analyzing the extent and nature of Social Security's income redistribution. To present the panoply of findings in full detail would require us to wade into several controversies tangential to the purpose of this book. Instead, here I will simply note some general, widely agreed-upon findings, leaving others to debate the many points of contention.

First, one's perspective depends on whether we are talking about the progressivity of income redistribution *within* the Social Security system or whether we expand our view to include income *outside* of the Social Security system. Remember, the Social Security system only "sees" worker income up to the cap on taxable wages. Income above the cap is basically outside of the system—in terms of both tax assessments and benefit credits.

This may seem like an arcane point, but it greatly affects conclusions concerning progressivity. If we look only at the money *within* the Social Security system, the system is (on average) progressive. That is, it redistributes income from high-earners to low-earners.

Looking outside the system, however, changes the view. Consider two high-income individuals, one earning $200,000 a year, the other earning $2 million. Both make the same contribution to Social Security, get the same benefits from it, and thus receive the same low return on their contributions. But the $2 million earner also has a great deal of other income that the Social Security system never touches. Thus, the $2 million earner has a *much smaller* fraction of his total income tied up in this particular low-return investment. Accordingly, a study that takes into account income *beyond* that affected by Social Security would conclude that the system is treating the $2 million earner more kindly than the $200,000 earner, simply by virtue of leaving more of his income alone.[10]

For simplicity's sake, we will focus here instead primarily on what happens *within* the Social Security system—with the money that it tracks, collects, and redistributes. Within this viewpoint, researchers have generally found that the system is somewhat progressive.

The progressive benefit formula, as we have noted, delivers a higher return to low earners than high earners. On the other hand, the system also generally provides higher returns to those who live longer and to those who are married—trends that favor higher-income groups.

On balance, researchers have tended to find that the progressive factor of the benefit formula outweighs these other regressive factors. They have generally found that the system overall treats lower earners better than higher earners. The Congressional Budget Office, for example, declared flatly in a 2006 report, "The Social Security system is progressive."[11] It went on to explain specifically that "the progressivity of the benefit formula more than offsets the regressive effects of differential mortality."

The CBO report elsewhere notes that the Social Security disability and survivors' benefit elements are somewhat more progressive than the retirement benefit system. This is qualitatively consistent with the findings of other researchers.

There seems to be broad agreement that on *average*, returns on Social Security (to the extent we look only within system revenues) are progressive. But it has also been found that this progressivity is far from consistent. That is to say, one's status as a low-income person is in no way a guarantee that one will receive a higher return.

A paper by Andrew Biggs reinforced the findings of others that Social Security is progressive on *average*, but also found that the progressivity was far from reliable:

Social Security replacement rates are generally progressive by lifetime earnings, whether measured on an individual or a couple basis. On average, as lifetime earnings rise, the replacement rate—the ratio of Social Security benefits to pre-retirement annual earnings—declines. . . . However . . . this effect is true only on average . . . redistribution by earnings level is not the only, nor possibly even the predominant, factor determining how well individuals are treated by the Social Security program . . . Only 31 percent of differences in individual replacement rates can be explained by differences in individuals' lifetime earnings. The remaining differences—69 percent—are attributable to other factors, particularly the many facets of the benefit formula that can cause individuals with identical lifetime earnings to receive different retirement benefits.[12]

In other words, Social Security is progressive on average, but to an individual participant this general trend may not turn out to be that important. So many factors affect one's individual return from Social Security, that one's own status as a low-wage or a high-wage worker is a very unreliable determinant of how one will be treated.

Aligning Income Redistribution with Policy Goals

Based on research to date, we know roughly how redistributive Social Security currently is. The policy question before us is: how redistributive do we wish it to be going forward?

There are at least three important aspects to this question:

1) How much do we want the system to redistribute income, on *average*? Do we want it to redistribute from high-earners to low-earners? If so, how much? Should it do more or less redistribution in the future than it does now?

2) How important is it that the redistribution be *consistent*? Is it sufficient to be progressive on average, or do we want the redistribution to be reasonably predictable in each individual case?

3) How *transparent* do we want the redistribution to be? Do we want individuals to know how much in benefits they are earning for themselves, and how much they are providing to others?

Let's briefly discuss each of these questions in turn.

Deciding Upon Aggregate Income Redistribution

With respect to how *much* income redistribution there should be altogether, there seems to be a broad bipartisan consensus that the system should remain at least as progressive as under current law. If one surveys the full spectrum of plans offered by both Republicans and Democrats, one finds that they generally seek to retain or enhance the system's progressivity.

Within this consensus, however, there remain significant differences concerning whether an increase in progressivity should be achieved by subjecting higher earners to higher taxes or to slower benefit growth.

The interest in increasing progressivity exists for a fairly predictable reason: Social Security faces a substantial projected shortfall under current law. To close this shortfall, someone's taxes must be raised or the growth in their promised benefits slowed. Many policymakers are troubled by the prospect of imposing either higher taxes or slower benefit growth upon the poorest members of our society. Hence, they seek to limit solvency-attaining measures so that they affect only the middle-to-high-income range. This value choice has the consequence of rendering the system more progressive than under current law.

As much as we might like to, it's not really practicable to exclude more than a minority fraction of the working population from the burdens of attaining sustainable solvency. Consider that by the end of the valuation period, roughly 26 percent of promised benefits remain unfinanced under current law. We'd therefore have to cut off benefits completely for at least (very conservatively estimating) the top one-seventh of the income spectrum to balance the system within available revenues.[13]

This is highly unlikely. To date, there has been very little interest on either side of the aisle in so changing Social Security that many Americans receive absolutely no benefits from it at all after contributing a lifetime of taxes.[14] It's more likely that a bipartisan consensus would seek to protect as many at the bottom end of the wage spectrum as possible, spreading the burdens incrementally throughout the upper portions of the spectrum.

As we previously noted, there is no consistent pattern of opinion across the political spectrum concerning how progressive the system should be. There are, however, fairly consistent differences as to whether higher income individuals should be asked to give up something on the benefit side or on the tax side. Conservatives are more willing than liberals, generally, to restrain the growth in benefits paid to high earners. Liberals are generally more willing than conservatives to raise taxes on higher earners and in some cases[15] to sever the contribution-benefit link altogether for a portion of Social Security taxation.

The question whether to raise taxes or restrain benefit growth for high earners is a value judgment. Social Security's idiosyncratic accounting methods, however, sometimes cause confusion as to who would be affected by various proposed changes. This confusion sometimes distorts the positions adopted by various advocates.

One source of confusion is the important distinction between *annual* wages and *lifetime* wages. Advocates have a tendency to talk about the tax side of Social Security in terms of *annual* wages. In any given year, it is often pointed out, only 6 percent of workers typically have wages above the tax cap.[16] A naïve listener, hearing this, might wrongly conclude that raising the cap on taxable wages would only raise taxes for 6 percent of workers.

In reality, however, people's earnings fluctuate from year to year. The total fraction of the workforce who can expect to earn more than the cap in at least one year during their careers—who would thus be affected by a wage cap increase—is actually around 20 percent.

By contrast, Social Security benefits are based not on annual wages but on *lifetime average* indexed wages. For many (indeed most) workers, there are some zero earnings years within that average due to work interruptions. Average lifetime earnings figures thus tend to be a lot lower than most of us generally imagine. Many would be surprised to learn that only 19 percent of workers retiring in 2007 had average lifetime indexed earnings of over $62,000.[17]

The confusion between average earnings and lifetime earnings can distort perceptions of how people would be treated in various Social Security proposals. A proposal to slow the growth of benefits for those with average earnings of $62,000 and up would actually affect *fewer* workers than an increase in the $106,800 taxable wage cap. Of course, it is not unknown for political actors to exploit this accounting confusion to exaggerate the pain inflicted by proposed benefit restraints and to understate the number of those who would be affected by a tax increase.[18]

Beyond these points of factual confusion there remain the inevitably subjective value judgments to be made. To render the system more progressive is to offer greater relative protection to those on the low-income end—something that many of us wish to do. On the other hand, doing too much of this risks undermining Social Security's political support among higher earners. Many seasoned analysts differ with one another on the right way to strike the balance between these two considerations. On this subject, individual policy positions often defy political stereotypes.

Consistency of Income Redistribution

Beyond questions of *average* progressivity, there is a question as to whether we should act to render Social Security's progressivity more *consistent*. This goal is at the root of proposals, like those of Biggs and others, to restructure the program into two tiers. As Biggs argues:

> While incremental reforms within the existing Social Security benefit formula could improve the targeting of its progressivity, a relatively simple combination of a flat dollar benefit paid to all retirees plus a personal account paying benefits proportionate to earnings could replicate the average progressivity in Social Security while improving the targeting of redistribution, thus improving the social insurance value of the Social Security program.[19]

In other words, Biggs's proposal would seek to make Social Security's progressivity more *reliable* by creating a first-tier benefit that everyone receives without regard to income and a second-tier benefit that involves *no* income redistribution. On average, this approach would be no more or less progressive on average than current Social Security, but it would improve the consistency with which this progressivity is delivered.

Transparency of Income Redistribution

Proposals like Biggs's to create a tiered Social Security system also speak to an additional value judgment concerning the *transparency* of the system's income redistribution. One needn't follow the Social Security debate for very long to appreciate that the current system isn't very transparent at all. Few people have any reliable sense of the proportion of their own benefit that they earned directly versus the proportion of their contributions redistributed to others.

Indeed, this opacity fuels many an otherwise avoidable argument. Disputes arise about the equity of the current system and of various proposed reforms, often because we are each visualizing very different pictures of what each person has paid for and of what each person should therefore receive.

Some of these points of contention could be clarified under a more transparent system. But how transparent do we *want* the system's income redistribution to be?

If we wished to be *totally* transparent with workers about what exactly their contributions are likely to buy, we'd probably create a highly complicated mess. We'd need to separately calculate the return each person should expect, respectively, in retirement benefits, in disability benefits, from the spousal survivors' (widows') benefit, in benefits for dependent children, and many other facets of Social Security. In addition to these direct returns, we'd need to spell out how much of each person's contributions were being redistributed to other people.

Moreover, reasonable calculations of any of these figures would be impossible without accounting for each person's age, wage income, race, sex, marital status, likelihood of disability, and many other factors. These calculations would vary enormously from one person to the next and would have wide ranges of imprecision. Instead of one broadly applicable explanation that most can understand, we'd have millions of individual projections of no significant reliability. Such complexity would defeat the purpose of increasing clarity.

We could, however, quite readily redesign the system to reveal very *broad* trends of income redistribution. For example, we could divide the current system—starting with the 12.4 percent payroll tax—into three parts, as shown in table 6.1.

Such a system would enable us to see fairly clearly what our Social Security contributions purchase. Everyone working today is paying part of his taxes (C) for no direct returns; this money instead goes to pay the unfunded benefits promised to older generations. In addition to this, each of us is buying some benefits for ourselves (A) while also paying to provide a safety net for our own generation's low-income workers (B).

Were we to split the system in this way, some things would rapidly become apparent. Some high-income people would realize that only a small percentage of their taxes are buying benefits for themselves, with most of their contributions going to pay for benefits for others.

Consider a young person entering the system today who expects to do quite well—someone who expects to earn at or above the taxable maximum for his whole career (and, to keep things simple, while never

TABLE 6.1   What the Social Security Payroll Tax Buys You

System Component	What You're Paying For	Your Expected Return
A	These contributions buy benefits directly for you	Your contributions times interest
B	These contributions are distributed to low earners of your own generation to provide a safety net	High if you're of below-average income, low or negative interest if you're above-average
C	These contributions are used to pay off the "legacy debt" of benefits owed to previous generations	Zero; no returns (−100 percent return rate)

marrying). Like all members of his generation, that person can expect to contribute roughly 3.7 percent of his wages simply to retire the system's inherited legacy debt—that is, paying benefits for previous generations with no expectation of receiving anything back.[20] (In our illustrative transparent system, this would be Part C.)

Of the remaining 8.7 points of his payroll tax (12.4 percent minus 3.7 percent), it might well turn out that 4 percentage points, times interest, would be enough to fund all of the benefits that he ever expects to receive once the system is made solvent.[21] In other words, not only would this person's expected return from Part C be zero, but from Part B as well. For this person, the system might appear as shown in figure 6.1.

Some of this income redistribution is partially visible in the current system. Today, a single maximum-income earner is able to visit the SSA Web site and learn that he expects to receive a negative return.[22] The reasons for the negative return, however, are not fully apparent.

By contrast, a low-income person of the same young age—though also expecting zero benefits from part C—would expect to be on the

FIGURE 6.1   Illustrative Benefit Earnings for a Maximum-Wage Earner in a Tiered, Transparent System

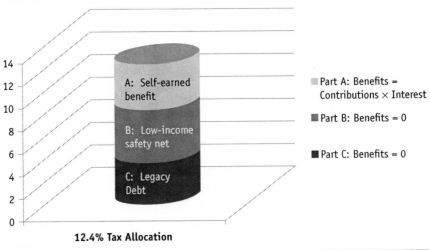

FIGURE 6.2   Illustrative Benefit Earnings for a Low-Wage Earner in a Tiered, Transparent System

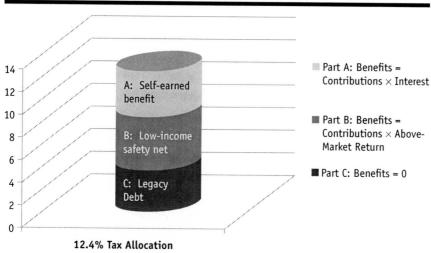

Part A: Benefits = Contributions × Interest

Part B: Benefits = Contributions × Above-Market Return

Part C: Benefits = 0

12.4% Tax Allocation

receiving end of income redistribution from part B's safety net (figure 6.2). That is, the low-income person would expect:

- A normal interest return on Part A
- An above-market return on part B
- And, again, nothing at all from part C.

Add it all up, and the low-income person would still receive a below-market interest rate from the system as a whole, but far higher than the higher-income person can expect.[23] The young low-income earner's return is pushed *upward* by systemic progressivity but is pushed *downward* even more by the continuation of pay-as-you-go financing.

Portraying the system in this way would manifest various coexisting value judgments embedded in current law. Specifically:

- *An earned benefit*: The value judgment that everyone should get something back for his contributions (Part A)

- *A progressive system:* The value judgment that everyone should contribute to a safety net for those least well-off (Part B)
- *Pay-as-you-go financing:* The value judgment to require younger workers to pay for the unfunded benefits of previous generations (Part C).

Would this kind of transparency be good or bad for Social Security? Some see in this type of system the danger that high-income contributors might withdraw support once they see more clearly what is going on. If they perceive that they are receiving nothing from Part B or Part C, political support might grow among high earners for expanding the earned benefit of Part A and for shrinking the other parts.

Some policy advocates have worried about precisely this effect. They desire functions A, B, and C to remain intermingled, obscuring the system's various forms of redistribution and forcing blunter political choices concerning the system as a whole instead of the relationships between its component elements. As an example of this concern, consider this passage written by some opponents of personal accounts:

> Moreover, most private-account proposals would make Social Security appear to be a worse deal relative to private accounts than would be the case, for another reason as well. A substantial share of the payroll taxes dedicated to Social Security are used to finance the cost of survivors and disability benefits and of raising benefits for those who worked for low wages throughout their careers. Any structure that encourages beneficiaries to compare the monthly check they receive from private accounts to the monthly retirement check that Social Security provides thus is likely to lead to serious misunderstanding by workers and beneficiaries of the relative value of the two systems.[24]

The system described in this passage isn't exactly the same as in our A-B-C example above. It is, however, similar in the essentially relevant respect. The proposal that this passage criticizes would have allowed workers to contribute 4 percent of their wages to a personal account, in exchange for accepting reduced benefits from the traditional Social Security system. Thus, this arrangement could potentially evolve into a system in which the personal account in effect becomes "Part A" above, with the highest-wage workers receiving little or no benefits from Parts B and C—and also in seeing this outcome quite clearly.

The authors of this passage are concerned that this would undermine support for Social Security based on a "misunderstanding." Desirable or undesirable, it would actually *not* be a misunderstanding. It would, instead, be an accurate reflection of how the system redistributes income. The policy question before us is whether we want this redistribution to become explicit and clearly delineated or to remain intermingled and thus obscured.[25]

Let us return now to summarize the fundamental value judgments raised in this section:

1) Do we *want* the system's current level of income redistribution? Do we want more? Do we want less?
2) How *consistent* do we want this redistribution to be?
3) How *transparent* do we want the redistribution to be? Do we *want* people to know how much of their money is being redistributed to others, or do we want to *obscure* that information, as the current system does?

On most of these questions, this chapter has taken a tone of agnosticism. There is no clearly right answer as to how redistributive the current system should be. On the question of transparency, however, the right course seems clearer. Without necessarily endorsing the particular transparency-increasing methods illustrated in this chapter, we can state with some confidence that the system's opacity does not well serve the public interest. At the very least, it does not well serve an informed public debate.

Without increased transparency in the system's income redistribution, it will be far more difficult for the public to assess whether this redistribution serves societal goals. Improving transparency should be an affirmative goal of Social Security reform.

CHAPTER 7

Decision Spectrum No. 4
Work Incentives

ANOTHER PRESSING POLICY QUESTION relates to the *incentives* Social Security provides to individuals. Do we want the system to reward or deter any particular behavior? If so, what?

The question of incentives is perhaps not as fundamental as the other three value choices framed in previous chapters (spending versus revenues, pay-as-you-go versus pre-funding, and income redistribution). A full understanding of many existing Social Security proposals, however, cannot be gleaned without appreciating the authors' emphasis on improving work incentives.

To explore all behavioral decisions affected by Social Security would require a chapter of far greater length than this one. Suffice it to say that incentive questions concern Social Security experts from across the political spectrum.

The 1994-96 Social Security Advisory Council unanimously opined that "conventional means-testing of Social Security is unwise."[1] The reasons for this unanimous view had much to do with incentives:

> The fact that benefits are paid without regard to a beneficiary's current income and assets is the crucial principle that allows—in fact encourages—people to add savings to their Social Security benefits and makes it feasible for employers and employees to establish supplementary pension plans. Moreover, means-testing would send the wrong

signal to young people and wage earners generally. The message would be: "If you are a saver and build up income to supplement Social Security, you will be penalized by having your Social Security benefits reduced." This message is both unfair to those who work and save and creates the wrong incentives.[2]

This doesn't mean that the council opposed requiring high earners to pay for most of the cost of attaining solvency; they actually favored it. But they unanimously sought to ensure that this was done in a way that didn't create undesirable incentives. Specifically, experts on both sides of the aisle sought to minimize Social Security's interference with other retirement saving that workers should be doing.

Of course, the very existence of Social Security itself inevitably deters some retirement saving. This is easy to understand. The promise of retirement benefits without individual saving is a manifest deterrent to that saving.[3]

Furthermore, as we have seen, the government itself does not save any Social Security contributions. Specifically, the Social Security payroll tax subtracts current income from individuals—some of which might otherwise be saved—and transfers the money to a government that spends *all* of it. Thus, even without the overt incentive problems of means-testing, Social Security has a problematic impact on saving generally and on retirement saving in particular.

Social Security's negative influence upon personal saving can be readily seen in analyses of reform proposals. The Congressional Budget Office, for example, found that a 2001 plan by the President's Commission to Strengthen Social Security to adopt a price-indexed benefit formula would substantially increase both personal saving and national economic growth. The principal reason for this finding was that upon shifting to a slower rate of growth in the Social Security benefit formula, individuals would do more personal saving.[4]

By contrast, CBO's analysis of the Diamond-Orszag Social Security proposal, which would have repaired system finances primarily by raising taxes, found that it would reduce economic growth.[5] The primary reason for this finding was that the higher payroll taxes and benefit promises would reduce personal saving.

Generally speaking, the higher the benefits promised by Social Security, and the higher the taxes imposed to pay for them, the less personal saving (and economic growth) there will likely be.

Even if we agree on the optimal size of Social Security benefits, we still face fundamental policy judgments concerning incentives: what positive behavioral incentives do we want the current system to provide? Or, more modestly, how can we ameliorate bad incentives?[6]

Due to space limitations, we will focus primarily on one particularly important incentive discussion: the system's effects on *work incentives.* How much should Social Security encourage or discourage participation in paid employment?

This question is of increasing concern to policymakers. As the baby boomers head into retirement, we face the prospect of millions of Americans no longer paying the payroll taxes needed to sustain Social Security and no longer contributing their work productivity to national economic growth.

At the same time, there is a growing realization that Social Security is currently designed in various ways to drive people out of the workforce. Among these are the nonworking spouse benefit, the statutory ages of benefit eligibility, and other disincentives, each of which will be described in the sections that follow.

The Nonworking Spouse Benefit

Social Security pays a benefit to a nonworking spouse equal to 50 percent of the benefit received by the household's primary wage earner. The signal sent to households by the structure of this benefit is very clear: Social Security since 1935 has been telling the spouse to remain home and out of the paid workforce.

In 2009, a typical "low-earner" retiring on Social Security received an annual benefit of less than $10,700, after paying a lifetime of taxes into the program.[7] Forty percent of women have wages at or below this "low-earner" level.[8] Meanwhile, the system would pay a benefit of over $13,800 to the nonworking spouse of a maximum wage earner, even if he or she hadn't paid a dime into the system.[9]

The decision to send a household's second earner into the workforce immediately results in a lower return on Social Security contributions. A typical married couple born today[10] can expect a 3.37 percent return on Social Security contributions if only one spouse receives wage income. If his or her spouse works (and has the same earnings potential), however, the return drops to 1.71 percent.[11]

Specifically, the current system provides extremely poor incremental returns on the contributions of women. A great deal of the additional payroll taxes paid by women are simply lost to the system, because the couple would have received a good portion of her same benefit even if she had not worked.

For example, a 2007 memorandum of the Social Security Administration showed that nearly 30 percent of women received no additional benefits whatsoever for their careers of contributions to Social Security, with an extremely negative average incremental return (minus 32 percent!) relative to what would have been received without paid employment.[12]

Social Security's nonworking spouse benefit offers women a tremendous monetary incentive to stay home. It is designed to recognize the substantial contributions made by stay-at-home spouses both to the family and to our society in general. This choice also usually involves a significant financial sacrifice (though the nonworking spouse benefit, it should be noted, is not contingent upon caring for a dependent child). The Social Security program offers a substantial monetary reward for that financial sacrifice.

The question facing policymakers is whether the design of the nonworking spouse benefit accurately reflects current societal values and needs. Do we want a system in which a low-income woman receives less for her lifetime of tax contributions to Social Security than a high-income woman receives for staying home? If not, then some changes will be necessary.

Normal, Early, and Delayed Retirement

Work choices appear to be greatly influenced by the Social Security eligibility age. When Social Security was first created, the age of retirement benefit eligibility was sixty-five. In 1961, however, the option of early retirement was created so that workers could claim retirement benefits as early as sixty-two.[13] Although one receives a reduced retirement benefit if one claims during early eligibility, more workers still choose to take benefits at age sixty-two than at all other ages combined.[14] Clearly, the existence of the early eligibility option has been taken as a signal to retire and to claim benefits as early as possible.

The typical male American alive in 1940, when the Social Security eligibility age was 65, had expected at birth to live to the age of 61.4.[15] For the typical male American alive today, the comparable life expectancy has jumped to 75.7. Even though we now live much longer than before, the average age of first Social Security benefit claims is now *earlier* than it originally was, largely because of the early retirement option.

Beyond the question of the signal sent by the retirement age, there is also the issue of the benefit adjustment for retirement benefit claims at different ages.

If you collect benefits before normal retirement age, your monthly benefits under law will be lower. This is to adjust for the expectation that you'll be collecting benefits for more years.

The adjustment is made to hold constant your expected benefits in retirement. That is, if you live as long as the average person, you expect the same total benefits no matter when you retire. This is designed to prevent gimmicking of the system through the selection of retirement age.

This is a sensible policy rationale as far as it goes. But some perceive a problem with it, namely that there is often a connection between when a person stops working and when he claims benefits. People who don't claim benefits are more likely to continue to work—and thus to pay more in payroll taxes. Thus, if the early-retirement benefit adjustment leaves their overall benefit expectations unchanged, working seniors might well be paying several years of additional payroll taxes into Social Security for *no* additional benefits.

A similar issue exists with the delayed retirement credit. If you retire *after* the normal retirement age, you get a delayed retirement credit—a benefit increase. It's designed to hold your expected lifetime benefits constant if you live a life of average length.

So, again, if you keep working and keep paying payroll taxes, you're unlikely to get much in additional benefits for those additional contributions. Some policy experts have thus suggested increasing both the penalty for early benefit claims and the reward for delayed retirement benefit claims. This provision has been included in many congressional Social Security reform proposals.[16]

Some have suggested combining an increase in the early retirement penalty with an increase in the early retirement age. This would improve work incentives on two fronts, while also preventing the steeper early-retirement penalty from impoverishing seniors who choose to retire at the earliest available age.

Others have suggested offering the delayed retirement credit (DRC) in a lump sum option. Today, the DRC can only be received as a relatively small addition to one's monthly retirement check, typically in the hundreds of dollars. Were the DRC available as a lump sum, it could well amount to tens of thousands of dollars for a typical worker. Some analysts have suggested that individuals may be far more receptive to postponing retirement if the reward is such a large lump sum than if the only option remains a seemingly small adjustment to a monthly check.[17]

Other Work Disincentives

Social Security has also been found to deter continued work—especially by seniors—in various other ways, including:

- Working seniors and their employers continue to be assessed taxes for the disability portion of Social Security even after the age when they are no longer eligible for disability benefits.

- Working seniors are assessed an earnings penalty for paid employment between the early (sixty-two) and normal (sixty-six) retirement ages. Benefits are reduced by $1 for every $2 earned over the earnings limit. Though technically the reduced benefits are simply *deferred* (they are paid later in the form of higher benefits received after the normal retirement age), the provision sends a clear signal to early benefit claimants that they should leave the workforce.[18]
- Different elements of the system combine in ways that effectively reduce the returns on continued work. For example, one part of the Social Security formula tracks your lifetime of wage earnings, determining your highest thirty-five years and averaging them to produce a single number (the AIME, or average indexed monthly earnings) representing your career earnings level.[19] But another part of the formula is designed to make benefits *progressive*—to treat you better if you're a low-income earner. Thus, the more years of earnings you have, and the more you thus increase the average of your top thirty-five earnings years, the worse your returns. As a result, by the time you reach your sixties, the returns on any further contributions you make to Social Security may be lower than at any previous point in your working life. (This quirk of the current system produces additional problems as well, such as the system inaccurately perceiving high-income immigrants or state government employees to be low-income individuals, based on their limited number of years contributing to Social Security.)

In sum, the current Social Security system is designed to drive seniors out of the workforce. In a recent paper, Andrew Biggs summarizes just how severely the system does so:

Social Security's 12.4 percent tax is the largest paid by most workers and Social Security benefits are the largest income source for most retirees. An individual considering whether to work or retire might ask, "What's in it for me? If I continue to pay into Social Security, how much additional benefit will I receive?" The answer: not much. The typical individual who works for an additional year before retiring will receive only 2.5 cents in additional benefits for each dollar of extra taxes paid to Social Security. This translates to a marginal rate of return of −49.5 percent.[20]

Although the precise figures differ from researcher to researcher, Biggs's qualitative finding generally agrees with what other studies have found.[21] Social Security's design creates strong disincentives to work, most especially among secondary household earners and seniors.

Like the other issues we've discussed, the question of work incentives in the Social Security system embodies a value judgment: how much should the system reward or penalize paid employment? Currently the program is on the "penalize" end of the spectrum for many.

When Social Security was designed in 1935, economic and cultural attitudes were in many ways different from today, especially with respect to women and seniors. Social Security's 1935 design, drawn in many respects to induce women and seniors out of the workforce, may not accurately reflect current societal values—nor our economic needs, given the impending retirements of millions of baby boomers. We thus face an important policy question as to whether we should alter Social Security's work incentives to better reward paid employment, especially by seniors and by secondary household earners.

Improving Social Security's Treatment of Work

Many proposals have been offered to improve incentives for paid employment, including:

- Reducing the Social Security taxes paid by seniors once they have reached a certain age or once they have contributed payroll taxes for a certain number of work years
- Raising the early and/or normal retirement ages
- Increasing the penalty for early benefit claims and/or the reward for delayed benefit claims

- Offering the delayed retirement credit as a lump sum
- Slowing the growth of benefit promises and payroll tax burdens by eliminating "wage-indexation" of the benefit formula
- Establishing personal accounts so that each year of an individual's contributions always funds some additional benefits
- Decoupling the system's "progressive" benefit formula from the wage history calculation, so that individuals accrue benefits equally for *each* year of work without limit on the number of years
- Reducing the future growth of the nonworking spouse benefit
- Eliminating the earnings penalty above early eligibility age

All of these proposals would improve the system's work incentives in various ways.

CHAPTER 8

Decision Spectrum No. 5

Is There a Role for Personal Accounts?

O NE COULD ARGUE THAT A DISCUSSION of personal accounts does not be-
long in this section of the book. Previous chapters introduced various spectra of value judgments without leaping forward to the *means* of
achieving them. Personal accounts, by contrast, represent a *specific policy
response* reflecting certain prior value judgments—that is, a means rather
than an end.

Personal accounts are an intensely polarizing, even emotional issue
among Social Security policy advocates. Some advocates cut right to the
finish line, declaring either the indisputable necessity of personal accounts or their unalterable opposition to them, without adequately reflecting first on what they want the Social Security system to accomplish and on whether personal accounts will move us toward or away
from those goals.

No discussion of the value judgments embedded in competing Social
Security proposals is complete without some exploration of personal accounts. To understand why personal accounts have become such a significant part of the Social Security debate, we must understand the
reasons that they have been proposed and opposed. Only then can we
make an informed determination of whether a personal account serves
or undermines our goals for Social Security.

Personal accounts are such an intensely polarizing issue that even a
factual recitation of the arguments for and against them is bound to

raise objections from one advocacy camp or the other. The following, however, attempts to fairly summarize some of the value judgments expressed by opposing sides.

Why Have Some Experts Proposed Personal Accounts?

There are many reasons why various policy experts have proposed incorporating personal accounts into Social Security. One of the leading reasons has been to establish a *savings* component within the program—that is, to shift from a pay-as-you-go program to a partially or fully funded program. The logic flows something like this:

1) Social Security is now a pay-as-you-go program.
2) This is bad, because it means that we aren't saving anything to meet the future retirement income needs of an aging population.
3) Pay-as-you-go is especially bad for younger generations, because as society ages and the ratio of workers to collectors drops, pay-as-you-go financing inflicts net benefit losses on younger workers.
4) Such ever-worsening outcomes would prevent Social Security from serving the needs of future generations as it has previous ones.
5) Ergo, we should turn away from pay-as-you-go and toward at least a partially funded system.
6) We know based on historical experience that the government won't save the money to even partially pre-fund Social Security if its funds are left on the federal ledger to be spent.
7) We also know, based on state and international experience, that governments can't resist politicizing the investments that they control.
8) Ergo, the only way we can have the effective savings component we need is to establish accounts under personal ownership.

This is a gross simplification, but it captures the basics of one important motivation behind personal account proposals. An important variant to this line of argument, however, arises specifically from the aftermath of the 1983 reforms. It goes something like the following:

1) Social Security is now a pay-as-you-go program.
2) This is bad, for all the reasons cited above.
3) But it's worse than that. Although it's actually pay-as-you-go, Americans wrongly *believe* that we're achieving some advance funding because we record a large Trust Fund on paper.
4) In reality, however, the government has not saved—and never will save—the money that is represented as being in the Trust Fund.
5) If our current system is effectively telling people that we're doing some saving even though we're not, the public will be badly misled with damaging consequences for retirement preparedness. Above all else, we need to correct this in a reformed program to *actually* save the Social Security money we now just pretend to save.
6) The only way we'll accomplish this saving is by taking part of the current 12.4 percent payroll tax away from the government—at least the part it was supposed to be saving all along—and sheltering it in personal accounts.

Those who disagree with this perspective might well offer two rebuttals:

1) The current system is *not* pay-as-you-go (that is, the Trust Fund embodies real saving).
2) Personal accounts are *not* more likely to result in the money being saved than if the government continues to manage the money.

Though there are certainly compelling arguments to be made against personal accounts, the savings argument cuts fairly clearly in their favor. Neither of the two rebuttals above holds up in light of the empirical evidence. As we reviewed in chapter 2, the most serious research has consistently found that Social Security has not amassed a storehouse of saving despite the accumulation of a Trust Fund. This invalidates rebuttal no. 1 above.

Rebuttal no. 2 is inherently speculative in that no one can say with certainty whether the government would spend just as much money in the future if it did not have access to Social Security money to spend. But various pieces of evidence strongly imply that rebuttal no. 2 also lacks a firm foundation. Among them:

- The empirical finding that government has historically engaged in more spending in the presence of Social Security surpluses is simply another way of finding that government otherwise spends less in their absence. In other words, government behavior would have to be qualitatively different in the future than it has in the past for rebuttal no. 2 to hold water.
- When the federal government has authorized collective investment schemes, such as that of the Railroad Retirement Trust Fund, it has engaged in "directed scoring" to allow it to double-count: in effect, both to invest the money and to spend it elsewhere.[1] Such tactics undo any effort to save through collective processes.
- By contrast, the federal government has *not* permitted itself to spend money held in personal accounts, even those that the federal government administers such as the federal employees' Thrift Savings Plan.
- Personal account proponents have frequently proposed to fund the saving in personal accounts not with debt but with other spending reductions. For example, the Bush administration proposed offsets to long-term Social Security benefit outlays[2] in addition to adjusting near-term spending targets in the unified budget[3] to offset the amounts to be redirected to personal accounts.
- It would be very unlikely for personal accounts not to amass at least *some* additional saving, given the empirical history that the government has tended not only to spend but to *overspend* Social Security surplus money. That is, even if the vast majority of savings in personal accounts were offset with continued federal spending, even the saving of a small fraction of the whole would represent a savings increase over current practices.

The empirical evidence on this particular point is consistent with personal account advocates' view. This doesn't by itself mean that personal accounts are necessarily the best policy; it only means that they would build some saving and thus some advance funding, whereas the current system does not.

Whether we *should* have a pay-as-you-go or a partially funded system is, of course, a value judgment. That the current system lacks a savings element, however, is more in the nature of an empirical finding.

Policy advocates disagree on the implications of this finding, but in their own different ways they acknowledge its correctness. For example, the ongoing heated arguments over how a transition to personal accounts could or should be financed (or, from the other vantage point, how they could not or should not be) embody an implicit recognition that such a shift from pay-as-you-go to partial funding would take place if personal accounts were created. If the personal accounts didn't involve real saving, there would be no transition to discuss.

It is an exaggeration, but not much, to say that if we want to move away from pay-as-you-go financing we will almost certainly need a personal account of some kind. To date, at least, no one has figured out how to efficaciously pre-fund Social Security *without* a personal account—not through the Trust Fund, not through a "lockbox" that the government can't find a way to pick, not through collective investment in stocks, nor through any other means.

It is theoretically possible to pre-fund Social Security without personal accounts. It would require, however, that government never run an on-budget deficit in the presence of a Social Security surplus. The government's long budgeting history demonstrates this to be implausible. Try to imagine, for example, the federal government refusing to run an on-budget deficit even in the midst of the economic turbulence of 2008–09.

This is why personal accounts come back onto the table whenever an expert or a group of experts arrives at the judgment that continuing solely with pay-as-you-go isn't an equitable arrangement. This finding starts a chain of logic that usually ends in a personal account being proposed in some form.

This is one reason why it is so counterproductive for policy advocates to insist on personal accounts (or any other option) being "taken off the table" at the outset of a discussion. It only makes sense to take personal accounts off the table if we have already decided that continuing with pay-as-you-go is an acceptable outcome. To date, no one in Congress has been willing to introduce a credible plan that would keep Social Security sustainably solvent through pay-as-you-go financing alone.[4]

That's a problem. It is understandable that some advocates vigorously oppose personal accounts; but if they also vigorously oppose what must be done in their absence, then our range of policy options becomes a null set.

This undoubtedly is one reason why some of the fiercest personal account opponents often succumb to simply denying the facts outright: that is, they deny the existence of the Social Security shortfall itself. Only by denying the problem altogether can one avoid the choice between personal accounts on the one hand and the implications of continuing pay-as-you-go on the other.

Closely related to the savings rationale for personal accounts is the rationale of creating a more manageable pay-as-you-go component of Social Security. In a nutshell, converting part of the system into a savings system means that the remaining pay-as-you-go obligations can be smaller. In 2001, for example, the President's Social Security Commission confronted a set of current-law projections for Social Security that appeared like figure 8.1.

The gray line on the graph represents Social Security spending; the black line Social Security taxes. The salient pattern on this graph is of near-term surpluses, followed by large and growing long-term deficits. Solely by introducing a small (2 percent of wages) personal account, the commission found (assuming, for simplicity, that every worker in America participates) that the picture would change to resemble figure 8.2.

This introduction of the small account would have the following implications for system financing:

- In the *near term*, the federal government would have less of a Social Security surplus to spend (see how the surplus area has largely vanished

FIGURE 8.1   2001 Social Security Projections

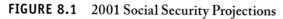

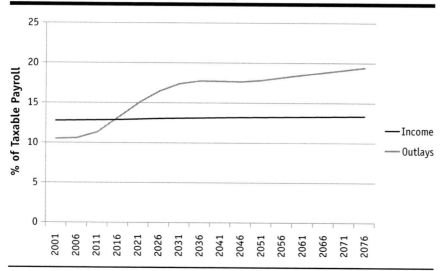

SOURCE: Based on data from a memorandum by the Social Security actuary published with the final report of the President's 2001 Social Security Commission.

FIGURE 8.2   2001 Projections: With Personal Account

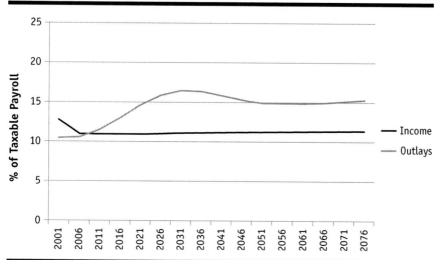

SOURCE: Based on data from a memorandum by the Social Security actuary published with the final report of the President's 2001 Social Security Commission.

on the left side of the latter chart) and the Social Security surplus would expire sooner (2009 versus 2016).

- Social Security's *long-term* costs and cash deficits would be significantly smaller under the personal account option, as a significant portion of future benefits would be paid from the personal account instead of by taxing future workers.

Would this make Social Security's finances worse or better? It depends on whom you ask and how they measure. If one assumes that the Trust Fund is "real"—that is, that the government saves Social Security money and accrues interest on that saving—then the personal accounts haven't improved anything. Indeed, over the seventy-five-year-window, the actuarial imbalance would be worse.

Without that (questionable) assumption, however, the picture looks very different. The personal account system would never experience annual cash deficits as large as the biggest current-law deficits. That is to say, if one believes that all near-term Social Security surpluses would otherwise be spent, and further that annual shortfalls in the traditional system would be de facto financed from worker taxes at the time benefits are paid, then the personal accounts *would* improve the financing outlook, significantly reducing the size of future annual shortfalls.[5]

A great deal of the debate over personal accounts flows from these debates over accounting. Depending on the metrics one uses and the assumptions one employs, personal accounts could seem either to improve or to worsen the system's fiscal stability. A good portion of the case for personal accounts rests on the view that some of the system's current accounting practices rest on assumptions belied by historical evidence.

Without understanding these underlying analytical disputes, it is hard to fathom why one expert makes one policy choice, whereas another makes a different one. Sometimes, experts try to "prove" that personal accounts hurt (or help) the system by citing a particular metric favorable to their case. But if the proof relies on a metric that another expert finds unsound, then the argument will be unpersuasive.

Additional considerations have also inspired proposals to create personal accounts. Another motivation pertains to creating additional flexibility in the delivery of benefits. Under current Social Security, you receive benefits only if you meet specific criteria, such as age, minimum number of work years, status as a nonworking spouse, or status as a surviving dependent child, among others.

It is very difficult, probably impossible, for any system of benefit formulas to be so well thought out, and so intricately precise, that it equitably treats every possible family circumstance. That's why we will always hear of tragic situations like that of a man who contributes to Social Security all of his life and then dies in his mid-fifties, without his family receiving anything from the program (or, at least, not until the other family members themselves reach eligibility age). Or, we hear about a woman who marries, drops out of the workforce to care for children, and then is divorced within ten years—having earned no benefits of her own, and entitled to none based on her former husband's earnings—despite the obvious personal sacrifices that she has made. No government-designed formula can eliminate every possible injustice.

A personally owned account, by contrast, doesn't care what one's family circumstance is, or whether it fits into the particular formula devised by government policymakers. It would create within the Social Security system an earned benefit that can be owned by any participant regardless of family structure.

Another reason for supporting personal accounts has to do with concerns about the over-annuitization of retirement benefits. Retirement planning means striking a balance between the income that one is assured of receiving regardless of how long one lives and flexibility as to when retirement saving is accessible. Social Security only provides retirement benefits in one form—as an annuity that lasts over the course of one's life. This is not optimal for many individuals, especially those with shorter life expectancies. Some analysts have found that Social Security forces many individuals to over-annuitize their retirement income assets and that personal accounts would help to mitigate this problem.

Of course, other less compelling reasons have been offered in support of personal accounts. One of them is that personal accounts would deliver higher Social Security benefits, on the assumption that workers would invest in higher-yielding securities (such as stocks). Such arguments, however, are flawed in at least two respects:

1) The low returns that today's young workers can expect from current Social Security are not a consequence of a particular investment. They are rather because of the burden of financing the legacy debt of a pay-as-you-go system. As a nation, we are stuck with those low returns. They are baked into the cake already; it is too late for today's retirees to pre-fund their own benefits. We *can* improve the returns for future generations through personal accounts, but only if our generation takes on *additional* financing burdens (that is, worsening our own returns, not raising them).

2) Some investment instruments, such as stocks, *do* offer higher investment returns over the long term—but only because they carry greater volatility and risk than other, lower-risk investments (a lesson being driven home with a vengeance as these words are being written). A personal account invested in stocks for the long term offers the *opportunity*, even perhaps the *expectation*, but not the *assurance*, of higher benefits. We can offer workers through personal accounts either a relatively *certain* benefit (if they invest in Treasury bonds) or the opportunity for a *higher* benefit (if they invest in a risk-bearing investment such as stock), but we can't offer both.

Thus, the argument that personal accounts will offer higher investment returns is compelling only if we also agree that we want workers' Social Security benefits to carry some investment risk. Not everyone agrees with that. Also, to the extent that it is argued that the higher returns can be provided to workers *without* their carrying some investment risk, this particular rationale for personal accounts lacks a sound foundation.

In fairness, it should be noted that the misleading argument of higher returns without risk isn't made solely by advocates of personal accounts. Indeed, many opponents of personal accounts have also made the same argument when advocating for the collective investment of the Social Security Trust Fund in the stock market.[6]

Some also favor personal accounts in part for philosophical reasons: specifically, because they would inject an element of personal ownership into the Social Security system. President George W. Bush often spoke to this value, as in this interview:

> If you look at a lot of our policy, we encourage ownership, and the reason why is because an ownership society is an optimistic society. It's a society in which the individual has got such a vital stake in the future of our country. So when somebody owns their own home, you know, that's their home. It provides (the) security of a home. It is an asset that they call their own. When you have your own health savings account, it's something you can carry with you. It means you're in charge of your health care decisions, not . . . somebody far away in an office complex that you'll never visit. When you have a personal savings account, a voluntary personal savings account as a part of a retirement system, it's your asset. You look at it on a quarterly basis to see whether or not you're getting a compound rate of interest that is suitable to your needs. Ownership really is a vital part of the American experience. And we want more people owning something. We just don't want ownership to be confined to a certain segment of society. We want everybody, every single person, to be able to say, "This is my asset. And I intend to pass it on to whomever I choose."[7]

Many on both sides of the aisle espouse this view of the benefits of ownership—of homes, of financial assets, and other items—especially for the poor. Many perceive positive differences between how owners act in contrast with renters, both with respect to maintenance of property and with respect to their personal outlook and happiness. "No one washes a rental car," goes the old expression. Many believe that Social Security would be improved if it contained this element of ownership—not just the promise of monthly checks but an asset that is securely under personal ownership and control.

Sources of Opposition to Personal Accounts

Of course, there are many conflicting concerns felt by opponents of personal accounts. Many strongly oppose personal accounts precisely *because* they would inject an element of personal ownership into what they believe should be purely a collective system of social support. As economist Mark Weisbrot once stated:

> Social Security is not a retirement account but a system of social insurance. It is a commitment by society from one generation to another; we all pay in, and we all draw out, because we never know how we will fare in our old age. The program also provides disability and survivors' insurance. The idea that "we are all in this together," on which Social Security is based, has always been unpalatable for those who believe in "every man for himself" and the law of the jungle.[8]

In this view, any individual ownership component threatens the desired organizing principle of Social Security, which is based intrinsically on mutual interdependence. A personally owned account, in this view, serves a contrary "every man for himself" mentality.

Once an individual has title to some assets of her own, it is feared, she might become more attached to that element of the system than to the collective good fostered by the system as a whole. Earlier we described an example of a hypothetical system that arouses this concern by separating redistributive and self-earned benefit elements.

We should emphasize how strongly this view is held among some opponents of personal accounts. For these advocates, the idea of personal ownership within Social Security is anathema, undercutting its foundational ethic. They see it as the unraveling of a system that is based above all else on shared benefits and shared commitments.

At the risk of perpetuating the back-and-forth arguments, we must recognize an inevitable consequence of this latter view: that which is not owned might never be delivered. Without an ownership element, one's Social Security payments remain at the mercy of the political process.

They might at one time be scheduled for one level, but nothing more than a change in law is needed to reduce them.

And, when scheduled benefits exceed resources, they are in fact reduced. This happened in 1977 and again in 1983. Without a substantial increase in future taxes, it will happen again.

All sides of the Social Security debate sometimes make internally inconsistent arguments. It is not unknown for *opponents* of ownership within Social Security to argue that currently scheduled Social Security benefits are a contract that cannot be reneged upon (in some of the more fantastic utterances even equating a reduction in benefits with defaulting on government debt).[9] But these two positions cannot be reconciled; if individuals do *not* own their Social Security benefits, then indeed they *can* be changed at any time.

The Social Security Administration's Web site offers a helpful summary of the situation with respect to ownership under current law:

> There has been a temptation throughout the program's history for some people to suppose that their FICA payroll taxes entitle them to a benefit in a legal, contractual sense. That is to say, if a person makes FICA contributions over a number of years, Congress cannot, according to this reasoning, change the rules in such a way that deprives a contributor of a promised future benefit. Under this reasoning, benefits under Social Security could probably only be increased, never decreased, if the Act could be amended at all. Congress clearly had no such limitation in mind when crafting the law. Section 1104 of the 1935 Act, entitled "RESERVATION OF POWER," specifically said: "The right to alter, amend, or repeal any provision of this Act is hereby reserved to the Congress." Even so, some have thought that this reservation was in some way unconstitutional. This is the issue finally settled by *Flemming v. Nestor.* In this 1960 Supreme Court decision Nestor's denial of benefits was upheld even though he had contributed to the program for 19 years and was already receiving benefits. Under a 1954 law, Social Security benefits were denied to persons deported for, among other things, having been a member of the Communist party. Accordingly, Mr. Nestor's benefits were terminated. He appealed the termination arguing, among other claims, that promised

Social Security benefits were a contract and that Congress could not renege on that contract. In its ruling, the Court rejected this argument and established the principle that entitlement to Social Security benefits is not [a] contractual right.[10]

The long and the short of the "ownership" argument is that whether personal ownership is desirable or undesirable within Social Security is a value judgment on which individuals of good faith can disagree. The flip side of the discussion, however, is that the *lack* of personal ownership means that benefits can be changed at any time, as they have been in the past, and undoubtedly will be again.

Closely related to these concerns are concerns about risk. We have seen that the current system exposes individual workers to political risk: the risk that their benefits, set by law, will be altered by law.

This political risk is closely related to financing risk. In theory, the government bears the risk associated with financing Social Security's defined benefits, instead of individual beneficiaries bearing investment risk as they do in a defined contribution system. But the government is us: to the extent that we fail to adequately finance scheduled benefits, the costs of that failure must be passed to some combination of beneficiaries and taxpaying workers.

The current Social Security system thus doesn't eliminate risk; rather, it simply allocates that risk via the political process.

Still, personal accounts could introduce within Social Security a new form of investment risk. To the extent that individuals are permitted to invest in different instruments, then their benefits might go up—or down—as a result of investment performance. For some policy advocates, permitting workers to assume any investment risk undermines the very point of Social Security. In one typical quotation, an opponent of personal accounts argues, "Why would you want to gamble with your future security when you can have the assurance of a steady fixed income from Social Security . . . ?"[11]

Without prejudicing the disposition of this particular value judgment, we do need to understand some factual caveats pertaining to it.

Just as personal account advocates must acknowledge that the opportunity for higher investment returns comes with higher investment risk, personal account opponents must acknowledge that more *certain* investment returns mean *lower* returns.

It's by no means an obvious analysis as to how much each of our incomes should be tied up in a steady and defined, but low-return, investment. Moses did not descend from Mount Sinai holding two tablets declaring that 12.4 percent of each of our wages was the optimal percentage to contribute to a low-return "guaranteed" investment.

If it were as simple as choosing a "guarantee" over a "gamble," then each of us would invest *all* of our retirement saving in "guaranteed" instruments. But smart planners don't do that, because doing so would reduce one's expected retirement income. Shrewd financial planners therefore mix more certain investments with higher-risk investments.

What is the optimal amount of money that each of us should invest in a low-return, defined-benefit investment such as Social Security?

Is it 12.4 percent of our wages? In that case, then we should only have personal accounts on top of Social Security, not within it.

Is it 15 percent? Then we should increase the Social Security payroll tax, even if it comes at the expense of our other investments.

Is it only 8 percent? Then it would make sense to have a personal account *within* Social Security, funded by part of the current payroll tax (or, alternatively, lower Social Security taxes and lower benefits as well).

Does the percentage vary from person to person? Then perhaps we should offer *voluntary* personal accounts.

Merely asserting that personal accounts are a "gamble" doesn't answer this important policy question. It might be possible to reach a broad bipartisan agreement that Social Security should devote a minimum percentage of each worker's earnings to a low-return, defined-benefit investment, free of individual investment risk. But that doesn't tell us whether 12.4 percent is the right amount of each of our incomes to devote to a guaranteed, low-return investment, or whether it makes more sense to split that 12.4 percent into different pieces with different risk tolerances. It's silly to make a religious point of the inviolability of

Social Security's current assessment before we determine whether that figure is based on any empirical rationale.

This debate is most important for low-income individuals who are least likely to have leftover discretionary income to save outside of Social Security. For high-income individuals, whether there are Social Security personal accounts need not affect their overall retirement investment risk. To the extent that Social Security currently forbids higher-income individuals from investing in stocks, they can counter the effect by investing more of their non-Social Security money in stocks. Anyone with sufficient savings outside of Social Security already has the ability to take on the investment risk that a Social Security personal account would allow. For these people, investment risk in Social Security is a much less tangible issue.

Where it makes a difference is for low-income people, who may not have additional income for saving after the 12.4 percent payroll tax is taken from them. Is their retirement security maximized by being forced to invest entirely into the low-return, defined-benefit investment of the current Social Security system? That's an analytical question—we need to study the evidence to determine the answer. But simply *asserting* the virtue of "guaranteed" benefits doesn't produce it.

It's important to disentangle genuine concerns about investment risk within Social Security from hyperbolic rhetoric about personal accounts embodying a "gamble." Clearly, many opponents of Social Security accounts do not truly equate them with gambling, as their rhetoric sometimes implies. If they did, then AARP would not encourage its members to set up personal accounts with its own financial services affiliates, nor would the Obama administration support automatic enrollment in IRA accounts. Support for other forms of personal accounts does not necessarily imply that they should be supported within Social Security, but it does demonstrate that they are not genuinely thought of as irresponsible gambling.

Again, none of this dismisses the concerns of those who oppose personal accounts within the system. We just need to remain alert to the reality that retirement security would be *reduced*—and a very real negative impact on seniors' income will result—if we fail to optimize the percentage of worker wages that we compel to be invested in a low-return, defined retirement benefit.

Opponents of personal accounts often express a closely related concern about investment risk: the value judgment that benefits should not vary from person to person based on luck or skill in investing. If you have the same wage history, age, and marital status as your next-door neighbor then you ought not, in this view, to be receiving a very different Social Security benefit simply based on whether you happened to invest your contributions in the right (or wrong) investment at the right (or wrong) time.

Again, this is a value judgment that transcends the numbers. It might be possible to show analytically that both you and your neighbor will be better off accepting some investment risk than continuing wholly with the current pay-as-you-go system. It might also be possible to show (and some analysts have) that under current-law Social Security, there is enormous variance in whether one's investment in the program will "pay off." But irrespective of the data, allowing individual investment risk is something many advocates find incompatible with their vision for Social Security; they are far more comfortable with other forms of risk—such as political risk, longevity risk, divorce risk—than they are with investment risk within Social Security.

Another objection raised to personal accounts is administrative cost. The current Social Security system has extremely low administrative costs. Creating personal accounts within Social Security would undoubtedly increase administrative costs, as it would require the federal government to track many things that it currently need not.

For example, it can now take longer than a year and a half before an individual's Social Security contributions are "reconciled" (properly credited to him) under the current system. These kinds of time lags can be tolerated in the current system, because it need not track or invest contributions in anything close to real time.

If personal accounts were created, then the administrative costs would have to be paid by someone. If they were paid by personal account participants, then those participants' accounts would need to earn a higher return than current Social Security, to offset the administrative costs and to receive the same total benefit.

This outcome could of course be avoided by paying for the administrative cost of personal accounts from general Trust Fund revenues. In this case, both those without accounts and those with them would be asked to foot the bill for account administration, raising fairness concerns. In either case, the total amount available to pay benefits would be slightly lessened by increased administrative costs.

These issues are real, though they are also often exaggerated. Most proposals to create personal accounts have been based on the model of the federal employee Thrift Savings Plan, which has extremely low administrative costs. The Social Security Actuary has estimated that replicating the basic features of the TSP would require an administrative cost of roughly 30 basis points (0.3 percent of account balances annually).[12] If the new system succeeded in having administrative costs closer to the actual TSP, then administrative costs would be far lower.[13]

Sometimes this issue has been exaggerated for political effect. In one particularly egregious example during the 2004 presidential campaign, a controversial paper was published within academia stating that creating personal accounts would lead to a "massive increase in payments to private financial management companies . . . the net present value of such payments would be $940 billion."[14] The publication of this paper raised issues regarding the propriety of the use of academic credentials to lend credibility to a set of factual representations, made in the heat of a presidential campaign, which should not have withstood serious peer review.

Among other mistakes, this paper ignored the actual data and design aspects of existing personal account proposals drafted on the model of the federal government's Thrift Savings Plan, so as to allege enormous payments to Wall Street that could only have arisen under a system vastly different than proposed. Under the TSP model for administering personal accounts, most administrative functions are performed by an arm of the federal government, without the windfalls to Wall Street imagined in this particular paper.

Another set of concerns about personal accounts involves the difficulty of avoiding unintended or inequitable consequences. Using personal accounts to pre-fund existing system obligations means allowing workers to shift part of their tax contributions—*and* part of their future benefit payments—to the accounts.

This introduces many questions. How much less should workers receive from traditional Social Security if they are allowed to move some of their taxes to an account? What amount ensures that system finances are not harmed? How do we ensure that progressivity is maintained? How would this change disability benefits or benefits for survivors? If a young widow inherits a personal account, can she access it immediately or must she wait until eligibility age, just as she must do in traditional Social Security? Can a husband choose to redirect some of his (and therefore his spouse's or widow's) Social Security benefit into a personal account, but then bequeath the personal account balance to another woman? Should you be able to receive the personal account balance as a lump sum and to spend it all, even if you end up in poverty? Or must you annuitize it (receive it as a stream of periodic payments) instead? Finally, if you can't withdraw it when you want, in the form you want, or bequeath it to whom you want, how much do you really own it?

Though existing personal account proposals offer answers to all of these questions, many personal account opponents are skeptical they will be adequately resolved in practice, and would thus prefer not to introduce the questions at all.

As we can see, the argument over personal accounts involves strongly held value judgments for many people. As is the case with some arguments *for* personal accounts, some arguments *against* them are not always well-grounded in fact.

One such weaker argument is that the introduction of personal accounts will undermine the "safety net" aspect of Social Security; that is, that the current system's progressivity and income redistribution cannot be maintained in a system containing personal accounts. One example of this argument comes from the Leadership Council of Aging Organizations, which declares flatly, "Privatization (sic) could destroy the progressive nature of the Social Security program."[15]

This is not necessarily true, for a couple of reasons:

1) A personal account is often introduced as a *component* of a larger Social Security reform plan. These plans typically preserve or even increase the progressivity of the Social Security system as a whole. A typical example is the Kolbe-Stenholm (later Kolbe-Boyd) proposal, which would be significantly more progressive than current-law Social Security. Such plans are usually designed to accomplish multiple objectives: both to introduce a savings component within the program and to increase its overall progressivity.

2) The personal account itself could be established in a progressive way. Many Social Security proposals would allow lower-income individuals to save a larger proportion of their Social Security taxes in a personal account than would be available to higher-income workers. Unlike the portion of one's Social Security contributions that is required to pay off the system's "legacy debt," the personal account could be expected to earn a Treasury bond rate of return or higher; this would mean that a larger share of a low-income worker's contribution is earning higher returns, which would add to the progressivity of Social Security as a whole.

These are but some of the many arguments made for and against personal accounts. Putting it all together, we can summarize various arguments in favor of personal accounts as saying that they would:

- Build savings within Social Security and end inequitable pay-as-you-go financing
- Create transparency by replacing illusory pre-funding with actual savings
- Reduce cost growth in the pay-as-you-go portion of Social Security
- Add flexibility in how benefits are received and by whom
- Mitigate the over-annuitization of retirement income

- Create an ownership component in the Social Security system
- Offer higher benefits through higher returns (sometimes speciously argued)

Concerns that weigh against personal accounts, in summary, say they would:

- Introduce an "every man for himself" element into a "we're in this together" system
- Introduce investment risk
- Lead to a transition cost of shifting from pay-as-you-go to a partially funded system
- Result in higher administrative costs
- Introduce complexities in ensuring equitable treatment of the disabled, spouses, and survivors
- Undermine the system's progressivity (sometimes speciously argued)
- "Solve" a problem that doesn't exist (always speciously argued)

CHAPTER 9

Putting It All Together

Balancing Value Judgments in a Comprehensive Plan

I N RECENT YEARS, MORE than a dozen proposals to shore up Social Security's finances have been scored by SSA's Office of the Actuary. Each of them reflects a different set of value judgments.

Sometimes a plan provision to further one policy objective has the effect of impeding another. For example, a plan author may wish to provide a stronger safety net against old-age poverty: that is, increased benefits certain to be received regardless of one's past earnings. Pursuing this objective, however, may set back another, such as improving the system's work incentives. The best authors develop creative ways to minimize conflicts between such competing objectives.

This chapter explains how various policy objectives have been reflected in some existing Social Security proposals.

Spectrum No. 1: Cost Growth/Revenues

At one end of this spectrum are proposals that would slow the growth of benefits sufficiently to sustain Social Security without raising taxes. Examples include the proposals of Senator Robert Bennett[1] (R-UT) and Congressman Sam Johnson (R-TX).[2] The Johnson proposal also contains a personal account, but for those who do not choose it, benefit

189

growth would be constrained to the extent necessary to avoid a tax increase. The proposal of Senator Lindsey Graham (R-SC) would similarly constrain costs, though workers would have the option of paying higher taxes for a higher benefit level if they so chose.[3]

At the opposite end are proposals that would close the solvency gap exclusively or almost exclusively by increasing system revenues. Examples include the Diamond-Orszag proposal (from economists Peter A. Diamond and Peter R. Orszag) and proposals by Congressman E. Clay Shaw Jr. (R-FL), and policy analyst Peter Ferrara. The Diamond-Orszag proposal contains some benefit restraints but the plan's offsetting benefit increases would exceed them through 2050.[4] All of the shortfall would be met by raising taxes through mid-century and the vast majority (roughly 80 percent by the end of the valuation period) thereafter. Averaged over seventy-five years, virtually all of the job would be done on the tax side. The Shaw[5] and Ferrara proposals[6] do not identify explicit tax increases but each requires that sufficient additional revenues be provided to Social Security to fill the financing gap without slowing the growth of scheduled benefits.

Other proposals are somewhere in the middle, splitting the difference between new revenues and cost restraint. The proposal of Congressmen Jim Kolbe (R-AZ) and Allen Boyd (D-FL) leans somewhat in the direction of cost containment. As with all plans, the precise balance depends on how one measures it and over what period. By mid-century, and roughly averaging the effects per SSA's actuarial method, the proposal is about 60–65 percent cost restraint and 35–40 percent additional revenues, though when looking at long-term cash operations, the proposal appears to lean more heavily in the direction of cost restraint (upwards of 85 percent).[7] The proposal of Senator Chuck Hagel (R-NE) is generally in the same range, requiring somewhat more in additional revenues than Kolbe-Boyd, though it does not explicitly identify all of these revenue sources.[8]

The Liebman-MacGuineas-Samwick (LMS) proposal[9] would lean the other way, relying somewhat more on additional revenues. By some measures, the LMS proposal would do the job almost entirely with additional revenues (the proposal's increase in the taxable wage base and additional personal account contributions would together infuse more revenue than required to attain seventy-five-year solvency through tax increases alone, and enough to get more than two-thirds of the way to sustainable solvency). By the out years, however, cost restraint would appear to dominate in the LMS proposal as well, eliminating nearly two-thirds of the cost increases projected under current law over the very long term.[10] (For reasons that are detailed in the endnotes, the true cost/revenue balance in each of these plans lies somewhere between the result obtained by reviewing seventy-five-year averages and the result obtained by reviewing out-year annual cash deficits.)

President Bush did not submit a complete solvency proposal so his precise position along this spectrum cannot be precisely quantified (and will thus be omitted from the following charts). His philosophical disinclination to raise taxes, however, is well known. Moreover, he expressed support for a progressive indexing concept developed by Robert Pozen. The Pozen proposal for progressive indexing would by itself have eliminated roughly two-thirds of the annual shortfalls through spending restraint over the long term.

FIGURE 9.1 The Revenue/Cost Spectrum

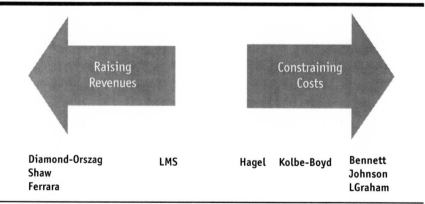

SOURCE: Based on data from "Proposals Addressing Trust Fund Solvency," Social Security Administration, http://www.ssa.gov/OACT/solvency/index.html.

Figure 9.1 very roughly characterizes the positions of various plans along this policy spectrum. Plans that rely principally on new revenues have been placed on the left, while plans that more tightly constrain cost growth are on the right.

Spectrum No. 2: Pay-as-you-go/Funding

Each of these proposals also falls at a distinct spot along the policy spectrum that ranges from pay-as-you-go financing to full funding.

At one extreme of this spectrum lie the Diamond-Orszag and Bennett proposals, which would continue wholly with pay-as-you-go. (Senator Bennett has expressed support for the concept of personal accounts, but his proposal as introduced did not include them.) In the Diamond-Orszag proposal, benefits would be financed primarily by steadily ratcheting various taxes upward over time. In the Bennett proposal, cost growth would be constrained so that the effective cost rate would rise to a peak in 2033 and decline thereafter.[11] Diamond-Orszag and Bennett thus represent opposite extremes on the cost/revenue spectrum, while occupying the same end of the pay-as-you-go/funding spectrum.[12]

At the opposite extreme lie proposals that would establish a wholly or predominantly funded system, such as the Johnson and Ferrara proposals. In each of these, the tax payments required for the traditional Social Security system would ultimately shrink to be significantly smaller than the investments workers make in personal accounts.[13] The larger personal accounts in these plans would mean greater transition costs today but, if successfully financed, improved treatment of workers in the long term.

Most other proposals are somewhere in the middle, allocating a minority of the 12.4 percent payroll tax to a personal account. The proportion of these plans that we describe as being in personal accounts is a function of how we measure it. A proposal to invest one-quarter of the payroll tax in personal accounts would actually result in a much *higher* fraction of benefits being in the accounts. This is because the accounts would directly finance benefits for the contributor, whereas much of one's traditional payroll tax goes out the door and never comes back—

buying benefits not for oneself but for a previous generation. To simplify, we will describe proposals as a function of the projected *taxes* that would be shifted to personal accounts.

An additional complication is that some proposals involve *voluntary* personal accounts, others *mandatory* personal accounts. Thus, a proposal in which workers may voluntarily invest 4 percent of their wages in personal accounts may actually result in less total advance funding than a proposal in which workers *must* invest 3 percent of their wages. Beyond this, some proposals put a ceiling on the age at which workers may invest in accounts or on the dollar amount each may contribute.

Again, to keep things simple, we will compare proposals according to the total amount of advance funding that the SSA Actuary expects to be achieved in each plan.

When one examines the various plans that occupy a middle ground between pay-as-you-go and full funding, one finds a remarkable result: every one of the plans listed here lies within a narrow band between 2.26 percent and 2.89 percent of national taxable wages. Specifically, here are the percentages that each would invest in personal accounts:

- L. Graham: 2.89 percent
- LMS: 2.76 percent
- Hagel: 2.67 percent
- Shaw: 2.28 percent
- Kolbe-Boyd: 2.26 percent

President Bush did not specify the size of investments in personal accounts beyond the first ten years of his proposal. He did, however, indicate that ultimately each worker would be able to voluntarily contribute 4 percent of wages to a personal account. Employing the Social Security Actuary's assumption of two-thirds participation in these voluntary accounts, then 2.67 percent of total taxable wages would be so invested, placing his proposal well within the mainstream of others put forward.

These proposals arrive within the same narrow band in different ways. The Bush and Hagel proposals, for example, would offer larger accounts, but they would be voluntary, resulting in less than 100 percent participation. The Kolbe-Boyd and LMS plans, on the other hand, would have smaller accounts, but they would be mandatory. Each of these plans is thus predicted to produce a comparable amount of advance funding for Social Security.

At one time, this would have been powerfully suggestive of the appropriate common ground for a Social Security solution. Except for those ideologically committed to opposing personal accounts (Diamond-Orszag), or, on the opposite side, committed to an almost wholly funded account system (Johnson, Ferrara), plan authors tended to arrive at roughly the same view of the optimal and most equitable amount of pre-funding: somewhere between 2.26 percent and 2.89 percent of projected taxable worker wages.

Of course, ideological passion will never be banished from the Social Security debate. If it were, however, it's quite possible that negotiators could have honed in on an optimal amount of advance funding relatively quickly.

FIGURE 9.2 The Pay-as-you-go/Funding Spectrum

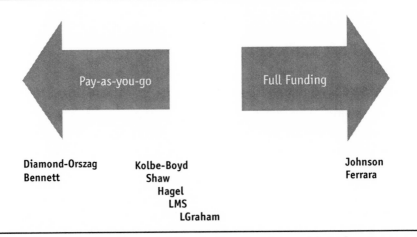

Diamond-Orszag   Kolbe-Boyd   Johnson
Bennett   Shaw   Ferrara
                        Hagel
                        LMS
                        LGraham

SOURCE: Based on data from "Proposals Addressing Trust Fund Solvency," Social Security Administration, http://www.ssa.gov/OACT/solvency/index.html.

Figure 9.2 roughly characterizes where various plans fall along this particular policy spectrum. Pay-as-you-go plans are on the left, fully-funded plans on the right.

Spectrum No. 3: Redistribution

A full analysis of the effect of various plans upon Social Security's income redistribution would require many dozens of pages. To broadly characterize the value judgments embodied in various plans, we will need to simplify considerably.

Further complicating matters is the fact that different plans have been evaluated by different agencies, employing different methods. Even separate offices within the Social Security Administration (such as the Office of the Actuary and the Office of Retirement Policy) employ different means of evaluating progressivity. This renders apples-to-apples comparisons difficult.

Evaluations of system progressivity also depend highly upon projections of returns from personal accounts. To simplify, we can employ the assumption that accounts will generally earn only a Treasury bond return, but not every analyst will agree that this is accurately reflective of likely reality.

So as not to be tripped up by these various analytical differences, we will employ simplified characterizations here that minimize their importance.

Most Social Security reform proposals generally fall into one of two categories: those that seek to *maintain* the approximate amount of current income redistribution and those that seek to make the system *more* progressive.

Plans that seek to roughly *maintain* the current amount of system progressivity include the LMS plan, the Diamond-Orszag plan, the Shaw plan, the Hagel plan, the Johnson plan, and the Ferrara plan.

Within this broad characterization, there are further minute distinctions. The Congressional Budget Office found that in the near term, Diamond-Orszag would offer some benefit enhancements to low earners; but over the long term, low-earner benefit growth would be restrained roughly proportionately to high-earner benefit growth.[14] In the Johnson plan, the traditional system's benefit promises would maintain the current proportion for high- and low-earner benefits, but a table in the Actuary's memo suggests that high-income participants in the personal accounts may do better than under current law.[15]

The LMS plan would roughly maintain system progressivity, but the precise findings depend on how the question is framed and whom one asks. The SSA Actuary's memo finds that low earners would actually carry a slightly greater solvency burden on the benefit side, though high earners would carry a higher burden on the tax side.[16] It also finds that the plan would be sustainably solvent. CBO, by contrast, found that the plan would *not* be sustainably solvent, but also that low earners would have higher benefits than projected by SSA.[17] The difference appears to lie in CBO having assumed the inclusion of certain low-income benefit enhancements (and thus costs) that are not included in the SSA analysis of the plan.

On the other side of the spectrum are plans that seek to shield low-income workers from the burdens of attaining sustainable solvency, thus increasing progressivity overall. Such plans include the Kolbe-Boyd (and previously Kolbe-Stenholm, for Texas Democrat Charlie Stenholm) proposal, the Bennett proposal, the Graham proposal, and the Pozen proposal to which President Bush gave support. The Kolbe-Boyd and Graham proposals would each redesign the basic benefit formula factors to provide additional income protections to low-income workers.

The Bennett and Pozen proposals would employ "progressive indexing" mechanisms to enable the benefits for low earners to grow more rapidly than the benefits for high earners. (Again, we describe the Bush/Pozen proposal here, but do not attempt to place it within the picture, due to its having been a starting point for solvency discussions rather than a completed plan.)

As we have previously noted, there is no stark partisan or even ideological pattern as to the relative progressivity of various Social Security plans. Some bipartisan proposals (LMS) seek only to maintain progressivity, others (Kolbe-Boyd) to significantly increase it. Some Republican

FIGURE 9.3 The Progressivity Spectrum

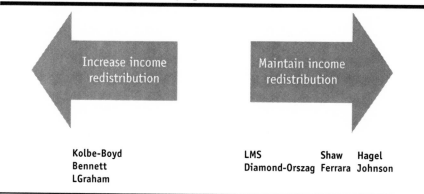

SOURCE: Based on data from "Proposals Addressing Trust Fund Solvency," Social Security Administration, http://www.ssa.gov/OACT/solvency/index.html.

proposals (Ferrara) seek only to maintain progressivity, others (Bennett) to significantly increase it. Some Democratic proposals (Diamond-Orszag) seek only to maintain progressivity, others (Pozen) to increase it. One can find plans authored by individuals of each party on each side of this particular spectrum.

Plans that would significantly increase system progressivity are on the left in figure 9.3, those that would not are on the right.

Spectrum No. 4: Incentives

Social Security plans may alter behavioral incentives in various ways, and there is no quick way to summarize them all.

Here we will gloss over several incentive issues that we have already implicitly covered. For example, increased personal saving could be prompted by reducing the growth of promised benefits or, alternatively, deterred by increasing the Social Security payroll tax. We have, however, already discussed the cost/revenue spectrum.

Similarly, establishing a personal account would create a vehicle for additional voluntary saving whereas continuing solely with a pay-as-you-go system would not. Again, however, this is a spectrum we have described already.

Here we will simply describe which plans embody willful judgments to improve certain other incentives. Perhaps the most notable plan in this regard is the Kolbe-Boyd (formerly Kolbe-Stenholm) proposal. This proposal would implement a number of reforms to reward work. It would steepen the penalty for early retirement and the reward for delayed retirement; it would reduce income redistribution from two-earner couples to one-earner couples. It would credit individuals for all of their years of earnings (not just the top thirty-five years). It would establish a minimum benefit that becomes more generous with the number of years worked.

Though we have not included it within our review to this point, a new proposal by economist Mark Warshawsky is notable for a number of changes it would make to stimulate additional employment. It would exempt seniors from the payroll tax once they have attained forty-five years of covered earnings and it would raise both the early and normal retirement ages.

The Hagel proposal would also reform the early retirement and delayed retirement credits to better reward continued work. In addition, it would somewhat increase the normal retirement age (to sixty-eight) though statistically this appears to have a smaller effect on retirement

FIGURE 9.4 The Work Incentive Spectrum

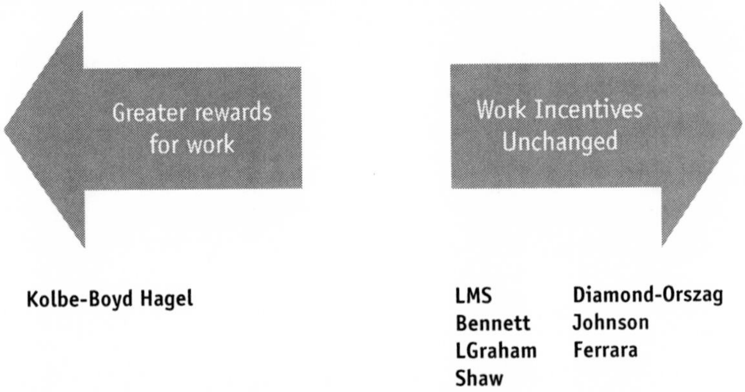
Greater rewards for work
Work Incentives Unchanged
Kolbe-Boyd Hagel
LMS
Bennett
LGraham
Shaw
Diamond-Orszag
Johnson
Ferrara

SOURCE: Based on data from "Proposals Addressing Trust Fund Solvency," Social Security Administration, http://www.ssa.gov/OACT/solvency/index.html.

decisions than does the early eligibility age. Other plans that would increase (or accelerate the current-law increase of) the NRA include the LMS and Bennett proposals.

Other plans (such as the Shaw and Graham proposals) contain small provisions that could improve work incentives on the margins, but nothing on the order of magnitude of the incentive reforms sought by the Kolbe-Boyd, Warshawsky, and Hagel proposals.

Figure 9.4 summarizes the approaches of various plans to labor force participation.

Summarizing the Plans

How can we assemble this complex information to arrive at a bird's-eye view of how these various proposals approach the Social Security problem? Table 9.1 fairly, if crudely, summarizes the various plans.

This simplified table obscures differences in the details of these proposals. Though Kolbe-Boyd and the LMS plan are described as occupying

TABLE 9.1 Plan Summaries

Plan	Cost Restraint or New Revenues?	Transition to Full/Partial Funding?	Maintain or Increase Progressivity?	Reform Work Incentives?
LMS	Middle	Partial	Maintain	No
Kolbe-Boyd	Middle	Partial	Increase	Yes
Diamond-Orszag	Revenues	No	Maintain	No
Bennett	Slow costs	No	Increase	No
Bush (Pozen)	Slow costs	Partial	Increase	No
LGraham	Slow costs (w/tax option)	Partial	Increase	No
Shaw	Revenues	Partial	Maintain	No
Hagel	Middle	Partial	Maintain (less?)	Yes
Johnson	Slow costs	Full	Maintain (less?)	No
Ferrara	Revenues	Full	Maintain	No

SOURCE: Based on data from "Proposals Addressing Trust Fund Solvency," Social Security Administration, http://www.ssa.gov/OACT/solvency/index.html.

the middle ground on cost growth, for example, Kolbe-Boyd would more constrain cost growth, while LMS would tap more additional revenues. Similarly, the progressivity column obscures differences of degree between plans.

The Bush proposal is listed as "slowing costs" although a fully fleshed-out plan was never specified. The most that we can accurately say is that the extent of the proposal publicly put forward relied upon cost restraint rather than revenue increases and would have increased progressivity while injecting partial advance-funding.

Despite glossing over details, Table 9.1 should provide a reasonably useful assessment of how competing value judgments are reflected in the design of various existing Social Security proposals.

PART THREE

The Debate Over Solutions

THE FIRST TWO PARTS of this book focus on how the past has led to the present: the evolution of the challenges facing Social Security and the resulting value judgments that now confront us. This third and last part of the book summarizes the spirited, ongoing debate over Social Security's future.

President Bush's 2005 Social Security reform initiative fostered a vigorous public debate about the scope of the problems facing the program and about the virtues and flaws of his substantive approach. Chapter 10 presents a chronology of that unsuccessful reform effort, which left Social Security in its current condition of "unfinished work."

Chapters 11 and 12 review some of the specific points of contention highlighted during the 2005 reform initiative. The purpose of these chapters is not to state the rightness or wrongness of particular policy viewpoints, though chapter 11 is blunt in critiquing some analytical misrepresentations. Instead, these chapters are provided to acquaint the reader with the arguments as they have been made from various perspectives.

This policy debate cannot be fully explained without some attention to matters of self-consistency, factual accuracy, and analytical rigor. For example, there are different defensible views that one can take about whether *gross debt* or *publicly held debt* is the best measure of federal indebtedness. But no matter which view is taken, it needs to be applied self-consistently. Without such an application of concepts to alternative approaches, one cannot arrive at a sensible evaluation of the best policy course.

We therefore review several of these points of contention, exploring the arguments on one side, the arguments on the other, and the consequences of a self-consistent application of each viewpoint. Chapter 11 reviews a persistent debate about the size and certainty of the current-law Social Security shortfall; chapter 12 focuses on the debate over policy choices.

Whereas chapters 11 and 12 recount the debate to this point, chapters 13 and 14 point to the future. Chapter 13 examines the ample common ground among reform proposals offered from individuals at different points along the political spectrum and also offers some subjective opinions about the best way forward. Chapter 14 reminds us of the enormous stakes in play and of our obligation to bequeath future American generations a Social Security program that strengthens rather than undermines their economic security.

CHAPTER 10

President Bush's Reform Initiative
A Chronology

DURING HIS TWO TERMS of office, and most especially in 2005, President George W. Bush expended enormous effort, time, and political capital on an initiative to reform Social Security. Despite the president's exertions, the legislation he sought was not enacted.

This chapter will provide a narrative chronology of the reform effort, focusing primarily on a small number of milestone events. The following chapters will review a few of the controversies that accompanied the initiative.

Reform Principles from the 2000 Presidential Campaign

President Bush was elected to office having firmly declared both his general intention to pursue Social Security reform and his specific reform principles. The principles, as described in a May 2000 document accompanying then-Governor Bush's speech at Rancho Cucamonga, California, were:

- Modernization must not change existing benefits for retirees or near-retirees.
- The Social Security surplus must be locked away only for Social Security.

- Social Security payroll taxes must not be increased.
- The government must not invest Social Security funds in the stock market.
- Modernization must preserve the disability and survivors' components.
- Modernization must include individually controlled, voluntary personal retirement accounts, which will augment the Social Security safety net.[1]

At least as notable as the substantive specifications was the announced determination of the candidate to tackle Social Security reform at all. Social Security had long been treated as the "third rail" of American politics ("touch it and you die"). If leaving well enough alone didn't threaten the nation with dire adverse consequences, that is undoubtedly what nearly all politicians would seek to do.

Not touching the rail, however, is an abdication of public responsibility (Senator Lindsey Graham employs the apt phrase "political malpractice") when the program is on a course that is both fiscally unsustainable and, as we have seen, inequitable for younger generations. This reality obligates those who aspire to positions of responsibility to touch the rail despite its high voltage; it equally obligates the voting public to determine its views of the best method of doing so and to support leaders who advance those views.

That a Republican candidate for the presidency had embraced Social Security reform was especially bold. As we have seen, up through the 1970s periodic changes to Social Security had usually involved politicians delivering more generous benefits, a course followed until 1972's benefit-indexing changes overcommitted program resources. Since this moment of overreach, subsequent Social Security corrections have involved more politically painful choices that politicians prefer to avoid.

This dynamic has placed those who advocate Social Security reform in the unenviable position of bearers of bad news, a position that political opponents are forever quick to exploit. For most of Social Security's history, Democrats have been more broadly identified with the program's creation and expansion, with Republicans being more frequently accused of wanting to undermine it. This political disadvantage has fostered an ongoing debate within the Republican Party, with one side of the party counseling to steer as far clear from Social Security politics as possible and the other side arguing that Republicans will be subject to the same political attacks whether they propose reforms or not.

Governor Bush was not heedless of the political risks of taking on Social Security reform. In his speech, he stated that "Social Security is also a test of presidential candidates—a measure of seriousness and resolve. Too many times, Social Security has been demagogued to frighten the elderly for political advantage. Too many candidates have traded on the problems of the system instead of correcting them, shoving them off for others to handle—to some future generation, some other president and some other Congress." Those words were true in 2000 and, sadly, they remain true now, with Social Security's problems much larger and nearer.

Beyond his bold general determination to take on Social Security, the candidate's specific reform principles provided clear clues to his policy thinking.[2]

Crafting policy principles in a presidential campaign is a delicate art. The candidate and the electorate have a mutual interest in revealing the candidate's philosophy of governance. Policy specificity serves that mutual interest. On the other hand, a responsible candidate must preserve his or her policy options, to allow for later maneuvering through congressional concerns or other changes of circumstance. Of course, the candidate must also take care not to unnecessarily undermine his own election prospects.

American voters reward presidential candidates who offer positive visions for the future. This introduces a distinct communications problem when dealing with a program like Social Security, whose resources are overcommitted under current law. The politician's irresponsible option, adopted by too many, is to say in effect, "I won't touch it," a promise that, once made, must either later be reneged upon or, alternatively, upheld to the great detriment of younger Americans. Governor Bush chose instead to say, in effect, "I do intend to touch it, but today's seniors will not be hurt."

By itself, however, this message would have fallen far short of a positive program for reform. The candidate's presentations on Social Security thus also stressed the element of his reform program (personal accounts) designed to improve the program's treatment of younger generations.

Inspection of Governor Bush's reform principles in detail reveals both a clear policy direction and an intention to preserve his flexibility in the event of an election victory.

Some of his reform principles did limit policy options, by design. They did so in ways indicative of his governing philosophy. At the same time, they took little off the table in practical reality.

For example, neither party's leadership believes it is appropriate to change benefits for those already in retirement; candidate Bush's reform principle eliminating that option simply recognized a widely shared value. As another example, investment of the Social Security Trust Fund in the stock market—ruled out in another campaign principle—had been recently condemned by a unanimous vote of the Senate and was inconsistent with the candidate's view of the appropriate role of government.

Finally, ruling out a payroll tax increase was in line with Governor Bush's lower-tax message and built upon similar views articulated by his predecessor, President Clinton.[3] There was no way, considering the broader themes of his candidacy, that candidate Bush would be more willing than President Clinton before him to raise the payroll tax.

Also like President Clinton, Governor Bush pledged to preserve the disability and survivors' components of Social Security. This was to allay concerns held by many (including reform proponents as well as opponents) that personal accounts may be poorly suited to deliver these other forms of benefits. Recognizing that the disability and survivors' components of Social Security also face fiscal challenges that require resolution, the principle left open the determination of the appropriate growth rate for such benefits going forward.

The principle that received the greatest attention was the candidate's commitment to establish personal accounts within Social Security. Perhaps most notable about the wording of the principle was that it left wide open a range of possibilities for designing such an account with respect to not only its size but also to whether it would be financed with projected payroll tax revenues or in some other way. Though the governor often spoke in favor of permitting young workers the opportunity to receive a higher return on their Social Security contributions, the principle as written did not stipulate the method of financing.

This was important because, by 2000, many advocates had begun to choose sides on the question of personal accounts and how they should be financed. A broad variety of individuals and organizations had embraced some kind of universal savings account available to all workers—from incumbent President Clinton to conservative Republican Senator Phil Gramm to the bipartisan Senate team of Judd Gregg and John Breaux, as well as AARP and Governor Bush's election opponent, Vice President Al Gore. Battle lines were being drawn over whether to finance these accounts with Social Security payroll taxes, but less so over the concept of accounts itself. By leaving open the method of financing, candidate Bush allowed himself room post-election to consider the ideas of a wide range of political actors if they chose to constructively participate.

This did not, of course, lessen the intensity of political attacks launched against him during the 2000 campaign based on his support for the personal account concept. These attacks exceeded the bounds of responsibility. Some came via predictable political channels, as when actor Ed Asner recorded phone calls to senior citizens in Florida alleging that Governor Bush's Social Security plan would cut their benefits.[4] But others came from reputedly non-political analysts who adopted an increasingly political posture, essentially inventing a Social Security plan, attributing it to the candidate, and trumpeting its specific adverse effects.[5]

Although the governor did not specify the method of financing the accounts, he did stipulate that personal accounts would be "voluntary."

This stipulation reflected his emphasis on personal choice and control, as well as a desire to reassure those who would prefer instead to remain wholly within the traditional Social Security structure. The requirement that the accounts be voluntary was a critical policy specification; it meant that the personal accounts would have to be designed carefully so that the system did not drift in and out of financial balance as different numbers of workers opted for them.

Although the reform principles were generally well designed to preserve a wide variety of policy options after January 2001, one proved less resilient in light of subsequent events: the second reform principle pledging that the Social Security surplus would be locked away for Social Security.

It was not difficult to preserve the *technical* application of this principle: to the extent that Social Security runs a surplus, as we have seen, its Trust Fund is credited for the amount of that surplus, times interest. This obliges the rest of the government to ultimately make budgetary resources available to honor the debt held by the Social Security Trust Fund and thus, in the narrowest sense, "locks away" this amount of revenue for Social Security.

But the only way to truly save the Social Security surplus is if government restrains its spending appetite sufficiently to balance its on-budget accounts in both good times and bad. At the time that both Vice President Gore and Governor Bush were pledging to "lockbox" the Social Security surplus, the government had been experiencing a surge of revenues as a result of the dot-com bubble. But the bubble was bursting. Although the candidates (and the voters) didn't yet know it, economic growth would turn negative in the third quarter of 2000 and again in the first quarter of 2001.[6] In reality, there would be no surplus to lock away; neither under then-current law nor under either candidate's platform.[7]

In fairness to both candidates, neither knew that the surplus each was promising to save would not exist. On the other hand, the "lockbox" buzzword of the 2000 campaign was always somewhat superfluous to the Social Security debate and should not have been treated as a substitute for genuine reform. A "lockbox" only works if the government is willing to always save the Social Security surplus and never to run a deficit—an expectation that looks particularly ludicrous from the standpoint of today's economy, deficits, and multiple deficit-ballooning federal crisis–management responses. Moreover, even if every penny of the Social Security surpluses since the mid-1980s had previously been saved, the program would still have been on a course toward insolvency.

Presidential campaigns involve many "gotcha" episodes, especially with respect to Social Security. Too often, candidates under pressure pledge not to raise the retirement age, not to change benefits for anyone, and not to raise taxes—in short, not to do any of the things that would repair program finances. (One of the less impressive aspects of American politics is that candidates sometimes get away with this while at the very same time pretending to support a strong Social Security program.) For a candidate who does not intend to meet his responsibility to safeguard Social Security, there is less of a cost to these idle pronouncements. But a candidate who intends to leave Social Security stronger than he or she found it cannot succumb to such political temptation.

Governor Bush was conspicuously careful during the 1999–2000 campaign not to constrain his policy options, even if it meant withstanding some serious political hits. For example, on *Meet the Press* on November, 21, 1999, this exchange took place:

> MR. RUSSERT: Would you look at—look at—raising the eligibility age for the boomer generation?
> GOV. BUSH: Yeah. Not for the short term. That may be an option for the boomer generation.
> MR. RUSSERT: For the long term.
> GOV. BUSH: As part of a tradeoff or as part of an opportunity for the boomers and (others) to be able to manage their own accounts.[8]

Obviously, the easiest thing for a candidate to do in that situation would have been to say, "No, I won't raise the retirement age." Then he would have dodged one political bullet while at the same time taking away one of his policy options if he later entered office. The fact that the candidate conspicuously declined to choose this course was an indication that he was dead serious about fixing Social Security and was more willing to withstand a near-term political hit than to constrain his subsequent opportunities for leadership.

That seriousness was later tested when Governor Bush was elected president. His Social Security reform ambitions would be affected by many factors, including the polarizing election fight of 2000 and subsequent legal disputes, the bursting of the dot-com bubble and ensuing economic downturn, the 2001 tax cuts, and the 9/11 terrorist attacks. Each would play a critical role in the coming Social Security debate.

2001 and the President's Commission to Strengthen Social Security

Almost immediately upon entering office, President Bush set about fulfilling his campaign promise to address Social Security, with the first step being the establishment of a bipartisan reform commission he had called for during the campaign.

On this issue as on others, the new president was committed to upholding the campaign promises that he had made. In this case, there was a potential internal conflict to be managed. He had run on a set of substantive reform principles. He had also run on establishing a Social Security reform commission. These two promises could have been in conflict if his commission had subsequently reported recommendations contrary to the principles on which he had run.

To ensure that both sets of campaign promises were met, the president's executive order wrote his reform principles into the organizing charter of the commission.[9] The commission was charged with developing bipartisan recommendations to "modernize and restore fiscal soundness to the Social Security system according to the following principles . . ." at which point in the text the campaign principles were reiterated.

The writing of these reform principles into the executive order constrained the commission from considering certain policy options, including cutting benefits for those in or near retirement, investing the Social Security Trust Fund in the stock market, eliminating the disability/survivors components, and raising the payroll tax. As we have earlier noted, however, this had only a slight practical effect on the commission's policy flexibility, leaving on the table an enormous range of potential changes to benefit formulas, the retirement age, and the method of financing benefits.

The commission was also instructed to develop recommendations to establish "voluntary personal retirement accounts." This meant the commission's recommendations would move into territory significantly different from that considered by, for example, the 1981–83 Greenspan Commission. The executive order was deliberately silent on the method of financing the voluntary accounts, leaving open various options, including the payroll tax, general revenues, or voluntary additional out-of-pocket contributions by workers. But the fact that the commission was explicitly charged with drafting such recommendations for a personal account element was something new.

One of the persistent controversies in the Social Security debate is when and whether it is appropriate to establish substantive preconditions for discussions. There are those who believe that fruitful dialogue can only occur if no preconditions are set. There are also those who refuse to come to the table *unless* preconditions are set. Throughout 2005, for example, some argued that personal accounts had to be "off the table" before Social Security discussions could take place, whereas others attempted to receive advance assurances that tax revenues either would or would not be part of the discussion.

The executive order wrote some such preconditions into the commission's deliberations, reflecting the commitment of the president to uphold the principles on which he had run. At the same time, the preconditions were carefully written in such a way as to maximize the latitude available to the commission and to incorporate policy views from both sides of the aisle, short of violating the president's campaign promises.[10]

The Bush administration was also aware that a number of bipartisan commissions had ended in paralysis and failure, including the Breaux-Thomas Medicare commission and the Kerrey-Danforth entitlement commission. President Bush did not want his commission to meet the same fate. Members were thus selected for the commission with a deliberate eye toward their willingness to work across the aisle with an open mind.

The commission was composed of sixteen members, equally divided among Republicans and Democrats. Perhaps the easiest selection was of recently retired Senator Daniel P. Moynihan as the Democratic co-chair. Moynihan was one of the great intellectuals in United States Senate history,[11] unsurpassed both in his institutional knowledge of Social Security history and in his stubborn independence. Moynihan had authored a Social Security plan in which personal accounts were designed as an "add-on" (funded by contributions above and beyond the payroll tax) , in contrast with the ongoing assumption that President Bush would prefer accounts funded with the existing payroll tax. These differences in policy backgrounds were less important to the administration than Moynihan's willingness to approach issues with fresh thinking and an open mind, and to bring his considerable knowledge and credibility to a difficult task.

The Republican co-chair, Dick Parsons of AOL-Time-Warner, was approached after Moynihan. He fulfilled the administration's desire to have commission co-chairs that between them bridged the public and private sectors and to have a match for Moynihan's public spiritedness, intellectual heft, and political independence.[12] Parsons left a profound impression on the members and staff of the commission by his willingness to master Social Security's fiscal challenges and by his determination to meet his public charge regardless of external pressure.

The other fourteen commission members brought an impressive array of credentials and expertise to the Social Security issue, including former members of Congress from both sides of the aisle, a former Social Security commissioner, a Social Security public trustee, and a previous member of a Social Security Advisory Council Technical Panel, in addition to several other noted economic experts and industry leaders. Here we will decline to list or describe the individual members of the commission, for fear of slighting their remarkable individual talents. Suffice it to say that all sixteen members of the commission worked strenuously to fulfill their mission, studying the issues carefully in a concerted effort to identify the best policies and withstanding more than a few episodes of political grandstanding at their expense.

The fact that commission members were selected in part based on a willingness to show an open mind on certain critical aspects of Social Security policy did limit to an extent the individuals deemed attractive candidates for the commission. The commission contained individuals who had previously expressed a preference for an "add-on" account, individuals who expressed a preference to instead redirect projected payroll taxes to personal accounts, and individuals who had never spoken on the question at all. It excluded, however, individuals who had manifested an absolute refusal to compromise on the important spectra of policy choices, some of which we reviewed in the last few chapters.

One publicly voiced criticism of the commission was that it excluded high-profile opponents of personal accounts on the left, which was true. What has less frequently been noted is that the commission also excluded those on the right who had expressed opposition to the historic structure of the Social Security program or who were adamant that the system should convert completely into a system of personal accounts. This resulted in the exclusion of experts on the right every bit as serious, knowledgeable, and talented as those omitted on the left.

The commission did not include any current members of Congress, reflecting the administration's goal of removing the commission's policy development to the extent possible from congressional politics. The upside of the decision was that the commission's policy product did not reflect the election concerns of sitting members. The downside of the decision, of course, was also that the commission's policy product did not reflect the election concerns of sitting members.

From the outset, the commission's task proved difficult. An atmosphere of mutual mistrust divided the political parties with an intensified fierceness after the bitter 2000 presidential election fight. Not only congressional Democrats but also congressional Republicans were wary of a commission that lacked direct representation from sitting members of Congress. Finally, there was the inherent political difficulty of the Social Security issue itself.

Conscious of these obstacles, commission co-chairs Moynihan and Parsons reached out to congressional leaders of both parties to solicit their policy views, to invite their participation (through either private communication or public testimony, as the member preferred), and to declare their receptivity to the gamut of policy ideas. The warmth of their outreach was not returned. The Democratic leadership declined their meeting requests (one key Democratic committee ranking member did make time to meet with the commission co-chairs, despite his professed skepticism over their policy mission).

Some Republicans were only marginally more enthusiastic. One Republican leader they met with expressed concern that the commission was launched without sufficient congressional Republican influence on the ground floor, so it should not be assumed that congressional Republicans would provide support at the end. Throughout the commission's deliberations, some Republican congressional aides also fed the press a steady stream of undercutting comments.[13] Even if these aides were few in number, they were naturally irresistible to reporters.

Republican reactions were diverse; some offices were supportive of both the policy goal and the process, others the policy goal but not the process, and still others neither. This contrasted with the Democratic side, in which budding expressions of interest in bipartisan work by individual legislators were stifled by pressure from the party leadership not to cooperate with the commission in any way.

Congressional timidity on reform was mirrored and fed by outside interest groups. The AARP set itself against the 2001 commission, as it had done against the 1983 reform effort and would again in 2005. There had been substantial quiet outreach from the White House to AARP's policy leadership before the commission's announcement, emphasizing that the commission's charter allowed for the structuring of savings accounts in the manner that AARP had indicated it favored. Despite this outreach, AARP blasted the commission with a press release issued on the very day of its formation, before the commission members had even come to know each other, let alone to deliberate on policy questions.[14]

These were all undoubtedly sour notes, and would indeed be harbingers of difficulties to come. That being said, Social Security reform is not for the faint of heart; responsibilities of fiscal stewardship require that it be pursued; and those who would achieve it must do so in an atmosphere where political sniping will always occur and must be withstood. The AARP has opposed the substance of every serious effort to sustainably shore up Social Security financing, including the 1983 reforms and on through to the present. Its opposition comes with the territory; reformers who aren't willing to withstand the opposition of AARP should find another issue on which to work.

None of this is to suggest that those who ultimately opposed the commission's substantive recommendations were necessarily acting on baser motives than those who supported them. In Social Security policy, at all times it is especially important to distinguish policy differences from sinister motivations. This vital principle, however, cannot be invoked to excuse condemning substantive recommendations even before they are made, distorting them after they are made, or declining to offer constructive alternatives.

Meanwhile, there were reasons for hope. Agree or disagree with President Bush's reform principles, the empirical facts remained that a president had been elected having promised to reform Social Security and that his candidacy had withstood aggressive fear-mongering among senior voters. Before him, too, President Clinton had spoken repeatedly about the need for reform, and had inspired individuals on both sides of the aisle to champion the cause. There was also ample common ground available for those willing to explore it.

In any event, it was clear that the formation of the commission could not by itself solve the continuing political problem of how to steer controversial Social Security reform legislation through a politically polarized Congress. This reality essentially limited the commission's primary function to putting meat on the bones of the president's reform principles and showing how they could be upheld in a financially sustainable Social Security system.

The commission's first significant product was an interim report outlining the fiscal challenge facing Social Security.[15] As we have seen, defining the problem is an indispensable part of the reform process. Often, experts disagree viscerally with one another on the appropriate policy response, largely because each maintains a different view of the problem to be solved. To lay the foundation for a policy consensus, the commission needed to lay out the different facets of the financing problem to be addressed in the course of reform.

The meat of the commission's interim report reviewed several of the points made in other post-1983 analyses of the Social Security shortfall, including the various Social Security Advisory Council and Advisory Board reports and trustees' reports. These analytical points included the lack of a saving component in the present Social Security system, the demographic origins of the financing shortfall, the relative certainty of the shortfall even under considerable variation in the assumptions, the inadequacy of a narrow definition of solvency, and the limited economic meaning of the Social Security Trust Fund balance.

To make these points, the commission reproduced text from various nonpartisan analyses, including those of the Congressional Budget Office, the General Accounting Office, the Congressional Research Service, and the Social Security Public Trustees. Regarding both its substantive points and format, staff who drafted the interim report were impressed by the design of a June 1998 Concord Coalition report on the Social Security problem, which had explained similar points with a concision and clarity greater than in typical government documents.

In crafting the interim report, the commission faced a few awkward messaging challenges. One of these concerned how to balance two complementary but not equivalent points, namely the size of the Social Security financing shortfall in the aggregate and the failure of the current program design to successfully facilitate saving. As we saw in the previous chapters, these are two important axes of the Social Security policy spectrum: first, the question of whether to fill the aggregate financing gap by raising taxes or by constraining costs; second, whether to shift from a pay-as-you-go system to a partially funded system.

These are both important questions, but they are not the *same* question. Revenues-versus-costs is essentially a question about system *size:* how large, generous, and expensive should the system be? The second question concerning pre-funding is more about *equity*; who pays, and when? In reacting to the interim report and in other contexts, some opponents of personal accounts manifested a tendency to see the commission's twin emphasis on saving, in addition to aggregate solvency, as a superfluous irrelevancy or worse.

By the twenty-first century, there were few political surprises left in the Social Security debate. Advocates of restricting cost growth to sustainable levels can expect to be attacked for "cutting benefits." Advocates of raising taxes can expect to be attacked for raising taxes. Advocates of personal accounts can expect to be attacked for transition costs and for subjecting beneficiaries to investment risk.

Some of the attacks on the commission's interim report, however, did come as a genuine surprise, especially where the commission had simply reproduced previous explanations of the realities of system financing, even to the extent of borrowing President Clinton's own submitted budget's explanation of the significance (or lack thereof) of the Trust Fund.

Despite this, the interim report itself, which contained no concrete policy recommendations, came under intense attack from some quarters essentially for its reproduction of previously accepted explanations of the problem. This was an indication that some policy advocates were doubling down, distancing themselves even from their own previous analyses, downplaying the reality of the financing shortfall, and challenging the criteria that had been developed by nonpartisan bodies in recent years to evaluate solutions.[16]

It was also a troubling indication of a broader flight from the previous analytical mainstream, reducing the pool of talent that could be brought to bear in an ultimate bipartisan negotiation. This trend, which accelerated in

2001 and continues through today, will make bipartisan compromise prohibitively difficult for as long as it lasts—no matter who leads the effort.

One important element of the environment in which the Social Security Commission operated was that in June a package of substantial tax cuts was enacted. The fact that the tax relief package was passed before the development of a specific Social Security policy has led critics of both the 2001 tax cuts and of the Bush administration's approach to Social Security reform to ask why the administration did not hold off on tax cuts and instead "use the surplus"—as President Clinton had suggested—for Social Security reform.

There are multiple answers to this question, some of which are clearly visible only in hindsight. In hindsight, as we have noted, we know that there was no on-budget surplus to use. Scorekeeping agency errors in economic forecasting and in the technical modeling of capital gains receipts had obscured the fact that even in the absence of tax relief there would be substantial on-budget deficits in the early years of the Bush administration.

Referring instead only to the information available at the time, a critical reason that the Bush administration moved first on tax cuts was that it faced a situation similar to (though of lesser magnitude) that which caused the Obama administration to run large deficits in 2009 and 2010. Specifically, the economy at the end of the Clinton administration was entering a downturn, contracting in the third quarter of 2000 and again in the first quarter of 2001.[17]

While Republicans and Democrats often disagree on whether the government should reduce taxes or increase its spending to fight economic contraction, there is a reasonably broad bipartisan consensus that an appropriate countercyclical government response will increase the deficit in the near term. Beyond this general agreement, federal tax receipts in 2000 were at their highest point as a share of the economy since World War II (20.9 percent of GDP).[18] The historic high in federal tax levels, the economic downturn, the desire to have a lasting positive impact on economic growth, and the new president's governing philosophy all pointed to the conclusion that Americans were being overtaxed and that substantial and lasting tax relief was in order.

In 2009, the new Obama administration faced a similar (if more severe) situation and also chose to stimulate the economy through various measures increasing the deficit in the near term. Consistent with its differing economic philosophy, the Obama administration's prescriptions relied mostly on additional spending rather than tax relief, and indeed are larger in the aggregate, driving the deficit to much higher levels. But the parallelism should not be missed: whether Republicans or Democrats, administrations of either party will take action to fight sluggish economic growth that has the near-term effect of increasing the deficit.

This is a critical reason why the idea of "using the surplus" to shore up Social Security was never a practicable solution. Economic downturns will always come; when they do, not only will any projected surplus likely turn into a deficit from the outset, but the federal government will also act to further increase that deficit in the near term, no matter which party controls the opposite ends of Pennsylvania Avenue.

It is also important to note that "using the surplus to shore up Social Security" is a potentially problematic concept even when the surplus actually exists. What is meant by the "surplus"? Social Security's Trust Fund is already credited for the surplus that it runs, indeed with interest, without regard to whether that money is actually saved. Thus, as reviewed in chapter 3, "using the surplus" for Social Security can only increase program resources under one of the following scenarios: Social Security's own revenues are double-counted in some way *or* non-Social Security tax revenues are transferred to Social Security.

The first of these options (double-counting) violates principles of transparent and honest accounting and worsens the debt facing younger generations, as discussed in Chapter 3.

The second option (bailing out Social Security with non-Social Security tax revenues) would both end the program's historic separation from the rest of the federal budget and do away with its longstanding self-financing structure and contribution-benefit link.

As previously reviewed, Social Security has long been distinguished in the public's mind from welfare because all contributions, whether from rich or poor, are linked to benefits. For the program to begin to rely on revenues attributed to no individual contributor would effectively end this principle and place Social Security in a financing category with other welfare programs.

Although the Clinton administration had proposed "using the surplus" for Social Security, there had never occurred a full and open public discussion about whether in fact to end self-financing and to terminate the contribution-benefit link. Though it is impossible to account for all individual opinions within the Bush administration, it is fair to say that the administration generally believed that Social Security should remain self-financing instead of shifting to welfare-style financing. Accordingly, even had the surplus continued, it should not be assumed that either the president or his commission would have supported turning to income-tax financing of Social Security.

The terrorist attacks of September 11, 2001 soon rocked the nation, transforming the priorities of the administration and pushing Social Security reform onto the back burner. Within the commission, there was some advocacy of extending the deadline for its final report. The president and his senior advisors concluded, however, that the postponement of Social Security reform did not argue for extending the commission's reporting deadline. Little would be gained by pushing the commission's final report into an even-numbered year when legislation was extremely unlikely to be enacted.

Still, the 9/11 attacks did mean that Social Security reform, difficult even before, was clearly not about to be the focus of near-term legislative efforts. If it was ever the case that the commission had the charge of fleshing out "the president's specific proposal," this became wholly untrue after 9/11. Now, the president would need to maintain policy flexibility going forward, not only immediately after the commission's report but possibly for years before legislation could be pursued in earnest. It would be counterproductive to unveil a single proposal that could be attacked but not promoted and defended with equal energy. Accordingly, what was now needed from the commission was a broader explanation of how Social Security's finances could be restored and personal accounts established, rather than a single all-encompassing proposal.

Before this moment, the commission members had worked very hard to master Social Security's financing issues and to narrow their individual policy differences. They could have reached unanimity—though not without further arduous internal negotiation—on a single Social Security proposal had it been deemed desirable for them to do so. The changed environment after the 9/11 attacks meant that this would not happen.

In the end, the commission produced a report of three reform options, spanning the critical spectra of options facing policymakers. One option would have solved the fiscal problem entirely on the cost restraint side; while another on the opposite end of the spectrum would maintain full scheduled benefits (and thus require additional revenues). (Because the commission did not recommend raising taxes, it declined to portray this latter option as fiscally sustainable). A third was in the middle.

Though each option contained a voluntary personal account, a score for each was also provided for a "0 percent participation" assumption, so that the results of continuing entirely with pay-as-you-go could also be seen.

One model was extremely simple, another extremely complex.

Basically, the commission report contained something for everyone to like, and for everyone to dislike (this of course did not prevent some from criticizing every option that had been put forward).

A few additional aspects of the commission's report are worth noting.

One is that the stipulation that personal accounts be *voluntary* constrained how the commission could design them. A particular policy challenge of such voluntary accounts is to ensure that the system remains financially sustainable regardless of the level of participation.

One possible way to achieve this is through a purely "add-on" account. If the account sits outside of, or on top of, Social Security, funded by additional out-of-pocket contributions by workers, then it need not affect Social Security finances in any way. Both the personal account contributions and the personal account benefits would be in addition to the traditional system, leaving the traditional system's revenues and benefit obligations unaffected.

The commission did not choose this route for a number of reasons. One was that, even if not formally termed a tax increase, it would have required workers to pay more out of pocket to receive a personal account while not securing the saving of any currently projected contributions. Second, this approach would have left pay-as-you-go in place: leaving all near-term Social Security surplus revenue on the table for the federal government to spend, perpetuating the misleading, illusory nature of Trust Fund accounting. Third, despite widespread rhetorical support for "add-on" accounts from some quarters, there was a resounding silence as to how they and a financially sustainable Social Security system could best be combined.[19]

The alternative approach, which the commission embraced, was to allow workers the opportunity to save some of their currently projected payroll taxes in personal accounts. This naturally meant that a proportional amount of future benefits, as well as taxes, would shift to the personal account. That is to say, if workers were given the opportunity to shift some of their Social Security investments into personal accounts, they would therefore be putting less into the traditional system and would thus receive less from it.

Whether one views this change as desirable or undesirable from the beneficiary's perspective depends in part on one's view of the personal account income.

Opponents of personal accounts will sometimes allege that they require additional "benefit cuts." These opponents would point out that the smaller amount contributed to the traditional system can buy less in traditional benefits than if all 12.4 percent were contributed there. A personal account proponent, on the other hand, would compare *both* forms of benefits (traditional benefits plus personal account benefits) in the reformed system to the benefits of the old system (see figure 10.1), and might also stress the second system's ownership element and the potential for higher returns in the aggregate.

This shift of both benefits and taxes into a personal account is the essence of partial advance-funding. In the near term, money is taken out

FIGURE 10.1   Continuation of Pay-as-you-go/Financing with Traditional System vs. Hypothetical Reform with Personal Account

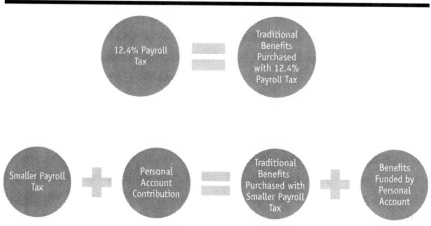

of the government's spending pool and put into a savings vehicle. In the long term, a portion of benefits is paid from the savings vehicle instead of by taxing future workers. In order to achieve true pre-funding, *both* things have to occur: we must both shift some money into saving today *and* take some of tomorrow's pay-as-you-go spending obligations off of the federal ledger.

But how to calculate the amount of traditional benefit payments to shift from the traditional system to a personal account? In the particular case of the commission plans, the answer was straightforwardly logical: the amount of the investment the worker shifted to the personal account, times interest.[20]

Designed in this way, personal accounts would not significantly alter the aggregate financial balance of the traditional system, regardless of participation rates. That is, the accounts themselves wouldn't significantly alter the amount of tax or benefit changes necessary to balance the traditional system in the aggregate.[21]

For example, in Commission Model 2, if no one participated in a personal account there would be no tax increase and benefits would generally be calculated with price-indexation. If, on the other hand, everyone participated in a personal account, there would still be no tax increase and everyone would receive both the benefits from his accounts *plus* the benefits from the traditional system, which in turn would be calculated by price-indexing, *minus* the contributions to the accounts (times interest).[22]

Constructing the personal accounts in this way would also leave the progressivity of the system essentially unaltered (exactly so, if the accounts earned the rate of interest used for the offset rate).

The commission's final report of recommendations inevitably attracted criticism from opponents of personal accounts specifically and from opponents of Social Security reform in general. As this chapter is intended to provide only a chronological narrative of the Bush administration's Social Security reform efforts, and not to settle every point of controversy, we will not enter fully into those debates here. Some of these controversies will be discussed in the following chapters. Readers who wish for further details on the debates over commission-related issues would do well to read the comprehensive papers of commission members John Cogan and Olivia Mitchell[23] and of former commission staff member Andrew Biggs.[24]

The Hiatus: Between the 2001 Commission and the 2005 Reform Initiative

After the 2001 commission and on through the 2004 elections, other pressing national priorities, most especially the war on terror, delayed action on Social Security. President Bush remained interested in pursuing Social Security reform throughout this period, but there was insufficient space on the crowded agenda for such an ambitious undertaking.

This does not mean that the issue lay dormant. A vigorous Social Security debate continued to play out, with many policy advocates introducing comprehensive reform proposals and sometimes critiquing those of others. In 2002–2004 alone, numerous plans were submitted to the Office of the Social Security Actuary for formal scoring: plan authors included Congressmen Clay Shaw (R-FL), Nick Smith (R-MI), Jim De-

Mint (R-SC), Jim Kolbe (R-AZ), Charlie Stenholm (D-TX), and Paul Ryan (R-WI); Senator Lindsey Graham (R-SC); and experts outside of Congress, including Robert Pozen, Peter Diamond, Peter Orszag, Robert Ball, and Peter Ferrara.[25] These plans (as we have seen) spanned a wide spectrum of policy choices.

Another notable bellwether event during this period concerned AARP. In 1998, President Clinton had tapped the AARP as a cosponsor of Social Security policy discussion forums, partnering with a bipartisan deficit watchdog group, the Concord Coalition.[26] President Clinton's reform effort eventually went awry when he became the subject of impeachment proceedings. The Bush administration attempted in 2003 to similarly facilitate a series of educational events on Social Security finances, cosponsored by AARP and the National Association of Manufacturers, or NAM.

Although both AARP and NAM would certainly want their respective efforts to be seen as facilitating an important discussion in the broader national interest, the concept behind the particular AARP/NAM partnership was that the two organizations between them embodied a balanced representation of constituencies for Social Security reform: AARP representing current (and future) beneficiaries, NAM representing the taxpayers (both individual workers and their employers) who pay the program's bills. The Social Security Administration was to act in the honest-broker role, providing objective analysis and logistical support.

Representatives of SSA, AARP, and NAM worked throughout 2003 to develop a common document of key facts and reform principles. During the summer, AARP and NAM finalized their agreement on the details of these documents and of their joint participation in the forums. As in all negotiations, the final wording of the documents wasn't precisely to the liking of any of the parties involved, but each signed on to them as a fair compromise between different perspectives.

In the autumn of 2003, AARP, NAM, and SSA began to conduct joint outreach meetings on Capitol Hill, explaining to members their vision for the forums. One forum was scheduled to be held in Minnesota in January, 2004.

Then in November, 2003, AARP threw its support behind a Medicare prescription drug benefit bill that had been a major focus of effort by the Bush administration. Almost immediately, AARP came under fierce criticism from the more partisan Democrats for agreeing to cooperate with a Republican administration on a major entitlement initiative. Numerous charges were leveled at AARP, including the allegation that its support for the drug benefit reflected its business interests[27] rather than an assessment of the public good.

The ferocity of the attacks stung the organization, which was unaccustomed to angering Democratic partisans. Soon thereafter, news reports broke that AARP was planning to participate in Social Security town hall meetings with NAM and SSA. This provided an additional avenue for some to caricature AARP (absurdly) as being the tool of Republican "privatizers" of Medicare and Social Security. Word began to leak out that AARP board members were growing nervous about the planned Social Security forums.

The final nail in the coffin of the Social Security forums came on December 15, 2003, when the Associated Press published an article indicating that AARP was pulling out of the forums. To add insult to injury, AARP staff was quoted in the article as saying that AARP did not want to be connected to "groups with partisan agendas."[28] It was a gratuitously unfair shot, given that AARP was actually in the process of appeasing a partisan attack while pulling out of joint sponsorship of nonpartisan forums that AARP had blessed months before.

Behind the scenes, AARP officials admitted to Bush administration staff that their reasons for pulling out of the Social Security forums had nothing to do with substantive concerns or with any misbehavior, partisan or otherwise, on the part of those who had worked to organize them. They essentially admitted that it had to do exclusively with the political heat that AARP was receiving from its left for supporting the prescription drug benefit legislation. AARP simply couldn't be seen, based on its internal political calculus, as working with the Bush administration on Social Security at that time.

AARP's sudden withdrawal from the forums destroyed the last vestiges of credibility for an organization that had little to start with on Social Security. From 1983 to the present, AARP had opposed the substance of each bill that would have made Social Security financially sustainable. Now it had shown that the organization's agreements could not be trusted and that it was unwilling to withstand significant political pressure, even if that pressure was unrelated to the substance of the Social Security discussion.

Worse yet, the public lost the benefit of the nation's leading elderly advocacy organization participating in a constructive discussion of the Social Security financing challenge. AARP would choose to present the issue henceforth in far less constructive tones.

In 2004, President Bush ran for re-election and Social Security was once again an issue on the campaign trail. The president highlighted Social Security reform at each of his public events. His message was consistent from one stop to the next: he would keep the promise of Social Security for current seniors; he decried efforts to scare the elderly; he argued that reform was necessary to safeguard the interests of younger generations. He reiterated his support for personal accounts and pledged to pursue legislation to shore up the program if reelected.[29]

The president hammered on these themes throughout the 2004 election campaign, laying out both what he planned to do and the principles he would observe while doing it. Some observers were nevertheless surprised, however, when he said the following in his first post-election press conference:

> I made Social Security an issue for those of you who had to suffer through my speeches on a daily basis, for those of you who actually listened to my speeches on a daily basis, you might remember every speech I talked about the duty of an American president to lead. And we must lead on Social Security because the system is not going to be whole for our children or our grandchildren. And so to answer your second question . . . we'll start on Social Security now. We'll start bringing together those in Congress who agree with my assessment that we need to work together."[30]

In Washington, it was considered newsworthy that a newly reelected president would seek to do exactly what he had been promising to do for months on the campaign trail. Too often in Washington, there is ample space between what politicians pledge to do while campaigning and what they choose to do once elected. President Bush was cut from different cloth.

Within the National Economic Council, analytical and policy development work had picked up considerably during the autumn months of 2004 to prepare for the possibility of the president's reelection and a subsequent push to achieve Social Security reform. This proved to have been a prudent investment of the agency's manpower.

The 2005 State of the Union Call to Reform and Personal Account Proposal

President Bush faced a Congress that was problematically composed with respect to Social Security reform. The legislature contained some members who fervently believed in the desirability of reform and were willing to brave political risks to achieve it. It also contained some members wholly unsympathetic to reform, both politically and substantively.

Between these poles were others who had to be brought on board if reform were to have a fighting chance: members who intellectually supported reform but were nervous about political risks as well as members who understood the intellectual case for reform but would nevertheless choose to fight it if so doing offered an irresistible political opportunity. The necessity of recruiting some from each of these camps to a majority coalition informed many of the tactical decisions that followed.

One of the first threshold decisions facing the White House was: should the president put forward a comprehensive Social Security plan? If so, what level of detail should it contain, and what should those details be?

Opinions abounded. At times it seemed as though every opinion offered was different, even though each (especially those from outside the administration) was offered with utter certitude. The following paragraphs generalize the various strains of opinion. These generalizations may not accurately apply in each individual case, but they convey a flavor of the chorus of opinions as heard within the White House.

Senior members of the House of Representatives generally opined that the president should hew to the model of the 2001 tax legislation; that is, put forward a specific plan to set a clear policy direction. Congress would then have to react to that plan. This view was premised on the belief that without the president setting a clear and specific policy direction, Congress was unlikely to coalesce on a way forward.

The Senate, on the other hand, contained a higher proportion of members who cautioned the president against proposing a specific plan. These senators, most especially moderate Republicans and Democrats, stressed that all Democrats (moderate or otherwise) would feel intense pressure to demonstrate first and foremost that they were not simply rubber-stamping "the president's plan."

In this view, the quickest way to oblige moderate Democrats to counterproductively *oppose*, for example, raising the retirement age or price-indexing was for the president to *embrace* raising the retirement age or price-indexing. To the average citizen, this may seem like petty nonsense and perhaps it is, but such is the nature of American politics with which all policymakers must deal.

Other factors were also weighed in the tactical discussion. One was that it is inherently easier to attack a specific reform plan than it is to defend it. This is to a large extent because current-law's scheduled benefits exceed projected program resources by trillions; no fiscally balanced reform plan can compete, superficially, with a scenario in which unfinanced benefits are promised to descend like manna from heaven. The plan that actually works will seem (wrongly) to inflict higher taxes, lower benefits, or both, relative to the status quo.

This dynamic will always allow advocates opposed to an agreement to wantonly tee off on it, an opportunity most readily seized by analysts unburdened by serious intellectual scruples. Responsible press coverage would in an ideal world act as a check on this tendency, but cannot everywhere be counted on. This perspective argued against any specific plan being put into the public space until back-channel negotiations had secured sufficient bipartisan buy-in to promote, defend, and pass it.

Arguing in favor of a specific plan, however, was the fact that reform opponents needn't and don't wait until there is an actual plan to launch attacks. In 2000, as we saw, a plan was simply invented and imputed to then-Governor Bush in one widely circulated paper. After 2001, many additional attacks were launched using one of the Social Security Commission proposals as a proxy for "the president's plan."

In this viewpoint, a failure to put forward a comprehensive plan would allow for such attacks but for no promotion of the specific advantages of reform. If instead a comprehensive plan were developed, staff could (prior to release) produce copious analyses showing why it was a good plan, which could influence the terms of subsequent debate. Without such a plan, only reform opponents would produce such numbers, analyzing provisions of their own invention and relying upon the most unflattering analytical criteria.

As the president began to meet with congressional leaders, certain tactical realities became clear. One was that members of the Democratic leadership were in a "you go first" mode. They were willing to respond to the president's invitations for high-level meetings and did not wish to publicly appear unwilling to discuss the future of Social Security. At the same time, they were not willing to offer specific ideas on how to fix the program's finances, nor were they willing to countenance members of their caucus doing so. (Democratic members Robert Wexler and Allen Boyd later did put their names on Social Security reform plans, despite drawing leadership displeasure for doing so.)

A cynical view of the Democratic leadership's attitude would be that it was focused primarily not on the substance of Social Security reform, but instead on the political opportunities offered by it. The more charitable view would be that it wanted to preserve its own policy and political flexibility and to see what the president would propose, as well as its impact upon public opinion, before deciding fully how to react. Regardless of which view one adopts, the Democratic leadership discouraged members from engaging in substantive discussions. Simultaneously, research was commissioned to determine how to most effectively attack Social Security reform proposals and their proponents.

Both sides of the aisle appeared to agree that the president needed to provide political cover for congressional action. It was unsurprising that Democratic leaders would want a Republican president to accept political exposure before they themselves were willing to accept it. But on the Republican side as well, the view was expressed that the president needed not only to make the general case for reform but also to absorb the political hits associated with the tough choices required to achieve solvency.

The easier part of the president's task was explaining the general need to strengthen Social Security. The aging of the population, and its effect on Social Security finances, was easily intuited. Surveys had fairly consistently shown that the public understood that the program faced a shortfall and further that it placed a high priority upon Congress moving to address it.[31]

This did not necessarily translate, however, into support for the specific measures necessary to shore up the program. Saving Social Security sounds good to average voters in the abstract; raising the retirement age or increasing their taxes does not. There would inevitably be a drop-off in public support as the discussion shifted from general goals to specific means. The president thus faced the task not only of explaining the need to deal expeditiously with the problem, but also of laying the groundwork for specific reforms.

This was an indispensable step in the reform process. With the Democratic leadership pressuring members against direct engagement, moderate Democrats would feel unable to vote for reform without some assurance of support from their local electorates. This was the critical hurdle that the administration needed to overcome.

Ultimately, the decision was made in favor of the counsel from centrist senators; the president would not embrace a specific solvency solution in the 2005 State of the Union address. The near-term tactical goal was to provide room for bipartisan discussions in which no senator on either side would feel the pressure of being either for or against "the president's plan."

An additional factor clinching this decision was that bipartisan negotiations were less likely to begin in the more politically polarized House. Moreover, the House Republican majority had no interest in passing a serious Social Security reform plan on a party-line vote, only to see it die in the Senate. Accordingly, the factors deemed likely to affect progress in the Senate played a significant role in the tactical assessment.

Once the decision not to put forward a specific solvency plan had been reached, the problem remained of how to generate adequate political cover for the choices that Congress must consider. This was handled by the president leaning further forward in the State of the Union speech than the vague goal of solvency, listing a broad range of specific solutions and declaring his willingness to consider them all. In this way, he would take the political hit for the specific options on the table while allowing negotiators maximum flexibility.

President Bush also took the extra step of saying that although he had listed specific options for consideration, he was also willing to consider others he had not mentioned. His specific words were:

> Fixing Social Security permanently will require an open, candid review of the options. Some have suggested limiting benefits for wealthy retirees. Former Congressman Tim Penny has raised the possibility of indexing benefits to prices rather than wages. During the 1990s, my predecessor, President Clinton, spoke of increasing the retirement age. Former Senator John Breaux suggested discouraging early collection of Social Security benefits. The late Senator Daniel Patrick Moynihan recommended changing the way benefits are calculated. All these ideas are on the table. I know that none of these reforms would be easy. But we have to move ahead with courage and honesty, because our children's retirement security is more important than partisan politics. I will work with members of Congress to find the most effective combination of reforms. I will listen to anyone who has a good idea to offer.[32]

There remained great concern within the administration that there had thus far been insufficient progress in moving from broad principles to specific reforms. In 2000, the president had run on a set of reform principles. In 2001, the Social Security Commission produced a spectrum of options rather than a single specific proposal. Again in the 2005 State of the Union address, the president would lay out updated reform principles and present a range of options, but no specific solvency plan.

Even as there was a decision to maintain policy flexibility for both the president and the congressional negotiators, it was recognized that a vital step forward was needed. There was a perceived need to put an actual proposal on the table. Without this, there existed a worsening risk of the press viewing the reform efforts only as a rhetorical initiative rather than as a serious legislative push.

The tactical answer chosen was to offer a specific personal account proposal with the State of the Union address. To understand how this decision fit into the larger policy challenge, let's remind ourselves of the four decision spectra we covered in previous chapters:

1) Costs versus revenues
2) Pay-as-you-go versus pre-funding
3) Progressivity and redistribution
4) Incentives

The personal accounts spoke primarily to policy question no. 2. By putting forward a specific personal account proposal, President Bush established a position on the appropriate amount of pre-funding.

Specifically, the president proposed to allow workers in Social Security to invest 4 percent of their wages in personal accounts up to an annual cap of $1,000. This was projected by the Social Security Chief Actuary to result in approximately $675 billion invested over the next ten years. The administration indicated that the accounts would eventually grow in size to allow all workers to contribute 4 percent of their wages to accounts, but did not specify a schedule beyond the first ten years.

The decision not to come forward with a specific solvency proposal temporarily deferred decisions on spectra 1, 3, and 4.

It is important to bear in mind these various decision spectra, because there was perplexity on the part of some reporters[33] as to the fiscal relevance and utility of personal accounts. A number of press questions were often put forward along the lines of, "Do the accounts help with solvency in the aggregate and, if not, why create them?"

There was an implicit (even if sometimes unwitting) rhetorical trap underlying these questions because, as we have seen, it is inherent in meeting the policy challenge of voluntary personal accounts that they *not* have a significant net effect on solvency in the aggregate. Otherwise, system solvency could deteriorate if personal account participation varied from projections.

But as we have also shown, just because accounts can be designed so as not to affect the *aggregate* balance between revenues and costs over all time, that does *not* mean that they do not play an important fiscal function. Specifically, they change the timing of when costs are felt, they can distribute the costs of financing more equitably across generations, and they would replace the counterproductive accounting illusion of pre-funding with real pre-funding, thus replacing mere accounting solvency with genuine solvency.

To frame questions primarily with respect to the one financing aspect that the personal accounts would *not* speak to has the obvious effect of glossing over critical fiscal policy reasons for introducing personal accounts.

The president's framework was developed to be responsive to many of the concerns raised about personal accounts. To hold down administrative costs, and to preempt concerns about Wall Street profiting from personal account administration, the administrative structure was modeled on the Thrift Savings Plan (TSP) in which federal employees participate. Administrative costs in TSP are extremely low,[34] with most administrative and recordkeeping functions handled by a government agency rather than by a private concern. Investment options in the TSP are confined to broadly diversified funds, so participants need not be experts in particular investment opportunities but can simply benefit from growth in the markets as a whole.

The benefit "offset rate" for the proposed accounts was set at a level to ensure that account holders who wished to replicate the Social Security benefit they would otherwise have received could do so, simply by investing their account entirely in T-bonds. In that instance the only real difference for the account holder would be the fact of personal ownership of a portion of an otherwise unchanged total Social Security benefit. This "offset rate" also served to ensure that the fiscal effect of the accounts would also approximate the desired neutrality for the system as a whole.[35]

The accounts were also designed to protect participants from market swings on the eve of retirement. The standard investment option[36] would have been a life cycle fund that became more heavily weighted toward bonds, investing less in stocks as individuals approached retirement.

The accounts were further designed to strike a balance between individual choice and protections against poverty in old age. Individuals would have flexibility—but only up to a point—over the rate at which they could withdraw funds from their accounts. They would not be permitted to withdraw so quickly from their accounts that their traditional Social Security benefits, plus a lifelong stream of monthly payments from their remaining account balances, were insufficient to keep them out of poverty.

This list of prudent design parameters is not to suggest that the personal account proposals were free of imperfections and unresolved complexities. Legitimate design questions remained, such as the diversity and administration of annuity options, the "time lag" between tax payments and credits to an account, inheritance of personal account balances prior to retirement age or outside of the family, prevention of the "zeroing out" of traditional benefits among the highest earners and in other quirky situations, and many other issues. But for the most part, the specifics of the Bush personal account proposal belied the caricatures that had been drawn by personal account opponents.

Nevertheless, the fact that the president had led with the personal account proposal instead of the solvency solution naturally invited questions from skeptics. Wasn't the administration simply offering the candy first, and leaving it to Congress to supply the bitter medicine later? Did the president's emphasis on the personal accounts demonstrate that he wasn't serious about fiscal sustainability, but only about his "ownership" agenda?

These questions were to be expected. In a certain sense, they were not unwelcome. Starting with the accounts alone provoked many calls from across the aisle for greater attention to Social Security solvency. This was far preferable to an alternative outcome, in which the president offered a specific solvency plan only to have such measures attacked as gratuitous and unnecessary. By criticizing the administration for its failure thus far to come forward with a specific solvency plan, the critics were performing a public service of sorts in acknowledging the need for such measures.

The purpose of this chapter is to detail the chronology, content, and rationale of the president's proposals and not to settle every point of substantive controversy, some of which will be described in the following chapters. One episode is worth reviewing here, however, because of its effect on press coverage of the president's State of the Union rollout.

To understand the issue, we must step back a bit and recall some basics about how a personal account works. The decision to invest in a personal account is a choice. It is a choice that involves investing money in one vehicle rather than another one. Specifically, it involves a choice to move some money *out* of the traditional Social Security system and *into* a personal savings account.

Any time an individual faces such a choice, she faces a trade-off. If a person chooses not to invest money in vehicle A, but instead in vehicle B, then she gets the return on vehicle B but not on vehicle A. This is inevitable, straightforward, and logical.

Because of the confusion sowed on this point, it may be useful to belabor it somewhat. Suppose that you were planning to invest $1,000 in a savings account that earned 3 percent interest. Suppose that you later changed your mind and decided to invest that money in a mutual fund instead. What would be the mathematical effect of that decision? You would *gain* the investment earnings from the mutual fund, but you'd *lose* the 3 percent interest you had previously planned to get from the savings account. The net effect would be the *difference* between one investment return and the other.

A voluntary Social Security account would operate in much the same way. If a person chose to invest some of his payroll taxes in a personal account instead of the traditional Social Security system, he would *gain* the proceeds from the personal account investment and *lose* the investment that he had chosen not to make in Social Security. The net effect would be the *difference* between one investment and the other. Again, this is straightforward and logical, and resembles the trade-offs and opportunity costs that individuals face throughout their lives.

Some opponents of personal accounts, however, portrayed this trade-off between one investment gained, and another declined, as involving some kind of debt with which personal account holders would be saddled. One paper described the choice to invest less in (and thus receive less from) traditional Social Security as a "liability account," making it sound as though account holders were taking on a formal liability rather than simply choosing to shift their investments.[37] Another used the term "margin loan," creating the misimpression that account holders were simply taking out loans that they would later have to repay.[38] Others actually produced hard numbers on the amount of personal account savings that would allegedly be reclaimed by the government, feeding these numbers into press coverage of the president's proposal the day after his speech.[39]

These distortions caused enormous confusion among reporters. The day after the State of the Union address, an article in the *Washington Post* proclaimed, "Participants Would Forfeit Part of Accounts' Profits,"[40] even including the details that, "If a worker sets aside $1,000 a year for 40 years, and earns 4 percent annually on investments, the account would grow to $99,800 in today's dollars, but the government would keep $78,700—or about 80 percent of the account. The remainder, $21,100, would be the worker's."

This was flatly untrue. Under President Bush's proposal, workers would have retained the *entirety* of their account balances. But the confusion was almost understandable given the concerted effort to distort what he had proposed. To its credit, the *Washington Post* later posted an admission that its story had been incorrect ("This article from The Washington

Post print edition incorrectly described how new private accounts would work under President Bush's Social Security plan")[41] but, clearly, enormous damage to public understanding had been done by the original distortion. In fact, many Web sites to this day repeat the original error as though it were fact.[42]

Those who propagated this distortion could fairly say that the *math* of the president's proposal in certain respects resembles what they had described. In other words, if a person withdraws from one investment earning a 3 percent return and shifts the money to another investment earning a 4 percent return, her gain is 1 percent of the principal. Similarly, if she borrows at a 3 percent interest rate and earns a 4 percent return on the borrowings, her gain is similarly 1 percent of the principal involved. In this superficial sense, a "loan" and an "opportunity cost" have similar mathematical effects.

This, however, does not excuse calling something a "loan" that is not one. A "loan" occurs when one person borrows money today and then later must repay the debt. The flow of funds is wholly different from that involved with a personal account. In the instance of an account, a person is simply choosing *not* to invest as much in one vehicle, and thus will receive less from it later because she had chosen to invest in something else. She is not *borrowing* anything, and she doesn't *owe* anything. She is instead choosing to contribute *less* to something, and thus will receive *less* from it later.

The bottom line is that an "opportunity cost" is not a "loan," and calling it one doesn't make it one. Some bloggers such as Donald Luskin took the propagators of the distortion to task.[43] But right out of the gate, an important policy issue had been blurred by an egregious factual distortion.

The unassailable proof that the description as a "loan" was a severe distortion, of course, lies in the fact that it was so readily misunderstood by reporters. The purpose of expert analytical pronouncements should be to inform and explain—not to confuse and distort. If the choice of the "loan" language has the effect of *confusing* understanding, then clearly it does not serve the goal of clarifying the policy issues. Had the proposal not been badly misportrayed by the "loan" terminology, the *Washington Post* wouldn't have misreported it as it did.

This again cuts to the fundamental question of whether the primary role of expert analysts should be to help one side gain political advantage or to clarify factual issues. Clearly, if the use of terminology leads to factual confusion, then it cannot serve that clarifying function and should be discarded.

After the 2005 State of the Union Address: From the Speaking Tour Through the Embrace of Progressive Indexing

The dynamics of the 2005 Social Security reform initiative are perhaps best understood by dividing the period after the State of the Union address into two phases. We can consider the first phase as the period immediately following the address, during which the debate focused primarily on the extent of the projected Social Security shortfall and on the ramifications of the president's personal account proposal. During this period, the need for measures to sustain system solvency was discussed primarily in the abstract, as there was no concrete solvency proposal to focus the discussion.

Later, on April 28, 2005, the president embraced "progressive indexing," a concept developed by former Social Security Commission member Pozen to address a large part (though not all) of the program's fiscal shortfall.[44] From this point onward, there occurred a debate over the merits of progressive indexing and over the president's reform proposals as a combination.

This second debate did not engender a consensus on the best means of shoring up Social Security and it came to a practical end in the wake of Hurricane Katrina. The response to Katrina redirected the administration's (indeed the nation's) attention in the autumn of 2005 and cut enormously into the president's political capital. Though analysts may differ on the relative effect of the Social Security debate before Katrina versus the political effects of Katrina itself, it's fair to say that after Katrina there remained little real chance that comprehensive Social Security reform could be enacted.

For ease of understanding, we will characterize—and grossly simplify—the starting tactical/strategic positions of various principal actors in the debate, including:

- President Bush
- Congressional Democrats
- Congressional Republicans
- The press
- Key interest groups
- The broader public

Obviously, none of these actors (other than the president) is an indivisible entity and wide divergences of views were found within each. We will thus describe the broad trends of opinion within each camp as the debate unfolded.

First, a general note: President Bush's concentrated efforts in 2005 to promote Social Security reform intensified a long-simmering debate. Individuals across the political spectrum held widely varying views about Social Security policy even before then, but the 2005 debate prompted many on all sides to voice those views more loudly and insistently than before.

In 2005, the Social Security discussion graduated from one dominated by such individuals as trustees, scorekeeping agency analysts, think tank experts, congressional policy staff, and individual proposal authors in Congress to a discussion involving many other high-profile actors, including political consultants, press secretaries, party organizations, congressional party leaders, and a U.S. president.

The expanding circle of those intensely discussing Social Security inevitably changed the tenor of the discussion. As it happened, previous points of shared bipartisan agreement gave way to an emphasis on—and widening of—the differences between ideologies and political parties.

The points of renewed controversy concerned not only policy differences but even the underlying facts of the discussion. The late Senator Moynihan was fond of saying that everyone is entitled to his own opinion, but not to his own facts. The Internet age, however, allows individuals across the political spectrum to engage in enormous selection bias, consulting only those facts consistent with their own prejudices and avoiding evidence that conflicts with them. This phenomenon permitted many actors on all sides to approach the discussion from standpoints of selective and incomplete factual evidence.

A sampling and explanation of these many points of controversy—including factual, analytical, and policy disputes—will be provided in later chapters. Here, we will simply review some critical episodes in the chronological narrative without characterizing the rightness or wrongness of different actors' substantive positioning in the context of the broader policy argument.

The President: Immediately after the State of the Union address, President Bush began to travel the nation in what was referred to as the "sixty cities in sixty days" tour. The purpose of the tour was similar to President Clinton's 1998 "year of discussion": to explain the issues facing Social Security and to build support for legislation to strengthen it.

The first five stops on the president's tour were in North Dakota, Montana, Nebraska, Arkansas, and Florida. These visits began a pattern that would continue throughout the speaking tour of concentrating appearances in what were regarded as "swing states."

Social Security reform could not pass on a party-line vote. Even though the Republican House majority had the ability to pass bills with single-party support, Senate Democrats if unified could block a purely Republican legislative initiative. In any event, Republicans in both chambers would be extremely disinclined to enact reform over unified Democratic opposition. The only way that reform could pass would be if there were significant bipartisan cooperation, most especially in the Senate.

The president's embarkation on his speaking tour reflected an analysis of the tactical landscape of the Social Security debate as it existed in early 2005, which featured such factors as:

- Public support for the general goal of reform but not yet for a specific approach
- The need to attract votes from both sides of the aisle
- The obstructionist posture taken by the congressional Democratic leadership
- The necessity of public support to permit moderate Democrats to resist pressure from their leadership and to vote for reform

Thus, the president hit the road to build public support for the votes of uncertain legislators while his senior aides were dispatched to Capitol Hill to hear the policy objectives and concerns of legislators of both parties.

Moderate Senate Democrats faced considerable pressure not only from their party leadership but also from the more partisan elements of their base to oppose any bipartisan deal to address Social Security. They could only withstand this pressure with adequate support from their constituents.

The president worked strenuously to broaden public understanding of the need to repair Social Security finances. The largest potential inroads from this strategy were in swing states, where moderate Democrats would need support for their reform votes from Republican-leaning electorates.

The president had mastered an effective in-person presentation of the Social Security problem. He explained how the impending retirements of the baby boom generation would soon swell the ranks of retirees. He explained, in simplified terms, how wage-indexation of the benefit formula causes benefits per person to rise faster than inflation. He explained how these factors would together add up to swelling program costs, indeed more costs than could soon be financed from incoming payroll tax revenues.

(As) a result of living longer, you've got people who have been made promises by the government, receiving checks for a longer period of time than was initially envisioned under Social Security. Secondly, the benefits that had been promised are increasing, so you've got more— and thirdly, baby boomers like me and (Senator) Hagel and a bunch of others are getting ready to retire. So you've got *more people retiring, living longer, with the promise of greater benefits.* The problem . . . is that the number of people putting money into the system (per beneficiary) is declining.[45] (Italics added.)

The president's simple message of "more people retiring, living longer, with the promise of greater benefits" was, at many stops, delivered as an accentuated summary. In brief and clear phrases, he summarized the essential forces—more retirees to support, a declining worker-collector ratio, and higher scheduled benefits due to wage-indexing—buffeting Social Security's finances.

President Bush framed the issue as one of stewardship and shared responsibility, calling upon legislators to eschew political opportunism in favor of bipartisan cooperation. He stressed his own personal commitment to this ethic as well as his willingness to openly consider all input regardless of source, short of violating his previous campaign promise not to raise the payroll tax:

Let me just say right off the bat, I'm open for any idea except raising payroll taxes to solve the problem. If anybody . . . has got an idea, bring it forth. I don't care if it's a Democrat [*sic*] idea, or a Republican idea, or an independent idea, I'm interested in working with the people who end up writing the law to come up with a good idea. And so all options are on the table, as I said in the State of the Union the other night. Bring them on, and we'll sit down and we'll have a good discussion about how to get something done. . . . I really mean that when I say that.[46]

The president, of course, had his own policy ideas as well. At each stop, he pivoted from his presentation on the system's aggregate shortfall to promoting the advantages of personal accounts for younger workers, highlighting the design elements that would ensure that investments would be prudently diversified and that participants would be protected from market swings on the eve of retirement.

Press coverage of the president's events was most intense at the outset, and naturally faded as the events continued. Thereafter, characterizations of his efforts were more widely disseminated in the form of third-party descriptions rather than by direct citizen exposure to words and images of the president himself. Some critics might validly say that the cogency of his event remarks was grossly amplified by audiences predisposed to be supportive. Even discounting for this acknowledged phenomenon, the presentations were genuinely educational for those who witnessed them.

Congressional Democrats: The congressional Democratic leadership basically faced three tactical options in responding to the president's initiative:

1) Acknowledge the reality of the Social Security problem, support the general goals of reform, and work to optimize (from their perspective) the policy choices in bipartisan legislation.
2) Acknowledge the reality of the Social Security problem, but express sharp disagreement over policy goals, and propose a fundamentally different approach.
3) Deny the urgency of the Social Security problem with the intent of obviating a perceived need for Democrats to join the president in offering solutions.

The choice made by the leadership was no. 3—to refuse to engage on the substance of reforms and also to deny the severity of the problem itself.

This was an interesting choice for several reasons, not least because it was at odds with the analyses of mainstream experts at scorekeeping agencies (and even at left-leaning think tanks) in recent years. In 2005, however, an increasing number of bloggers, analysts, and reporters began to publicly downplay or even deny the problem itself.[47]

Other Democrats continued with approach no. 2, acknowledging the reality of the shortfall while attacking President Bush's policy ideas.[48] It's fair to say, however, that those in camp no. 3 were more vocal in the national political discussion and few Democratic actors in camp no. 2 publicly challenged those in camp no. 3.

The gamble was also interesting because surveys consistently showed, even throughout the reform initiative, that the public appreciated the reality of Social Security's financing shortfalls and supported congressional action to repair them.[49] By denying the reality of the problem, the Democratic leadership was betting that offering no alternative solutions could remain a politically tenable position.

A prototypical example of this rhetorical stance was given by a prominent Democratic leader in a televised interview:

> What we're saying is there is no crisis. This is a manufactured crisis. Social Security, if we don't do anything, it's safe for approximately the next fifty years. When I mean safe, people will draw 100 percent of their benefits. And if we still decide to do nothing after that, people will still draw 80 percent of the benefits. We have to do something to take care of the out years, but it's a manufactured crisis. And the president, you know, all you have to do is see what some of the real right-wing groups have talked about over the years. They don't like Social Security. They want to get rid of it. This is an effort to get rid of Social Security.[50]

From a substantive perspective, a few elements of this statement are worth noting.

One is that the claim that Social Security was safe "for approximately the next fifty years" implied a rejection of the estimates of the Social Security trustees, accepting instead the more optimistic projections of the Congressional Budget Office. CBO has since revised its estimates to be more in line with those of the trustees, and both agencies have been obliged by the recent recession to adopt more conservative projections.

Second, the view that no action is necessary for decades is contingent upon a particular view of the Trust Fund. Under last year's projections, payroll taxes will fall short of benefit obligations in 2016, and from that date onward the program will have to rely increasingly on redeeming the assets in the Trust Fund to cover annual cash shortfalls before ultimately reaching the point of insolvency. We saw in chapter 2 how interpretations of the Trust Fund affect one's view of the immediacy of the problem.

Third, the projected insolvency date is not a useful proxy for the amount of time before substantive changes must actually be negotiated and implemented. Unless we are content to allow those already receiving benefits to suffer sudden benefit cuts of 24 percent, then we must act considerably sooner than the point of insolvency. The window for avoiding certain inequities in the treatment of adjacent birth cohorts is closing just a few years from now.

A fourth notable element was the decision to attack not only the substance of the president's position but also the *motivation* underlying it, in the statement, "This is an effort to get rid of Social Security." Although the statement contains a reference to "right-wing groups," the statement does not indicate whether all who have pursued Social Security reform with personal accounts (including many Democrats) were similarly motivated by a desire to destroy Social Security. In the politically polarized America of 2005, there was no shortage of those willing to attribute policy differences to malicious intent.

This particular rhetorical tactic significantly raised the stakes, as it recast differences over Social Security's future as a battle between heroes (defending the status quo) and villains (those seeking to destroy the program). This made it much less likely that congressional Democrats could agree to *any* Social Security reform if President Bush's own ideas were defeated.

It could hardly be expected that, having said that everything was fine for the next fifty years, the Democratic leadership could thereafter turn around and embrace a realistic Social Security fix containing tough medicine in either raising taxes or slowing benefit growth. Thus, by embracing these tactics, the Democratic leadership had in effect decided not only to fight President Bush's proposed reforms, but to impede *all* reforms to produce sustainable solvency in the near term.

As a result, neither in public nor in private would the Democratic leadership engage with the administration or countenance its caucus members doing so. Senior administration officials sought and received numerous meetings with members of Congress and their staffs at which the most that was usually offered was a sheepish, "We agree with you that there is a problem, but we can't support your proposal, and we aren't in a position to offer any counterproposals to yours."

The remarks excerpted here were not an isolated instance. They were repeated throughout 2005 and were a reliable indicator of a fundamental tactical/strategic choice made by the congressional Democratic leadership.

Congressional Democrats also adopted a position that personal accounts (often referred to as "privatization," as discussed below) had to be "off the table" before any Social Security discussions could begin.[51]

Whatever the merits of this as a political strategy, it was antithetical to prospects for serious negotiations. First and most obviously, there is no such thing as a good-faith negotiation in which one party asks another to decline from even presenting his policy views, giving away critical ground even before talks begin. Second, all were quite aware that President Bush strongly favored the very thing that it was insisted be off the table. (Of course, many Democrats felt that President Bush, although he had not ruled out negotiations with anyone, had also imposed a comparable precondition by declaring his opposition to raising the payroll tax.)

Third, and perhaps most important from the standpoint of this book, taking personal accounts off the table would carry not only tactical but also strong policy implications: namely, as we saw in chapter 5, that Social Security would remain funded solely on a pay-as-you-go basis. But whereas in 2005 there were several congressional proposals to achieve sustainable solvency with personal accounts, there were none that would achieve sustainable solvency without them. The one recent proposal scored as attaining sustainable solvency without personal accounts—the Diamond-Orszag plan—is one that no representative or senator of either party had been willing to touch.[52]

In other words, if personal accounts had been taken off the table and if the universe of plausible approaches was accurately reflected in the congressional plans introduced to date, then the remaining set of available negotiated outcomes would have been a null set.

Fourth, this bluff was actually called. Later in 2005, GOP Senator Robert Bennett of Utah, despite his own support of personal accounts, attempted to garner support for a proposal lacking them. Although the Bush administration continued to support personal accounts, it was informed of and supported Bennett's move, recognizing that personal accounts had become an excuse for the opposing political party to avoid negotiations. Bennett's proposal attracted no more support from across the aisle than the personal account proposals had.

This does not mean that all advocates of the "take personal accounts off the table first" negotiating position were cynically creating an environment in which no negotiated solution would be possible. Supporters of the mantra included both those who were opposed to any negotiations and moderate Democrats who were in principle willing to negotiate but who simply opposed personal accounts. It is also possible that, having heard so many negative things about personal accounts, these moderates assumed that little or no substantive damage could be done by taking them off the table.

This, however, is precisely why it is important to evaluate our own respective value judgments first about how best to attain sustainable solvency before leaping to rule out options. If we simultaneously rule out one set of policy options, while also ruling out the consequences of their absence, then we have nowhere else to go.

Again, this is not to suggest that the only viable Social Security solution must contain a personal account. Indeed, past a certain point of delay, it may be too late for personal accounts to play a useful pre-funding role. But in 2005, the empirical fact in evidence was that no one in Congress was willing to embrace a solution to achieve sustainable solvency that lacked personal accounts. This considerably constrained the field for available action.

In addition to denying the general problem, Democratic political strategists developed several themes that were employed throughout the

2005 debate: specifically, that personal accounts would cause large benefit cuts and would add enormously to the national debt.[53] The merits of these various claims will be discussed in another chapter.

Another tactical decision made by Democratic opponents of reform was to refer repeatedly to President Bush's reform initiative as "privatization." That term carries intensely negative connotations for most voters because "privatization" as commonly understood in other contexts, such as school administration or trash collection, means turning over a public function to a private entity to run. President Bush had not actually proposed "privatization" of Social Security, instead proposing the creation of savings accounts administered by the federal government. The use of the term "privatization" implied that important Social Security functions would be thereafter run by Wall Street. This would naturally provoke fear in the typical senior, who did not want the administration of traditional Social Security benefits to change.

Congressional Republicans: The attitudes of congressional Republicans were diverse. Intellectually, most believed that Social Security required reform. Within that broader conceptual agreement, there were significant differences.

Perhaps the most significant internal divide was about personal accounts; specifically, whether personal accounts alone could partially or even wholly resolve Social Security's financing shortfall. This view that personal accounts could be a "free lunch" solution for Social Security was fed by some outside groups who argued that the administration's advocacy of additional solvency-achieving measures was fiscally unnecessary and politically damaging. Again, we will explore the validity of this perspective in a subsequent chapter.

Congressional Republicans were understandably concerned about being tied to a politically difficult Social Security solution in the absence of Democratic support. Thus, the president's efforts to build public support for reforms in swing states represented by Democrats addressed Republican needs as well as those of moderate Democrats.

While some congressional Republicans charged ahead to develop specific reform proposals, and others sought to engage their Democratic counterparts in direct discussions,[54] Republican party caucuses held back from committing to a specific reform approach until they could better gauge the success of the president's efforts and the prospects for bipartisan collaboration. At the same time, Republicans with jurisdiction held hearings to explore the fiscal shortfall and the options for attaining sustainable solvency.[55]

The press: Here I will not attempt a general characterization of the press coverage of the reform effort. Certainly, as we have seen, there were some high-profile examples of uncritical reporting in some instances and outright factual errors in others on key points.[56] This is unremarkable; all participants in the public discussion make mistakes. Nor can we expect total and unvarying objectivity in any arena where characterizations must be made by subjective human beings.

Rather than characterize the tilt of press coverage in any particular fashion, therefore, we will review in the next chapters some of the substantive issues that arose in press coverage of the debate.

One facet of that coverage is, however, worth noting here. It is that 2005's elevation of Social Security into a political issue meant that it would be reported as such, and not purely as a substantive matter. The political objectives of various actors—President Bush's to achieve reform, the Democratic leadership's to block it, as well as the tactical differences among Republicans—were naturally of interest to the press. As a result, many stories took on a character of "Who will win the battle between President Bush and the Democratic leadership?" or of "Infighting among Republicans."[57]

Some such stories were published even before the president had rolled out his personal account proposal in the February State of the Union address, and many well before he fully joined the specific solvency discussion at the end of April. In much of the press coverage, the political collision was the major story to report upon even before the policy debate was fully joined.

This certainly had an impact, because the answer to the question, "Can Congressional Democrats block the president's Social Security reform initiative?" was always a trivial "Yes." If the issue was perceived as a political challenge, in which Bush "won" by achieving Social Security reform, and congressional Democrats "won" by blocking reform, then defeat for the initiative was inevitable, there being no way to compel a congressional minority to act against its interests in a political contest.

Only if strengthening Social Security is understood as a common need of the American public and a common responsibility shared by Republicans and Democrats is there any prospect for bipartisan collaboration in the effort. Whenever the issue was reported as a shared responsibility, the public interest thus advanced; whenever it was reported as a political collision, the public interest retreated.[58]

It is also worth noting that wherever the press unwittingly adopted the anti-reform rhetoric of "privatization," this significantly handicapped the contest. Since none of the major players actually favored privatizing the system, use of the term was inappropriate and virtually assured to foment popular opposition. Frustrating though it was to the White House, the anti-reform buzzword continued to appear in press reports. To its great credit, the *Washington Post* in 2006 pushed back on this distortion, editorializing that the president's proposal "did not involve privatization: The accounts, which were to be optional, were to be designed and administered by the government, with no opportunities for Wall Street salesmen to foist enormous hidden fees on unsuspecting workers."[59]

Interest groups: The role of interest groups in the Social Security debate was also in a certain sense unremarkable. Coalitions formed both to promote reform[60] and to oppose it.[61] Two particular aspects of interest group involvement may be worthy of note.

One was the increasingly shrill voice of AARP, the nation's most powerful elderly organization, indeed perhaps the most powerful lobbying organization of any stripe. The organization ran television ads that equated the injection of personal accounts into Social Security with recklessly tearing down one's home when only a repair of the kitchen sink was necessary. The ad contained inflammatory images of a family's beloved home being reduced to rubble.[62] In another animated ad posted on the AARP Web site, those favoring personal accounts within Social Security were depicted as thieves with super-elastic arms that crept and reached their way into people's homes to steal their retirement nest eggs.

By resorting to such hysterical rhetoric, AARP set itself uncompromisingly against the sort of open-minded discussion of policy options outlined in earlier chapters and undercut its ability to be taken seriously in future reform discussions. AARP's was a scorched-earth approach to the Social Security debate, endeavoring to leave standing no future prospects for compromise.

Another interesting element of the involvement of interest groups was the close coordination between analyses of think tank and academic experts and the rhetorical purposes of political advocates. We previously saw how, during the 2004 campaign, a questionable paper was published under an academic heading, abetting exaggerated political claims regarding the administrative costs of personal accounts.[63] This pattern continued in 2005, as a further example shows.

When the president's 2001 Social Security Commission proposed that personal accounts have a "benefit offset rate" that was lower than the Treasury bond rates projected by the Social Security trustees, some analysts alleged that the differential meant that the accounts were being "subsidized" with a "sub-market interest rate."[64] In other words, the critique was that the finances of the traditional system were being weakened in order to make the personal accounts more profitable and attractive.

In part to address these criticisms, President Bush's proposal set the total benefit offset rate (including administrative costs) to equal the trustees' projected interest rate of 3 percent above inflation. Quickly, another paper was produced within academia that argued the precise opposite of the previous attack: now the criticism was that the interest rate was too high, and many who cited this paper claimed that most (70 percent) participants in personal accounts would lose money.[65] (This paper, by Yale economist Robert Shiller, did not actually claim this in its median projection of U.S. returns, but this was the figure within the paper most readily seized upon by reform opponents.)

Almost immediately, ads began to appear parroting the finding that under President Bush's proposal, 70 percent of account participants would get lower benefits. In fact, some of the same quarters that had attacked the 2001 commission's proposed accounts as being "subsidized" (via a too-low interest rate) turned around and then attacked the president's 2005 proposal on the basis of Shiller's analysis, saying that it would lead to net benefit cuts through a too-*high* offset rate. These attacks were launched despite the fact that the administration's new proposal had actually been crafted to meet the earlier criticisms of these same opposition analysts.

It is not necessary to critique every element of Shiller's paper to be concerned by this sequence of events. Substantively, the "problem" identified by the paper is easily remedied simply by allowing the benefit offset rate to be set at the realized, rather than a predicted, Treasury bond rate. In that case, personal account holders investing in Treasury bonds would be no worse off, no matter whose projections for interest rates are right. The paper contained some other substantive problems as well.[66]

Of greater concern was the direct pipeline between ostensibly objective research and political advocacy, with scant concern for internal consistency among those citing the various academic "findings." The press cannot be expected to sort out these inconsistencies without clarifying help from experts. Too many experts neglected this clarifying role in the interest of feeding effective—though internally conflicting—political messages to reporters and to advocacy groups.

The general public: As for the broader public, generalizations are tricky, given the diversity of the electorate and shifting attitudes over time. The following paragraphs attempt to provide a sense of public attitudes in the first few months of 2005.

Generally speaking, there was wide agreement in early 2005 that the Social Security shortfall existed and needed to be dealt with. A March

29–30 Fox News Opinion poll found that 32 percent of respondents said that changes to Social Security needed to be made "immediately" and another 14 percent said they'd be needed in the next year or two. Only 9 percent said that no changes needed to be made. Of respondents under age fifty-five in the same poll, 77 percent said that they were either very or somewhat concerned that Social Security would not be able to pay their full promised benefits under current law.[67] Similarly, an ABC/Washington Post poll conducted in mid-March 2005 found that 71 percent believed that Social Security was heading for a crisis and 67 percent believed that "major" changes were necessary.

These are but two of several polls taken in early 2005; any of a number of surveys could be cited from around this time showing that the public generally appreciated the need to deal promptly with Social Security.

With respect to specific policy options, public opinion in early 2005 is more difficult to gauge, even in hindsight. The Fox News poll cited above found that 60 percent favored allowing individuals the option of investing in a voluntary personal account. By contrast, in March a CBS/New York Times poll found diminishing support for personal accounts.[68] Perhaps the most significant aspect of the Times/CBS poll was the finding that if the personal accounts could be tied to specific consequences such as benefit cuts and increased debt, support diminished much further. Again, we will explore the legitimacy of these associations in a later chapter.

By mid-spring, there were signs that the administration had at least won the debate over the existence of the Social Security problem. In repeated surveys, the public signaled its agreement that Social Security faced a shortfall. The Senate in March unanimously passed an amendment from Senator Lindsey Graham saying that the president and Congress "should work together at the earliest opportunity to enact legislation to achieve a solvent and permanently sustainable Social Security system." Even many press commentators critical of the president's specific proposals nevertheless were willing to criticize the Democratic leadership for its problem-denying posture.

Despite this, by April Congress was no closer to moving on specific reform legislation, even though a number of legislators had developed specific plans. Meanwhile, the debate continued to swirl inconclusively around the concept of personal accounts.

Clearly, further steps were needed to advance the ball on specific Social Security reform. The alternative was stasis in Congress with reform detractors eventually winning a battle of attrition. Reform opponents did not need to win; they only needed not to lose, a political advantage that required further action to overcome. On April 28, the president took a significant step to move the debate forward, embracing the idea of "progressive indexing" of the benefit formula, a concept developed by a former Democratic member of the Social Security Commission, Robert Pozen.[69]

The basic idea behind "progressive indexing" was as follows. The current benefit formula is financially unsustainable within a constant tax rate. It causes the benefits paid to each new class of retirees to be higher than the one before by the amount that wages grow in the interim. This growth is generally faster than the rate of inflation, with the result that benefits rise in real (inflation-adjusted) terms over time. This benefit formula, combined with a rising number of beneficiaries, causes Social Security cost burdens to rise faster than the underlying tax base.

Under Pozen's proposal, benefits for the poorest 30 percent of workers would continue to grow at this "wage-indexed" rate of growth. Benefits for the very wealthiest Americans (less than 1 percent of the population) would grow only at the rate of inflation. Everyone else's benefits would grow at a rate somewhere in between. The idea was that the wealthiest among us do not need benefits that grow faster than inflation, and any benefit growth above inflation should be most generous for those in greatest financial need.

Progressive indexing was not a complete solution to Social Security's financing problem. Depending on the particular assumptions, it would close roughly two-thirds of the program's long-term annual shortfalls.

The embrace of progressive indexation set a direction for the debate while still leaving room for congressional negotiators to put their stamp on a complete solution. As we have seen, many Social Security proposals attempt to protect low-income participants in a manner similar to Pozen's concept. President Bush's embrace of progressive indexing added his blessing to this element of many reform plans.

Pozen's simple concept of "progressive indexing" had already won substantial external support before the president formally embraced it. On March 15, a *Wall Street Journal* editorial praised the concept in the same issue that Pozen's own op-ed piece promoted his vision.[70] Pozen had also visited with members of Congress to promote his plan, and a number of moderate senators on both sides of the aisle had praised the approach. If any reform concept attracted significant bipartisan support among legislators in early 2005, progressive indexing was it.

This by itself would have been insufficient to win the president's support, but the Pozen proposal also meshed neatly with President Bush's own policy values.

Recall earlier how the embrace of personal accounts had expressed President Bush's position along policy spectrum 2 (replacing pay-as-you-go financing with partial pre-funding). Embracing progressive indexing expressed the president's policy preferences on two other spectra as well:

1) Favoring cost control over raising taxes
3) Increasing the system's progressivity, to better treat the poor.

Because the Pozen proposal was only a partial solution, it still left room for different directional choices by Congress on spectrum 1 (the means of closing the remaining solvency gap) as well as decision-making along spectrum 4 (incentives).

Although intensive internal work had been done to develop options for comprehensive reforms, coordinated by the National Economic Council with the support of several administration agencies, progressive indexing was not among the proposals developed internally. That work was done by Pozen himself, working with the Social Security Actuary's office. Once the product was fleshed out, it was fed through the administration's internal analyses to determine whether it comported with the president's thinking with respect to containing costs and improving the relative treatment of the poorest Americans. It did.

Once the president had formally embraced progressive indexing, that concept (nearly as much as personal accounts) became the focus of intense substantive debates, some of which we will review in later chapters.

Suffice it to say here that the combination of progressive indexing and personal accounts reflected President Bush's vision for Social Security: partially pre-funding future benefits, constraining the unsustainable growth of system costs, and improving the relative treatment of those most in need.

The Fadeout of the Reform Effort: From Progressive Indexing through Katrina

The president's embrace of progressive indexing injected a new topic into the Social Security debate. Henceforth, the debate would also encompass progressive indexing, as it already had swirled around personal accounts and the severity of the underlying problem.

Proponents of the proposal noted that it would constrain cost growth without cutting benefits from today's levels, that it would channel more system finances toward lower earners, that it would not raise taxes, and that the personal accounts offered the potential for higher benefit returns. Opponents described the proposal as "cutting" benefits, also arguing that personal account benefits were risky and that the transition to them would cause an unacceptable near-term increase in federal debt.

The relative merits of these various arguments will be explored more fully in later chapters. Here we will simply note that there were both legitimate and illegitimate criticisms to be made of the Bush administration's proposal. Legitimate criticisms included the opposing argument that it would be better for higher-income individuals to foot the bill for solvency through higher taxes than by slower benefit growth. Others expressed the concern that if progressive indexing were continued indefinitely, benefit levels would converge for the upper 70 percent of the wage income spectrum, effectively severing the contribution-benefit link.[71] Others argued that the personal accounts would not truly pay for themselves because of revenues lost via pre-retirement account inheritances and administrative costs.[72]

Still other discerning critics noted that if the accounts did ultimately grow to receive 4 percent of wages, this would eventually be more than enough to fund all of the benefits that the highest-wage workers would be promised under progressive indexing. This could therefore mean that the highest-wage workers would receive all of their benefits from personal accounts and none from the traditional system (behind the scenes, the administration was developing refinements to avoid this outcome, but these were never completed and released).

At the same time, less legitimate attacks were launched. Often these attacks were riddled with internal inconsistencies. Sometimes the interest rate assumptions used to minimize the Social Security shortfall were inconsistent with the assumptions used by the same critics to allege benefit losses in personal accounts.[73] Sometimes one baseline of comparison was used to allege benefit cuts and a different one to allege an increase in federal debt, again by the same critics. Sometimes critics employed current-dollar figures to magnify the "transition cost" of personal accounts, while using smaller "present-value" dollars to describe the projected shortfall of the current system, fostering severe misimpressions of their relative magnitude. Sometimes the same critics said in one paper that the president's proposal was not actually progressive,[74] while saying in another that it would put too much of the financing burden on higher-income retirees and thus turn the program into welfare.[75] Sometimes it was wrongly implied that there would be "benefit cuts" from today's levels, instead of accurately conveying that benefits would continue to grow in real terms and that the "cuts" would only be from far higher benefits in the distant future that could not be paid under current law without a substantial tax increase.[76]

Again, while there were many legitimate concerns to express about the administration's proposals, the debate often obscured the nature of the real trade-offs facing policymakers. If every criticism from every angle is thrown on the wall, some of them will ultimately stick—even, sometimes, mutually contradictory ones.

The peculiar nature of this debate led ultimately to a paradoxical outcome: by summer of 2005, the public was expressing opposition to "the president's Social Security proposal" while expressing support for its substantive specifics. A CBS/New York Times poll in June of 2005[77] asked, "What if the government decided to address Social Security's financial problems by having future Social Security benefits grow more slowly than they do now for middle- and high-income people, while allowing benefits to grow as scheduled for low-income people?" By a 59 percent to 35 percent majority, respondents said this would be acceptable. This, of course, described the president's proposal for progressive indexing.

The same poll showed that respondents agreed with President Bush on the urgency of the problem: in fact, 57 percent said the problem was so serious that it needed to be fixed "right now." Moreover, a compendium of polls taken before and after the president's sixty-day tour showed that support for personal accounts had held steady, rising slightly from 46 percent to 49 percent.[78]

The same June CBS/New York Times poll that showed support, however, for the *substance* of President Bush's progressive indexing proposal showed 62 percent *disapproving* of his handling of the Social Security issue.

This may seem paradoxical but it shows the power of descriptive language in driving attitudes. To take but one stark example: whereas the *New York Times* found that 59 percent of respondents were supportive of the concept of a slower rate of growth for middle- to high-income workers, a CNN/USA Today/Gallup poll the previous month asked whether individuals would be supportive of a proposal to "curb" benefits for middle- or higher-income workers. Described with this terminology, 54 percent opposed the idea.[79] When other polls described a proposal to "reduce" benefits, they generally found opposition as well.

This is a case study in why opinion polls should not drive public policy. The same policy might produce public support or opposition based on how it is described. The political battle thus involved the *words* to be attached to reform as much as it did the substantive implications of reform itself. This is one reason why this book has been so critical of the misuse of artful language by policy experts where this has fed political advantage at the cost of understanding.

A May 2005 CBS News poll[80] provides another example of how surveys can yield confusing direction. The poll reported that 62 percent of respondents favored raising the (then) $90,000 cap on taxable wages. The same poll found that a 50–40 majority favored reducing the benefits of those earning $100,000 or more, while a 55–35 majority *opposed* limiting the rate of benefit growth of those with incomes between $50,000 and $100,000.

This might seem like coherent guidance to policymakers. But how can these dollar figures be translated into action? A significant problem is that Social Security taxes are levied on *annual* wages, whereas the benefit formula is based on *lifetime averaged indexed* wages. These are very different.

Many of us have some years where we earn more than the cap on taxable wages, but many of us have surprisingly low wage *averages* because we also had years where we worked part-time, or in a low-paying job, or didn't work at all. Plus, the Social Security system doesn't "see" any income over the cap, so such income doesn't pull up one's average for benefit calculation purposes.

As it turns out, a full 22 percent of workers have wages at some point above the wage cap (then $90,000, now $106,800) but only 19 percent of workers have lifetime "average wages" (used for benefits) higher than even $62,000.[81]

Given all this, what does the original question mean? Does it refer to annual wages or to lifetime average wages? Does it refer to one concept on the tax side, and another on the benefit side? Does anyone even know?

If this poll refers consistently to *lifetime average* wages as seen by the Social Security system, then it would only have us raising taxes or slowing benefit growth for less than 1 percent of the population—the small percentage with lifetime average taxable wages at the taxable maximum. That's not going to get us very far.

If, on the other hand, we're talking about *annual* wages in each question, then we'd affect 22 percent of workers on the tax side and a similar number of workers on the benefit side. The benefit changes, however, would affect people with lifetime wage *averages* below $60,000, despite the way the question is worded.

Inevitable confusion on these points is, of course, readily exploited by political advocates. In 2005, some circulated figures alleging large "benefit cuts" under President Bush's proposal for those earning only $58,000,[82] describing that person as "middle class." In reality, a person at that AIME level in 2005 was in the upper 15 percent of all wage earners.[83] A benefit change at that wage level and above would have affected *fewer* workers than raising the cap on taxable wages, a measure advocated by many of those same critics.

If these quirks and points of analytical inconsistency are obscured from members of the public, it is nearly impossible for them to sort out the implications of what is being asked and to give meaningful guidance to policymakers. It also makes it too easy for policy advocates to sell a favored policy choice or attack a disfavored one without clarifying for the public how many people would actually be affected.

As a general rule, when surveys referred to benefit "cuts" or "reductions," they produced public opposition. Political consultants also quickly found that negative responses to personal accounts could be generated by using words such as "privatization," "risk," "debt," or the "stock market," and throwing in references to the Chinese for good measure.[84]

By the summer of 2005, the Social Security initiative was in an awkward place. The president had succeeded in making the case that reform was necessary. No such consensus, however, had developed on the substance of reform. Survey respondents supported the substance of progressive indexation but could also be readily induced to express opposition if the same proposal was described so as to imply an actual reduction in benefits. This induced sufficient nervousness within Congress to prevent many from casting a supportive vote.

Although reform opponents had launched effective political attacks, they had also over-reached. Claims about the adverse consequences of reform had been so exaggerated that the passage of a law would have produced a rapid refutation of the claims. Seniors would have continued to receive their checks, no one's benefits would have been "cut" from current levels, the system's fiscal balance would have improved,[85] and there would not have been a near-term transition cost of $2 trillion or anything close to it (according to CBO and the SSA Actuary).

All this would ultimately have redounded to the political benefit of those who passed reform and embarrassed those who fought it. This, of course, raised the stakes still further; it made it politically essential for opponents that reform not happen at all.

Despite public understanding of the necessity of reform, obstructionists had one critical advantage: the status quo was not felt to be as difficult a place, politically, as any particular solvency solution. The currently insolvent system promises trillions more than it is currently taxing to deliver. A solvent system would correct that imbalance, and thus would appear to tax more, offer lower benefits, or both.

Surveys[86] showed opposition to each of the following ideas: raising the retirement age, raising the payroll tax, and "cutting benefits." Thus, without sufficient public shaming of the irresponsibility of inaction, all obstructionists needed to do was to sow enough doubt about any reform proposal put forward.

In this environment, President Bush's congressional allies had to make a determination on how to proceed. The tactics decided upon were different in the House than in the Senate because of the differing political situations in each chamber. House Republicans, even with the power to pass a bill on a party-line vote, needed a demonstration that the Senate could pass something. This put an enormous onus on Senate Republicans to first see how much could be accomplished on the toughest questions.

Senate Finance Committee Chairman Chuck Grassley (R-IA) worked feverishly to explore the substantive ground available for progress. Receiving no encouragement from across the aisle, he turned to fellow Republicans to determine whether it made sense to move forward on solvency and personal accounts together, on personal accounts first, or on solvency first without accounts.

At first it appeared that opposition from some Republicans to personal accounts meant that a solvency-without-accounts approach might be the appropriate first step. But soon it became clear that even the Republicans who expressed concerns about personal accounts were unwilling to back measures to attain solvency in their absence (a familiar story on both sides of the aisle). This left the chairman with nowhere to go.

House Republicans, by contrast, found it easier to produce support for personal accounts than for the difficult measures to ensure sustainable solvency. They thus coalesced behind the "GROW account" bill. This legislation simply sought to save the amount of the near-term Social Security surplus in personal accounts that would pre-fund a small portion of Social Security's future liabilities. It was not a full Social Security solution and its backers did not pretend that it was. Instead it simply put its sponsors on record as supporting the creation of personal accounts and opposing the continued spending of the Trust Fund money, while leaving open their options with respect to system solvency.

Heading into the August recess, the Social Security initiative was already in trouble. Reform opponents had grown increasingly comfortable defending the status quo, while reform proponents had been unable to agree on a unified approach. Congressional Republicans were unwilling to move without Democrats, and Democrats declined to move. Republicans promised there would be votes on Social Security accounts after the August recess, but it remained to be seen how this would lead to a successful bicameral legislative conference.

If opponents had persistently nudged back the Social Security reform cause throughout the spring and summer of 2005, Hurricane Katrina blew it into another county. The hurricane devastated New Orleans and the entire Gulf Coast and the administration suffered fierce criticism for its response. The hurricane and its aftermath both absorbed the administration's energy and cut deeply into the president's support, leaving insufficient political capital to revive the Social Security reform effort.

Although Katrina marked the point at which the Social Security reform effort faded away, the effort was imperiled before Katrina hit. This has naturally prompted many post-mortems and criticisms of the substance and tactics of the administration's reform initiative. We will review the substantive controversies in later chapters.

The failure of the 2005 Social Security reform effort opens the Bush administration to appropriate critiques of its choices. We should be careful to note, however, that the failure of one effort does not necessarily imply that a different proposal or a different tactical approach would have been successful. To succeed would have required a sufficient number of congressional Democrats to break from their leadership and to engage in crafting a bipartisan Social Security reform solution. Although the administration could endeavor to make this attractive to moderate Democrats, it had virtually no control over that outcome, at least relative to the Democratic leadership.

We cannot fairly judge the tactical choices of the Bush administration without comparison to a successful alternative scenario. Before President Bush's 2005 effort, President Clinton failed (for different reasons) to achieve Social Security reform. Two years after President Bush's 2005 effort, new Treasury Secretary Hank Paulson was rebuffed in similar overtures to congressional Democrats, despite the esteem in which he was held across the aisle. One needn't believe that the Bush administration tactics were perfect to observe that a successful alternative path has yet to be found. Indeed, without the active cooperation of congressional Democrats, it likely will not be found.

Substantively, opponents of President Bush's reform proposals will say that they failed because they would have "cut" benefits too deeply and because the personal accounts imposed an unacceptable transition cost, among other shortcomings. But we can only sensibly evaluate this charge in comparison with an alternative means of sustaining Social Security solvency. If reform opponents had rallied behind and generated public support for continuing the pay-as-you-go system on a sustainably solvent basis, offering higher benefits and imposing higher taxes than President Bush's proposal, this would substantiate the criticism.

Quite conspicuously, however, reform opponents did not do this. Instead they downplayed the Social Security problem, inviting comparisons not between President Bush's proposal and an alternative solution, but between his proposal and the unsustainable status quo. Again, it is not difficult to make any reform solution look bad in comparison with a system that is purporting to offer trillions in benefits more than it is charging for. But we can only judge the merit of the proposals in comparison with an alternative that can actually pass into law.

Since the 2005 Social Security reform effort, party control has shifted at both ends of Pennsylvania Avenue, in both the presidency and Congress. As of this writing, we are still waiting to learn what the superior alternative might be.

CHAPTER 11

The Certainty and Severity
of the Social Security Shortfall

O UR REVIEW OF THE SUBSTANTIVE controversies begins with the foundational question: does Social Security even face a shortfall requiring prompt correction?

Some experts believe that there is no need for further belaboring of the question of *whether* Social Security faces a shortfall, and that the discussion can safely turn to what to do about it. Yet both during and after the 2005 debate, the very existence of the Social Security financing problem was itself a focus of contention. When, for example, President Barack Obama's administration floated the idea of shoring up Social Security's finances in early 2009, a barrage of criticism was unleashed from the left, arguing in apparent earnest that there was no Social Security shortfall requiring correction.

Without consensus agreement even on the necessity of action, agreement on the policy response will remain prohibitively elusive.

Other controversial issues that we will explore in the next chapter are worthy of an even-handed treatment, detailing the thoughtful arguments on both sides. This one, however, does not warrant such agnosticism. The "Social Security faces no shortfall" canard is an urban myth, built upon one false predicate after another.

The persistence of this myth is one of the more remarkable phenomena of our Internet age. There is practically a cottage industry of bloggers who attack any mention of the Social Security shortfall as a bogeyman.

This movement is disturbingly anti-empirical in nature, as we will here document in some detail. Some individuals who regard themselves as educated about Social Security finances surprisingly still fall for it; but it is virtually impossible to do so after attaining significant familiarity with the details of the trustees' projections.

All of the information necessary to refute the contention that "there is no Social Security shortfall" is readily available online to anyone who cares to view it. And yet it continues to be argued in many places— occasionally even among reporters, columnists, and legislative staff— that the Social Security shortfall is a product only of the overheated imaginations of the Social Security trustees, based on overly conservative projections. That this continues to be said by some is testimony to the durability of self-perpetuating myths in an era offering a diversity of information sources.

First, let us quickly gloss over the semantic questions and then focus our attention squarely on substantive issues. On the semantic side, some asserted that President Bush's rhetoric exaggerated the problem, criticizing him in particular for referring to the Social Security problem as a "crisis." In truth, President Bush rarely applied the term "crisis" to Social Security except in the context of avoiding a *future* crisis, referring to the issue far more frequently as a "problem."[1] (Actually, it was President Clinton who used the term "crisis" much more frequently, often describing the "crisis" as "looming."[2])

President Bush was also criticized for allegedly exaggerating the system's problems by applying the term "bankrupt" to Social Security's projected condition at the point of insolvency. Some critics argued that the system would not be "bankrupt" at the insolvency point because it would still have incoming revenue sufficient to pay three-quarters of promised benefits at that date.[3]

The president's terminology, however, was correct. Most of us would not consider that an individual (or General Motors or United Airlines) must have absolutely *no* income to be considered "bankrupt." Instead we would consider the term "bankruptcy" to apply to a condition in which one's assets are depleted and in which projected future income is insufficient to discharge one's debts: precisely the condition now anticipated for Social Security in 2037.

The main purpose of this section, however, is to settle arguments not about semantics but rather about substantive facts, to which we will now turn.

The myth that the current Social Security projections are too conservative and that the problem might vanish of its own accord typically rests on the following components:

- The trustees are arbitrarily projecting that future economic growth will be less than it has been in the past.
- Were it not for these overly conservative assumptions, the Social Security shortfall, or a good portion of it, would disappear.
- In the past, the trustees have generally been too conservative in their projections and it's likely that they are being too conservative again.

Each of these contentions is false. Let us examine them each more closely.

Economic growth.   National aggregate economic growth is a product of two factors: growth in the number of workers and growth in economic output per worker (productivity).

The more workers we have, and the more they produce, the more our economy grows.

Over the past forty years, productivity growth has averaged 1.7 percent annually. The trustees are projecting that this will continue for the indefinite future, as shown in figure 11.1.[4]

No economist can say what future productivity growth will be. It could be higher or lower than in the past. The trustees are *not* projecting, however, that it will slow down relative to the recent historical average.[5]

What *is* changing is the rate of growth of the American workforce. Starting in the early 1960s, the enormous baby boom generation began to join the ranks of workers. This swelled total worker numbers,

FIGURE 11.1   U.S. Productivity: Historical and Projected

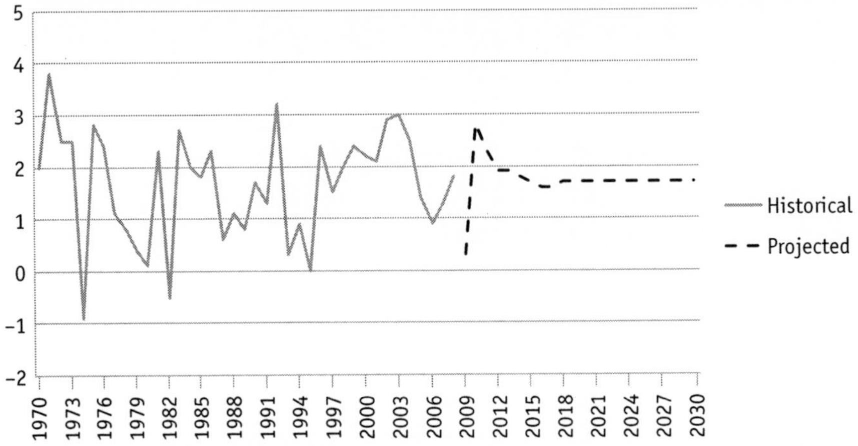

SOURCE: Based on data from the 2009 Trustees' report.

resulting in high annual workforce growth rates lasting through the late 1980s.[6]

The first baby boomers, born in 1946, were turning sixty-two by early 2008 and began to depart the workforce. The net growth of our labor force is, of course, the amount of workers entering it minus the amount of workers leaving it. The generation now leaving the workforce is of unprecedented size; moreover, the members of this same generation did not have as many children as their own parents did.

The inevitable result can be seen in figure 11.2. Future labor force growth will not be anything close to what it was over the previous several decades.

Because the total growth of our economy is the product of labor force growth and productivity growth, slower labor force growth means slower aggregate economic growth. It's thus not slower *productivity* growth that shapes the projections but rather *demographics.*

It's important to understand how firmly fixed these trends are. The baby boomers are already with us and are now heading into retirement, claiming benefits at a rate at least as high as previously projected. The

FIGURE 11.2   U.S. Labor Force Growth: Historical and Projected

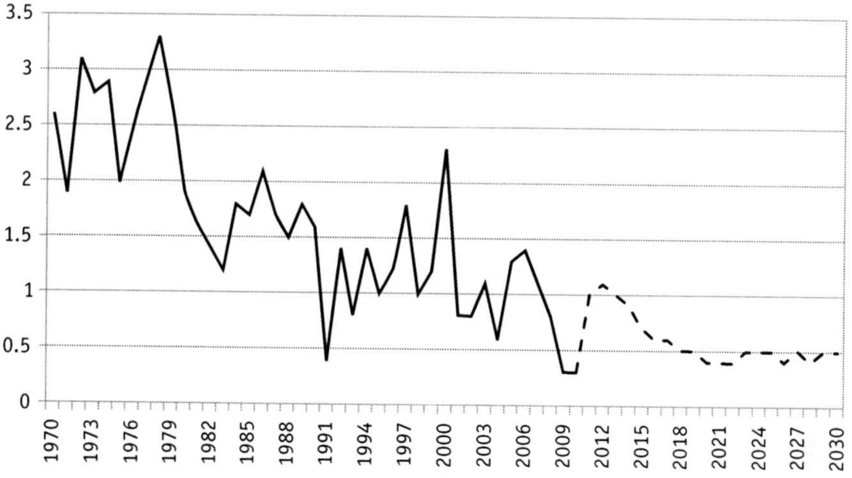

Source: Based on data from the 2009 Trustees' report.

generation behind them has already been born. Immigration levels might affect the numbers somewhat, but aren't large enough to avert the broader trend toward slower workforce growth.

Over the next several decades, therefore, the annual rate of workforce growth is projected to be less than one-third what it was from the early 1960s through the early 1990s. Thus, even if future productivity *vastly* exceeds recent historical norms (and there is no particular reason to believe that it will), future aggregate growth rates will be significantly lower than in the past. This doesn't mean that individual workers' incomes will grow more slowly—it merely means that the total number of workers will grow more slowly.

This concept isn't, or shouldn't be, so hard to understand. If one state's population grows faster than another, for example, its economy grows faster, too. In 1997, New York's economy was bigger than Texas's. By 2007, Texas's was larger.[7] Was this because Texans had been more productive than New Yorkers over that decade? No—New York's productivity had actually grown faster in the interim. Texas's economy had grown faster primarily because its population had grown faster.

There is no basis for the charge that the trustees are positing a slow-down in economic growth for no particular reason. The trustees are simply noting that our labor force is growing more slowly—not our productivity. This is why many external bipartisan review panels have repeatedly signed off on the trustees' assumptions as reasonable.[8]

This has not stopped some from wrongly implying that the trustees are arbitrarily departing from historic patterns in their future economic projections. Former Labor Secretary Robert Reich did this in a recent blog post: ". . . (g)o back into American history all the way to the Civil War—including the Great Depression and the severe depressions of the late nineteenth century—and the economy's average annual growth is closer to 3 percent. Use a 3 percent assumption and Social Security is flush for the next seventy-five years."[9] This statement glosses over the demographic realities that will influence total growth rates.

There are endless further examples of the charge that the trustees are being excessively conservative in their economic projections. A 2007 *Newsday* column stated that the trustees' report "deliberately uses the most conservative or pessimistic assumptions."[10] A series of articles in the *Christian Science Monitor* have cited critics of the trustees' economic projections, even putting in one 2006 headline that the projections for the shortfall were "suspect."[11] In an April 2007 online discussion of Social Security finances, a *Washington Post* reporter declared flatly that the trustees' estimates were "remarkably pessimistic" and that the "situation is not nearly as dire as they say."[12] Bloggers repeat this canard almost daily.

Although no one can predict future productivity growth with accuracy, future productivity growth would need to be *much* faster,[13] in the light of demographic trends, to maintain future aggregate GDP growth at rates that these sources claim we should rely upon. Positing an increase in productivity growth sufficient to offset this enormous demographic change, needless to say, would solve a lot of problems besides Social Security. If achieving higher productivity growth is so easy, why aren't we doing it already?

One additional nuance is worth mentioning for precision. Social Security revenues are not, strictly speaking, a function of economic or productivity growth but of *wage* growth. Social Security doesn't directly levy a tax on productivity, but on *wages*. And, historically, wage growth has not been precisely the same as productivity growth, largely because workers receive compensation in various other forms such as health benefits.

The rising amount of total compensation provided through health benefits has cut into the growth of wages subject to the Social Security tax. Over the past forty years, real wage growth has averaged 0.8 percent above inflation. The trustees are actually projecting that this will *increase* somewhat in the future, averaging 1.1 percent above inflation over the long term.[14] Thus, in no sense are the trustees imposing an arbitrary slowdown in future revenue growth; quite the opposite.

Obviously, no one can precisely predict the future of the American economy. But critics of the trustees' projections need to explain why they see fundamentally different demographic trends than the rest of the analytical world sees or why future productivity and wage growth will both be *much* higher in the future than they have been in the past.[15]

The relative importance of economic growth to the projections. The second component of the myth is that not only are the trustees' economic growth assumptions unduly conservative, but most or all of the projected Social Security shortfall would disappear if they weren't.

This is also untrue.

The vast majority of the Social Security problem remains even under a wide range of possible economic growth scenarios. This information is readily available to anyone who cares to examine the trustees' report in detail.

The trustees' report each year contains a stochastic analysis showing how much the fiscal outcomes vary under a wide range of possible economic and demographic projections.

In 2009, the trustees' intermediate projections were that the program would enter permanent annual deficits in 2016, requiring increasing amounts of general revenues thereafter to redeem debt held by the Trust Fund until the point of insolvency in 2037 (see table 11.1).[16]

TABLE 11.1 Potential Variations in the Trustees' Projections

Projection	Annual Deficits	Insolvency	Cost in 75th year (% of taxable wages)
Intermediate	2016	2037	17.68
2.5th percentile	2009	2030	13.29
10th percentile	2010	2032	14.64
50th percentile	2014	2036	17.93
90th percentile	2017	2043	22.30
97.5th percentile	2019	2052	25.05

SOURCE: Based on data from the 2009 Trustees' report, http://www.ssa.gov/OACT/TR/2009/VI_ stochastic.html#100970.

The median projection of this analysis actually shows permanent deficits arriving in 2014, with insolvency in 2036, both a bit *earlier* than the particular combination of variables constituting the trustees' intermediate projections.

Regardless, the qualitative picture doesn't really change even at the far extremes of the projections. The 10th percentile of possible outcomes shows permanent deficits arriving in 2010, the 90th percentile in 2017, with the insolvency date ranging only from 2032–2043. The qualitative gap between annual costs and revenues remains in each plausible run.

Even looking all the way out to the 95 percent confidence band— from the 2.5th percentile to the 97.5th percentile—one finds that permanent program cash deficits would still arrive sometime between 2009 and 2019. Suffice it to say that if there exists only a slim 2.5 percent chance of permanent annual cash deficits being postponed even *three years* beyond the trustees' intermediate projection (from 2016 to 2019), the debate over whether we have a fiscal problem ought to have ended some time ago.

A review of this chart reveals that the problem is simply not going to vanish of its own accord. Permanent deficits are just as likely to arrive this year as they are to be postponed even until 2017. It's just as likely that program costs will eventually absorb over 25 percent of worker wages as it is that insolvency will be postponed even fifteen years beyond the trustees' intermediate projection. We can play with the trustees' projections as much as we like, and we'll only produce as many reasons for further alarm as we will reasons to wish the problem away.

So, where does the notion come from that faster economic growth might by itself make the problem disappear?

The notion comes from the irresponsible citation of a particular hypothetical scenario contained within the trustees' report called the "Low-Cost Scenario." The Low-Cost Scenario is not intended to be a plausible benchmark and is instead a compendium of every unlikely variation in the projections that might conceivably shrink the Social Security shortfall. So improbable is this scenario that it does not even appear within the 95 percent confidence band of possible outcomes.[17]

Under the Low-Cost Scenario, longevity grows more slowly over the next seventy-five years than it has over the last thirty.[18] The scenario assumes that fertility levels permanently return to 2.3 percent, levels not seen since the early 1970s.[19] It assumes that real wage growth will permanently return to 1.7 percent every year, a level attained in only nine of the last thirty years.[20] And it assumes many other highly improbable economic and demographic outcomes.

Any one of these particular projections might turn out to be true, but the chances of them *all* being true are negligible. Many of them in fact are negatively correlated with each other. For example, it makes no sense to assume that both fertility rates *and* labor force participation rates for women will be much higher than the intermediate assumptions, when these two outcomes tend to vary inversely. These are among the reasons why the peculiar combination of variables in the Low-Cost Scenario is too implausible even to appear within the 95 percent confidence band of possibilities.

This particular made-up scenario, however, would remain solvent, at least in the technical sense of retaining a positive Trust Fund balance, which is what allows some to point to the existence of this absurdly unlikely illustration as "proof" that the problem might well vanish on its own.

Worth singling out, however, is the misleading implication that faster economic growth *by itself* is enough to bring the solvent Low-Cost Scenario to pass. For example, a recent MarketWatch column entitled "Why Social Security Isn't Going Broke" stated, "The actuaries' own low cost projection assumes an average annual growth rate of 2.9 percent between now and 2085. . . . Guess what? Under the actuaries' low-cost projection, the Social Security system never runs out of money!"[21] Secretary Reich conveyed the same misimpression in his recent piece.[22] One particularly confused piece in the *American Prospect* in early 2009 argued that even the "low-cost" scenario was "pessimistic."[23]

A naïve reader could be forgiven for believing, based on such remarks, that economic growth alone might eliminate the shortfall as per the Low-Cost Scenario—instead of this happening only via a vast compendium of additional improbable changes to the assumptions, such as in longevity and other demographic variables.

In reality, however, changes to the economic growth projections alone do not change the Social Security picture all that much under current law, because both the system's revenues *and* its benefits are tied to national wage growth, due to wage indexation of the benefit formula. Faster wage growth means that more tax revenue comes in; it also means that more money is paid out later.

Thus, faster growth tends only to improve the near-term picture for Social Security somewhat, pushing out the dates of the first cash deficits and of insolvency. On the other hand, slower growth moves those dates closer—as we are seeing with the effects of the current recession. But neither changes the *aggregate* imbalance in a significant way (as noted earlier, a landmark paper by Gokhale and Biggs found that in a system with a declining worker-collector ratio, faster growth could somewhat increase the present value of the system's total structural shortfall).[24]

The trustees' report is clear on the point that faster earnings growth (without ample assistance from demographic forces) will not by itself eliminate the Social Security shortfall. For example, it shows that even under the Low-Cost Scenario's projection that real wage growth will implausibly more than *double* its historic rate over the next seventy-five years (from 0.8 percent annually to 1.7 percent), this by itself would only postpone insolvency for seven years (from 2037 to 2044) and fail to eliminate even *half* of the seventy-five-year actuarial imbalance.[25]

In sum, the assertion that the Social Security shortfall might well disappear if economic growth accelerates within plausible bounds has no credible factual foundation.

The trustees' projection history. The third element of the myth is that the Social Security trustees have a track record of being overly conservative in their past projections, and thus their current projections should be taken with a grain of salt. As one senator asserted in a statement typical of this view, "They (the trustees) have been wrong because they have consistently understated economic growth. I believe, in all likelihood, they are wrong again."[26] Many bloggers have echoed the theme that the trustees' projection history is one of inaccuracy and excessive conservatism,[27] with some even going so far as to say that the trustees' low-cost scenarios (which we described above) were a better guide to future events than their intermediate projections.

This, too, is untrue.

In reality, the Social Security Trustees have an impressive projection record of exceptional (at least for federal government scorekeepers) accuracy and consistency. And, exactly contrary to the myth, to the extent that the trustees' projections have been imprecise, they have tended to be somewhat too *aggressive* (that is, too optimistic about program finances) rather than too *conservative* (too pessimistic on the finances).

This contradicts the relentlessly promulgated stereotype of the trustees' projection record, but any complete examination of the data makes it inescapably clear.

In 2007, I presented a paper at the American Enterprise Institute (AEI) that examined the trustees' projection record from the last major reforms in 1983 through 2005. It turned out that the trustees' reports over that period had done reasonably well in predicting the state of the system by 2005, the inevitable errors being generally in the direction of being too aggressive. Specifically, reality most often turned up somewhere between the trustees' intermediate and high-cost scenarios, with the mythmakers' low-cost scenarios being by far the least accurate.[28] This finding held up under a number of different methodologies.

These were just the findings, however, through 2005. Since then, Social Security's finances have taken a significant turn for the worse due to our ongoing recession. Social Security's cash surpluses in 2009 and 2010 were last year projected to be a mere $19 billion and $18 billion, respectively. The thin 2010 surplus then projected was roughly the same size (after adjusting for inflation) as predicted in what may have been the single most conservative previous trustees' report in their projection history, the 1996 report.[29]

(For perspective on the range of trustees' estimates, consider that in 1983 it was predicted that Social Security would enjoy a 2010 cash surplus of 2.51 percent of taxable payroll, which in today's dollars would be $143 billion.[30])

Some, including the Congressional Budget Office (CBO) in its latest projections, are now predicting that Social Security will instead enter cash deficits *this year*. Not a single trustees' report since 1983 has predicted that cash deficits would be encountered so early; each one has predicted that the date of first cash deficits would arise between 2012 and 2021. In other words, there now exists a reasonable chance that of the last quarter-century of trustees' reports, not a one of them would have been conservative *enough*.

Ironically, given the charge that the trustees have been too conservative on the economics, the over-optimism of the majority of their reports was driven mostly by too-rosy projections of the economics. In 1983, for example, the trustees relied on projections of 1.5 percent real wage growth going forward[31] (the historical average over the past forty years has been 0.8 percent).[32]

More recently, the CBO in 2008 actually increased its long-term real-wage growth assumptions to 1.4 percent annually—almost to the level of the discredited 1983 assumption—right on the eve of the national economic downturn. CBO thus produced a spectacularly mistimed 2008 projection, badly exaggerating Social Security's fiscal health (especially in the near term), causing immediate embarrassment to the respected score-keeping agency.[33] By early 2009, CBO had to abruptly change course and provide sharply worsened near-term estimates to congressional staff (and has more recently backed off slightly from its long-term real-wage growth assumption, reducing it to 1.3 percent).

Rarely have so many people seized an opportunity to be so spectacularly wrong. There was never a factual foundation for the argument that the trustees had been unduly conservative, but the arrival of the current recession has made possible a scenario that couldn't possibly make the critics look more foolish. That is: a situation in which every single trustees' report since the last major reforms may actually have *understated* the problem. Many analysts knew that the critics were wrong; without anticipating the depth of the current economic downturn, however, we could not know they would be *this* wrong.

As of this writing, the most recent available trustees' projection is still that Social Security cash deficits will materialize—not this year, but in 2016. A review of the projection history reveals that as incoming data has replaced previous projections, this has generally tended to move Social Security's anticipated problems *closer* in time, not further away. And, as the problems have moved closer, they have also become more certain.

Even without anticipating the likely further worsening in the projections, one can clearly see that the trustees have generally erred on the side of fiscal optimism. So, what has been the basis of the myth that they have an overly conservative projection history? In short: cherry-picking.

Looking at figures 11.3 and 11.4, one can see that the projections reached their most conservative extreme in the mid-1990s. If one treats these atypical reports as being representative of their overall projection record, one could create the misimpression that the trustees are generally too conservative. This is precisely what many bloggers have done.[34]

Such cherry-picking, however, misrepresents reality in several ways.

First, the trustees' assumptions have been tweaked since the mid-1990s reports; thus the assumptions in those reports are not a fair guide to the accuracy of their *current* projections.

FIGURE 11.3   Annual Trustees' Projections for the Arrival of Social
Security Deficits

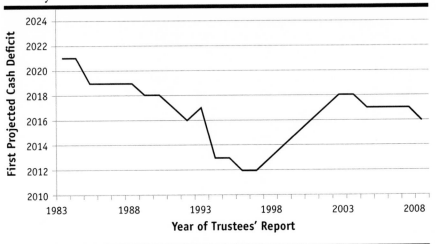

Source: Based on data from the 1983–2009 Trustees' reports.

FIGURE 11.4   Annual Trustees' Projections of Social Security
Insolvency Date

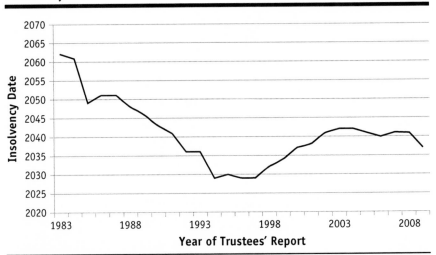

Source: Based on data from the 1983–2009 Trustees' reports.

Second, as can be easily seen, the mid-1990s reports aren't representative of the trustees' projection record as a whole and give an impression opposite of the reality that they have tended to err on the side of fiscal optimism.

And third, the mid-1990s trustees' reports were too conservative in part for a very good reason; they were issued on the eve of a surge of real-wage growth in the mid- to late-1990s that caught all government scorekeepers—not just the trustees—by surprise. This wage growth surge pushed Social Security's projected problems back by a few years, after which they resumed their inexorable march closer in time.

Amazingly, even as the current recession has driven Social Security finances to a point worse than projected in nearly every trustees' report since 1983, some have continued to beat the drum of "overly pessimistic projections."[35] That this would continue to be said even in the face of recent economic data is a demonstration that the myth is anti-empirical at its core.

On the issues that we will hereafter explore, there are valid points of view on all sides of the question. This is not one of them. As I stated in my 2007 AEI paper, "The American public is not well served by the myth that the perceived Social Security shortfall arises only from projections in the past that have proved too conservative. This myth both mischaracterizes the trustees' track record to date, as well as the factors that significantly affect the fiscal picture going forward." This is even more true today.

CHAPTER 12

President Bush's Reform Initiative

The Policy Controversies

B EYOND THE DEBATE OVER Social Security's fiscal health under current law, 2005 featured a vigorous and fascinating debate about the policy judgments made by President Bush. This chapter reviews a few of the more consequential of these policy controversies.

A General Observation About Social Security Analysis

To understand the Social Security debate, it is important to understand generally how one's assumptions can predetermine one's conclusions.

As an example, consider the following pictures of two alternative future courses for Social Security. Even if you don't habitually like graphic explanations, please stay with this one; it's important to everything that follows in this chapter.

Figures 12.1 and 12.2 project future income and outgo for two hypothetical Social Security programs. Each has a black line showing incoming tax revenues and a gray line showing outgoing obligations (which, for our purposes, could go either toward immediate spending on benefits or into near-term investments to fund future benefits).

Each system depicted here has an incoming stream of revenue equal to exactly 12.5 percent of worker wages in every year over the next seventy-five years.

FIGURE 12.1   Hypothetical Social Security System A

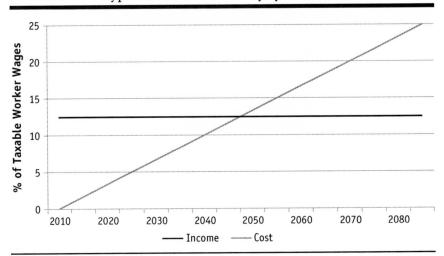

What is different about the two systems is the time flow of their outgoing obligations. System A owes no payments at all until after 2010, but over time the costs of System A rise uncontrollably. Not only does System A face enormous annual deficits fifty to seventy-five years from now, but it is obvious that it is on an unsustainable course that deteriorates still further beyond that.

System B, by contrast, is in *perfect* balance every year. Every single year, as far as the eye can see, the program's annual income and its annual outgo are exactly balanced, down to the penny. (To make this easier to see on the graph of System B, the black line has been turned into a dashed line.)

Which system would we prefer to have? It should be obvious that System B is by far the more responsible course. System B faces no foreseeable shortfalls in any year and it's quite possible that it never will.

System A is clearly unsustainable. Not only is it unsustainable beyond seventy-five years, it's clear that it faces massive problems even within the seventy-five-year window. Within that time span it will eventually only be producing half of the annual income needed to meet annual obligations.

FIGURE 12.2   Hypothetical Social Security System B

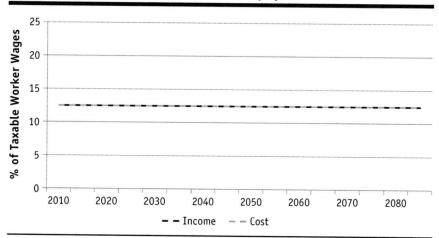

Why are we comparing these two hypothetical systems when it is patently obvious that System B is superior to System A?

Here's why: because if policymakers had inherited the dysfunctional System A, and had proposed responsible reforms to convert it to System B, then a smart (if devious) expert at a think tank would be able to write a policy paper, based entirely and faithfully on the projections of the Social Security Actuary, that said all of the following things:

1) Converting to System B requires a multi-trillion-dollar transition cost.
2) Even after seventy-five years, this transition cost wouldn't be fully paid off.
3) Converting to System B actually *worsens* the system's actuarial balance.

That may seem ridiculous, but this is *exactly* the methodology that has been used to attack Social Security reform proposals in recent years—most especially proposals like President Bush's that include personal accounts. Let me explain:

The reason that System B shows a multi-trillion-dollar "transition cost" relative to System A is that System A projects large near-term surpluses, indeed stretching into the trillions. Switching to System B would eliminate them.

Of course, as we have seen, the government is unlikely to save all of the surpluses that arise under a system like System A. But some current actuarial methodologies simply *assume* that it will. The fact that System B is in perfect balance every year doesn't eliminate the analytical finding that it would involve a massive transition cost, because its perfect annual balance is deemed inferior to System A's near-term surplus (even if A's surplus is spent).

This assumption is critical because it cuts to the heart of competing views of Social Security and larger federal budgetary policy. An advocate of System B will likely be skeptical that the trillions of near-term surpluses projected in System A will ever be saved. System A's advocates may argue back that the government really will save the money.

It is trivially easy for a clever expert, instead of exploring the empirical evidence as to which view is correct, to make a series of sobering cautionary pronouncements about System B simply by *assuming* that none of the large near-term surpluses in System A will be spent.

Not only that, but the scorekeeping would *also* find that the "transition cost" of System B would not be fully paid off even after seventy-five years.

As we can see above, System B is in perfect balance in every single year. But System A is actually presumed to have a *positive* effect on federal debt over seventy-five years because it assumes that the near-term surpluses will be saved and that they will *earn interest*. The interest-compounded value of these surpluses, it turns out, are greater than the huge deficits in the latter part of the valuation window.

This in turn relates to the third finding of our hypothetical critical paper, which is that converting to System B actually *worsens* the program's actuarial balance.

This is because—strange though it may seem—the ongoing definition of "seventy-five-year actuarial balance" would actually be *positive* for System A. Existing discounting methods shrink the measured size of the long-term shortfall so that System A's deficit in 2085 appears to be much smaller than its surplus in 2010. This is because it is implicitly assumed that the surplus in 2010 will be saved and will earn interest, and thus has a value to government finances that more than offsets the size of the 2085 deficit.

Before we get too deep into the intricacies of Trust Fund accounting and actuarial methodology, we need a simple reality check: in the real world, it's ridiculous to claim that System B is inferior to System A.

System B is in perfect balance in every single year. There is absolutely nothing fiscally irresponsible about the perfectly balanced System B, by any stretch of the imagination. System A's viability, on the other hand, depends on several implausible assumptions about government behavior.

Any methodology that finds System A to be superior to System B is highly flawed; if it is not thrown out entirely, it should at least be used sparingly with full disclosure of its shortcomings.

In any reasonable hard science, if a theory fails to make a sensible empirical prediction then it is thrown out. In Social Security policy, however, there is sometimes a tendency to throw out reasonable *policy* in deference to flawed *scorekeeping.*

Without a full understanding of this, there is no way for the press, let alone the layman, to appreciate the nature of much of the Social Security debate. One needn't be an advocate of President Bush's particular reform proposal to be troubled by the exploitation of flawed metrics to obscure fiscal realities and to present unrealistic images of the effects of alternative courses.

The absurd methodological conclusions critiqued here are precisely those that some have invoked, either naively or misleadingly, to argue against the reforms urged by President Bush and others. Of course, there are valid fiscal concerns to raise about his or any reform proposal; but to understand fiscal realities we need metrics that lead to sensible empirical results.

None of this is a criticism of the excellent work of the Social Security Actuary's office; indeed, the Actuary's office has taken pains to produce further analytical measures to help others avoid these conceptual mistakes. Rather, it is an observation that *within* the excellent projections of the actuary there are metrics that can be (and sometimes are) abused.

In this author's opinion, the fiscal effects of reform proposals should be judged, to a great extent, by this simple yardstick: *how much they reduce the size of Social Security's projected annual cash deficits, measured as a percentage of worker wages in each year evaluated.*

Others could validly disagree with this perspective and may have equally compelling scorekeeping ideas to offer. But if our policy debate is to produce anything close to a reasonable outcome, any methodology that finds that System A is preferable to System B ought not to be the basis for policy conclusions. If readers have reached any particular conclusions about Social Security policy that turn out to have been based implicitly on such methods, they would do well to wipe clean their slates of perception and to approach the policy problem anew.

Having made this general point, let us now turn to several specific controversies that came to the fore in the 2005 reform effort.

Slowing the Growth of Benefits Versus "Benefit Cuts"

Earlier, in chapter 4, we discussed the value judgment of whether the Social Security shortfall should be addressed by raising taxes or by slowing cost growth. When President Bush embraced progressive indexing, he put himself on record as favoring a solution based on cost containment.[1]

In chapter 4 we also explored the factors that have caused many others to believe that the solution should focus primarily on containing the growth of costs instead of on raising taxes. One such motivation is that under current law the real purchasing power of Social Security benefits and the cost burdens facing future workers are both projected to rise dramatically.

Figures 12.3 and 12.4 reproduce the 2005 projections both for system cost growth and for scheduled benefit levels for medium-wage workers (in 2005 dollars).

In the context of these trends, the logic behind progressive indexing is:

FIGURE 12.3   Growing Social Security Cost Burdens on Workers: 2005 Projections

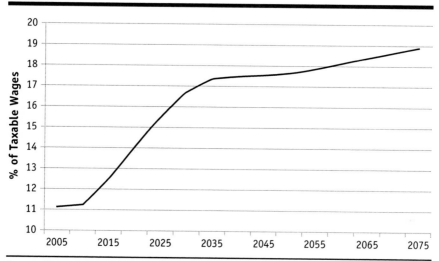

SOURCE: Based on data from the 2005 Trustees' report.

FIGURE 12.4   The Growth of Benefits Relative to Inflation: 2005 Projections (Medium-Wage Earner)

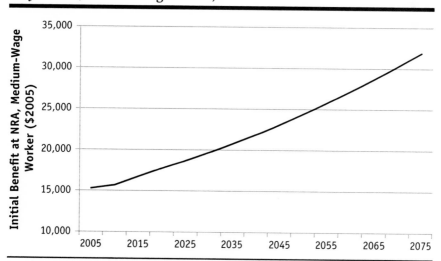

SOURCE: Based on data from the 2005 Trustees' report.

1) The rate of Social Security cost growth must be slowed.
2) Low-income people should be protected from the effects of slower benefit growth to the extent possible.
3) Thus, most benefit growth beyond inflation should flow to those lower-income workers who have less income outside of Social Security.
4) Benefits should continue to rise for everyone, rich and poor, but need not rise significantly faster than inflation for the better-off among us, in view of the burdens this would impose on younger generations.

Progressive indexing would have changed 2005's cost projections to appear as in figure 12.5. It wouldn't eliminate the surge in costs as the baby boomers retire but it would enable the cost burden to ultimately level off and glide back toward historic norms.

Under progressive indexing, the growth of benefits for medium-wage workers would look as shown in figure 12.6, low-wage workers as shown in figure 12.7, and high-wage workers as shown in figure 12.8.

FIGURE 12.5 Social Security Cost Growth Under Progressive Indexing: 2005 Projections

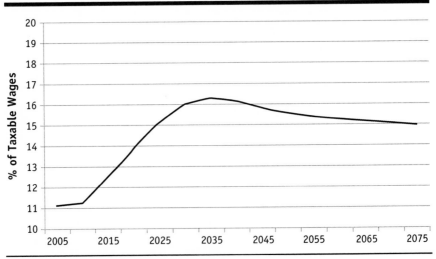

SOURCE: Based on data from the 2005 Trustees' report.

FIGURE 12.6   Real Benefit Growth Under Progressive Indexing: 2005 Projections (Medium-Wage Earner)

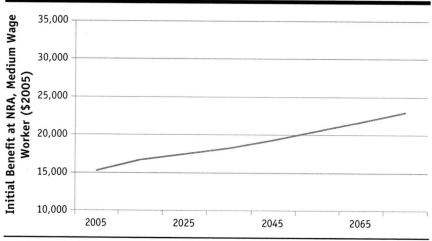

SOURCE: Based on data from the 2005 Trustees' report.

FIGURE 12.7   Real Benefit Growth Under Progressive Indexing: 2005 Projections (Low-Wage Earner)

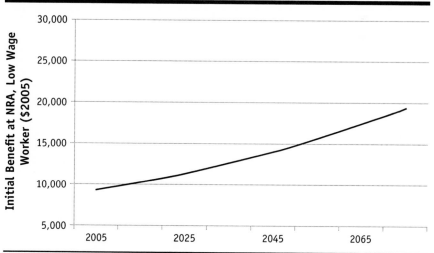

SOURCE: Based on data from the 2005 Trustees' report.

FIGURE 12.8   Real Benefit Growth Under Progressive Indexing: 2005
Projections (High-Wage Earner)

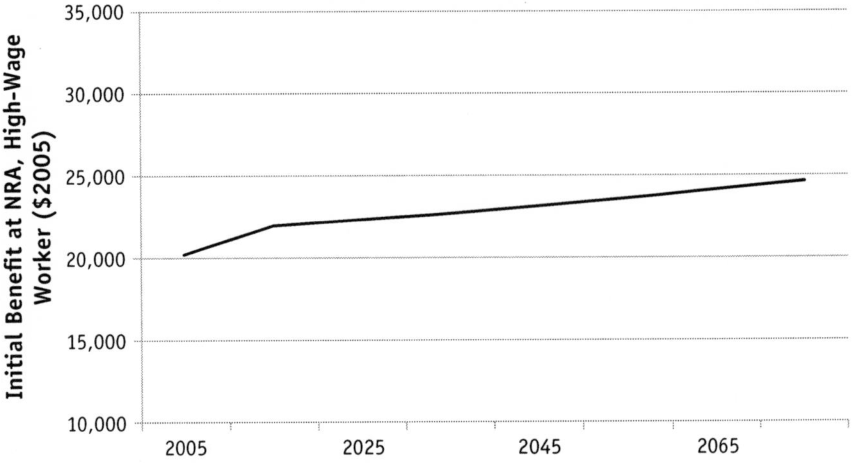

SOURCE: Based on data from the 2005 Trustees' report.

These pictures give a visual sense of how progressive indexing would
work. Workers at all wage levels would continue to see their benefits rise
in real terms (except for the very highest 1 percent, whose benefits
would rise only with inflation), but the slope of the rise would be higher
for the poorest among us.

Over time, of course, this would mean that benefits for low-wage workers would begin to approach those for medium-wage workers, and those
of medium-wage workers to approach those of high-wage workers, and so
on—unless progressive indexing were "turned off" and replaced with another formula.

Criticisms of the approach varied in their cogency. Among these
criticisms were:

• Progressive indexing would dramatically "cut" benefits.
• Progressive indexing, despite its name, would hit Americans of modest
income hard.

- Progressive indexing would make the system *too* progressive, almost like welfare, and ultimately sever the connection between contributions and benefits.
- Progressive indexing was badly designed because it would impose the most severe "cuts" when they are least needed for solvency (specifically, when real wage growth—the difference between wage growth and price growth—is high).

Let's review these in turn.

The charge that progressive indexing would "cut" benefits can be raised in both responsible and irresponsible ways. In the politically charged environment of 2005, there were naturally many examples of attacks that fostered skewed perceptions.[2] As one such criticism stated, "Progressive price indexing would reduce annual benefits for an average wage-earner who is twenty-five today and retires in 2045 by 16 percent or $3,523 (in inflation-adjusted 2005 dollars), relative to the benefits that the worker would receive under the current benefit structure. For an average earner who retires in 2075, the benefit reduction would be 28 percent, or $7,629 in today's dollars." This statement is meticulously worded but has the effect of fostering confusion, as we shall see.

In a sloppier, more egregious statement, a press release from a House of Representatives leadership office asserted, "Workers earning $58,000 a year would be hit with a 42 percent benefit cut for survivors and retirees."[3]

Though the two statements differ in their levels of irresponsibility, there are problems with each. One is that the use of terms such as "reduce" and "benefit reduction" connotes to many listeners that something is declining rather than rising over time. The first statement's comparison with the "current benefit structure" is precise in one narrow sense but conveys a misleading impression.

The specific word "current" in the first statement's phrase of "current benefit structure" is likely to lead to confusion. The numbers in the statement don't actually refer to what workers at those wage levels receive today, nor to what they would receive in the future under current law. They refer instead to benefit levels in the distant future far higher than the current system can finance, which would require a change in law to be provided and which would also require future workers to carry a cost burden of more than 19 percent of their wages (under 2005 projections).[4]

The second statement is more egregious in appearing to imply that workers *now* earning $58,000 would experience a "42 percent benefit cut" when nothing of the kind would happen to anyone in the near term—nor, in fact, to workers earning $58,000 even in the future.

The second statement was based on the SSA Actuary's depiction of a "high-wage worker" who in 2005 would have had a lifetime average wage of roughly (believe it or not) $58,000. The citation of this figure in this context is irresponsible in several respects. First, no near-term beneficiaries at all would actually have been affected. Second, while the effects of progressive indexing would become significant for high-wage workers in the distant future, such workers would then be earning *far* more than $58,000. It is difficult to stretch an interpretation of this statement into one that accurately conveys the effects of progressive indexing.

The coexistence of these criticisms' varying degrees of irresponsibility is not an accident. The second, more irresponsible type of statement was often made by someone who had heard and believed the more carefully worded first statement. This demonstrates that despite the meticulous defenses of the first statement's terminology, its overall effect was to lay a foundation for subsequent confusion. If terminology repeatedly has such an effect, then it should be modified—even if a polemical justification for it can be found.

As with other controversies, the debate over "benefit cuts" highlights the importance of self-consistency in our analysis of alternative reform approaches. As we have seen, the charge was made not in comparison with current benefit levels but relative to the "current benefit schedule" in the distant future. If one accepts this basis of comparison, then one must apply it *consistently*—which in this case would mean finding that the president's proposals would *reduce* federal debt by trillions over that same time span.

Sometimes, however, critics simultaneously employed two inconsistent baselines to attack President Bush's proposals—that is, using the *current-revenues* baseline to charge that his proposal would increase federal debt while using a different *current-benefit-schedule* baseline to allege that his proposal would cut benefits. Shifting between baselines produces nonsensical results—in this case, the nonsensical result that the proposal would *both* increase debt and cut benefits over the long term. Depending on one's basis of comparison, one could self-consistently make one charge or the other, but not both (figure 12.9).

As we saw in chapter 4, there are legitimate arguments for opposing value choices: on the one hand, for constraining the growth of costs, and on the other, for raising system revenues. An honest assessment of alternative approaches, however, requires a self-consistent frame of reference as well as an acknowledgement of the trade-offs involved with each choice.

FIGURE 12.9   Comparing Reforms to Current Law

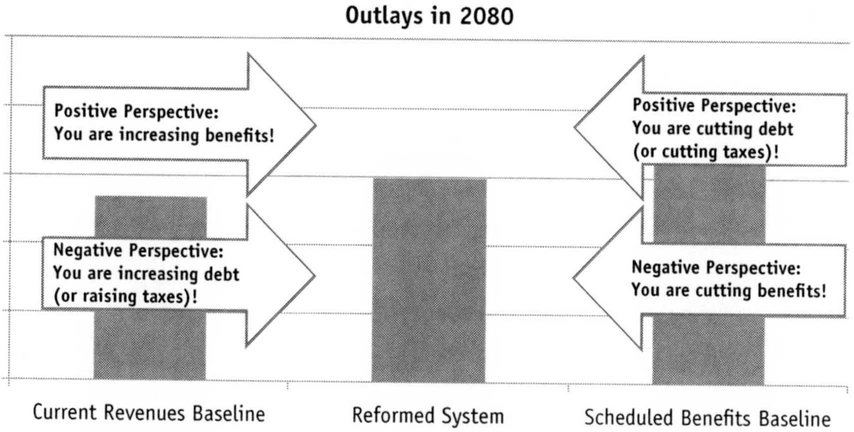

Outlays in 2080

Positive Perspective:
You are increasing benefits!

Positive Perspective:
You are cutting debt
(or cutting taxes)!

Negative Perspective:
You are increasing debt
(or raising taxes)!

Negative Perspective:
You are cutting benefits!

Current Revenues Baseline   Reformed System   Scheduled Benefits Baseline

SOURCE: Based on data from the 2005 Trustees' report.

To justify comparisons of the president's proposals *not* with current levels, but instead to a far higher level of future benefits that the current system cannot pay, there needs to be a witting embrace of far higher future tax burdens. Referring blandly to the "current benefit structure" does not convey a clear sense of this trade-off. Indeed, it obscures it.

Another criticism of "progressive indexing" is that it would adversely affect the benefits not only of high-income Americans, but also those of modest income. Again, there are legitimate and less legitimate ways to express this concern.

Progressive indexing would slow the rate of growth of benefits for the upper 70 percent of the lifetime wage spectrum, while providing everyone with benefit growth equal to or higher than inflation. It is legitimate to argue that benefit changes should be confined to a *smaller* number of workers—*if* it is also acknowledged that we would then need to raise taxes for a *large* number of workers. It should not, however, be implied that a benefit change could be easily implemented to achieve a comparable amount of fiscal progress while leaving these "middle-class" workers untouched.

Some numbers help to demonstrate the point. Roughly 26 percent of scheduled benefits exceed projected tax revenues over the long term.[5] If solvency is to be achieved by constraining cost growth, the minimum number of individuals affected would be at least 15 percent—and that only if we were willing to completely cut off benefits for millions of Americans who have paid into the system all of their working lives.

This, of course, is highly unlikely. Consider that the so-called "$58,000 worker" cited above was actually in the top 15 percent of the lifetime wage distribution.[6] We know, based on the criticisms cited earlier, that few would support reducing this person's benefits to zero. If we're not willing to cut off such workers' benefits entirely, then we need to spread the burdens among a larger group.

Once we acknowledge practical limits on how much our political system is willing to change benefits, then we are in a box in which any solution based on cost restraint will affect the vast majority of Americans one way or the other. Let's look at the numbers to see the contours of this box:

- Progressive indexing as described here (exempting the bottom 30 percent of workers and the disabled from changes) would close *70 percent* of long-term annual shortfalls under 2005 projections.[7]
- Include the disabled in the progressive formula, and progress climbs to *81 percent* of projected shortfalls filled.[8]
- Increase the number of those totally exempted from benefit changes to the bottom 40 percent, and we're down to *68 percent* of the annual cash flow problem solved.[9]
- Exempt the bottom 50 percent and we're not even close—only *51 percent,* or roughly half, of the cash flow problem solved.[10]

In other words, if we want to affect only half of the population, then we're only going to solve about half of the problem, unless we are willing to also start considering more drastic measures such as actually *reducing* benefits relative to inflation or severing the contribution-benefit link altogether.

Thus, the criticism of progressive indexing's impact on middle-income Americans isn't really about *who* is affected; the middle class will participate in any solution based on containing costs. The legitimate counter of a critic, therefore, would be not to imply that middle-income people can be exempted but to argue instead that they should be assessed higher *taxes.*

This is a perfectly legitimate position to hold—but again, we must be forthright about what such tax increases can actually accomplish and how many people would be affected.

For example, one of the most popular ideas among those who want to raise taxes is to lift the cap on wages subject to the Social Security tax. This cap is currently $106,800. In 2005, it was $90,000. Many have suggested raising this cap (which now captures about 84 percent of all wages earned nationally) so that it covers 90 percent of total national wages. This would mean raising the cap to about $180,000. It is sometimes represented that this would solve a large portion of the shortfall—roughly 43 percent under those same 2005 estimates[11]—while affecting very few workers.

These numbers, however, don't tell the whole story. They assume that the government always saves and earns interest on all Social Security tax revenue that it collects. As we have seen, this is not how the government operates. The figures above disguise the fact that the system would still face substantial annual deficits going forward.

In actuality, raising the cap in this way would only reduce Social Security's long-term cash imbalances by a minor amount—roughly 10–15 percent, depending on the year the estimate was made.[12]

A glance at figure 12.10 shows that raising the cap on taxable wages in this way would not come close to solving the problem—or even half of it. The large gap between the gray and black lines would be simply replaced by a nearly-as-large gap between the dashed and dotted lines. This doesn't necessarily mean that we shouldn't raise the cap; it does mean that it doesn't get us very far in solving the problem.

Moreover, the number of workers affected would *not* be insignificant. Remember, Social Security benefit levels are determined based on

FIGURE 12.10 Projected Social Security Costs/Revenues After Raising the Cap on Taxable Wages

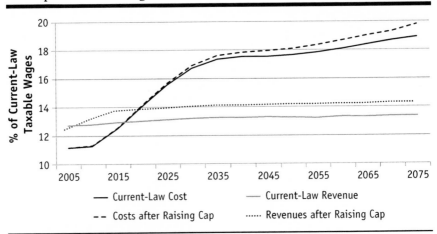

SOURCE: Based on data published online by the SSA Office of the Actuary, 2005.

lifetime wages, not annual wages. So, in order to get an apples-to-apples comparison between benefit changes and tax changes, we need to look at tax effects on a lifetime basis as well.

Although it is often noted that only 6 percent of workers have wages income above the cap in any particular year, *22 percent* of workers have income above the cap at some point in their careers, and thus would pay higher taxes even as we solve only a small fraction of the shortfall.[13]

Thus, there is almost no way to avoid affecting large numbers of workers in a complete Social Security solution. We have examined progressive benefit changes that would affect 70 percent of workers while fixing 70 percent of the problem, as well as changes that would affect roughly 50 percent of workers while fixing 50 percent of the problem. We have examined progressive tax changes that would affect 22 percent of workers while fixing about 10 percent of the problem. One needn't spend a great deal of time on these calculations before concluding that any fix that repairs 100 percent of the fiscal problem, while leaving the contribution-benefit link intact, will inevitably affect a solid majority of workers—including the middle class.

If definitions are not consistently applied, one can create a gross misimpression of the ease of leaving the majority of workers on Social Security untouched. One columnist, for example, referred to progressive indexing as a "gut punch to the middle class,"[14] implying that it would gratuitously target middle-income earners so as to leave the rich untroubled. Earlier, we cited the example of the charge being made that "workers earning (only) $58,000 a year would be hit with a 42 percent benefit cut for survivors and retirees."[15]

Partisans' glib reliance on such figures often misleadingly conflates the distinct concepts of annual income and lifetime income. "Raising taxes on those earning more than $90,000 a year" sounds to the naïve ear like it will affect fewer workers than "cutting benefits for those earning a mere $58,000." But actually, that's not the case. There are actually *more* workers with annual wages at some point above $90,000 than there are with "lifetime average earnings" (at least as defined in their Social Security records) of $58,000.[16]

In sum, one can fairly find fault with progressive indexing's impact upon the "middle class" if one is willing to put forward an alternative solution that fixes a comparable amount of the fiscal problem while leaving the middle class unaffected. Thus far, there has been an utter absence of such plans.[17]

Another concern expressed about progressive indexing was that it would make Social Security *too* progressive—that is, that by allowing a faster rate of benefit growth for lower-income individuals it would undermine the support of higher-income workers for Social Security. Some noted that if progressive indexation were carried out in perpetuity, it would lead ultimately—after more than a century—to the upper 70 percent of the wage distribution receiving the same benefits regardless of their contributions, in effect severing the contribution-benefit link.

As we saw in Chapter 6, there are different opinions on whether Social Security's current level of progressivity should be *increased* or merely *maintained*. President Bush's proposal put him on the side of *increasing* progressivity—tilting the system's benefits more toward the poor. Some on the right believed that Social Security was already progressive enough and should not be made more so. Some on the left worried that a more progressive benefit structure would undermine support from higher earners. And many on both sides (including President Bush) wanted the system's contribution-benefit link to be preserved.

These are important concerns. To properly weigh them, the following points need to be borne in mind.

The first point is very simple: do we make the system more progressive? Yes or no?

If we say yes, then higher earners will take a bigger hit as we restore solvency. If we say no, then the burdens of achieving solvency must be spread throughout the entire wage spectrum—including low earners.

Either choice is defensible. It is *not* possible, however, to hold lower-wage workers harmless *without* requiring higher earners to take a disproportionate hit in the course of achieving solvency.

Also, we need to be consistent about it. Sometimes the same quarters attacked progressive indexing both for being too progressive[18] and for not being progressive enough.[19] It's not reasonable to attack the proposal from both directions at the same time; this leaves no place to go to arrive at a "better" proposal. As a longtime senator was fond of saying, "Don't tell me what *not* to do. Tell me what *to* do."[20]

It is correct to note that, if carried out ad infinitum, progressive indexing would ultimately lead to a flat benefit received by all of the top 70 percent of the wage spectrum. But progressive indexing (especially if combined with other measures to ensure solvency) need not be carried out ad infinitum to keep the system in balance. In fact, the proposal's author, Robert Pozen, subsequently suggested "turning off" progressive indexing by a certain date specifically to avoid this outcome.

Finally, progressive indexing was also criticized for being poorly designed to impose the largest benefit "cuts" when least needed from a fiscal perspective.[21] Specifically, the argument was made that "if real wage growth were stronger in future decades than the trustees currently project, progressive price indexing would result in deeper benefit cuts, even as the Social Security shortfall was getting smaller on its own."

This criticism reflects at least two misunderstandings of Social Security finances.

First, saying that progressive indexing results in "deeper cuts" in a faster-growth scenario is a distortion of perspective. It's not that progressive indexing would provide for *slower* benefit growth in a higher-wage-growth scenario; it's that *wage-indexation* would provide for *faster* benefit growth. Benefits under progressive indexation wouldn't actually be "cut more" in a faster-growth scenario, they would actually grow more rapidly. Saying that progressive indexation would result in "deeper benefit cuts" in this scenario reflects some confusion as to how each line would move in an alternate faster-growth scenario. See the figure 12.11.

The other point of confusion is that the present-law Social Security structural shortfall does *not* truly get smaller by itself in a faster-growth

FIGURE 12.11   Under Both Wage Indexing and Progressive Indexing, Benefits Grow Faster as Wages Grow Faster

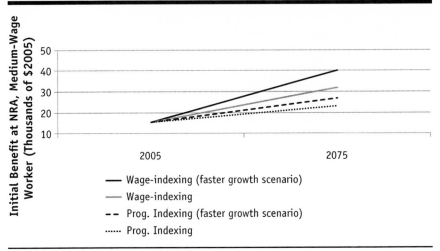

Source: Based on data from the 2005 Trustees' report with additional calculations by the author.

scenario, as the Biggs-Gokhale paper shows. The shortfall simply seems smaller largely because, in a faster growth scenario, the higher taxes would arrive before the higher benefits are owed.

This timing lag between faster revenue growth and faster benefit growth would push out the projected insolvency date somewhat, thus reducing the seventy-five-year actuarial imbalance but not the total structural imbalance. Thus, it's not actually the case that the total Social Security shortfall would be growing smaller of its own accord in a scenario in which progressive indexing produces more savings. That is an accounting illusion fed by reliance on incomplete metrics.

This all being said, there are many legitimate concerns that could be expressed about progressive indexing. A better-founded criticism of progressive indexing could have been offered but rarely was: that the re-indexing would produce cost savings too gradually.

In the near term, when payments to the baby boomers were causing costs to spike upward, progressive indexing would produce only modest savings. Over the long term, when costs would largely stabilize even under current law, progressive indexing would continue to worsen returns for later generations for as long as it continued. One could argue instead for a proposal that saved the same total amount of money but saved more in the near term, less in the long term, distributing the burdens of change more equitably across generations.

Perhaps the reason this criticism was not voiced more aggressively was that many critics were downplaying the need not only for progressive indexing but for other cost-containment measures; in this context, it might have been unnatural for them to argue for *additional* near-term cost-saving measures. Looking objectively at progressive indexing's technical imperfections, however, this probably would have been a more compelling criticism than most actually offered.

Regardless, President Bush's "progressive indexing" proposal was robustly debated with respect to important and sincerely held value judgments. Foremost among them were the appropriate amount of cost restraint and the appropriate level of system progressivity. Arguments on all sides of this question varied in the firmness of their foundations.

Before we leave our account of the 2005 debate over progressive indexing, there is one thing we need to remember: much of the progressive indexing debate was not about progressive indexing itself but about the terms that will be used to understand *any* proposal to slow the growth of system costs.

Look at where we are today and where we are heading. In 2009, a medium-wage earner retiring at the normal retirement age received a benefit of $17,600[22] and it cost 12.35 percent of worker wages to provide full benefits to all beneficiaries.[23] In 2085, a medium-wage worker retiring at the normal retirement age is being told to expect a benefit of $38,560 (in today's dollars); it would cost 17.78 percent of each worker's wages in that year to fund all such benefits.

If we instead applied progressive indexing, the retirement benefits of a medium-wage worker might rise only from about $17,600 today to about $26,530 in 2085, and the cost of supporting those benefits might rise to about 14.1 percent of workers' wages.[24] Would we say that medium-wage worker benefits have risen 50 percent by 2085 (relative to the 2009 level) or that they have been cut by 31 percent (relative to the benefit schedule requiring higher taxes)? See figure 12.12.

A 31 percent benefit cut, obviously, sounds terrible. Try to find support for that in a public survey. If that's how we frame the debate, then almost certainly the political dynamic would be to try to avoid such drastic "cuts"—and thus push far higher tax burdens onto our grandchildren.

If we as a society knowingly approve of this outcome, fine. If, however, we arrive at this outcome primarily because the public wrongly believes that reform would actually *reduce* benefits below current levels, and doesn't accurately understand the costs of paying for higher future benefits, that is not fine at all. We need a debate that enables the public to make an informed choice about where it wants to go.

Thus, this is as much about how we define the terms of debate as it is about the specifics of progressive indexing. Policy advocates know this, which is why tremendous energy is often expended to define the terms of debate so that they lead inevitably to a particular result.[25]

FIGURE 12.12   A 50% Increase or a 31% Cut?

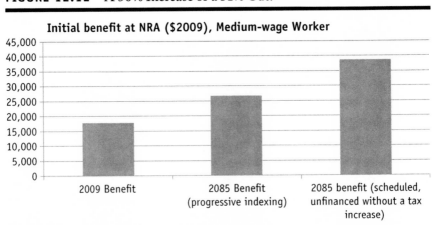

SOURCE: Based on data from the 2005 Trustees' report.

Progressive Indexing and Personal Accounts:
The Combined Effects on Workers

President Bush proposed two components of Social Security reform in 2005: progressive indexing and personal accounts.

Sometimes the merits of these ideas were debated separately. Sometimes the debate concerned their combined effects. Considering them separately:

Progressive indexing would slow the growth of benefits relative to wage-indexing—though still allowing a rate of benefit growth exceeding what currently projected revenues can fund. Thus, additional measures would be needed to fully close the fiscal gap.

The effect of *personal accounts* would be to shift a portion of projected revenues *and benefits* away from the traditional system (and into the accounts). This affects both the government and the individual.

For the government: the accounts would take spending money *away* from the government in the near term while *reducing* the amount of benefits that need be paid by taxing workers in the future.

For the individual: the worker with an account would direct some payroll taxes to it in the near term and thus put *less* than the full 12.4 percent payroll tax into the traditional system. In the long term, the worker will get *some* (new) benefits from the accounts, while getting *less* from the traditional system than if he'd declined a personal account.

So, what happens when we put these two effects together?

For the *government*: In the near-term, the fiscal effects of progressive indexing and of personal accounts would run counter to one another, with personal accounts being the bigger effect. Progressive indexing would save money, but very little, in the near term. This is because current and near-term retirees would not be affected while those coming afterward would be affected only very gradually. Meanwhile, however, personal accounts *would* have a significant near-term effect, taking money out of the government's spending pool and sheltering it in personally owned savings. So, in the very near term, the accounts would increase the government's budgetary pressure while progressive indexing would relieve it only a little.

In the long term, both personal accounts and progressive indexing would reduce the government's spending obligations. With each passing year, progressive indexing produces more savings (unless it is turned off). At the same time, the government balance sheet would benefit more and more from no longer having to pay the growing portion of benefits previously pre-funded through personal accounts.

In sum, therefore, the combination of progressive indexing and personal accounts would *increase* pressure on the federal budget in the near term and significantly *decrease* it in the long term. The quantitative analyses of supporters and critics alike agree on this.

The Bush administration did not deem the combination of progressive indexing and personal accounts alone to be an adequate answer to Social Security's shortfall; thus, looking only at these two measures provides a distorted and incomplete picture of the fiscal effects of the administration's vision for comprehensive reform.

We can, however, get a sense of the relative magnitude and time flow of only the two provisions described above. SSA projected that the combination of progressive indexing and personal accounts would have a positive effect on federal cash flow by 2032, with the net improvement growing significantly each year thereafter.[26] (A complete solvency plan would likely reach this point earlier, for example by 2029.)

These net fiscal effects (for the government) were a hotly debated controversy, to which we will return in the next subsection. Here we will simply note that contrasting conclusions depend significantly upon the metrics employed, on conflicting assumptions about how the accounts would be financed, and on whether progressive indexing was enacted in combination with other solvency measures.

Here, we will first turn to the question of the combined effects of progressive indexing and personal accounts upon the individual worker.

For the worker, progressive indexing would not have affected current or near-term retirees. Its effects would have been greatest for the youngest workers—the retirees of the future. Relative to wage indexing, progressive indexing would be a slower rate of benefit growth, resulting as well in a slower growth in tax burdens. The effects of the change would grow the further out one looks, affecting younger generations the most.

A medium-wage worker retiring last year might receive a benefit of $17,600 under current law. Under progressive indexing, this wouldn't have changed. In 2085, wage-indexing would have scheduled a benefit of over $38,000 (in 2009 dollars) for a medium-wage worker, as well as imposing an effective tax burden of nearly 18 percent. Progressive indexing, by contrast, would promise that worker a benefit of over $26,000 (in 2009 dollars) and impose an effective tax burden of closer to 14 percent (figure 12.13).

So we see the effects of progressive indexing are nonexistent for the retirees of today, but very significant for the retirees (and taxpaying workers) of 2085.

Now consider the personal account. The personal account's total effect on benefits is somewhat in the eye of the beholder. Let's consider the example of the Pozen proposal for a personal account (as distinct from the Bush proposal). For the medium-wage earner above, we would

FIGURE 12.13   Benefits Under Progressive Indexing + Personal Accounts

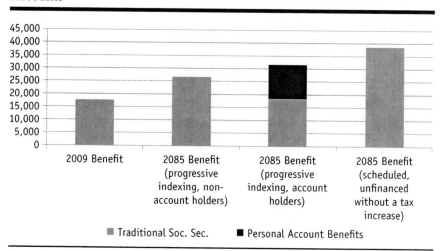

SOURCE: Based on data from the 2005 Trustees' report and SSA OACT memo on the Pozen proposal. Updated for the Bush administration's lower benefit offset rate and 2009 benefit projections.

predict that the "expected yield" on the accounts would result in a total benefit of close to $31,000—about $18,500 from the traditional system and the remaining $12,500 from the account.[27]

These numbers are not presented to imply that these benefits can be precisely predicted. They are instead presented to illuminate conflicting perspectives in the debate over benefit levels. Personal account advocates would point out that expected total benefits would go *up* for those who opted for the accounts—from about $26,500 to $31,000. A personal account opponent, however, would note that this is only a *projection* and argue that it neglects the element of *risk* in the personal account portfolio. (Many personal account proponents would also acknowledge this.)

Many on both sides would therefore argue that the true benefit value, even for the account holder, would be the "risk-adjusted" benefit of $26,500. This figure represents the benefit that the account holder can receive with certainty (by investing in Treasury bonds).

Some personal account opponents would go further and note that there is some risk that the accounts could produce a benefit *smaller* than $26,500—if the holder invests in risk-bearing securities and if the returns are less than the Treasury bond rate. (In response, a personal account proponent would argue that the likelihood of stock investments, for example, returning less than a Treasury bond rate over a full forty-five-year working career is small based on historical experience, even with the recent downturn.)

At the extreme end of the discussion would be personal account opponents who would argue the proposal would "cut" benefits for account holders all the way to $18,500. In their minds, the only "true" benefits are those that come from the traditional Social Security system. This is the implication behind oft-repeated statements such as, "If you cut benefits to fix Social Security finances, and then divert additional revenue to personal accounts, you'll have to cut benefits further to make up that lost revenue."

This argument is problematic at best. It is certainly valid to note that, in this example, the personal account benefits might carry a level of investment risk higher than the traditional base benefit of $18,500. It is misleading, however, to ignore the personal account benefit altogether and to say starkly that the personal account itself has caused this individual an "additional benefit cut." At the very least, the "risk-adjusted" value of the personal account holdings should always be included in any estimate of total benefits.

Opponents of personal accounts consistently treat the revenues directed to personal accounts as a real-world phenomenon with real-world fiscal effects. Whenever that is done, the benefits from the accounts must be counted, too. Analytically, it makes no sense to count the revenues invested in the accounts but not the benefits that they would fund. (Moreover, doing so predetermines the policy answer; from that distorted analytical vantage point it would never make sense to invest *any* projected revenues in personal accounts, no matter how generous the benefits they provide.)

Taken together, we can summarize the opposing perspectives on the combined effects of progressive indexing and personal accounts as follows. Some opponents might refer to *both* the progressive indexing and the personal accounts as "cutting benefits" because they make comparisons to a higher "scheduled benefit" amount and because they exclude the personal account benefit. Proponents would instead refer to progressive indexing as a responsible rate of benefit growth and would argue that the accounts likely *increase* total benefit expectations. Such conflicting perspectives apply to many proposals to combine personal accounts with traditional solvency solutions.

Now let's turn to the specifics of President Bush's personal account proposal. He embraced larger personal accounts than in the original Pozen plan. Although a phase-in schedule was never specified, it was stated that ultimately the policy goal was to enable all workers, regardless of income, to invest 4 percent of their wages in the accounts.[28]

Obviously, if workers invested *more* of their wages in larger personal accounts, then they would receive *more* of their benefits from the accounts and *less* from the traditional system than in the example we gave above.

Now consider how conflicting perspectives would view this change. Personal account proponents would view the larger accounts as a good thing because they would increase the total median expected benefits that workers can receive.

Personal account opponents, by contrast, would *not* derive solace from a higher expected (risk-bearing) investment but instead would view the smaller proportion of benefits coming from the traditional system with greater alarm.

In the particular case of President Bush's proposal, a further concern was raised. Some critics noted that it might eventually be possible for some higher-income workers to receive *no* benefits from the traditional system, drawing benefits only from the personal accounts.

While this might seem improbable upon first hearing, remember our explanation in chapter 6 of how it might come to pass. The majority of the Social Security taxes of high earners pays for the benefits of previous generations as well as provides a safety net for those less well off. It is not at all out of the question that a personal account accepting 4 percent of a higher-income worker's wages would be sufficient to fund the full benefits he expects to receive from traditional Social Security (especially if progressive indexing is adopted).

Calculations performed within the administration showed that in practice only a very small percentage of beneficiaries might be at risk of having their traditional benefits "zeroed out" by personal accounts, with most of these instances arising only after several decades.

That being said, this criticism was a legitimate concern—and it concerned policymakers on both sides. It concerned the Bush administration because the president's goal was to have personal accounts as a *supplement* for traditional Social Security benefits, not as a complete replacement for them. It concerned critics to the administration's left because it meant that the personal accounts of the highest earners might not "pay for themselves" on the government's long-term balance sheet. It also concerned analysts with various policy leanings, especially when it became better understood that the phenomenon might arise in other quirky circumstances (such as unusual marital histories), in addition to the very highest earners.

It is worth stressing that in the big picture, this phenomenon would play a small role at most. One's picture of the plan's overall fiscal effects would be affected far more by technical assumptions about discount rates and the political economy of government spending decisions than by this issue.

That being said, the criticism was a legitimate one. If a detailed long-term proposal had ultimately been presented, it would likely have needed to contain either a provision to prevent this "zero-out" effect or a provision to limit the accounts of the highest earners to something less than 4 percent of wages.

Progressive Indexing and Personal Accounts: The Combined Effects on Government Finances

The combined fiscal effects of comprehensive reforms including personal accounts were hotly contested in such detail that some generalizations are necessary to provide an efficient treatment of the 2005 debate. We will therefore briefly mention the respective points on which reform proponents and opponents agreed and disagreed, and then explore those points of contention more fully.

Table 12.1 may be useful in illuminating the points of agreement and disagreement.

TABLE 12.1   Effect of Reform Elements on Social Security/Government Finances

Provision	Near-Term	Long-Term	Overall
Progressive indexing	Small (positive)	Positive	Positive
Personal accounts	Negative	Positive	Disputed
Combination	Negative	Positive	Positive

The typical reader may be surprised to see the many areas of agreement on the table. We will substantiate the chart's characterizations on the following pages.

In addition to the points of agreement and dispute listed on this table, there was another: whether it was fair to judge President Bush's reform initiative *only* by the combined effects of the partial proposal of progressive indexing and personal accounts.

Neither the Bush administration nor its critics saw progressive indexing and personal accounts taken together as sufficient to repair Social Security's finances. The president did not present them as a complete proposal for Social Security solvency. Instead, as we have seen, he sought for tactical reasons to maintain flexibility on the components of a complete solvency solution, embracing progressive indexing to set a direction for that discussion.

Obviously, any fiscal analysis of a *partial* solvency solution will be less favorable than one that analyzes a full comprehensive plan of the kind the president favored but was unable to negotiate with Congress.

To the extent that we want to examine only the *partial* solution of progressive indexing, figures 12.14 and 12.15 may be useful. Figure 12.14 shows the 2005 projections for "current law." The black line shows the unsustainable projected growth of Social Security spending, the gray line system revenues. The chart shows a brief period of surpluses lasting through 2016 and then yawning deficits thereafter.

Progressive indexing as designed by Robert Pozen[29] would change that graph to look like figure 12.15.

We can see that the progressive indexing shrinks the long-term shortfalls but does not eliminate them. Now let's look at the Pozen proposal, including his proposed personal accounts (shifting to 2004 assumptions, under which the integrated Pozen proposal was scored).

We can see from figure 12.16 the combined effects described in our table. In the near term, the accounts would reduce federal revenues and thus cut into near-term surpluses. In the long term, annual operations would be improved, even relative to progressive indexing alone. (In an apples-to-apples comparison under 2004 projections, 2032 would be the

FIGURE 12.14   Social Security Costs and Revenues: 2005 Projections

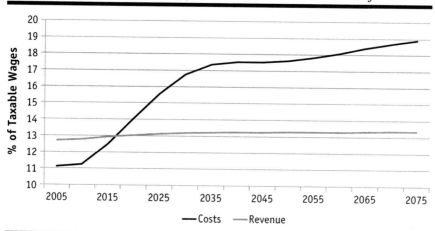

SOURCE: Based on data from the 2005 Trustees' report.

FIGURE 12.15   Progressive Indexing Alone: 2005 Projections

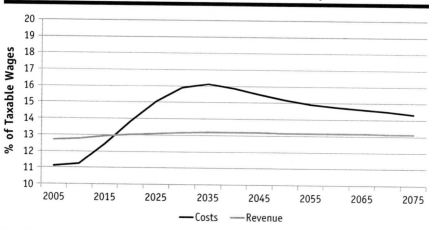

SOURCE: Based on data from the 2005 Trustees' report.

FIGURE 12.16   Progressive Indexing + Accounts: 2004 Projections

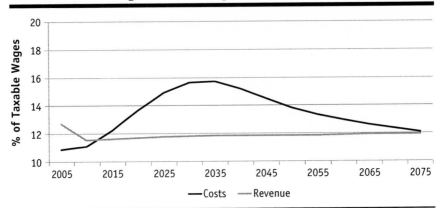

SOURCE: Based on data from the 2004 Trustees' report.

date at which the new system's annual cash flows permanently become more manageable than under current law.)

This brings us back to our table and to our characterizations of the conflicting viewpoints of reform proponents and opponents.

Both sides generally acknowledged the fiscal effects of progressive indexing in isolation: very small up front, larger over time, but always improving the fiscal balance sheet.

As for personal accounts, proponents as well as opponents generally acknowledged that they would increase pressure on the federal budget in the near term. Both sides also acknowledged that (as proposed) they would reduce the system's long-term annual benefit payment obligations in the manner shown on the last graph.

The disagreements were on the following points.

First, the *magnitude* of the near-term pressure: Opponents saw—and portrayed—the near-term budgetary pressures arising from personal accounts as much larger than proponents saw them.

Second, the *debt* effects: Opponents assumed that all investments in personal accounts would be financed by debt. Proponents did not. This led to conflicting interpretations of the accounts' effects in the aggregate—even over the long term, by which time the accounts would clearly reduce annual federal benefit-payment obligations.

Third, the appropriate *measure* of net aggregate effects averaged over time: Opponents generally relied upon a measure of actuarial balance that would find the personal accounts in isolation to have an adverse impact. Proponents believed that this particular measure was biased against personal accounts (among other flaws) and that better measures showed the accounts to be a net fiscal positive in the aggregate.

The first two differences here are interrelated. One reason that personal account opponents saw the near-term fiscal effects of personal accounts as being so large was that they assumed, implicitly, that they would be debt-financed. As a result, they added large and growing interest service to the "transition cost" of personal accounts.

Whether personal accounts were to be financed with debt is an important issue, though the assumption of debt-financing is clearly a departure from how government programs are typically scored: for example, the $862 billion stimulus package enacted early in 2009 was entirely debt-financed but the costs of such debt are not included in the $862 billion figure commonly used to describe it. Obviously, if one compounded the costs of such debt over decades, the cost of the stimulus package would appear to be much larger.

In addition, many criticisms of personal accounts used nominal/current dollars in finding a large "transition cost."[30] This sometimes led to confusion when comparisons were made with the size of the current-law shortfall, usually expressed in "present value" dollars. (Present-value dollars are discounted by a rate of interest above inflation.) One legislator was heard saying in one policy meeting, "The president wants to take on a transition cost of $2 trillion over ten years just to fix a problem that is only $3.5 trillion over seventy-five years!" —apparently not realizing that the two figures were completely incomparable because they used different types of dollars. If the standard of nominal-dollars-plus-interest were applied to the current-law shortfall, it would stretch into the *hundreds* of trillions over the next seventy-five years.

Finally, some (but not all) opponents of personal accounts also employed a "100 percent participation" assumption for the accounts in contrast with the SSA Actuary's assumption of two-thirds participation. A CBO analysis later found a one-third participation rate to be more likely.[31] The assumption of 100 percent participation significantly increases estimates of the near-term budgetary pressure created by the accounts.

Opponents of personal accounts, based on these techniques, charged that they would lead to a massive increase in federal debt. This charge cuts to the heart of a fundamental analytical difference between personal account proponents and opponents—that is, whether Social Security money would be more likely to be saved if it were not kept within the pool of available federal spending money. In dissecting this particular controversy, it is vitally important to understand the difference between an analytical *finding* and an *assumption*.

Current actuarial methods implicitly *assume* that Social Security money is, in effect, saved. Whenever the government collects a Social Security surplus, the Trust Fund is credited with that surplus and with the interest that it "earns" regardless of what the government actually does with the money. Personal account advocates, obviously, disagree with the assumptions underlying that methodology.

As we have seen, academic literature has found that the presence of Social Security surpluses has indeed fueled *additional* federal spending relative to that which would have occurred in the absence of the surpluses. This is essentially a finding that the government would have spent *less* had the Social Security surpluses not been available.

The current actuarial method, however, *assumes* that any redirection of federal revenues—whether to personal accounts or anywhere else—will leave government spending unchanged and that the government will engage in additional borrowing to make up the difference. Again, this is an *assumption*; it is not an analytical *finding*.

Obviously, if one *assumes* that any investment in personal accounts causes an increase in debt, then this tilts the analytical playing field considerably and undercuts perhaps the primary fiscal argument for personal accounts. Indeed, it basically predetermines the outcome of the fiscal analysis.

As it happens, the Bush administration did *not* propose to finance personal accounts with debt. So many papers were released projecting a mountain of sobering fiscal effects based on the assumption of debt-financing that this will no doubt come as a surprise to many readers. But the Bush administration actually proposed to offset the "transition cost" of personal accounts over its five-year budget window.

The administration had set a target of cutting the deficit in half over five years, and it fit the proposed near-term "transition cost" of personal accounts within that preexisting target. In effect, this meant that other spending had to be reduced to pay for the accounts up front.[32]

Offsetting the up-front "transition cost" of the personal accounts in its budget meant that the administration had to make some tough choices. One of them was to make the personal accounts much smaller than they might otherwise have been; the administration chose (also for administrative reasons) to phase in the accounts gradually by the ages of participating workers. This phase-in reduced the size of the investments requiring offsets in the near-term.

Critics of the administration's approach might validly point out that the administration left open the question of how the accounts would be financed in future years, when they were fully phased in and larger. This is a fair concern. This does not change, however, the fact that analyses based on the *assumption* that the accounts would be wholly debt-financed are inconsistent with what the administration actually proposed. Such an assumption thus should not have been the basis for hyperbolic estimates of the large debt the accounts would supposedly have created.

Finally, even if every dollar in personal accounts *did* result in an additional dollar of publicly held debt, the net effect on total saving would be zero (the additional saving in personal accounts would be exactly offset by additional publicly held debt of the federal government). That is, the *worst*-case outcome would be one in which the overall savings/debt picture was unchanged.

This is very important to bear in mind, because it was often forgotten when criticisms of personal accounts were voiced. The sequence of the analysis was something like this:

1. It was proposed that $X be saved in personal accounts.
2. Some were concerned that if $X were saved in personal accounts, the government would borrow $X to make up the difference.
3. This would undo any gains of saving $X, because $X in saving would be offset by an increase of $X in other debt.

But sometimes, one side of this picture was forgotten altogether. The concern that there *might* be an increase of $X in debt was a result of the fact that $X *would* be saved elsewhere. The worst-case outcome here is a wash; no net effect on savings. If the government spent *any* less as a result of the $X being directed into savings, then the overall fiscal picture would have improved.

A personal analogy might be helpful here. Suppose you have been spending all of your money, and you decide that you need to start saving. So you go down to your bank to set up an automatic savings program, and you plan to contribute $100 a month to it.

Is that a wise thing to do? Most people would think that it is. The argument of personal account opponents, however, was equivalent to saying that since you were spending all of your money before, and since you were proposing to save $100 a month now, you'd go out and borrow $100 to make up the difference. And so they said: "Don't do it! You'll wind up awash in debt!"

Obviously, this argument neglects the fact that at *worst*, you'd be no worse off than you are now. But perhaps more importantly, it neglects the fact that you are intending to alter your spending behavior to allow for that $100 to be saved. Even if you hadn't fully specified how yet, most financial advisors will tell you that the discipline of automatically saving $100 a month will be good for your finances because you'll be less likely to otherwise spend that $100.

Another analytical difference between account advocates and opponents had to do with the scorekeeping arcana. Specifically, if we *assume* that personal accounts are debt-financed, then:

- They will appear to *worsen* system finances when using the post-1988 definition of "seventy-five-year actuarial balance."
- They will leave system finances *mostly unchanged* (aside from small effects from administrative costs and inheritances) if we instead look at the *total* system balance under post-1988 methods.
- They would *improve* system finances if we measure the *total* system balance using the pre-1988 "average cost" actuarial method.

This is difficult to explain succinctly without delving deeply into dreary methodological details. The key factors to understand are as follows.

First, the qualitatively different results under these different metrics arise *only* if the accounts are debt-financed. The accounts (even taken alone) improve the overall fiscal picture if they build saving where the Trust Fund does not.

Why does taking a seventy-five-year view of the program bias the analysis? Let's run the experiment and see. Suppose that a young worker chooses to shift some money into a personal account today; at the same time, his scheduled traditional Social Security benefit is changed by an equal (and offsetting) amount in present value. If we only look at the system's finances over five years and also ignore the amount of "pre-funding" set aside, we'll see only one side of this exchange: we'll see the "loss" of system revenue redirected to the account, but not the fact that a portion of future unfunded obligations has been eliminated through pre-funding. This will make it appear that total system finances have been *worsened* even though they've remained basically unchanged.

But whether we look at the system over five years, ten years, or seventy-five years, we'll always have the same analytical problem. For millions of workers, we'll see the effects of shifting their tax revenues to the accounts but not the fiscal improvement arising from pre-funding some of their benefits. In order to see the *total* effects of the reform, we need to look at *both* sides of the equation for every worker.

Another personal illustration may be helpful in understanding this analytical issue. Ask yourself: Is it helpful or harmful for you, starting at the age of twenty-five, to put $100 a month aside in retirement saving, or nothing? We could look at it in either of two ways. One way would be to assume that it is harmful because you're out $100 each month for the next forty years. That puts more pressure on your personal budget for four decades. In fact, it will be years further into retirement before you will have enjoyed as much spending money as you would have had all along by not saving.

The opposite way to look at it is to say: That's silly. You're not $100 "worse off" for forty years because you're *accumulating savings* to meet your future wants. So even if you have $100 less available each month for the next forty years, you're never truly worse off.

That's the basic analytical divide between personal account opponents and proponents. Opponents would say the system is worse off because there is less money otherwise available to spend in the near term. Proponents would say that's nonsense—that money didn't disappear, it's being amassed to fund future benefits. In fact, the system is *better* off because we're keeping that money from being spent.

Sometimes observers wonder why this issue exists, even as a scorekeeping phenomenon. Shouldn't everything come out the same, given that both the Trust Fund and the personal accounts are represented (at least on paper) to be forms of pre-funding? Why should one form of prefunding be better or worse than the other from a scorekeeping standpoint, if we assume that each is equally effective?

Part of the answer lies in the fact that the Trust Fund provides *general* funding authorization, not funding for a *specific individual*. Thus, every bond in the Trust Fund over seventy-five years is assumed to be available to fund *any* benefit claims that arise *within those seventy-five years*.

By contrast, *some* of the revenue invested in personal accounts within seventy-five years would go to pay benefits to some specific individuals *after* seventy-five years—and thus, such revenue is not available to fund benefits within the seventy-five-year window. Accordingly, a seventy-five-year-look at the system (or any time-limited period) causes the net effect of the personal accounts to appear negative.

Finally, we should note that the presumed fiscal effect of personal accounts depends as well upon the discount rate employed in our calculations. Recall that under the Bush administration proposal, the amount of future benefits pre-funded would be equal to the investment in the accounts times interest. Since this interest rate was the same as the discount rate assumed in the post-1988 actuarial method, the fiscal effects of the accounts would be roughly neutral over all time.[33]

Under the pre-1988 method, however, which measured Social Security shortfalls by the size of the tax rate on wages required to fund them, the accounts would have been a net *positive* for system finances over all time. This is because the administration's proposed account offset rate (the rate of cost savings) exceeded the implicit interest rate used in the pre-1988 methods.

This is a lot of technical information to jam into one chapter subsection. But we can summarize it fairly succinctly.

On the chart at the beginning of this chapter, we listed the net aggregate effect of personal accounts upon system finances as being "disputed" between personal account proponents and opponents. As we have seen, the disputes arise from different assumptions about:

- Whether the accounts are financed with debt
- Whether money in the Trust Fund is equally likely to be saved as money in personal accounts
- Whether one looks at both the revenue and spending sides for all generations studied
- The discount rate used to compare federal spending over long periods of time

About the combined effects of progressive indexing and personal accounts, however, there was no actual controversy: both personal account opponents and proponents agreed that the net effect would be *positive* for system finances as a whole.

This may come as a surprise, because the tenor of much criticism of the proposals seemed to imply that they would worsen system finances. But buried within the analyses even of the proposals' harshest critics were acknowledgements that the net effects of the proposals were to improve system finances.[34] The differences here, again, involved whether it was fair to judge the overall effects of reform only by certain partial specifics, when the president was on record as favoring a complete fix; and whether it made sense to judge the overall fiscal effects of reform solely via scorekeeping metrics seen as biased against personal accounts.

By using methods seen by advocates as biased against personal accounts, and by judging the effects of *partial* reforms, reform opponents depicted the president's proposals as fixing far less of the fiscal shortfall than reform proponents did. But they both agreed that the net fiscal effect of even the partial proposals would have been an improvement over current law.

A very important summary point should be made about these scorekeeping controversies. They are not *solely* about whether they shed a favorable or unfavorable light on personal accounts. One's view of these questions might well be overly influenced by one's position in the impassioned personal account debate. That would be a mistake.

As we detailed in chapter 3, a number of advisory councils and technical panels have unanimously found inadequacies in the traditional method of calculating Social Security's "seventy-five-year actuarial imbalance." They reached these conclusions not because they were carrying water for one reform approach or another, but simply from the standpoint of bookkeeping transparency, accuracy, and objectivity.

Were it not for the more recent, intense political debate about Social Security reform, it is likely that there would remain a wide consensus among Social Security experts that certain scorekeeping metrics are inadequate to portray either the course of current law or the effects of reform proposals.

As it has happened, however, the very methods previously found faulty by so many advisory councils and technical panels also happen to be the very methods that can be used most readily to place reform proposals—including personal accounts—in the most unflattering light. This inevitably creates a great temptation for reform opponents to lean heavily on methodologies that otherwise might well have been abandoned or, at the very least, highly qualified and surrounded by other more complete ones.

At the start of this chapter, we reviewed some of the absurdities that can arise from naively applying certain methodologies without adequate attention to whether they produce a sensible analytical result. It should not be necessary to sympathize with President Bush's policy views to be concerned about the application of scorekeeping methodologies that lead inevitably to flawed conclusions.

The reader is thus urged not to base an opinion of the scorekeeping controversies above upon his or her degree of instinctive sympathy or opposition to President Bush's proposals. All reform proposals—not only personal account proposals, and not only his—should be evaluated by scorekeeping methods that withstand skeptical analytical rigor.

Applying a Self-Consistent Measure of Federal Debt

Those who followed the Social Security debate of 2005 are well aware that the effect of reform on federal debt was an intensely debated issue. What is too little appreciated is how much of this debate turned on issues of self-consistency in defining the meaning and significance of federal debt.

What is the best measure of the federal debt? There are competing perspectives on this question.

There are basically two ways that one can look at the federal budget and the federal debt. One is the *unified budget* view and the other is the *on-budget* view.

The unified budget view is basically as follows: what matters is the *total* operations of the federal government: its total tax revenue, its total expenditures, and the amount of borrowing from the public that it must do to make up the difference.

In the unified budget view, it doesn't matter how much of the incoming tax revenue is divided between this tax source and that one, nor does it matter how much the government spends on this program in comparison with another. It doesn't matter how the government keeps its internal books and divides its accounts. It doesn't matter whether the government maintains separate "trust funds" nor whether IOU's are issued from one government account to the other. All that matters is the *total* amount of taxing and spending the government does, and thus the amount that it must borrow from external sources.

In the unified budget view, then, the meaningful definition of debt is the borrowing "from the public." What *doesn't* matter is the borrowing done between internal government accounts.

If the government were an individual, the "unified budget" view would hold that what matters is the total amount that the individual earns, the total amount the individual spends, and the amount of borrowing the individual must do to make up the difference. It doesn't matter whether the individual spent more on travel than on clothing this week and intends to spend more on clothing than on travel next week. Nor does it matter whether the individual keeps his own "travel account" and "clothing account" and writes down IOU's from one account to the other as his spending patterns vary. What matters is the individual's *total* creditworthiness as seen by other creditors and the amount of borrowing he must do from other people.

The contrasting view of the budget is the *on-budget* view. In this view, it *does* matter how the government's operations are subdivided, and it matters what is termed "on-budget" and "off-budget."

In the "on-budget" view, the debt that matters is not the debt borrowed from the public, but the *gross* debt—the total debt issued, not only to the public, but also between internal government accounts.

To understand the practical difference between the two perspectives, consider a situation in which the government has a $300 billion "on-budget" deficit and a $300 billion "off-budget" surplus.

In the unified budget view, the government as a whole is in balance; it does not have to go out to do any net borrowing in the private markets to run its operations.

In the "on-budget" view, by contrast, the government is running a $300 billion deficit, and this is in no way mitigated by the presence of a $300 billion off-budget surplus. In the "on-budget" view, the $300 billion on-budget deficit *does* add $300 billion to the debt—it just adds it in the form of debt held by another government account instead of debt borrowed from the public.

The point of this illustration is not that one view or the other is correct. It is reasonably fair to say that most federal budget experts believe that what is *economically* significant is the unified budget, and the debt held by the public. It is not economically significant how the government keeps its internal books; what is economically significant is the amount that the government must go out into the markets to borrow, competing with other borrowers for credit.

It is reasonable, however, to take the view that the "on-budget" approach has a *legal* significance. There may be no economic restriction on how much debt the government can issue between its own internal accounts, but the debt has a *legal* significance in representing the government's full faith and credit. The government could at any time issue $1 trillion in bonds to the Social Security Trust Fund, by fiat. It wouldn't have to go out into the markets to borrow this money—but it would represent a binding obligation.

It should also be noted that the debt subject to statutory limit is roughly the *gross* debt[35]—meaning debt held by government trust funds in addition to debt held by the public. Whenever such debt (including the Social Security Trust Fund debt) threatens to exceed this statutory cap, legislation is required to raise it.

Less important than the correctness of either budgetary view is the necessity of *self-consistency* in understanding the debate about debt and Social Security reform. Unfortunately, individuals on all sides of the Social Security debate are guilty of gross inconsistencies in how they discuss debt.

For our purposes, the critical difference between the unified budget view and the on-budget view of the Social Security Trust Fund is that the unified budget view does not regard debt held by the Trust Fund as economically significant, whereas the on-budget view does.

In the unified budget view, the Trust Fund merely represents the government's internal bookkeeping; it sheds no light on how much actual saving has been done, nor does it determine how much borrowing the government must do from the markets. Those things are determined solely by the *total* budget balance. In the on-budget view, however, the debt held by the Trust Fund is just as meaningful as debt held by the public.

Again, one can argue for either view. But each comes with its own set of logical implications. Table 12.2 summarizes some of them.

The unified budget view, as we've stated, does not regard the Trust Fund debt as economically meaningful, as it is merely debt exchanged between government accounts. Also in the unified budget view, the key

TABLE 12.2   A Self-Consistent View of the Budget

Factor	Unified Budget View	On-Budget View
Important deficit figure	Unified deficit	On-budget deficit
Important debt figure	Publicly held debt	Gross debt
Trust Fund debt economically meaningful?	No	Yes
Critical fiscal date for Social Security	2016	2037
Would the transition cost of personal accounts funded by projected payroll taxes, if not offset, increase federal debt?	Yes	No
Would the debt issued to finance such accounts be new debt or simply replace existing debt?	New debt	Existing debt

date for Social Security would be 2016—the date that incoming Social Security tax revenues are projected to be exceeded by benefit obligations. At that point, Social Security becomes a drag on the unified budget.

In the "on-budget" view, however, the Social Security Trust Fund debt *does* matter, and thus the key date for Social Security would be 2037, the date at which the Trust Fund balance is depleted to zero.

These descriptions are often inconsistently applied. For example, proponents of personal accounts are more likely to argue that 2016, not 2037, is the key fiscal date for Social Security and that the Trust Fund is not "real"—reflecting the unified budget view. But if they do that, then they must also acknowledge that personal accounts *do* have a transition cost, if they are financed from projected payroll taxes. They are not simply replacing one form of federal debt with another. If there is a failure to offset the investment in personal accounts up front, then they *would* add to the federal government's debt in the near term (offsetting the savings accruing in the accounts) because the publicly held debt would be more "real" than the currently issued Trust Fund debt. Personal account advocates who take a unified budget view must acknowledge this.

By the same token, opponents of personal accounts need to acknowledge that if the Trust Fund is "real" and if, as they argue, Social Security is fine under current law through 2037, then personal accounts funded from payroll taxes do *not* have a transition cost. In the on-budget view—the view in which Trust Fund debt is meaningful—any additional publicly held debt arising from the transition to personal accounts would be completely offset by a *reduction* in debt held by the Social Security Trust Fund (because the payroll taxes would go to the personal accounts, not to the Trust Fund, reducing the amount of debt issued to it).

From an "on-budget," "gross debt" perspective, therefore, a personal account funded by payroll taxes would have no transition cost in the form of additional federal debt. Personal account opponents can argue either that Social Security is fine until 2037 or that the transition cost of personal accounts would add to federal debt—but they consistently can't argue both.

A numerical example may help to clarify the point: the Obama administration's first budget predicted that "gross debt" will be roughly $18.4 trillion by the end of fiscal year 2014. Of this, roughly $12.6 trillion would be "debt held by the public," the rest of it held by government accounts such as the Social Security Trust Fund. Even if the Bush administration had proposed to fund personal accounts entirely with debt held by the public, the total gross debt in fiscal year 2014, including debt held by the Social Security Trust Fund, would still be $18.4 trillion. The chief difference would be that $13.2 trillion of that total was held by the public.

For a summary of these points, see table 12.3

Again, the purpose of this section is not to declare one perspective superior to the other (though this author favors the unified budget view). It is that we can only have a sensible debate if we each employ self-consistent thinking as we analyze these issues.

If a personal account advocate holds that personal accounts have no transition costs, but asserts that the current system's problems come to a head in 2016, then he is being inconsistent. If a personal account

TABLE 12.3   Personal Accounts and Budget Views

If personal account *proponents* take a **unified budget view**, they must acknowledge:	If personal account *proponents* take an **on-budget view**, they must acknowledge:
Personal accounts, if not otherwise offset, would have transition costs that would increase near-term debt.	Social Security is projected to be solvent until 2037.
If personal account *opponents* take a **unified budget view**, they must acknowledge:	If personal account *opponents* take an **on-budget view**, they must acknowledge:
Social Security's financing shortfall arises in 2016.	The transition to personal accounts would not increase near-term debt, but simply replace one form of debt (Trust Fund debt) with another.

opponent asserts that the current system is fine for decades, but that personal accounts funded from payroll taxes have an enormous transition cost, then he too is being inconsistent.

One can argue for either the unified or the on-budget view of the federal budget; but whichever one we adopt, we need to employ it consistently. Otherwise we will not be able to sensibly compare alternative policy choices.

Is There a Free Lunch Available?

Not all of the controversies surrounding President Bush's Social Security proposals pitted his administration primarily against critics to its left. In some aspects of the debate, the criticism emanated more from those considered to be to its right.

One of these points of controversy had to do with whether there was a "free lunch" solution to Social Security—specifically, whether personal accounts alone could lessen the need for other changes to benefits, taxes, or both to make the system financially sustainable.

To appreciate this conflict, let's remember the nature of the current problem. In a nutshell, the Social Security fiscal problem is one in which scheduled benefits far exceed projected revenues, as seen in the familiar chart shown in figure 12.17.

A first glance at this projection suggests that we need to either move the spending line down by reducing the growth of scheduled benefits or move the revenue line up by raising taxes.

Politicians don't generally like to do either of these. In the peculiar political environment of Social Security, it's even tougher. It's terribly hard for Democrats to vote for such medicine after downplaying the system's problems and attacking other proposals for "cutting benefits." It's also hard for Republicans to do it, risking political attacks that they are somehow against Social Security and its beneficiaries.

Thus, there is a perpetual search for a free lunch—a third way that might avoid the need for tough choices on either taxes or benefit levels.

FIGURE 12.17 The Social Security Outlook

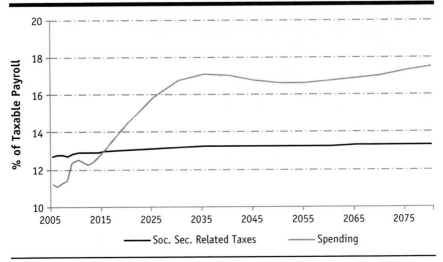

SOURCE: Based on data from the 2009 Trustees' report.

The predominant way that this impulse is expressed is to ask, "Can we get a better return on our investment on Social Security? Is there a way to better optimize the benefits that we pay, relative to the taxes that we collect?"

This is a reasonable question, and there are respects in which the answer is "yes." But there are limits and trade-offs associated with that answer.

A typical expression of this concern about the current system's poor returns is as follows:

> Workers would get much higher returns and benefits if they could save and invest their payroll taxes in personal accounts. Studies by the Cato Institute, the Heritage Foundation, and others show that, for most workers today, the real rate of return Social Security would pay, counting all of the promised benefits, is 1 to 1½ percent. For many, it would be zero or even negative. A negative return is paying a bank to hold your money rather than receiving interest. In contrast, the long-run real return in the stock market going back before the Great Depression is at least 7 percent to 7½ percent, and arguably more. The long-run real return on corporate bonds has been 3½ percent.[36]

We need to understand two very important issues introduced in this statement.

One is the low rates of return paid to current and future workers under the present Social Security system. As we have seen, one large reason for these low returns is that most of the taxes paid by today's workers go to pay the benefits of previous generations. That happens because of the collision between pay-as-you-go financing and a declining worker-beneficiary ratio.

As we have seen, this is one motivation for transitioning from a completely pay-as-you-go system to one that is at least partially pre-funded. Personal accounts have been proposed as likely the most effective available means of doing so.

The key point to understand here is that we cannot now change the fact that current and future generations will inevitably face lower returns than past generations (unless current and future workers are excused from paying the unfunded benefits that older generations have been promised).

The most we can do is to redistribute these lower current and future returns. They will decline perpetually if we continue wholly with pay-as-you-go; alternatively, we could choose to arrest the decline by shifting partially to a funded system. (We could, alternatively, cause them to dip first and later to improve over time by shifting to a more fully funded system, if transition generations today were willing to accept especially low returns on their own contributions.)

In other words, it is the shift from *pay-as-you-go* toward *pre-funding* that would improve returns for future generations.

A second issue introduced in the passage on the previous page is the returns received on *particular forms* of investing. This is a different issue and not to be confused with the first. For a given level of saving, stocks historically offer a higher long-term rate of return (and risk) than, say, government bonds. An individual investor can, with a given amount of saving, pursue higher returns, but only if he accepts higher risk.

This leads to the following summary of what personal accounts can and can't do:

Personal accounts can be a means of transitioning from a wholly pay-as-you-go system to a partially funded system. This can improve the intergenerational equity in meeting the financial shortfall going forward. It does not, however, intrinsically lessen (or worsen) the shortfall facing current and future generations in the aggregate.[37]

Personal accounts can offer the opportunity to invest in securities offering higher expected returns but also higher risk. They cannot increase the amount of a "guaranteed"[38] benefit generated by a given amount of funding.

Sometimes these points can be conflated. The reason that personal accounts can offer higher potential returns to younger generations is that they would benefit from current generations agreeing to restrain their consumption, to build saving, and thereby to transition away from the pay-as-you-go system. It is not because the opportunity to invest in stocks would itself enable the payment of higher Social Security benefits risk-free.

Now, it *is* the case that, over the long term, stocks generally outperform bonds. Long-term investors in stocks benefit from the "risk premium"—that is, from their willingness to accept variation and uncertainty in their investment returns. Stock Investor A may wind up with very different returns than Stock Investor B, if they are ten years apart but otherwise pursue the same strategies. Over enough time (a very critical stipulation), both Stock Investor A and Stock Investor B can be relatively certain that they will get higher returns than Government Bond Investor C.

No one, however, knows exactly what "enough time" is. In the meantime, the only way for Stock Investor A and Stock Investor B to be certain to receive a return even as high as Government Bond Investor C is to also invest in government bonds. If Investors A and B want to enjoy C's relative impunity from risk, then they need to give up their upside gains as well.

This is the crux of the personal account investment issue. Individual account holders can generally expect, over a working career, significantly higher returns if their investment opportunities are diversified. President Bush and many other personal account advocates often spoke of this potential for higher returns as a positive argument for personal accounts. But it can only be offered if the account holders are willing to accept the investment risk that goes along with it. (The value judgment as to the acceptability of investment risk in the Social Security system was explored at length in chapter 8.)

Where policy advocates sometimes get into trouble is in promising *both* higher returns *and* the benefits of a government-provided "guarantee." As private sector investors well know, it would be wonderful if one could receive the historic stock market return with the certainty of a government bond return. Neither the private markets nor the government, however, can provide this (not, at least, without taking a loss).

The government thus cannot use risk-bearing investments by itself to close the gap between incoming tax revenues and outgoing Social Security defined benefit payments. In fact, as it turns out, the least expensive way for such defined benefits to be financed is through investment in low-return, riskless securities.[39]

If it were possible to tap higher investment returns without risk, as one Bush administration economist privately noted, then most of our budgetary problems could vanish overnight. All that would be necessary would be for the government to borrow at a Treasury bond rate, invest in stocks, using the proceeds of higher returns to pay off all of its debt and to fund many other spending desires at the same time without resorting to taxation.

The Bush administration recognized these economic realities, which put it in the analytical company of the Congressional Budget Office and most academic economists. This meant that the administration could tout the potential for higher returns for personal account holders but could not represent that the accounts themselves would fix Social Security's finances.

This precipitated many criticisms from the right. A typical argument from this side was that Republicans needed to be supporting only a plan that "includes no tax increases or benefit cuts"[40] and that personal accounts would avoid the need for such measures. Congressional Republican staff heard many arguments that benefit changes were unnecessary and that Social Security could be made sustainably solvent through the establishment of personal accounts alone.

There indeed were some Social Security proposals that would have attained sustainable solvency, and which would have established personal accounts, while not slowing the growth of promised defined benefits in any way.[41] These plans attained solvency, however, only by providing substantial additional general revenues to Social Security, an avenue equally available for shoring up the system in the absence of personal accounts. Within Republican ranks, there existed some confusion as to whether it was the personal accounts or the assumption of trillions in revenue infusions that produced the finding of sustainable solvency for these plans.

Although the fault lines between the administration and "free lunch" advocates of personal accounts were highly public in 2005, it was not only ostensible conservatives[42] who made such arguments. There were "free lunch" advocates on the left as well who advocated investing the Social Security Trust Fund in the stock market as a means of closing the shortfall. Such advocates included the Clinton administration,[43] AARP,[44] and various Democratic authors of specific proposals.[45]

Advocacy of collective Trust Fund investment in the stock market is actually an even more egregious version of the "free lunch" mistake. Personal account advocates are on reasonable ground when they argue that personal accounts offer the potential for higher returns; indeed, those who invest in stocks over a full working career can reasonably expect substantially higher returns. The problem arises instead when proposal authors attempt to combine the accounts' potential for higher returns with the *certainty* of a defined benefit.

This flaw, however, exists with *all* existing proposals to invest the Social Security Trust Fund collectively in the stock market because they make an explicit goal of fully maintaining the defined-benefit (risk-free to the worker) nature of benefit payments. Investing the Trust Fund in the stock market can only increase the government's risk and potential losses when financing a stream of defined-benefit payments, in contrast with a personal account proposal in which individual account holders accept some downside consequences of investment risk.[46]

In summary, the 2005 debate raised the question as to whether there was a "free lunch" solution to Social Security that did not involve changes in benefits or taxes. Some personal account advocates, Trust Fund stock investment proponents, legislators, and interest groups said yes. The Bush administration—and most mainstream analysts—said no.

A Summary of the Substantive Debate of 2005

There is an inherent danger in a chapter such as this in that some readers will be sympathetic to President Bush's proposals and others will not be. This will inevitably color attitudes toward the arguments cited here.

It's vital to recognize that regardless of one's preferred vision for the Social Security system, we each share a stake in our own vision being evaluated by objective, self-consistent means and in being fairly compared to the alternatives. Only then can the case for our own value judgments be heard and properly understood.

Of course, President Bush's proposal would have had great implications both for individual workers and for the federal budget. It is appropriate that there be vigorous debate over these implications and that they be compared—whether flatteringly or unflatteringly—with alternative policy choices.

At the same time, it is important to understand that much of the debate in 2005 wasn't specifically about President Bush's proposals at all, but instead about the means of evaluating *any* reforms to repair Social Security's finances.

In the course of the 2005 debate, I had many conversations with friends, analysts, and policy advocates from across the aisle. Sometimes I would object to a particular line of attack, pointing out that it could be made against *any* fiscally sound proposal. The justification was often given to me that their first priority had to be to defeat President Bush's proposal, and that the effect on the future debate was a secondary consideration. Only later would they worry about how to reconcile the shape of an eventual reform package with the previous criticisms. This, unfortunately, can have the adverse effect of skewing even a subsequent policy debate and of making it much harder for the public to accept choices that must inevitably be made.

The Social Security debate occurs on multiple levels. One cannot understand it without understanding these issues:

- What is the legitimate concern expressed about a particular proposal and what are the trade-offs of pursuing an alternative course?
- Which arguments are less legitimate and made primarily for political effect?
- What is the tactical effect of each argument—how does an argument reframe the terms of the debate *beyond* the specific proposal in question?

Table 12.4 provides examples of these multiple levels of meaning, pertaining to the controversies detailed in these and other chapters.

The point of this chart is not to slight anyone's motivations. It is, rather, to convey the importance of understanding that an argument that "President Bush's proposal would cut benefits" isn't *solely* about the merits or demerits of that proposal. It's also about establishing the terms of debate for the next stage of the discussion.

The public does not like the idea of "cutting benefits." Thus, if "cutting benefits" is defined in relation not to today's benefit levels but to a far higher level of future benefits requiring much higher future taxes, then obviously this tilts the discussion toward the higher-tax outcome—without anyone arguing explicitly for "higher taxes." The public needs to be aware of this.

Similarly, the argument that progressive indexing would "apply the *same* magnitude of benefit reductions to a worker whose annual earnings average $90,000 as to one whose annual earnings average $9 million" is even less about President Bush's proposal, because the same would have been true of *any* change to the existing benefit formula. Framing the argument in this way doesn't lead us to refining the proposed benefit

TABLE 12.4 Fair and Unfair Policy Arguments Concerning Bush Administration Proposals

Point of Contention	Legitimate Criticism(s)	Unfair Criticism(s)	Tactical Effect of Unfair Criticism
"Cutting benefits"	It is preferable to have a higher rate of benefit growth (even though this means higher taxes).	Implying that benefits would be "cut" relative to current levels, or relative to the levels payable under current law.	Redefine frame of reference so that it compares with far higher benefits promised in the distant future rather than today's benefit levels, thus biasing toward tax increases.
Too progressive/not progressive enough	Preferable to have alternative benefit changes that are more or less progressive than progressive indexing.	Simultaneously alleging that proposal is both more and less progressive than current law; misleading implications that middle class can be excused from the solution on both the benefit and tax sides.	Bias toward tax increases by using "lifetime wages" to describe those affected by benefit changes but using "annual wages" to describe those affected by tax changes, and by redefining system progressivity to cover wage income currently untaxed by Social Security.
Transition cost/increase in debt	The cost of transitioning to a partially pre-funded system (personal accounts) is more than this generation should take on; future generations should simply foot the growing bill for pay-as-you-go.	Implying that proposed personal accounts (referred to as "privatization") introduce new costs instead of pre-funding *currently* projected costs; ignoring the saving that would occur and focusing exclusively on the debt that *might* accrue; depicting debt as a stand-alone negative effect rather than simply cutting into the savings gain.	Steer the debate toward metrics (75-year actuarial balance) implicitly biased in favor of pay-as-you-go and against pre-funding of any kind.

(continued)

TABLE 12.4 Fair and Unfair Policy Arguments Concerning Bush Administration Proposals (continued)

Degree of own-ership/control in personal accounts	Personal account owners would not have unlimited ownership/control; they could not withdraw pre-retirement, nor could they with-draw their full balances upon retirement if doing so would put them into poverty.	Calling the personal accounts a "loan," suggesting that participants will not own the assets in the accounts, and wrongly implying that participation confers a debt on the participant rather than simply the opportunity cost of not putting that money into the traditional system.	Confuse press coverage of personal accounts for political effect.
Can we invest our way out of the problem without tough choices?	The opportunity to invest in stocks and other securities offers the potential for higher benefits if some investor risk is tolerated.	Stating that higher defined benefits can be assured through investment in higher-return securities.	Enable political figures to position themselves to appear to favor a solvent system without embracing the difficult choices involved in getting there.
Social Security shortfall being exaggerated	There really isn't one; at most, critics could point out that the Social Security system has enough revenue to continue to pay the majority of benefits in a worst-case scenario, but this does not excuse further delays in action, nor does it excuse groundless claims that the problem might largely vanish.	This is a phony, manufactured crisis, based on overly conservative assumptions.	Avoid being tagged with the irresponsibility of abetting a fiscally unsustainable status quo and a mounting cost of repair.

changes. Instead, it lays the groundwork to alter the historic design of Social Security, to require additional tax contributions on all income between $90,000 and $9 million.

The very act of criticism inevitably suggests the preferability of an alternative policy direction. Even if one ultimately agrees with that alternative policy direction, one first needs to understand how the terms of discussion can steer us toward particular policy outcomes.

The controversies discussed in this chapter are but a few of those that attended President Bush's 2005 reform proposals, but they are the main ones: the effects on benefits; the fiscal effects of progressive indexing and of personal accounts, separately or in combination; the severity of the current-law problem; and the desirability or plausibility of approaches avoiding the choices the president made.

President Bush's specific proposals unquestionably brought to the forefront many impassioned disagreements about the best future for Social Security. At the same time, substantial common ground has nevertheless emerged to be seized by our political leaders, if only they are willing. We will review these areas of common ground in the next chapter.

CHAPTER 13

Seizing the Common Ground

T HAT THERE ARE STARK divisions about the best future for Social Security is well known. To this point, this book has focused on those many areas of controversy.

Less appreciated by the press and general public is how much common bipartisan ground exists on Social Security policy. Serious Social Security proposals from the left to the right exhibit a remarkable degree of substantive overlap. If policymakers from both sides of the aisle found it in their respective interests to reach a Social Security accord, they would discover that many of the features of such an accord are already apparent.

Of course, it would require arduous negotiation to overcome the remaining stark policy differences. Nevertheless, by examining Social Security proposals put forward in recent years, we can discern the outlines of the substantive box in which most policy advocates have voluntarily placed themselves. These areas of agreement are already sufficiently defined so that the remaining areas of disagreement could be approached as a fairly localized problem, one readily overcome with sufficient leadership, courage, and good will.

This chapter will describe the areas of common ground on which such a bipartisan Social Security accord could be based.

Naturally, we must be careful not to go so far as to assert *universal* acceptance of all of the positions described in this chapter. There will always be someone who will take a position outside the mainstream of practicable bipartisan action.

There will always be, for example, someone out there asserting that there is no Social Security shortfall at all; there will always be someone out there willing to cut benefits for current low-income retirees. No bipartisan accord, however, can be constructed by catering to the views furthest outside the mainstream.

The field of practically available options can be gleaned by examining the common ground exhibited by Social Security proposals developed to date. Let us now survey that common ground.

Reform Principle No. 1: Sustainable Annual Social Security Cash Flow

The first area of common ground relates to the scorekeeping: the measures by which reform will be judged.

As we have previously seen, it is widely recognized that the scorekeeping metrics employed in the 1983 reform effort suffered from significant flaws. Chief among them was that balance over seventy-five years was defined in a way that allowed for enormous annual *imbalances*, with no safeguards to ensure that surpluses in earlier years could or would be saved to finance huge deficits in later years. This scorekeeping led to a policy outcome that was assured of unraveling over time. Because the program was not put on a sustainable path in 1983, the 1985 trustees' report almost immediately showed a system out of balance again; this imbalance has grown steadily worse over time.

Since 1983, there has emerged a strong consensus that the previous method of computing a "seventy-five-year actuarial balance" was inadequate to thoroughly assess the fiscal consequences of reform legislation. As we saw in chapter 3, countless bipartisan advisory councils, technical panels, commissions, and scorekeeping agencies have repeatedly echoed the viewpoint that flawed accounting should not similarly undermine the next Social Security fix.

At the same time, however, there remain many divisions among analysts today. Analysts differ on whether an "infinite horizon" measure (actuarial balance over all time) is the proper correction for the flaws in the "seventy-five-year balance" measure. Analysts differ on how to treat the Trust Fund. Analysts differ on the right discount rate to apply to Social Security's future shortfalls. Analysts differ on the adequacy of various definitions of "sustainable solvency."

There is one standard, however, that it is widely agreed should apply to any Social Security solution. It is the standard of *balanced and sustainable annual cash flows* by the end of the valuation period.

In plain English: however far out in time we choose to look, by that point in time the incoming tax revenue generated by Social Security should be at least as high as the outgoing benefit obligations—and should be on a trend to stay that way.

For more than the last decade, the Social Security Actuary has routinely analyzed all Social Security proposals by this standard. The actuary evaluates not only whether the plan is fiscally balanced over seventy-five years but also whether incoming tax revenue and benefit payments are in balance in the *seventy-fifth* year. One plan author after another from the left to the right has submitted to this standard.

This is an important minimum standard to avoid the two major flaws in the 1983 scorekeeping. Specifically:

- By insisting that a reform plan be in *annual* balance by the seventy-fifth year, this standard avoids a solution based on the gimmick of assuming that an enormous future deficit is somehow "balanced" by our today running a surplus that we actually spend.
- As long as the trend line is in the right direction, there is no "cliff effect" in the seventy-sixth year; that is, no inherent reason to suppose that the system will be immediately out of balance again.

This superior scorekeeping standard is even useful for meeting the objections of those who are skeptical of any "permanent" solution to Social Security. For one thing, there's no inherent reason why seventy-five years must be the only time frame over which to apply this standard. It could just as easily be applied over fifty years, if policymakers decided that they were skeptical of our projection ability beyond that time. (In practice, however, it is actually more difficult to get to sustainable cash balance over fifty years than over seventy-five, due to demographic realities.)

Also, it doesn't prejudice one interpretation of the Trust Fund over another. Before the point that annual cash balance is again achieved, policymakers could choose to redeem most of the debt held by the Trust Fund with general revenues—or not. The only requirement would be that the system be returned to sustainable annual cash operations at some later point within the valuation period.

Finally, it doesn't actually *mandate* that the whole job be done at once; that is, policymakers could choose to close 75 percent of the long-term annual cash gap rather than 100 percent. (This author would favor a complete solution, because anything less means that we are passing substantial hidden costs to future generations without identifying them.) The metric would simply acknowledge transparently that a partial, unsustainable solution hadn't done the full job; it would level with the public that there were more sacrifices yet to come.

Obviously, it's not enough that Social Security be in balance *only* in the last year of the valuation period; it needs to be in balance in the aggregate on the long road to that last year. The standard of sustainable annual cash flows must be in *addition* to the traditional solvency standard, not in lieu of it.[1]

In any event, serious Social Security reformers from the left to the right have consistently submitted to the standard of sustainable annual cash flows when evaluated by the Office of the Social Security Actuary. Any credible bipartisan negotiation will need to do no less.

Reform Principle No. 2: Protecting Current and Near-Term Retirees

An examination of recent Social Security proposals reveals another widely shared value: these proposals generally make *no changes to benefits for current retirees or current disabled beneficiaries.*

Some (such as President Bush) have overtly stated as a fundamental reform principle that future changes to Social Security should not affect those now receiving benefits. This is a principle premised upon basic fairness: it is only acceptable to change benefits if those affected have a reasonable chance to plan for and adjust to those changes.

For today's seniors, it's too late to do that; they've retired with a certain set of benefit expectations based on the government's representations, and they can't go back and live their working lives over again. We must honor the promises that were made to them.

Not every plan author has stated this reform principle so starkly as President Bush. But it is generally honored in proposals across the political spectrum.

The closest thing to an exception to this principle involves the computation of the Consumer Price Index (CPI), the measure of inflation used to calculate retirees' annual Cost of Living Adjustment (COLA). Numerous economists have opined that the current method of calculating the CPI overstates actual inflation and have proposed shifting to a new "chain-weighted" CPI as a more accurate measurement. Obviously, any changes to the method of computing CPI would affect future COLAs for current retirees and other beneficiaries.[2]

Although policymakers on both sides want to leave current beneficiaries unaffected, there will and must always be ongoing efforts to ensure that inflation is computed as accurately as possible. Accordingly, modifications to CPI's methodology should always be permitted where appropriate.

An accurate CPI should be pursued for its own sake—in all governmental calculations—and is thus an issue transcending Social Security reform. But if a refined CPI has the effect of reducing the Social Security deficit, this obviously reduces the amount of other changes that Social Security policymakers must make.

CPI accuracy issues aside, however, there is a wide consensus that Social Security reform should not affect those now receiving benefits. This creates a defined policy box in which the effects of measures to achieve solvency must be distributed among those now in the workforce and those yet to enter it.[3]

Reform Principle No. 3: Protecting Low-Income Workers

Existing reform proposals also reflect a striking bipartisan consensus on the treatment of low-income workers. The essence of this consensus is to minimize the impact of reform on the benefits of low-income workers if they claim benefits at the Normal Retirement Age or later.[4]

Some proposals (like the Shaw and Ferrara plans) make no changes whatsoever to the growth in benefits for the lowest-income workers. These plans achieve solvency primarily by increasing Social Security revenues. The Kolbe-Boyd proposal, CBO found, would generally result in net benefit *increases* for lower-income households, even beyond the current benefit schedule.[5]

The Liebman-MacGuineas-Samwick proposal makes progressive changes to the benefit formula and establishes personal accounts, the funding for which would come disproportionately from higher earners. A low-income earner who received only a Treasury bond return on her personal account would have total benefits, by the latter part of this century, more than 40 percent higher than low-income beneficiaries receive today (and within roughly 15 percent of the far higher future levels of the current scheduled benefit formula).[6]

The Bennett proposal would attain sustainable solvency primarily by implementing "progressive indexing," which would hold scheduled benefit growth harmless for the bottom 30 percent of the wage distribution. The Bennett proposal also includes provisions to accelerate the current-law rise in the retirement age and to adjust benefits via "longevity indexing" for life expectancy. By the end of the valuation period, benefits for low-income individuals under the Bennett plan would be comparable to those under the LMS plan.[7]

The Hagel proposal includes longevity indexing, an increase in the normal retirement age and an increase in the penalty for early retirement. Thus, as with the Bennett proposal, low-income workers in the Hagel plan who claimed benefits at the Normal Retirement Age would see their total benefits affected by longevity-indexing only.

The Diamond-Orszag plan is in a place similar to these other proposals. Like the Bennett and LMS plans, it would implement benefit changes affecting the lowest-income retirees, but in the distant future benefits for low-wage workers would be more than 40 percent higher than they are today and within roughly 15 percent of the higher future benefit levels of the current formula.[8] Earlier in the valuation period, Diamond-Orszag's benefit changes are even gentler, in no way constraining the growth of total system costs for roughly the next fifty years.

The proposal of Senator Graham has somewhat complex effects; at first glance it would appear to change benefits for the lowest-income workers more than the other proposals listed here. But the proposal also subsidizes the personal accounts of low earners from general revenues, with the result that total benefits for the lowest earners would be within the general parameters outlined by the other plans.

The common ground here is significant. Benefit changes in all of these plans are limited to roughly the amount to which low-income individuals would be subjected if benefits were adjusted *only* for growing life expectancy. Beyond this, low-income individuals would not be affected as long as they claimed benefits at the Normal Retirement Age or later. The only exception among the proposals listed in chapter 9 is the Johnson plan.

This suggests a policy box in which bipartisan negotiations might operate: beyond taking into account the longer lifetimes over which benefits will be received, total benefits for the lowest quarter of the wage distribution should be maintained at the full rate of growth of the current, wage-indexed formula. (Moreover, with one exception noted below, existing plans also generally protect low-income workers from payroll-tax increases as well.)

If this principle were observed by bipartisan negotiators, it would therefore mean that any further changes to benefits would be applied only to the top three-quarters of the wage distribution.

Here, there are, of course, sharp differences. Some plans would affect the upper 75 percent of the wage distribution through higher taxes, others by constraining the growth of benefits. But they all recognize, one way or the other, that this population must foot most of the bill for rendering Social Security financially sustainable.

The reader will observe that 75 percent of the wage-earning population is a large fraction of the whole. It means that many Americans of below-average income will be affected by any solutions we impose from this point onward. But as we saw in the last chapter, the Social Security financing shortfall is already of such size that it cannot be solved with measures that affect only the highest-income Americans. Had we acted earlier, we could have confined changes to a smaller fraction of the income spectrum.

Unfortunately, those who have obstructed reforms and counseled delay have already brought us to the point where the vast majority of younger Americans, including many of below-average income, must contribute to the solution. There is a cruel irony in this outcome, for those who have obstructed action sometimes justify their conduct by citing the value of Social Security to the most vulnerable in our society. But the math cannot be escaped; the longer we continue to wait, the deeper any solution must dig into the pockets of the less well-off.

Of course, there is a more optimistic way of looking at it as well. We are still at the point where we can avoid a payroll tax increase, we can avoid changing benefits for those in retirement, and we can offer benefit growth above inflation for all Americans.[9] With a few more years of delay, however, even this will no longer be true.

Given the apparent bipartisan agreement to hold harmless the benefits of low-income workers, plans to attain sustainable solvency must focus their effects on benefit levels for the top three-quarters, on their taxes, or on some combination of the two. They do so in a variety of ways.

The Liebman-MacGuineas-Samwick proposal would gradually reduce the factors in the upper two of the three regions of the benefit formula, in addition to raising the cap on taxable wages and requiring all workers to make additional contributions to personal accounts, among other provisions.

The Kolbe-Boyd proposal also changes the top two bend point factors and implements a change in the cap on taxable wages, though the balance of the plan is weighted much more heavily toward cost restraint than is the LMS plan. Because Kolbe-Boyd actually *increases* benefits for the lowest earners, whereas LMS would expose them to roughly the mathematical equivalent of longevity indexing, Kolbe-Boyd must impose tighter constraints on benefit growth on the higher-income end.

The Bennett proposal achieves most of its progress toward sustainable solvency by imposing progressive indexing on the upper 70 percent of the wage distribution.

The Graham proposal would reduce the rate of benefit growth for most workers through price indexing, while also requiring general income taxpayers to finance transition costs[10] and to subsidize the personal accounts of lower earners.

Many proposals would fill the gap primarily on the revenue side. The Shaw, Ferrara, and (to a large extent) the Hagel proposals would fill the shortfall by requiring additional general revenues to be provided to Social Security. In practice, this would mean a good deal of the gap would be filled by those who directly pay income taxes (roughly the upper half of the wage distribution), but anyone who pays taxes to the federal government would be affected in some way.

The Diamond-Orszag proposal would also solve virtually the entirety of the fiscal problem with tax increases: a combination of payroll tax rate increases that would affect all workers,[11] an increase in the taxable wage cap, and a further "legacy charge" that would hit roughly the top fifth of the wage distribution. The Diamond-Orszag proposal thus differs from the others in requiring low-income workers to pay higher payroll taxes, though it is in a similar place with respect to their benefits.

With respect to the treatment of the upper three-quarters of the wage distribution, the policy differences are indeed large: some proposals (Diamond-Orszag) would increase their payroll taxes; others (Shaw, Ferrara) their general revenue obligations; others (Bennett) would slow their benefit growth; and others (LMS, Hagel, Graham, and Kolbe-Boyd) would combine these effects.

There is, however, *no* sustainable proposal that avoids affecting the upper 75 percent of the population in one way or another. Nor is there any proposal that would apply more than modest effects to the benefits of the bottom 25 percent.

Thus, we begin to see the outlines of an accord taking shape. Today's beneficiaries would be left out of it entirely. The benefits of the bottom quarter of the wage distribution going forward would be mostly untouched—except for possible longevity indexing. According to an SSA memo, adjusting benefits for life expectancy can close roughly one-quarter of the projected actuarial shortfall.[12]

There is thus an apparent consensus to allocate the vast majority of the cost of repair among the top three-quarters of the wage income distribution going forward.

The debate is thus not about *whether* young middle- to high-income earners need to participate in the Social Security solution, but *how*. The plans already put forward give us many diverse options for doing so, but they all reflect an agreement on *whom* to affect.

Reform Principle No. 4: Avoiding Surplus Revenues

An important question in the Social Security debate is whether new tax revenues should be "on the table." Republicans generally don't want to raise the Social Security tax; Democrats generally don't want to constrain benefit growth sufficiently to avoid a tax increase. But amid this stark policy divide there is an implicit agreement uniting the two sides.

A review of existing Social Security proposals shows a vital principle commonly held by authors across the political spectrum: a determination to avoid the 1983 mistake of permitting the government to collect and spend significant surplus Social Security tax revenues.

As we have discussed, the 1983 reforms predicated actuarial balance on a foundation of large annual *imbalances*—large near-term surpluses followed by large and growing long-term deficits. To the extent that these near-term surpluses were spent, this meant that the so-called actuarial balance was illusory.

As we have seen, analysts often argue about program accounting, about the economic significance of past surpluses, and about the Trust Fund. But when it comes time to craft tangible proposals, a significant implicit bipartisan agreement emerges—an agreement *not* to do what was done in 1983, i.e., *not* to raise near-term Social Security taxes in a manner that could be exploited to finance unrelated government spending.

This observation may surprise the reader, because it is well known that analysts of opposing political parties often take conflicting views of the Trust Fund—even of its past history—and that the political parties differ sharply on whether the Social Security shortfall should be fixed, in whole or in part, by raising revenues.

It is, nevertheless, the case that proposals from both sides of the aisle generally avoid predicating a Social Security solution on raising *near-term* revenues for the *traditional* (non-personal-account) part of the Social Security system. Implicitly, plan authors on both sides recognize that doing so would simply result in the money being spent.

Proposals to make Social Security sustainable thus generally take one of four approaches to new tax revenues:

- Don't collect new revenues at all (Bennett).
- Collect new revenues only to the extent needed to offset payroll tax revenue redirected to personal accounts — that is, *not* to increase total revenues for the traditional system (Kolbe-Boyd, Graham, Hagel, Ferrara, Johnson).
- Collect new revenues only to finance "add-on" personal accounts (LMS, Shaw; a proposal by the late economist Edward Gramlich that we have not discussed is also so constructed[13]).
- Phase in the new revenues gradually so that they are collected essentially as needed to meet increasing benefit payments (Diamond-Orszag).[14]

This is an important principle, because it suggests that a bipartisan accord to achieve sustainable solvency is not so simple a matter as picking from a menu of revenue and cost-containment options. If the product of such a process were a significant surge in federal government spending money in the near term, it would be unlikely to find significant support on either side of the aisle.[15]

The desire to shelter Social Security money from being spent is clearly a motivating concern of personal account proponents. But, as we see above, the concern is not held only by those who would invest Social Security payroll taxes in personal accounts. Each of the various "add-on" account proposals—Liebman-MacGuineas-Samwick, Shaw, and Gramlich—studiously avoids raising revenues for any purpose other than to fund personal accounts. Furthermore, proposals by opponents of Social Security personal accounts (Diamond-Orszag and Ball) have phased in their revenue increases only gradually as needed to pay benefits or have failed to garner congressional support—or both.

The question of whether to raise Social Security revenues will continue to be passionately debated. But in the end, it's highly unlikely that negotiators would agree to raise traditional Social Security taxes in the near term, allowing the government more spending money.

Some Republican proposals don't raise taxes at all. Some Democratic proposals would gradually raise the tax rate over time. Bipartisan proposals tend to raise revenues *only* to finance funded accounts. Those appear to be the only likely outcomes.

Reform Principle No. 5: Personal Retirement Savings Accounts

Another area where there is some bipartisan consensus is—believe it or not—on the question of individual retirement savings accounts.

Many readers might find this to be a surprising, even absurd statement. After all, virtually no issue in the Social Security debate has been more polarizing than the question of whether Social Security revenues should be invested in personal accounts. Many individuals feel so strongly about personal accounts that they will not even begin to negotiate Social Security's future with those advocating an opposing view of the question.

Yet an examination of the proposals introduced to date, in combination with an examination of other positions that key players have taken, reveals a strong consensus on the desirability of voluntary personal retirement savings accounts for workers generally.

First, there is the fact that every author of a recent legislative proposal to render Social Security financially sustainable supports personal accounts of one kind or another. Only one such legislative proposal— that of Senator Robert Bennett—would not establish personal accounts within the Social Security system, and even he favors personal accounts. He introduced his proposal without them in the hopes of attracting bipartisan support (which, it turned out, the account-less proposal did not).

This of course does not mean that Social Security personal accounts are widely supported by legislators of both parties. But there is a clear divide in the enthusiasm level: many personal account supporters have been willing to draft comprehensive proposals to make Social Security financially sustainable. No congressional opponents of personal accounts have been willing to do so.[16]

At the very least, this is reflective of the difficulty that plan authors experience in attempting to craft a salable, equitable Social Security proposal that continues wholly with pay-as-you-go financing. No legislator was willing to touch the one sustainable such proposal authored by personal account opponents: the Diamond-Orszag plan.

This may not seem to prove much beyond the fact that opponents of Social Security personal accounts haven't been willing to put their names to specific reform proposals. But there is more to it; it turns out that many such prominent opponents have elsewhere signaled their *support* for a universal savings account if it is funded separately from the Social Security payroll tax. Support for this concept has included both the Clinton and Obama administrations.[17]

The policy principle that unites both supporters of Social Security personal accounts on the one hand and supporters of USA (Universal Savings Accounts) and auto-IRAs on the other[18] is the view that workers should generally be provided with an opportunity to have automatic payroll deductions placed in personal retirement accounts.

Supporters of Social Security personal accounts would require the *government* to make this savings opportunity available with a portion of the payroll tax. Supporters of auto-IRA would require *employers* to make this opportunity available by deducting an additional percentage of worker wages. The support for one approach or the other, however, is very wide and very bipartisan.

Clearly, whether such an account is inside or outside of Social Security, whether it involves an additional mandate upon employers, and whether it requires additional contributions from workers are all issues on which there are sharp disagreements. To allow for the continued possibility of a bipartisan Social Security accord, it is essential that these discussions take place in the context of a broader discussion that encompasses the future of Social Security. To move one or the other approach to creating personal accounts separately from the Social Security discussion would destroy a considerable portion of the remaining prospects for a Social Security accord.

Many Republicans would not want to raise Social Security revenues at all. Others might be willing to do so, but only to reimburse the Trust Fund for revenues redirected to personal accounts. Some have shown themselves willing to bring in additional revenues to fund "add-on" personal accounts. But none have been willing to raise taxes for a Social Security solution in which no personal accounts are involved.

Across the aisle, some Democrats have been willing to constrain benefit growth to sustain the traditional system without tax increases, as long as new revenues are provided for another component of the system, such as personal accounts. Others have been willing to sign onto plans that would raise revenues sufficiently to partially offset revenue redirected to personal accounts. Outside of Congress, some Democratic authors have been willing to raise revenues to balance the system without incorporating personal accounts. But no recent plans with Democratic congressional cosponsors lack *both* personal accounts *and* new revenues.

Accordingly, it is clear that if there is to be a bipartisan Social Security accord, there needs to be a decision as to how to implement the broadly shared vision of a universal retirement savings account. The possibilities include personal accounts funded by payroll taxes as included in various Social Security proposals, add-on personal accounts as in the LMS and Shaw plans, or accounts wholly outside of Social Security, as in the John-Iwry concept (from David John of the Heritage Foundation and Mark Iwry, then of the Brookings Institution), among others. There will be strong supporters and strong opponents of each choice.

If, however, these decisions are made wholly apart from a Social Security reform discussion, it will likely kill the last remaining prospects for a bipartisan Social Security deal. There is little practical likelihood that Republicans would agree *both* to tax increases on workers under Social Security *and* to a separate mandate upon employers that would be funded with additional out-of-pocket contributions by workers.

The personal account is the element that could make additional revenues acceptable to Republicans and also the element that could make a traditional solution without tax increases acceptable to Democrats. Without the personal account in the mix, bridging this divide could well prove impossible.

Given the vast bipartisan support for a universal payroll-deduction retirement savings account of some form, it seems clear that a personal account element—of some kind—needs to be somewhere in the solution.

In a nutshell: there is broad agreement that we should have a financially strengthened base Social Security benefit which delivers defined—albeit low—returns and which provides a progressive safety net against old-age poverty.

There is similarly broad agreement that some kind of universal savings account into which workers can automatically deposit a portion of their wages would be a good thing.

What we need to do is to figure out what percentage of each worker's wages should be invested in the base safety net benefit, what percentage should be automatically deducted to a savings account, the degree of consent required from the worker, who should administer that savings account, and how.

Everything else is so much noise—semantics, politics, and presentation. Let's stop pretending that the same savings account, if administered one way, represents responsible retirement planning, but administered another way represents a reckless gamble and the destruction of the Social Security system. Once we put aside such juvenilities, we can begin the adult work of determining how to combine the features of our national retirement system that are broadly agreed to be desirable.

Some Subjective Opinions about an Optimal Reform Framework

To this point, I have tried to steer clear of promoting my own policy opinions, focusing instead on presenting background facts, analysis, and various sides of the ongoing Social Security debate. In general, as I am not an elected policymaker, I tend to see my role as facilitating the policy judgments of those so designated by the voters rather than promoting my own vision for reform.

That being said, one's ability to advance the discussion is limited if one is unwilling to offer solutions. The following section thus provides my own subjective take on optimal Social Security policy, presented with the aim of providing concrete options for policymakers going forward.

I hasten to note that offering these ideas in no way suggests discomfort with the policy proposals with which I have been associated in the past. I served President Bush for eight years, and before him Senator Judd Gregg and Senator Alan Simpson. In each of those roles I worked on policies that I was comfortable promoting and defending. The ideas offered here instead reflect my current assessment of substantive issues and the state of the debate to this point.

First, I reaffirm my agreement with each of the bipartisan consensus reform elements that we have reviewed to this point:

- Reform should lead to sustainable annual cash flows throughout and beyond the chosen valuation period.
- Apart from the continual process of improving the CPI, reform should not change benefits for those now receiving them, whether retired or disabled.
- Reform should not reduce net scheduled benefits for the bottom quarter of the wage distribution, with two important caveats: we should allow for proportional adjustments to reflect greater longevity and our assessment of total benefits must count *all* benefits provided by the system (including any benefits funded through personal accounts).[19]
- Reform should not create an illusory solvency by raising taxes in a manner that simply provides the government with additional near-term spending money.
- Personal accounts should be somewhere in the mix, whether funded with the payroll tax or with other contributions.

These represent the elements of reform proposals introduced in Congress to date, and I am comfortable with all of them.

We now enter the realm of the subjective value judgments outlined in chapters 4–9. In making these subjective judgments, I am now moving away from identifying preexisting common ground.

The positions outlined below are *within* the common ground established in the above five principles, but they do not necessarily occupy the center of that common ground. Indeed, I doubt that they do. The subjective views below are those I would express were I personally involved in a negotiation to determine the best possible future course for Social Security.

Spectrum No. 1: New Revenues versus Cost Containment

In fixing the shortfall, I prefer constraining the growth of costs to raising taxes, primarily for the following reasons:

First, because we can. At this point, we can still allow benefits to continue to grow in real terms, above inflation, without raising taxes. In other words, the purchasing power of seniors and their protections against poverty can continue to be strengthened without a tax increase.

Second, the system is already heavily tilted toward increasing benefits and costs. Even if we fixed the problem *entirely* on the cost containment side, future benefits and cost burdens for future workers would still be higher than they are today.

Third, there is wide recognition that younger workers will be assessed higher taxes to deal with the more rapidly growing costs in federal health care programs. Indeed, federal policymakers recently added still *further* to these growing costs and tax burdens. Given the magnitude of these pressures, I believe it would be ill-advised to also rely on higher taxes to fix Social Security. There is already considerable risk of future generations actually having a lower after-tax standard of living than we have enjoyed.

Fourth, raising taxes represents a further aggressive claim upon the resources of future generations. Constraining costs better retains their flexibility to deal with future needs that we cannot anticipate. We are already making enough aggressive claims upon their economic resources without adding more.

Finally, the primary argument for raising taxes is to maintain constant replacement rates (the ratio of benefits to preretirement earnings) going forward. Maintaining replacement rates is indeed an important goal of retirement planning, but it is misapplied with respect to current Social Security. Current Social Security is a pay-as-you-go system without a saving component; hence, benefits for one generation can only be increased by collecting higher taxes from another. It is thus essentially a zero-sum game; one generation's overall retirement income replacement rate comes at the expense of another's. If we want to actually add to overall retirement income to maintain constant replacement rates, we should do this through a *saving* component, not through the pay-as-you-go portion of Social Security.

For these reasons, I believe that traditional Social Security should be balanced by cost containment rather than by tax increases. I would add two caveats:

No. 1, this conclusion only applies to the *traditional*, defined-benefit, pay-as-you-go portion of Social Security. One could make a reasonable case for contributing additional revenues to a funded component, and some bipartisan proposals do exactly that.

No. 2, there are reforms that may make sense from a larger policy perspective that could result in additional revenues for Social Security. The most obvious of these is to reform the taxation of health insurance.

Today, those who receive health benefits through their employer are not taxed for the value of those benefits, while the cost of health insurance is subject to tax for those who purchase it on their own. Some have suggested leveling the playing field by determining a standard amount of health insurance benefits excluded from taxation for everybody. Everyone's health premiums below a certain amount would be shielded from taxation, and everyone's health premiums above that would be taxed.[20]

This is primarily a health insurance reform, proposed to increase fairness, to broaden coverage, and to contain health care cost growth. Recent health care legislation has taken a different approach to expanding coverage, leaving most of the current law's problematic tax treatment in place. But if this differential tax treatment were reformed going forward, and also applied to the payroll tax, then it could result in additional revenue for Social Security, depending on the level of the exclusion and how it is indexed to grow.

Once we have decided to balance the system primarily by containing costs, exactly how should we do so? To fully answer this, we would need to get ahead of ourselves and have answers to other policy considerations. I would think through the problem this way:

Pay-as-you-go or advance funding? Once we know how much (if any) of the system we want to convert to a funded system, we will also know the total amount of benefits we want to provide through the remaining pay-as-you-go system, and can draw up the benefit formulas accordingly. We will get to that question next.

How much progressivity? Answering this question can guide us as to how specifically to draw up the benefit formula to have the desired effects upon workers at different income levels.

Work incentives? We need to determine whether and how to change the benefit formulas to improve work incentives.

Timing? We need to decide how *fast* to phase in the benefit changes. Here we have two important considerations. One is rooted in demographics. As can be seen in the following chart (figure 13.1), the vast majority of the projected cost increase will occur over the next twenty-five years, with only minor changes after that. To achieve maximum equity in worker cost burdens, most of the benefit changes should therefore be phased in over the next twenty-five years. The other important consideration is the benefit expectations of individual workers. Benefit changes phased in over less than forty-five years will affect the benefits of those already in the workforce; on the other hand, benefit changes that continue to compound over more than forty-five years will hit younger workers more severely without their having an opportunity to make up the difference (unless they work for longer than forty-five years). Based on these considerations, most benefit changes should be fully phased in within forty-five years, and as close to twenty-five years as can be accomplished without unfairly cutting already accrued benefits.

Spectrum No. 2: Advance Funding or Pay-As-You-Go

I believe that some advance funding within Social Security would be optimal because continuing permanently with pay-as-you-go exacerbates intergenerational inequities by worsening participants' returns as the ratio of taxpaying workers to beneficiaries declines.

What is the optimal way to accomplish such funding? We can approach the problem via the following two steps:

1) Calculate the size of voluntary personal accounts that would leave the fiscal balance of the system unchanged while leading to the fairest treatment of different generations. For ease of reading, I

FIGURE 13.1 The Social Security Outlook

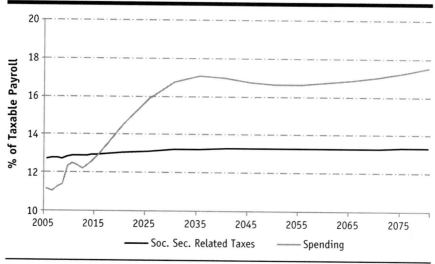

SOURCE: Based on data from the 2009 Trustees' report.

have confined the technical explanation of this calculation to an endnote.[21]

2) As in the LMS and Kolbe-Boyd plans, set up mandatory payroll-deduction accounts of that size *without* an associated offset to Social Security benefits. Instead of designing an individual benefit offset, gradually adjust the traditional benefit formulas to keep the system in balance while also creating the desired overall effect on benefit growth for the two elements (traditional and personal account benefits) in combination.

Why do it this way?

The calculation in step no. 1 enables us to determine the optimal amount of advance funding from an intergenerational fairness perspective. Indeed, if we were determined to have voluntary accounts, then we'd need to be sure that they were designed this way—actuarially neutral for each individual, so that maintaining solvency was not premised on participation projections.

Step no. 2 helps us to avoid design complexities that have vexed proposal authors. We avoid issues such as whether a worker's widow or surviving dependent child is affected by a benefit offset, if that worker decided to bequeath his personal account to someone else. We avoid any risk that the personal account benefit offset might "zero out" the traditional benefit. And we also avoid many political concerns, including misperceptions that the personal accounts themselves "cause" further "benefit cuts."

In the end, it's just simpler to contribute X percent of each worker's wages to personal accounts without attempting to design benefit offsets to fairly cover every possible family circumstance.

Note that the determination of the optimal amount of advance funding to accomplish through personal accounts leaves us agnostic on two vital issues:

- Whether the personal accounts are funded by projected payroll taxes, by a tax increase, or by other out-of-pocket contributions by workers
- Whether we call the personal accounts Social Security accounts, Universal Savings Accounts, auto-IRAs, or anything else.

The labeling is not important to me, but it may well be important to others. Many legislators may have spoken out strongly *against* Social Security personal accounts, but have spoken out in *favor* of automatic deduction of worker wages into an "auto-IRA." The two concepts are basically the same (administrative issues aside) once we have decided that these personal accounts will sit atop the basic Social Security benefit, without triggering an additional benefit offset.

Whatever we have to call the personal accounts to maximize political comfort for legislators is fine with me. The key is finding agreement on the optimal personal account size while assessing *in combination* the effects of the accounts and the traditional Social Security solvency solution for individual workers and for the national retirement system as a whole.

As it happens, the optimal size of a personal account to maximize intergenerational equity is somewhere around 2.5 percent of projected taxable worker wages.[22] This would be closer to the neighborhood of 2.25 percent of future taxable wages if we changed the taxation of health insurance premiums as described earlier.

The policy question becomes whether to accomplish this by automatically deducting an *additional* 2.25 percent of worker wages or whether workers should be permitted to save any of their *current* payroll taxes. My personal policy preference is to facilitate the saving of a portion of now-projected payroll taxes so that it need not all come from additional out-of-pocket contributions by workers, who face the prospect of large future tax increases as it is. I say this as a subjective value judgment, recognizing that saving any payroll taxes in personal accounts is a theological taboo for some others.

The precise balance of payroll tax savings versus additional out-of-pocket contributions would be calculated to ensure sustainable system finances when combined with other changes meant to strengthen progressivity and the safety net against poverty, to improve work incentives, to reform the taxation of health insurance, and to attain sustainable solvency.

Again, I care little how we label the funds invested in the accounts, though others care strongly. If we concluded that we should invest 1.5 points from projected payroll taxes in personal accounts, requiring an additional 0.75 points in additional out-of-pocket contributions, I wouldn't care whether we structured the first 1.5 percent as a "carve-out" of payroll taxes or simply cut the payroll tax to 10.9 percent and structured the personal accounts as a pure 2.25 percent "add-on." Authors of existing proposals have structured accounts both ways, sometimes making impassioned arguments for one approach or the other. I could accept either choice.

I would prefer to *administer* the accounts through the existing Social Security administrative structure rather than by imposing an additional mandate upon employers, as in existing auto-IRA proposals. Administering the accounts through Social Security would also minimize (or eliminate) the fees beneficiaries pay to financial services providers.

Spectrum No. 3: Progressivity

In chapter 6, we discussed various aspects of the Social Security progressivity question:

1) The *degree* of income redistribution within Social Security
2) Its *consistency*
3) Its *transparency*

Let's take these in reverse order. My personal view is that *transparency* in income redistribution is desirable. This is most readily accomplished by explicit separation of Social Security contributions into components that are redistributed and those that are not.

If it is decided that a personal account is the best means of achieving some advance funding, then there is an obvious method to increase the transparency: splitting the current, somewhat-redistributive system into two tiers. This would involve a *more* progressive basic benefit, combined with a *non-redistributive* personal account.

Figure 13.2 highlights another concern that I share: that increased *consistency* in progressivity is desirable. Research has shown that the progressivity of the current system is very haphazard, with variances in income redistribution overwhelming systemic averages. This means enormous inefficiencies in providing income security protections for the less well-off. The excellent research of Andrew Biggs has shown that a two-tiered system—with a non-redistributive personal account overlaying a more progressive basic benefit—would significantly increase the consistency and certainty of protections for the poor, even if the total amount of income redistribution remains unchanged.[23]

Turning next to the question of the total *amount* of progressivity: most existing plans seek to either maintain or somewhat increase system progressivity. To the extent that proposals protect low-income workers from the costs of restoring the system to sustainable solvency, it is inevitable that overall progressivity will increase.

FIGURE 13.2 Toward a More Transparent System

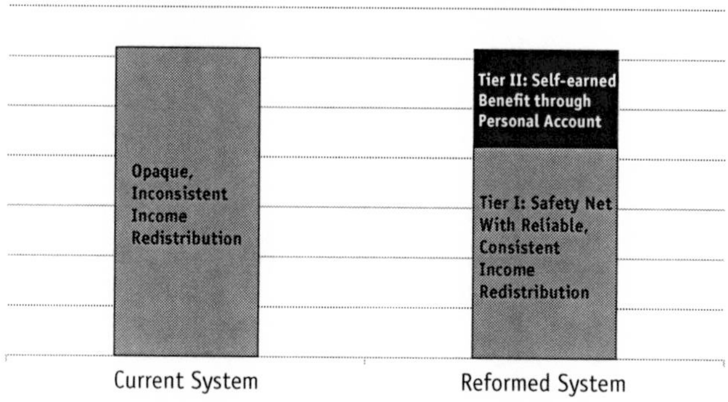

My own views are consistent with the aims of these other proposal authors. There are two specific methods that I believe are worth considering to increase the progressivity of the basic benefit.

1) Create a new bend point at 175 percent of the current-law first bend point. First, this reminder for the readers who have forgotten the meaning of "bend points." The Social Security benefit formula is rather like a system of tax brackets in reverse. Whereas the income tax system imposes *higher tax rates* on those with more income, the Social Security system delivers *lower benefit returns* to those with more wage income. Currently, there are three benefit brackets—90 percent, 32 percent, and 15 percent—the borders between which are indexed for national wage growth. The 90 percent bracket delivers high returns to the lowest earners; the 15 percent bracket delivers low returns to the highest earners.

Most Social Security proposals change benefits in some way to attain solvency. Some raise the retirement age, some re-index the growth of the borders between the bend point factors, others index the bend point factors themselves. Some proposals leave the 90 percent bend point factor alone but gradually reduce the 32 percent and 15 percent factors (while allowing continued wage-indexation of the borders between brackets). See figure 13.3.

FIGURE 13.3   Progressive Bend Point Factor Changes

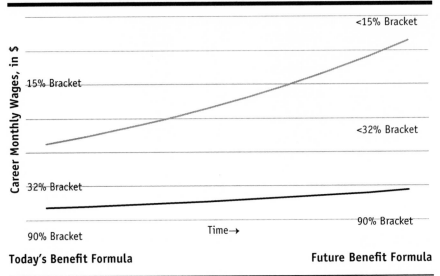

SOURCE: Based on data from the 2009 Trustees' report.

Some explanation of the above picture may be helpful. On the left, one sees today's benefit formula. All wage earners have some income in the lowest 90 percent bracket. The lowest-wage workers are entirely in that 90 percent bracket and thus receive very high returns on their contributions. Middle-income workers are in the 32 percent bracket; the highest-income workers are in the 15 percent bracket.

Under the change depicted above, the borders separating the brackets would continue to grow over time as under current law. In the future, the amount of income in the 90 percent bracket would be higher than today. The 32 percent and 15 percent multipliers would be gradually reduced. For example, many proposals would reduce the 15 percent factor to 10 percent. Shifting to a "two-tiered" system with a personal account would permit us to reduce it significantly further, because higher-income individuals would elsewhere receive improved returns, free and clear, from their personal accounts.

Changing both 32 percent and 15 percent factors would affect benefit growth for roughly 90 percent of future workers.[24] To protect more low-income workers, we could create a new bend point at 175 percent of the current first bend point. Below that line, the current 90 percent and 32 percent factors would be untouched, while above it the 32 percent and 15 percent factors would be gradually reduced. These adjustments to the upper two bend point factors could be the principal means by which solvency is achieved.

This approach would leave the first-tier benefit for more than 20 percent of workers wholly untouched. The combination of these basic benefits with personal accounts would mean that the vast majority of lower-than-average income wage earners would receive total benefits *meeting or exceeding* those scheduled under current law (even those requiring a tax increase to fund), if their accounts only earned a Treasury bond rate of return. To offer such a result in the context of newly stable Social Security finances would be an enormous step forward in retirement income security.

2) Create a new minimum benefit that rises with the number of years worked. I also maintain a concern about gaps in the current system that permit individuals to fall into poverty in old age even after putting in several years of taxpaying work.

One way to avoid this is to establish a new "minimum benefit" that rises with the number of years of employment. Even if modest, it would be a substantial increase over the current-law benefits of many low-wage workers.

One potentially attractive formula is to provide a minimum benefit equal to 15 percent of the average wage index for all workers with twenty-eight years of earnings, increasing it to 25 percent of the average wage index as the number of earnings years increases to thirty-eight.

One challenge in devising minimum benefit protections of this sort is to avoid destroying work incentives; if one's minimum benefit does not rise appreciably with continued work (and continued tax contributions), that will have adverse effects on work decisions. The particular formula above nicely balances the competing objectives of targeting additional benefits on the lowest-income households while also likely improving work incentives.

The net result of these two changes would be a system in which:

a) Overall progressivity would increase.
b) The traditional Social Security benefit (our newly-designed safety net) would be nearly flat for roughly the top 80 percent of the wage distribution.
c) To the extent that benefits for higher earners are greater, this would be due primarily to the personal account component.

Hence, Social Security's progressivity would be *greater, more consistent,* and *more transparent.*

Spectrum No. 4: Work Incentives

The current Social Security system punishes continued work by seniors in multiple ways. This would be a problem at any time, but is particularly so now when so many seniors are facing difficult decisions on whether to extend their working careers in response to adverse financial market and economic conditions.

I agree with those who have advocated reforms to improve work incentives. Such proposals offer two notable advantages:

• Most of them would directly improve system solvency, reducing the severity of other tough choices that must be made.
• Few such proposals have become as politically polarized as other contentious issues, such as personal accounts, price indexation, and raising the payroll tax.

We previously described many of these provisions in chapter 7. Below is a summary of several provisions that I believe are worth considering:

1) *Eliminate the payroll tax for those with more than forty-five years of earnings.* For various reasons, the return on payroll taxes paid by seniors is very low. This change would provide a significant positive incentive both to working Americans and to potential employers. Obviously, the first-order effect would be to reduce payroll tax revenue, increasing long-term annual deficits by roughly 8 percent. This, however, neglects the broader economic and budgetary benefits of continued productivity by seniors.

2) *Exempt seniors from the disability tax.* Once reaching retirement age, seniors are currently taxed to fund disability benefits they can no longer receive (disabled seniors instead receive retirement benefits). This could be corrected by exempting seniors from the disability tax and concurrently changing the respective retirement/disability tax rates from 10.6 percent/1.8 percent to 10.5 percent/1.9 percent. This would have a minor effect on long-term deficits (less than 1 percent).

3) *Steepen the penalty for early benefit claims and reward for delayed benefit claims.* As previously discussed, the current adjustments do not account for the value of extra payroll taxes contributed through further work, meaning that individuals often pay more in payroll taxes for no expected benefit increase. This could be corrected by increasing the early retirement penalty from 20 percent to 25 percent for those claiming three years before normal retirement age, and increasing the delayed retirement credit from 24 percent to 30 percent for those who claim three years late. This would reduce long-term cash deficits by roughly 10 percent.

4) *Offer the delayed retirement credit as a lump sum.* A typical person who delays retirement by three years beyond the Normal Retirement Age might only expect a $300 a month benefit increase under the current system, but could well warrant a $50,000 lump sum if offered in that form. International experience suggests that workers may be far more willing to delay retirement benefit claims if offered a lump sum. This would be actuarially neutral and would improve work incentives without a cost to system finances.

5) *Gradually raise the early and normal retirement ages.* This would be by far the most controversial proposal in this section but it is the most straightforward response to population aging and flawed work incentives. Current law has the early and normal retirement ages ultimately reaching sixty-two and sixty-seven, respectively. Very gradually raising the early eligibility age to sixty-seven and the normal retirement age to sixty-nine (through 2072) would shave roughly 20 percent off of the long-range deficit.

6) *Reform the AIME formula.* The current system only counts, indexes, and averages one's top thirty-five earnings years when computing benefits. Thus, a senior's part-time job might well entitle her to no new benefits at all. One way to fix this would be to apply the benefit formula, not to the *average* of one's lifetime earnings over a truncated period, but to *each* earnings year. For example, the current benefit formula could be divided by forty and then applied to *every* year of work so that benefits keep accumulating as long as work effort does. This would correct several current problems of the system. It would not only address work incentive issues, it would also fix problems in handling immigrants and state employees, who might be well-off but who only work under Social Security for a few years (the current lifetime-income-averaging formula often mistakes these people for low-earners). This reform would improve work incentives, help steady low-wage earners, and make Social Security function much more like a well-designed private-sector pension plan. It would also reduce long-term deficits by roughly 15 percent.

7) *Cap the growth of the non-working spouse benefit.* Currently it is possible for the nonworking spouses of high-wage earners to get higher spousal benefits than those earned by other low-wage workers over a full working lifetime. This reform would continue to recognize the value of stay-at-home work, but would cap the benefit so that it does not exceed the inflation-adjusted value of a benefit earned, through 2012, by someone who earned and paid taxes on half the average wage over an entire working career. This would significantly increase

the rates of return on work by women and would close roughly 5 percent of the long-term annual shortfalls.

8) *Eliminate the earnings limitation above early retirement age.* Technically this is not a "penalty" but a deferral of benefits for those who work between early and normal retirement age, but it clearly has a deterrent effect on continued work. Current actuarial methods treat the earnings limitation as fiscally neutral, but repealing it would have the benefit of incentivizing additional work.

9) *Direct the Social Security Administration to better educate near-term beneficiaries of the benefits of continued work.* In the past, SSA far too often encouraged people to retire and to claim benefits at age sixty-two. This not only embodied a negative work incentive, it also increased the risk that individuals would retire too early, claim lower annual benefits than they would have by waiting, outlive their savings, and ultimately wind up in poverty. SSA is already taking steps to improve this, and a number of useful online information sites have leapt into the breach, better educating seniors about the benefits of delayed benefit claims. This is a welcome informational trend and should be accelerated.

If all or most of these reforms were enacted, not only would Social Security finances be improved but seniors would be at lower risk of poverty in old age, and the nation would greatly benefit from the continued productivity and tax contributions of its senior citizens.

Summary

In my view, the ideal Social Security reform package would contain several work incentive reforms; include progressive benefit changes to attain sustainable solvency and strengthen low-income protections; reform the taxation of health benefits;[25] and establish personal accounts to achieve the fiscal benefits of partial pre-funding.

A proposal that includes all these elements would have the following beneficial effects:

- Sustainable solvency without tapping general income tax revenues
- Intergenerational equity
- Enhanced retirement security, especially for low-wage households
- Improved work incentives
- Manageable transition costs
- The benefits of savings in personal accounts without the complexity of benefit offsets

The fiscal effects of such a proposal can be seen in figures 13.4 and 13.5.

A few quick words about the graphs so that it is clear what they show. First, everything is shown as a share of taxable worker wages—the share of each wage dollar devoted to Social Security. To keep things apples-to-apples, everything is expressed in terms of *current-law* taxable wages (the proposal would change the definition of taxable wages to include some health insurance premiums, generating confusion if we didn't so translate).

The black line on each chart shows how under *current law*, costs rise rapidly over the next twenty-five years, then continue to grow further over

FIGURE 13.4 "Ideal" Social Security System

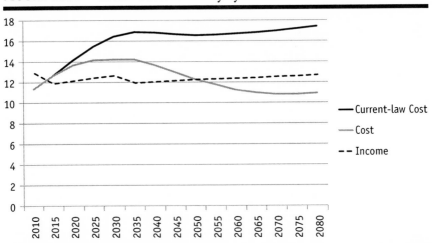

SOURCE: Calculations by the author based on data from SSA.

FIGURE 13.5 "Ideal" Social Security System (Including Accts)

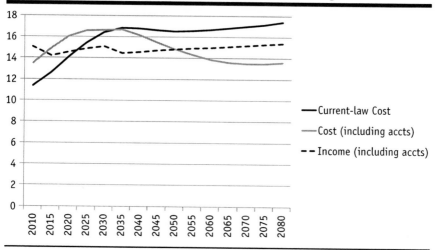

SOURCE: Calculations by the author based on data from SSA.

the long term. The grey line on the first chart shows that under the re-formed system, costs would grow less rapidly in the near term and would later return to today's levels as a share of worker wages. If you think of an auto-IRA or a Social Security account as part of workers' "costs," then look at the second chart instead, at the grey line. Either way, the trend is similar.

The fiscal effects of this approach compare favorably to other state-of-the-art Social Security proposals. We can substantiate this by a variety of measures.

One measure is to examine how much of the projected imbalance over the next seventy-five years the proposal would eliminate. Under the actuaries' post-1988 methodology, the proposal would eliminate 100 percent of the imbalance, as would several other proposals.

But we can further strengthen the test by subtracting any credit given to proposals for assuming infusions of general revenues or for assuming the cost-free redemption of the existing Trust Fund. Using this tougher standard, this proposal would be in first place among existing plans, eliminating 85 percent of the shortfall, with the runners-up being the LMS plan (83 percent), Diamond-Orszag (80 percent), Kolbe-Boyd (65 percent), and the plan of former Congressman Nick Smith[26] (64 percent).

In earlier chapters we were critical of even this method of score-keeping, because it assumes that balance can be achieved by large annual *imbalances*. A tougher, more realistic standard is to examine the extent to which different proposals would eliminate projected annual cash shortfalls, measured as a percentage of taxable worker wages. By this standard, the LMS plan finishes in first place (83 percent), followed by the plan we have described here (75 percent), and then by Kolbe-Boyd (74 percent), Nick Smith (71 percent), and Diamond-Orszag (66 percent).

These various plans represent different philosophical approaches to restoring Social Security to balance. I have strong policy disagreements with some of these plans, in particular with the Diamond-Orszag plan. But from a purely fiscal perspective, the five plans listed here clearly represent the gold standard among existing Social Security proposals.

Putting It All Together: The Common Ground

The specific reform ideas offered in this chapter represent my own subjective policy views. They are provided as constructive substantive input to policymakers and might well be some distance afield from the political center of gravity.

Based on the Social Security discussion to date, however, we can say with some confidence that a practicable bipartisan accord would have the following features:

- Sustainable annual cash flows
- No changes in benefits for current beneficiaries
- Minimal changes in benefits for the lowest-income quarter of the wage distribution (specifically, no more than those that recognize increased longevity)

- No additional net revenues beyond those invested in a saving component or phased in as needed to pay future benefits
- Some kind of universal retirement savings account

These are the basic conceptual elements of a deal waiting to be struck. What we need to do is to find the specific place where a consensus agreement can be reached, amid the ample common ground already staked out. And that brings us to our final chapter.

CHAPTER 14

We Must Do Better

To fulfill our shared responsibility to secure Social Security's future, we all need to do much better, starting now.

That statement warrants qualification: we needn't necessarily do better if we don't care about Social Security's financial stability, intergenerational fairness, or efficacy in serving societal goals. In that case, we can keep on doing just as we are doing: allowing these aspects of the program to inevitably deteriorate while we impugn one another's motives and demonize the actions required to place Social Security on a stable and effective track.

We must, however, do better if we believe that Social Security's financial stability is important and that Social Security should serve future generations at least somewhat as it has served us.

Even if we care about nothing beyond these principles, we need a loftier Social Security policy discussion than we now have.

It doesn't matter whether you favor personal accounts or oppose them with every fiber of your being. It doesn't matter whether you believe the system should be fixed wholly by tax increases or by cutting costs. No matter where you are on these various spectra of action, the sooner we can reach a bipartisan agreement and implement reforms, the better that Social Security will function by your own favored standard.

A stable and effective Social Security system will not be maintained unless all of us do better than we have done so far: Republicans,

Democrats, seniors, young people, the press, academics, think tank experts—every relevant player in the debate, including this author. This book was written with an eye not only toward doing more, but doing *better*: doing better in explaining the value choices before us; doing better in exploring the common ground already laid down; and doing better in laying down a factual and analytical foundation for future discussions. Still, there is much more for this author to do in the future along with everyone else.

We need to listen to policy opponents and to treat their concerns as signifying something other than malicious intent. Where we cannot agree with their suggestions, we need to develop alternative means of addressing their concerns.

Opponents of personal accounts need to fully hear why many proponents favor them. Opponents need to understand the motivating concerns (which include the generational inequities of pay-as-you-go, the lack of transparency in Trust Fund accounting, and the over-annuitization of retirement income, among others described in this book) that have led so many to propose personal accounts, rather than to dismiss the concept as the centerpiece of a dastardly plot. If, after obtaining this understanding, no design of personal account is still deemed acceptable, then we need to determine whether there are other means by which these valid concerns can be addressed.

Similarly, personal account proponents need to more clearly understand why so many strongly oppose personal accounts within Social Security. Proponents need to determine whether personal accounts can be devised in a way that meets these concerns, or whether their own concerns can be addressed with an alternative policy.

The same goes for virtually every aspect of the Social Security debate. If one side is disinclined to raise taxes, and the other is disinclined to contain costs sufficiently to avoid a tax increase, a way forward between these two extremes must be found. Either the two sides must find a middle ground between their respective positions or else they must find a creative alternative to a tax increase, as in many of the bipartisan proposals that we have discussed.

Doing better means more than listening to one another. It also means being more candid about the downsides of proposals that we ourselves favor.

Proponents of personal accounts must acknowledge that the opportunity to offer higher investment returns can only come if participants also accept some investment risk. They must acknowledge that personal accounts alone cannot overcome the gap between the program's projected taxes and its defined benefit promises.

Opponents of personal accounts must acknowledge that continued delay and a failure to create a savings component within Social Security mean that future generations must pay far more, to receive the same or lower benefits, than they would in a funded system.

Opponents of raising taxes need to acknowledge that slower benefit growth is the necessary alternative choice to a tax increase. Opponents of benefit "cuts" must acknowledge that the alternative is much higher taxes for future workers.

Policy advocates on both sides need to recognize the trade-offs implicit in the status quo. It's intellectually dishonest to pretend that a reformed system has only disadvantages relative to current law. The financing hole in the current system has yet to be filled in, and the effects of this resolution are as of yet unknown. We don't know precisely how the shortfall will be manifested, but it is pure sophistry to compare reform proposals to a false construct in which the current system's shortfall is never felt in either higher taxes or lower benefits.

Neither Democrats nor Republicans should refuse to come to the bargaining table. If personal accounts are truly an awful idea, it doesn't hurt Democrats if Republicans are the ones who raise it. If raising taxes is an awful idea, it doesn't hurt Republicans if Democrats are the ones who raise it. Only those lacking the courage of their convictions need to insist on having their own way even before discussions commence.

If there is a segment of society whose conduct on Social Security has been most disappointing, it is probably the community of experts within think tanks and academia. These individuals enjoy an unusually protected role in the debate. Politicians of course should lead and not merely follow, but it is inevitable that political calculations must always enter into their thinking. The press bears a responsibility to understand issues and to report on them objectively, but it's inevitable that to a certain degree they will be at the mercy of their own preconceptions, the limits of their technical expertise, and the representations of expert analysts. Seniors have a responsibility to be conscious of how government policies affect younger generations, but it's inevitable that seniors' lobbying groups will look after their organizational and parochial interests.

In contrast with these other groups, however, policy experts within academia and think tanks have the least excuse for not doing better. Ideally, this group would bend the least to external political or parochial pressures, be the least susceptible to a herd mentality, and earn the deference they receive while presenting the salient issues to the press and public.

On these pages, however, we have reviewed several examples of intellectual shortcuts being taken, whether willfully or accidentally, to foster profound misimpressions. Too often, "experts" have fueled the ill-founded prejudices of their surrounding communities, minded the predilections of their funding sources, and slanted their messages for political advantage. Perhaps more than any other group, the intellectual class of American society has poorly served our citizens in the Social Security debate.

There is simply no excuse, for example, for credentialed academics and think tank experts to continue to write that the projected Social Security problem is merely a figment of overly conservative projections. Nor is there any excuse for academics to issue what are effectively press releases for political campaigns under their academic letterheads. These episodes not only undercut the quality of the Social Security discussion, they fundamentally degrade the role and reputation of academia. The role of experts should be to illuminate the issues, not to obfuscate them for the purpose of fostering political advantage.

More generally, we as a society must do better, and I believe we will. The question is when. We are living through some growing pains of the information age. The explosion of free information sources and the personal mobility of modern American economic life have paradoxically permitted us to increasingly segregate ourselves along cultural and political lines.

More than ever before, we can choose to live and to socialize with people who share our political predispositions. More than ever before, we can engage in systemic selection bias, frequenting information sources that support our prejudices, implicitly filtering out information that contradicts them. Even some of the nation's most hallowed newspapers have succumbed to the worst manifestations of these trends, their editorial pages offering little more than blinkered, ill-informed scorn of those of different cultural backgrounds and different political views.

In our latest information age, we have not yet figured out how best to overcome these trends; that will come with maturation. Americans will increasingly grow to realize the intellectual perils of sealing themselves off from disagreements. Reality will persistently shove itself forward, to contradict our fondest wishes and deepest beliefs. Each time it does, we will learn more lessons about the importance of attending to inconvenient truths.

For the Social Security debate, the process cannot move quickly enough. Each year that we dither, the cost facing younger generations grows larger. We must do better—and soon.

Our children and grandchildren are depending on us.

NOTES

1. A Memorandum to the President and Congress

1. Technically, forty quarters of earnings.

2. If we count the 6.2 points from the employer as money that otherwise would have been added to wages, the total effective tax rate would actually be closer to 11.7 percent. We use the 12.4 percent figure here, however, because it is what most policymakers are accustomed to citing.

3. http://www.socialsecurity.gov/pressoffice/factsheets/HowAreSocial Security.htm

4. In 2009; the figure rises automatically each year with national average wage growth. See http://www.ssa.gov/OACT/COLA/cbb.html.

5. Some individuals, such as those who die before retirement age, may contribute to Social Security while receiving nothing back. Others (such as the first generation of recipients) may have received benefits despite paying virtually nothing in. But generally, the entitlement to benefits exists for all those who pay into the program.

6. Benefits are subject to the income tax for individuals with income above $25,000 and couples above $32,000. These amounts are fixed in law and are not indexed to rise from one year to the next. For individuals with more than $34,000 in income, and couples with more than $44,000 in combined income, 85 percent of the benefit is subject to taxation, with the taxation of 50 percent coming back to Social Security and 35 percent transferred to Medicare's Health Insurance program. These rates are phased in for those with lower income. See http://www.ssa .gov/OACT/TR/TR08/VI_glossary.html#1005808 and http://www.aarp.org/ research/socialsecurity/benefits/aresearch-import-362-FS88.html.

7. http://www.ssa.gov/OACT/TR/2009/IV_SRest.html#271967.

8. http://www.urban.org/publications/1001065.html.

9. http://www.ssa.gov/OACT/TR/2009/lr6f8.html.

10. http://www.ssa.gov/OACT/TR/2009/III_cyoper.html#84778.

11. One of many Social Security acronyms, the average earnings figure is

called the AIME, or average indexed monthly earnings. See http://www.ssa.gov/OACT/ProgData/retirebenefit1.html for further details. Wage-indexation is applied up through the year that the individual attains age sixty.

12. See http://www.ssa.gov/OACT/COLA/piaformula.html for further specifics. The "primary insurance amount," or PIA, is 90 percent of the AIME through $744, plus 32 percent of the AIME above $744 and below $4,483, plus 15 percent of the AIME above $4,483.

13. http://www.ssa.gov/OACT/ProgData/nra.html.

14. http://www.ssa.gov/OACT/quickcalc/early_late.html.

15. http://www.ssa.gov/OACT/COLA/colaapplic.html.

16. This is generally true, though there are also features of Social Security that cut into its progressivity, such as redistribution according to longevity and marital status. I will explore these nuances more carefully in a later chapter.

17. http://www.ssa.gov/OACT/NOTES/ran5/index.html. See "Internal Real Rates of Return for Hypothetical Workers," April, 2009, Table A.

18. http://www.ssa.gov/OACT/TR/2009/III_cyoper.html#84778.

19. http://www.socialsecurity.gov/policy/docs/statcomps/di_asr/2007/background.html.

20. http://abcnews.go.com/WN/LifeStages/Story?id=3732745&page=1.

21. http://www.ssa.gov/OACT/TR/2009/lr4b2.html.

22. http://www.ssa.gov/OACT/TR/2009/lr6f7.html. For perspective, $1.4 trillion is more than twice what was spent in 2009, during a time of war, in all areas of national defense combined. See http://www.whitehouse.gov/omb/budget/Historicals/, Table 3-1.

23. http://www.ssa.gov/cgi-bin/awards.cgi.

24. http://www.ssa.gov/cgi-bin/awards.cgi.

25. http://www.ssa.gov/OACT/TR/2009/lr4b2.html.

26. In addition to these demographic factors, the ongoing economic recession has also precipitated a further increase in benefit claims; the principal cause of the overall surge in claims, however—the retirement of the baby boom generation—has long been anticipated.

27. http://www.ssa.gov/OACT/TR/2009/lr4b2.html.

28. http://www.ssa.gov/OACT/TR/2009/lr4b1.html.

29. Ibid.

30. http://www.cms.hhs.gov/ReportsTrustFunds/downloads/tr2008.pdf.

31. We say "the equivalent of" because the funding sources for Medicare are various. The combined cost of Medicare Parts A, B, and D are projected to exceed total costs of Social Security by the 2030s, however, meaning that if Medicare costs were expressed as a percentage of taxable worker wages, the total share of taxable wages going to these programs would be roughly one-third within a gen-

eration. See http://www.cms.hhs.gov/ReportsTrustFunds/downloads/tr2009.pdf, Table III.A.2.

32. The question is sometimes raised as to whether this outcome would be avoided if the economy grows faster than the trustees now project. The short answer is no, as chapter 11 will substantiate. The cost burden as a percentage of worker wages, under current law, only admits of slight fluctuations from current projections.

33. http://www.ssa.gov/OACT/TR/2009/lr4b1.html.

34. In 2016 (under 2009 projections), the amount of cash that the government would need to produce is still less than the amount of interest credited to the Trust Fund. Thus, even as the government must produce additional cash and make interest payments to the Social Security Trust Fund, the Trust Fund balance would continue to grow through 2023. See http://www.ssa.gov/OACT/TR/2009/lr6f8 .html. A helpful analogy is that of a mortgage. If the Trust Fund is analogous to a mortgage owed by the government, it starts paying cash to service the mortgage in 2016. But since the amount paid in 2016 is less than the interest on the mortgage, the total mortgage debt continues to grow. Only in 2024 do the payments become large enough to pay down interest and some principal as well. The payments, nevertheless, start in 2016; interest payments require cash to service in the same way that principal redemption does. Another important point that will be discussed in some detail later is that the nature of the bonds in the Trust Fund is that they are called as needed. Accordingly, the rate at which Trust Fund debt is repaid has little to do with the duration of the bonds in the fund and everything to do with tax and benefit levels. If we enacted a benefit increase for 2017, we would redeem more debt in that year. If we slowed the rate of benefit growth between now and then, we might not need to redeem any debt until 2017. If the workforce suddenly and inexplicably expanded by 25 percent, we would not redeem debt until the 2020s. The government's transactions with Social Security are essentially determined by the tax and benefit balance, not by the durations of the bonds themselves.

35. This is not to suggest that price inflation is the only appropriate way to compare benefits across generations, as this is a topic of debate among policymakers. The point is only accentuated, however, if we use wage-replacement to compare the worth of benefits. With that as our basis of comparison, the choice between tax increases and replacement-rate declines is already before us, with the trade-offs growing worse every year.

36. See previous discussion under "Social Security Benefits." page xxx.

37. http://www.ssa.gov/OACT/TR/2009/IV_LRest.html#267012.

38. http://www.ssa.gov/OACT/TR/2009/IV_LRest.html#267012.

39. See http://www.ssa.gov/history/reports/adcouncil/report/findings.htm #principles , http://www.ssab.gov/Publications/Financing/tech99.pdf, http://www

.ssab.gov/documents/2003TechnicalPanelRept_000.pdf, and http://www.ssa.gov/
OACT/TR/TR08/IV_LRest.html#254423.

40. http://www.ssa.gov/OACT/solvency/provisions/tables/table_run214
.html.

41. This will be explained in greater detail later in in Chapter 6.

42. http://www.cnn.com/2005/ALLPOLITICS/03/22/pollsoc.sec/index
.html; http://www.ssa.gov/OACT/TR/TR05/IV_LRest.html#wp267528.

43. It bears repeating that even if one only sees the problem arising in 2037,
the solution, to be equitable, would need to be enacted and phased in far sooner.

2. 1983: A Temporary Rescue

1. http://www.youtube.com/watch?v=0-91W5LS0E8.

2. http://www.youtube.com/watch?v=JCDjqy5_V2w&feature=related.

3. Ronald Reagan was actually born in 1911, before Woodrow Wilson became president. President Reagan remains, along with William Jefferson Clinton, one of only two presidents whose middle name is the surname of a previous
president.

4. http://www.doleinstitute.org/archives/wordsSocial.shtml. (Courtesy of the
Reagan Library.)

5. http://www.ssa.gov/history/reports/trust/1981/1981.pdf, page 2. This in-
ability to pay benefits would occur when program assets declined to 9 percent of
the amount obligated for the following twelve months. Benefits, according to the
1981 Trustees' Report, were generally paid on the third day of a month, whereas
contributions flowed in throughout the month. Thus, without a cushion on hand,
some benefit payments would need to be delayed. See p. 38, http://www.ssa.gov/
history/reports/trust/1981/1981a.pdf.

6. http://www.ssa.gov/history/reports/trust/1982/1982.pdf.

7. http://www.ssa.gov/history/reports/trust/1981/1981a.pdf, p. 27.

8. http://www.ssa.gov/OACT/TR/TR08/VI_cyoper_history.html#90303.

9. http://www.ssa.gov/history/reports/trust/1988/1988c.pdf, p.87.

10. http://www.ssa.gov/history/imf.html.

11. http://www.ssa.gov/history/idapayroll.html.

12. Congress runs for reelection in even-numbered years.

13. This feature was supported by those seeking to limit the growth of Social
Security as well as by those looking to expand it; the hope on the part of fiscal
conservatives was that annual inflation adjustments would dull Congress's appetite for election-year benefit expansions.

14. Some allege that such larger benefit cuts have been proposed, but these
neglect the benefits provided through personal accounts in such proposals. Put-

ting aside the question of how benefits are financed, the total amount of benefits need not be reduced from current promises by more than 2 percent of taxable payroll over the next seventy-five years.

15. In present-value terms.

16. http://www.ssa.gov/history/reports/hsiao/hsiaoChapter1.PDF, p.8.

17. Statement of Henry Aaron, Gardner Ackely, Mary Falvey, John Porter, and J. W. van Gorkom, *Social Security Financing and Benefits, Report of the 1979 Advisory Council*, pp. 212-15.

18. http://www.ssa.gov/OACT/TR/TR08/lr5b1.html.

19. http://escholarship.bc.edu/cgi/viewcontent.cgi?article=1028&context=retirement_papers.

20. http://www.ssa.gov/history/reports/gspan8.html.

21. The bipartisan Medicare Commission http://thomas.loc.gov/medicare/members.html included Republicans appointed by Republicans, and Democrats appointed by Democrats. It failed to pass recommendations. The Kerrey-Danforth Commission of 1993-94 was technically appointed by President Clinton via executive order, http://www.ssa.gov/history/reports/KerreyDanforth/Kerrey-Danforth.htm, though Republican appointments were negotiated with congressional Republican leadership. It too failed to reach agreement.

22. http://www.ssa.gov/history/greenspn.html

23. The Kerrey-Danforth Commission contained twenty-two elected members among thirty-two total members, quickly divided along party lines, and was unable to report recommendations. The bipartisan President's Commission to Strengthen Social Security in 2001 was able to reach unanimous agreement but, containing only outside experts, was unable to secure congressional backing for its proposals.

24. http://www.ssa.gov/history/reports/gspan18.html. The intermediate scenario is represented by the II-B column, whereas III is a high-cost (financially pessimistic) scenario also developed by the trustees.

25. http://www.ssa.gov/history/reports/gspan5.html. See also http://www.ssa.gov/history/reports/gspan7.html. Congress closed the remaining gap mainly by phasing in a gradual increase in the normal retirement age from sixty-five to sixty-seven, which is still being phased in. Presently, the NRA is sixty-six.

26. http://budget.senate.gov/democratic/testimony/2007/Novelli S2063103107.pdf.

27. "Retired People's Group Rejects Moynihan Plea," *New York Times*, February 18, 1983. More recently, AARP has been best known for its opposition to personal accounts, but it has further opposed at least one element of every recent bill that would render Social Security financially sustainable, with or without accounts. AARP expressed opposition to price indexing, progressive indexing, and other measures. It opposed progressive indexing in http://www.aarp.org/research/

press-center/presscurrentnews/aarps_response_to_proposed_progressive_price_
index.html and price indexing at http://www.aarp.org/research/socialsecurity/
reform/rother_ss_testimony.html. No proposal for permanent Social Security
sustainability has been introduced in Congress that has not drawn fierce opposition
from AARP to at least one of its elements. For information on all of these plans,
see the Social Security actuaries' memos at http://www.ssa.gov/OACT/solvency/
index.html.

28. http://www.washingtonpost.com/wp-srv/liveonline/advertisers/aarp
050405.html.

29. See part 2 of published testimony before the House Ways and Means
Committee, February 22 and 23, 1983, testimony of AARP Executive Director
Cyril Brickfield. AARP opposed all of the major benefit and revenue changes in
the Greenspan Commission recommendations, singling out the COLA changes,
the payroll tax increase, and the benefit taxation increase for targeted criticism. As
its counterproposal, AARP proposed a series of measures as a "starting point for
non-payroll tax sources of revenue for Social Security," including a general increase in income taxes and raising taxes on the oil and gas industries, among others. AARP's recommendations would have severed Social Security's contribution-
benefit link, as none of these revenue influxes would have been credited toward
benefits.

30. The 1985 trustees' report showed the program heading out of balance
again, and the long-term shortfall steadily worsened thereafter.

31. http://www.ssa.gov/OACT/TR/TR08/lr4b1.html.

32. http://www.ssa.gov/OACT/TR/2009/lr6f2.html.

33. hhttp://www.ssa.gov/OACT/TR/2009/III_cyoper.html#142447. This is
the combined total in the old-age, survivors, and disability trust funds. The individual trust funds are subsets of this $2.4 trillion.

34. Some would say it has all been spent—but on things other than Social
Security benefits.

35. http://www.ssa.gov/OACT/TR/2009/lr4b1.html.

36. Trust Fund interest credits will exceed the amount of bonds redeemed in
2016, but redemptions will need to occur in 2016 in order to maintain full benefit
payments. Simultaneously with the bond redemptions, additional bonds will be
issued, reflecting the interest earnings of the fund. The government will need to put
up additional cash, under 2009 projections, starting in 2016.

37. There is a vigorous debate about whether Social Security's authority to pay
full benefits expires with Trust Fund depletion. While there is no absolute consensus, the prevailing opinion appears to be that Social Security can only provide
benefits to the extent that resources in the Trust Fund allow.

38. http://www.ssa.gov/OACT/TR/2009/lr4b1.html.

39. http://www.ssa.gov/history/reports/trust/1983/1983c.pdf, p.74.

40. http://www.huffingtonpost.com/dean-baker/president-elect-obama-sug_b_156113.html.

41. See http://www.ssa.gov/OACT/TR/2009/lr6f2.html. For example, in 2030, the total cost of paying benefits is projected to equal 16.76 percent of taxable worker wages. Payroll taxation and benefit taxation is expected to cover 13.2 percent. The remaining 3.56 percent, roughly 21 percent of the total, would be paid from the Trust Fund. In fact, the Trust Fund is never projected to hold more than four years of benefit payments, per http://www.ssa.gov/OACT/TR/2009/lr4b3.html—a far cry from the claim that twenty-one years of full benefit payments from 2016-2037 have been prefunded.

42. http://www.ssa.gov/OACT/TR/2009/IV_LRest.html#267012.

43. http://www.pbs.org/newshour/bb/congress/jan-june05/reid_2-17.html. The Democratic leader was referring to a CBO report that projected solvency through 2052. CBO's projections have since moved closer to those of the trustees.

44. http://www.aarp.org/money/social_security/a2003-04-02-ssfinancing.html

45. Henry J. Aaron, Barry P. Bosworth, and Gary Burtless, *Can America Afford to Grow Old?* Brookings Institution, 1988. The quotation refers to OASDHI, which includes the Medicare Health Insurance Trust Fund. The principle is the same as if the quotation had referred to OASDI (Social Security) alone.

46. Testimony of Dan Crippen and Barry Anderson before the House Ways and Means Committee, February 23, 1999.

47. "Social Security and Surpluses: GAO's Perspective on the President's Proposals," General Accounting Office, February 23, 1999.

48. "Social Security Taxes: Where Do Surplus Taxes Go and How Are They Used?" CRS, April 29, 1998

49. FY2000 Budget, Analytical Perspectives, p.337.

50. http://www.csss.gov/reports/Report-Interim.pdf, p.18.

51. For a full review of the literature describing the economics of the Trust Fund through 2001, see Andrew Biggs's "Perspectives on the President's Commission to Strengthen Social Security," Cato Institute, August 22, 2002.

52. Henry J. Aaron, Alan S. Blinder, Alicia H. Munnell, and Peter R. Orszag, "Perspectives on the Draft Interim Report of the President's Commission to Strengthen Social Security," The Century Foundation, (July 23, 2001): 3.

53. See http://www.cbo.gov/doc.cfm?index=3948&type=0 and http://www.cbo.gov/doc.cfm?index=4324&type=0.

54. http://papers.ssrn.com/sol3/papers.cfm?abstract_id=425581

55. "Are Trust Fund Surpluses Spent or Saved?" http://www.nber.org/aginghealth/winter05/w10953.html. "The authors find a strong negative relationship

between the surpluses: an additional dollar of surplus in the trust funds is associated with a $1.50 decrease in the federal funds surplus." Bosworth and Burtless reported similar findings in a survey of public pension programs internationally. See http://www.brookings.edu/~/media/Files/rc/papers/2004/0105useconomics_bosworth/200401bosworthburtless.pdf.

56. Paul Krugman, "Inventing a Crisis," *New York Times*, http://www.pk archive.org/column/120704.html.

57. http://www.nber.org/digest/may05/may05.pdf.

58. Indeed, the omnipresent Wikipedia states in http://en.wikipedia.org/wiki/Social_Security_(United_States)#Amendments_of_the_1980s that the "Social Security system began to generate a large short-term surplus of funds, *intended* to cover the added retirement costs of the 'baby boomers'." But experts at think tanks ranging from Heritage http://www.heritage.org/Research/SocialSecurity/bg683.cfm ("The 1983 amendments to the Social Security Act, intended to place the system on a sound financial footing, assumed that Congress would build up large reserves in the Social Security Trust Fund over the next two decades, while the proportion of Americans in the labor force was large, so that retirement funds would be available for the baby-boom generation when it entered retirement age") to NASI, http://www.aspeninstitute.org/atf/cf/%7BDEB6F227-659B-4EC8-8F84-8DF23CA704F5%7D/Social%20Security%20and%20Private%20Savings.pdf ("This is not a crisis . . . this is precisely what the 1983 reforms intended to happen") describe the intentions similarly.

59. http://www.ssa.gov/history/myersorl.html.

60. Ibid.

61. http://www.ssa.gov/history/reports/gspan17.html.

62. *Congressional Record*, 1990, *S14755-6*. Italics added.

63. *Congressional Record*, 1990, *S147556*. Senator Moynihan also in these remarks referenced the opinion of Barry Bosworth, who reportedly expressed more optimism at the 1988 hearings that Social Security surpluses could be saved. Our excerpt here focuses on the views of Moynihan and Myers and their accounts of this not having been foreseen back in 1983.

64. Congressman Jake Pickle, Letter to the *Wall Street Journal*, May 17, 1983. Another letter from the Social Security Chief Actuary on May 11 also stated that "Social Security is essentially a pay-as-you-go system."

65. http://www.ssa.gov/history/reports/gspan5.html.

66. http://www.ssa.gov/history/reports/gspan18.html.

67. http://www.ssa.gov/OACT/solvency/provisions/index.html.

68. "Social Security Financing Reform: Lessons from the 1983 Amendments," Congressional Research Service, 1997, https://www.policyarchive.org/bitstream/handle/10207/446/97-741_19970724.pdf?sequence=1.

69. http://digital.library.unt.edu/govdocs/crs/permalink/meta-crs-484:1, CRS-6.

70. http://digital.library.unt.edu/govdocs/crs/permalink/meta-crs-484:1, CRS-11.

71. http://www.ssa.gov/history/reports/trust/1988/1988c.pdf, p.87.

72. The calculation in this paragraph assumes that future real wage growth continues at the historic rate of the past forty years. The same point can be made using different assumptions. Using the trustees' assumptions across the board, a deficit of 4.4 percent of taxable payroll in 2080 would appear smaller, in present-value (PV) dollars, than a deficit of 3 percent of taxable payroll in 2050. The qualitative point here is that the PV calculation does not capture the relative size of tax burdens facing different generations.

73. With the Trust Fund having built up to a significant balance by 1988, the changes in the trustees' report in that year avoided the potentially embarrassing outcome of having actuarial balance calculations and Trust Fund accumulations that produced two different pictures of system solvency. When the Trust Fund balances had been smaller, with no expectations of their being built up, this concern had not been as pronounced. By the mid-1990s, however, the shortcomings with all such actuarial averaging calculations were being more widely recognized, as noted in the reports of the 1994-96 Social Security Advisory Council, the 1999 and 2003 Technical Panels of the Social Security Advisory Boards, and more recent reports of the Social Security Trustees.

74. http://www.ssa.gov/history/reports/trust/1988/1988c.pdf, p.87.

3. The Warning Bell Tolls . . . and Tolls

1. http://www.ssa.gov/OACT/TR/TR08/VI_LRact_bal.html#102608.

2. Ibid. It appears at first glance as though there was a slight improvement in the long-range outlook in the 1988 report, but this is an artifact of the change of methodology implemented that year. Using consistent definitions of actuarial balance, the long-range balance deteriorated in the 1988 report as well.

3. Ibid. Again, this is not apparent at first glance because the actuarial methodology had changed in 1988. With the changed methodology, the newly re-emerged deficit did not appear larger until 1994. Using consistent methods, it was already larger by 1992.

4. http://www.aei.org/docLib/20070910_BlahousExtendedRemarks.pdf. The citation from that paper is www.ssa.gov/history/reports/trust/1985/1985c.pdf, p. 72.

5. Terms such as "optimistic" and "pessimistic" may be less than apt with respect to Social Security finances because longer lives strain program finances

whereas shorter lives "help." Nevertheless, terms such as "optimistic" are often applied to financial projections, especially when referencing variables such as economic growth.

6. http://www.ssa.gov/history/reports/trust/1983/1983d.pdf and http://www.ssa.gov/history/reports/trust/1983/1983a.pdf, p. 37.

7. http://www.ssa.gov/OACT/TR/2009/V_economic.html#133682.

8. http://www.ssa.gov/history/reports/trust/1988/1988c.pdf, p. 87.

9. Aaron, Bosworth, and Burtless, *Can America Afford to Grow Old?* Brookings Institution, 1988.

10. *Congressional Record*, 1990, S147556.

11. Carolyn L. Weaver, editor, *Social Security's Looming Surpluses* (Washington, DC: AEI Press, 1990): 51.

12. Ibid., 54–55.

13. Ibid., 32–33.

14. http://www.ssa.gov/OACT/TR/TR08/VI_LRact_bal.html#102608.

15. The SSAC was technically appointed by Secretary Shalala, but the appointments reflected consultations with legislators on both sides of the aisle.

16. http://www.ssa.gov/history/reports/adcouncil/report/findings.htm#principles.

17. The Social Security Advisory Board was created by Congress in 1994 as a longstanding body, in contrast with the previous quadrennial Social Security Advisory Councils.

18. Report of the 1999 Technical Panel on Assumptions and Methods of the Social Security Advisory Board, p.37.

19. There are still some exceptions among those who have not submitted proposals for Social Security actuary scoring. For example, AARP continues to produce analyses of reform proposals based on the seventy-five-year actuarial balance metric, with scant attention to the standard of sustainable solvency.

20. Report of the 1999 Technical Panel on Assumptions and Methods of the Social Security Advisory Board, p. 31.

21. http://www.ssa.gov/OACT/TR/2009/VI_stochastic.html#100970.

22. http://www.davidlanger.com/article_s67.html, http://tpmcafe.talkingpointsmemo.com/talk/blogs/bruce_webb/.

23. In some of the Republican personal account proposals, a small piece of the investment gain would go to the beneficiary; but even in these, the vast majority of the upside gain would be clawed back by the government to shore up its books.

24. We're using 2009 projections for cash deficits (2016) and the insolvency date (2037) here, to keep things familiar. In the late 1990s, projections for the insolvency date were different, and shifted from year to year.

25. http://www.gao.gov/archive/1999/a399076t.pdf.

26. http://www.gao.gov/archive/1999/a399076t.pdf.

27. Douglas Elmendorf, Jeffrey Liebman, and David Wilcox, "Fiscal Policy and Social Security Policy in the 1990s," NBER Working Paper 8488, September 2001.

28. Ibid., 62.

4. Decision Spectrum No. 1

1. Examples include books with titles such as *Social Security: The Phony Crisis*, *The Plot Against Social Security*, and *Social Security and Its Enemies*.

2. http://www.ssa.gov/OACT/TR/2009/lr4b2.html.

3. http://www.ssa.gov/OACT/TR/2009/lr6f10.html.

4. http://www.ssa.gov/OACT/TR/2009/lr6f2.html.

5. http://www.ssa.gov/OACT/TR/2009/lr4b2.html.

6. http://www.ssa.gov/OACT/TR/2009/lr6f10.html.

7. http://www.ssa.gov/OACT/TR/2009/lr6f2.html.

8. http://www.ssa.gov/OACT/COLA/wageindexed.html.

9. Over the past forty years, real wage growth has averaged 0.8 percent—that is, 0.8 percent faster than inflation.

10. Gokhale and Biggs, "Wage Growth and the Measurement of Social Security's Financial Condition," from *Government Spending on the Elderly*, edited by Dimitri B. Papadimitriou (New York: Palgrave Macmillan, 2007).

11. http://www.ssa.gov/OACT/solvency/provisions/benefitlevel.html.

12. http://www.ssa.gov/OACT/NOTES/ran7/index.html.

13. http://www.ssa.gov/OACT/TR/2009/IV_LRest.html#267012.

14. http://www.ssa.gov/OACT/TR/2009/lr6f5.html.

15. http://www.ssa.gov/OACT/TR/2009/lr6f4.html.

16. This proposal was not included in health care legislation recently passed by Congress but remains a policy option going forward.

17. http://www.socsec.org/feature.asp?menuid=%7B8FF7DF6B-697C-4F31 -9BCF-23166EA8D639%7D.

5. Decision Spectrum No. 2

1. Sylvester J. Schieber and John B. Shoven's *The Real Deal* (New Haven, CT: Yale University Press, 1999) contains an excellent presentation of the early debate over advance funding.

2. The declining rates of return can be seen here: http://www.ssa.gov/OACT/ NOTES/ran5/index.html. Anything less than a 2.9 percent real rate of return is a net loss in present value terms under OACT methodology. These figures, however,

assume that Social Security is actually partially pre-funded through the Trust Fund. If these calculations recognized the pay-as-you-go nature of the system and the cost to young workers of redeeming Trust Fund debt, worsening net benefit losses would be even more apparent.

3. "Scaled" refers to the Social Security Actuary's methodology of simulating the growth in annual earnings for a typical worker, as opposed to unrealistically assuming a constant income every year.

4. http://www.ssa.gov/OACT/TR/2009/lr6f10.html and http://www.ssa.gov/OACT/TR/2009/lr4b1.html.

5. http://bostonreview.net/BR29.2/diamondorszag.html. This was the estimate at the time that Diamond and Orszag wrote. Estimates of the current legacy debt have since risen with time. The sentences deleted here from this passage refer to the legacy debt's impact on the Trust Fund; those sentences are deleted here to prevent confusion in the context of this chapter's discussion of the limited meaning of the Trust Fund. The basic point of the passage remains salient even without reference to Trust Fund accounting.

6. We are deliberately simplifying. For a typical worker of the distant future, an 11.8 percent account, invested entirely in Treasury bonds, would be sufficient to fund projected Social Security benefits. An 11.8 percent account would fund a higher amount than scheduled benefits for most workers, though less for others. A system of larger accounts would increase the certainty that workers would receive more than currently scheduled benefits, whereas a system of smaller accounts would reduce that certainty. For simplicity, this illustration will gloss over these benefit allocation issues to focus on the qualitative point regarding the intergenerational distribution of burdens.

7. This analysis assumes that the transition to personal accounts has not been funded by borrowing. If that is the case, then the new saving has not occurred. In such a case, we would not have a fully pre-funded system and the explanation here would not apply. This illustration understates the ongoing gains of advance funding for future generations, as costs of the pay-as-you-go system would continue to rise indefinitely beyond the 2085 date shown here.

8. See Schieber, http://www.mrrc.isr.umich.edu/publications/policy/pdf/Schieber.pdf.

9. Steven Nyce and Syl Schieber, "Productivity Rewards and Pay Illusions Caused by Health and Retirement Benefit Cost Increases," Watson Wyatt Worldwide, August 2009.

10. But not gross debt. Later in the book we will review how definitions of federal debt are often inconsistently applied in the Social Security debate. If we regard the Trust Fund as "true" debt, then funding a transition to personal accounts would

not cause an increase in federal indebtedness. It would (if not offset) cause an increase, on the other hand, if we defined debt as debt held by the public.

11. Memorandum from the Social Security Actuary, February 2005. CBO estimated that the actual investments in the voluntary accounts would have been closer to $300 billion over ten years.

6. Decision Spectrum No. 3

1. http://www.usatoday.com/news/washington/2006-09-20-wealthy -americans_x.htm; http://www.aei.org/publications/pubID.27704/pub_detail.asp; http://thegspot.typepad.com/blog/2008/04/against-means-t.html

2. Perhaps the closest thing to a pattern is that conservative Republicans are more willing to restrain the growth in benefits paid to high earners, Democrats more willing to raise the taxes on high earners. In a typical example, President Bush proposed "progressive indexing," which would greatly increase income redistribution over time by constraining the growth of benefits on the upper part of the wage spectrum while imposing no such constraints on the bottom 30 percent. A paper from the left-leaning Center on Budget and Policy Priorities http://www .cbpp.org/cms/?fa=view&id=297 argued that the proposal would "weaken support greatly for Social Security." Similar concerns have been expressed from the left with respect to other proposals to increase the progressivity of income redistribution within Social Security. On the other hand, there are also counterexamples. The Democratic Diamond-Orszag proposal included a provision to impose a "legacy tax" on high earners, a provision to which many moderates and conservatives objected because it would sever the contribution-benefit link.

3. For a complete explanation of the formula, see: http://www.ssa.gov/OACT/ COLA/piaformula.html.

4. http://www.ssa.gov/OACT/NOTES/ran5/index.html. See April 2009 calculations, Table 3.

5. http://www.ssa.gov/OACT/NOTES/ran5/index.html.

6. http://www.ssa.gov/OACT/NOTES/ran5/index.html. See Table 3. For this calculation and others it is important to cite Table 3 rather than Table 1, because Table 1 represents an insolvent system.

7. In 2010 the level stayed the same as in 2009 for technical reasons associated with growth and decline in the Consumer Price Index.

8. A classic example of this is the Obama administration's advocacy of the "Making Work Pay" tax credit. This tax credit was provided to individuals who do not pay the income tax, using the argument that these individuals deserved "relief" from the burden of paying payroll and other taxes. Obama advisor Austan Goolsbee

portrayed this not as a spending program but as tax relief on multiple occasions: "These people pay taxes — payroll taxes (and others)," said Goolsbee in a 2008 CNN story: http://money.cnn.com/2008/10/31/news/economy/taxes_welfare/index.htm?postversion=2008110308. The administration, however, structured the tax credit so that it did not cause a corresponding reduction in Social Security benefits—the full amount of the payroll tax remained credited to the Social Security Trust Fund. Thus, the administration rhetorically treated the payroll tax *both* as a tax burden to be relieved and as establishing an entitlement to benefits to be continued.

9. This confusion was also on display during a 2010 debate over a finding by the Tax Policy Center that 47 percent of households pay no income taxes. Some immediately sought to dismiss the significance of the finding, noting that these individuals do generally pay Social Security and payroll taxes. See http://www.nytimes.com/2010/04/14/business/economy/14leonhardt.html for one example. For better or for worse, however, Social Security benefits and contributions are connected, both individually and in the aggregate through the separate Social Security Trust Fund accounting. One can argue whether Social Security finances *should* be separated from the rest of the federal budget, but as long as they are, it is inconsistent to speak of payroll taxes as part of the general tax burden rather than as a payment toward one's own Social Security benefits.

10. As an example, see the work of Julia Lynn Coronado, Don Fullerton, and Thomas Glass, http://www.nber.org/cgi-bin/printit?uri=/digest/may00/w7520.html, who are among the researchers who evaluate total system progressivity, encompassing wage income outside of the Social Security system as well as within it. Again, this is an analysis of the effect of the Social Security system in isolation. The $2 million earner gets a much lower return on his income tax contributions than a $200,000 earner.

11. http://www.cbo.gov/ftpdocs/77xx/doc7705/12-15-Progressivity-SS.pdf.

12. http://www.aei.org/publications/filter.all,pubID.29198/pub_detail.asp. Biggs is not the only researcher to focus on the wide variations in returns. A December 2001 paper by Jeffrey Liebman, "Redistribution in the Current Social Security System," similarly concluded, "Because much of the redistribution that occurs through Social Security is not related to income, the range of transfers received at a given level of lifetime income is quite wide."

13. This is a conservative estimate of what percentage of the overall wage spectrum draws 26 percent of total benefits.

14. Even proposals to limit less than the highest 1 percent of wage earners to inflation-indexed benefit growth have provoked controversy.

15. See the Diamond-Orszag and Ball proposals.

16. http://www.nasi.org/usr_doc/Reno_Presentation_2-25-05.pdf.

17. http://www.ssa.gov/OACT/NOTES/ran5/index.html.

18. See http://www.commongroundcommonsense.org/forums/index.php?showtopic=27743&st=0&start=0 for a typical example.

19. http://www.aei.org/publications/pubID.29198/pub_detail.asp.

20. http://www.ssa.gov/OACT/TR/2009/IV_LRest.html#267012.

21. This assumes that Social Security is made solvent with progressive benefit changes and without tax increases.

22. http://www.ssa.gov/OACT/NOTES/ran5/index.html.

23. http://www.ssa.gov/OACT/NOTES/ran5/index.html.

24. http://www.cbpp.org/cms/?fa=view&id=297.

25. Some policy opponents would also oppose balancing system finances within current tax rates for similar reasons; instead they favor raising taxes so that in effect Part B, instead of paying zero benefits to the highest wage-earners, pays at least something to workers at all wage levels.

7. Decision Spectrum No. 4

1. Report of the 1994-96 Advisory Council on Social Security. "Volume I: Findings and Recommendations": 18.

2. Ibid.

3. Numerous studies have found that the pay-as-you-go nature of Social Security (and other entitlements) has a depressive effect upon individual saving. One such paper is by Jagadeesh Gokhale, Laurence J. Kotlikoff, and John Sabelhaus, "Understanding the Postwar Decline in U.S. Saving: A Cohort Analysis," at http://ideas.repec.org/p/nbr/nberwo/5571.html. As stated in the paper: "The decline in U.S. saving can be traced to two factors: The redistribution of resources from young and unborn generations with low or zero propensities to consume toward older generations with high consumption propensities, and a significant increase in the consumption propensities of older Americans."

4. "The cut in benefits would reduce households' spending and boost their saving before retirement . . . According to CBO's simulations, national wealth (the sum of private wealth and cumulative budget surpluses) would be 10 percent to 12 percent higher in 2080 than it would be under the baseline scenario." "Long-term analysis of Plan 2 of the President's Commission to Strengthen Social Security," Congressional Budget Office, http://www.cbo.gov/doc.cfm?index=5666&type=0.

5. "Calculations based on a life-cycle growth model suggest that, under the proposal, real (inflation-adjusted) gross national product (GNP) could be between 0.7 percent and 0.8 percent lower in 2025—and between 1.5 percent and 1.7 percent lower in 2080—than it would be under the trust-fund-financed benefits baseline scenario." Congressional Budget Office, "Long-Term Analysis of the Diamond-Orszag Social Security Plan," http://www.cbo.gov/doc.cfm?index=6044&type=0.

6. The growing fashion among federal policymakers to consult the findings of behavioral economics in designing public policies has resulted in several ironies. A typical proposal arising from this attention to behavioral economics is the initiative to mandate automatic enrollment in employer-provided savings accounts, based on the rationale that people will make suboptimal personal financial decisions unless the "choice architecture" is better defined for them. Whatever the virtues of this particular policy idea, a great irony lies in the fact that the proposed choice-framer (the federal government) rarely examines and corrects its own suboptimal choice architecture (as evidenced in the construction of federal entitlement program costs to grow at an unsustainable rate without a change in law) or its own adverse impact upon the supposedly suboptimal individual decision-making (such as the enormous disincentives to save that arise from pay-as-you-go financing of Social Security and Medicare).

7. http://www.ssa.gov/OACT/TR/2009/lr6f10.html.

8. http://www.ssa.gov/OACT/NOTES/ran5/index.html.

9. http://www.ssa.gov/OACT/TR/2009/lr6f10.html.

10. These are 2009 figures; calculations for 2010 will be nearly the same.

11. http://www.ssa.gov/OACT/NOTES/ran5/index.html.

12. April 2007 memorandum from SSA to Charles Blahous.

13. http://www.ssa.gov/history/1960.html.

14. http://crr.bc.edu/images/stories/ib_8-7.pdf.

15. http://www.ssa.gov/OACT/TR/2009/V_demographic.html#155199, Table V.A.3. This figure is based on "period life expectancy," which incorporates life expectancy trends to date. By contrast, "cohort life expectancy" incorporates future longevity improvements yet to occur over the remaining lifetime of each individual. The figure cited here thus reflects an average of life expectancy trends up through 1940. The longer life expectancy of younger male Americans alive in 1940 would be reflected in "cohort life expectancy." We use "period expectancy" consistently here for apples-to-apples comparisons.

16. http://www.ssa.gov/OACT/solvency/index.html.

17. http://openlibrary.org/b/OL21309135M/Should-a-lump-sum-payment -replace-social-security%27s-delayed-retirement-credit%3F.

18. http://ssa-custhelp.ssa.gov/cgi-bin/ssa.cfg/php/enduser/std_adp.php?p_ faqid=403&p_created=974129313&p_sid=U6Vjatwj&p_accessibility=0&p _redirect=&p_lva=&p_sp=cF9zcmNoPTEmcF9zb3J0X2J5PSZwX2dyaWRzb 3J0PSZwX3Jvd19jbnQ9NzUsNzUmcF9wcm9kcz0mcF9jYXRzPSZwX3B2P SZwX2N2PTEuMyZwX3BhZ2U9MQ**&p_li=&p_topview=1.

19. It also indexes them into today's terms using wage-indexation, but that detail is peripheral to our main point here.

20. http://www.aei.org/publications/filter.all,pubID.29723/pub_detail.asp.

21. See, for example, John Laitner http://papers.ssrn.com/sol3/papers.cfm ?abstract_id=1090913 and Barbara Butrica, Karen E. Smith, and C. Eugene Steuerle, http://papers.ssrn.com/sol3/papers.cfm?abstract_id=920832.

8. Decision Spectrum No. 5

1. http://www.senate.gov/legislative/LIS/roll_call_lists/roll_call_vote_cfm .cfm?congress=107&session=1&vote=00347.

2. February 3, 2005 memorandum of the Chief Actuary of the SSA.

3. http://georgewbush-whitehouse.archives.gov/omb/budget/fy2006/pdf/budget/overview.pdf. The administration's budget target was to cut the deficit in half by 2009. The amount of additional savings that had to be found in 2009 to meet the target while financing personal accounts was relatively small, owing to the phase-in schedule for the accounts. This, however, supports the main point in the paragraph, which is that political economy factors affected *both* the design of the Social Security proposal and larger budget decisions, to enable the transition investments to personal accounts to be fully offset.

4. A proposal by Senator Bennett (R-UT) would achieve solvency but with the aid of general revenue transfers. Bennett has also expressed support for personal accounts.

5. Final Report of the President's Commission to Strengthen Social Security, Actuaries Memo, pp. 32 and 34. A small part of the out-year improvement in this particular example arises from this model's particular offset rate of 3.5 percent above inflation. The qualitative characterizations would remain true, however, in a plan with an offset rate equal to 3 percent, the assumed Trust Fund interest rate in the 2001 trustees' report.

6. See the Robert Ball Social Security plan, report of the 1994–96 Social Security Advisory Council, p. 25. Also the Clinton administration's Social Security proposal.

7. http://www.foxnews.com/story/0,2933,158960,00.html.

8. http://www.zmag.org/zspace/commentaries/2143.

9. http://www.prospect.org/csnc/blogs/beat_the_press_archive?base_name =washington_post_jihad_on_socia&month=04&year=2009.

10. http://www.ssa.gov/history/nestor.html.

11. http://www.socsec.org/.

12. http://www.ssa.gov/OACT/solvency/PresComm_20020131.html.

13. http://www.factcheck.org/false_attacks_over_windfalls_to_wall_street.html.

14. http://faculty.chicagobooth.edu/austan.goolsbee/research/ssecfees.pdf.

15. http://www.lcao.org/docs/principles/ss_private.pdf.

9. Putting It All Together

1. http://www.ssa.gov/OACT/solvency/RBennett_20090212.pdf.

2. http://www.ssa.gov/OACT/solvency/SJohnson_20050215.pdf.

3. http://www.ssa.gov/OACT/solvency/LGraham_20031118.pdf. The Graham proposal does contain some revenue increases but the cost restraints alone are sufficient to balance the traditional system. The revenue increases are intended to offset the up-front transition cost of personal accounts, even though the accounts are designed so that they will not add net costs to the system over time.

4. http://www.ssa.gov/OACT/solvency/DiamondOrszag_20031008.pdf. See Tables 1 and 1a. Cost rates on Table 1 are expressed as a percentage of taxable payroll, which can be translated into a percentage of current-law taxable payroll using information from Table 1a. Total system costs under the plan only become less than current-law in the later part of the valuation period (beyond 2050).

5. http://www.ssa.gov/OACT/solvency/CShaw_20050512.pdf.

6. http://www.ssa.gov/OACT/solvency/PFerrara_20031201.pdf. Specifically, the proposal assumes that increased corporate tax revenues will be collected and non-Social Security spending reductions will be enacted, with the savings transferred to Social Security. Regardless of the source of the revenues, the proposal embodies the value judgment that Social Security revenues should be increased rather than its cost growth reduced.

7. http://www.ssa.gov/OACT/solvency/Kolbe_20051104.pdf. The different percentages are arrived at by comparing the effects of spending and revenue proposals in the actuarial balance calculation in the seventy-fifth year and in other isolated years. See footnote on Liebman-MacGuineas-Samwick for some additional qualifications of these numbers.

8. http://www.ssa.gov/OACT/solvency/CHagel_20050310.pdf.

9. By Jeffrey Liebman, Maya MacGuineas, and Andrew Samwick.

10. http://www.ssa.gov/OACT/solvency/Liebman_20051117.pdf. A precise quantification of the balance between costs and revenues in LMS is elusive because some of the long-term cost reduction is achieved by outright restraints upon benefit obligations, while some has been achieved—as in Kolbe-Boyd and Hagel—by moving some cost burdens into the near-term via pre-funded accounts. As a result, a seventy-five-year actuarial summation of the cost/revenue balance overstates the plan's total reliance on revenues whereas an analysis based on costs in the seventy-fifth year overstates the role of cost containment because it implicitly includes savings arising in that year from advance funding as opposed to pure cost restraint. As indicated in chapter 9, the aggregate reliance of a personal account plan on revenues versus cost restraints lies somewhere in between these two possibilities.

11. http://www.ssa.gov/OACT/solvency/RBennett_20090212.pdf, Table 1.

12. The Diamond-Orszag proposal was unveiled with the inadvertently ironic title, "A Balanced Approach." Though the proposal is a serious and honestly scored plan, it represents a pole in the Social Security policy discussion: neither constraining total system costs at all through 2050 nor incorporating any genuine prefunding at any point. The cost/revenue spectrum and the pay-go/funding spectrum are probably the two most fundamental and contentious debates in Social Security policy; the Diamond-Orszag proposal rejects the middle ground on each.

13. http://www.ssa.gov/OACT/solvency/SJohnson_20050215.pdf and http://www.ssa.gov/OACT/solvency/PFerrara_20031201.pdf. This is true of the Johnson plan irrespective of stock return assumptions. Whether it is true of the Ferrara proposal depends on stock return assumptions, but it is a stated goal of the proposal. Even in a low-return scenario, the size of the personal account contributions would be competitive with the traditional system tax rate under this proposal.

14. http://www.cbo.gov/ftpdocs/60xx/doc6044/12-22-Diamond-Orszag.pdf.

15. http://www.ssa.gov/OACT/solvency/SJohnson_20050215.pdf. See table B1.

16. http://www.ssa.gov/OACT/solvency/Liebman_20051117.pdf.

17. http://www.cbo.gov/ftpdocs/70xx/doc7041/02-08-LMS_Proposal.pdf.

10. President Bush's Reform Initiative

1. "Renewing America's Purpose: Policy Addresses of George W. Bush, July 1999-July 2000," http://campus.murraystate.edu/academic/faculty/mark.wattier/Purpose.pdf, p. 221.

2. The author did not participate in the crafting of the campaign reform principles, and is describing them primarily as an outside observer. The author joined the administration in February 2001.

3. President Clinton, during an April 7, 1998, Social Security forum, said, "I do agree with those of you who say it ought to be possible for us to save Social Security without a payroll tax increase. I don't think we ought to automatically rule out any ideas over the next thirty to fifty years, as some would do, but I think that we plainly know that we can do this and provide for increased strength of the system without a payroll tax increase, given current assumptions. So I believe that will be possible." President Clinton also later stated, "But we all know that there are basically only three options: we can raise taxes again, which no one wants to do because the payroll tax is regressive. Over half the American people who are working pay more payroll tax than income tax today . . ." Social Security Y2K event, December 28, 1998. See http://www.socialsecurity.gov/history/clntstmts.html.

4. Peter Marks, "Accusing Fingers on Each Side as Campaign Becomes Nasty," *New York Times*, October 28, 2000. See http://nucnews.net/nucnews/2000nn/ 0010nn/001028nn.htm.

5. http://www.socsec.org/facts/issue_briefs/pdf_versions/11issbrf.pdf. "Governor Bush's Individual Account Proposal: Implications for Retirement Benefits," by Aaron, Blinder, Munnell, and Orszag. This study purported to show the "reductions in Social Security benefits" that would arise under Governor Bush's proposal. To fully appreciate the techniques employed in the paper requires an understanding of the program's various analytical metrics, some of which are explained in the following chapters. Essentially, the study subtracted an amount of revenue from Social Security over the next seventy-five years (on the assumption that this amount would be redirected to personal accounts) to arrive at alarming figures for "benefit cuts" arising from this revenue redirection in combination with preexisting revenue limitations under current law. The paper relied heavily on analytical metrics that implicitly assume that any lessening of reliance on Trust Fund saving will also reduce benefits, portraying the consequences of these assumptions as ostensible findings. The paper defined the revenues available to finance Social Security benefits as those credited to the Social Security Trust Fund, bypassing the empirical question of whether funds invested in personal accounts would be more or less likely to build saving than the current Trust Fund mechanism and thus to enhance the ability to finance future benefits. The paper also relied upon the metric of seventy-five-year actuarial imbalance as modified in 1988, which as we have seen implicitly treats the Trust Fund as genuine interest-earning saving regardless of actual federal fiscal practices, which also biases analyses against partial advance funding. Finally, the piece employed charged language of "reductions" in benefits without the context of the scheduled rise in the inflation-adjusted value of benefits under current law, or the inseparable trade-offs that exist between benefit levels and tax burdens as discussed in chapter 4. Finally, the paper ignored the fact that none of the personal account proposals recently introduced within Congress mirrored the proposal the paper had invented and imputed to the candidate, and thus there was little basis for assuming the particular plan postulated for the paper. The paper was unexceptional in reflecting the particular policy views of a set of economists. Of concern in this instance was that, rather than examine whether the empirical evidence supported these views, the paper instead employed an analytical framework that implicitly assumed the superiority of a certain approach to financing and presented the results not as an inevitable outgrowth of that assumption but as an analytical finding. The tenor of the paper was also concerning in that it suggested that, during a campaign and possibly during a legislative reform effort, some

prominent analysts would devote their energies to increasing one side's political leverage rather than engaging to illuminate the various policy trade-offs for policymakers and for the public. This flight from the analytical mainstream reduced the pool of talent available for a subsequent bipartisan educational and policy development effort.

6. http://www.economagic.com/em-cgi/data.exe/var/rgdp-qtrchg.

7. In January 2001, CBO projected a total budget surplus of $313 billion for 2002, the first year that the new president's policies would be in effect. See http://www.cbo.gov/doc.cfm?index=2727&type=0&sequence=1. Of this, the on-budget surplus was projected to be $142 billion. By January 2002, CBO had revised that to a unified deficit of $21 billion (including an on-budget deficit of $181 billion), with $148 billion of the deterioration attributable to the slower economy and another $94 billion attributable to technical adjustments, largely in the treatment of capital gains receipts. http://www.cbo.gov/doc.cfm?index=3277&type=0&sequence=1. By August of 2002, CBO made a further $104 billion downward revision in technical adjustments. http://www.cbo.gov/doc.cfm?index=3735&type=0&sequence=1. After all the adjustments had been made, it turned out that the new president had not inherited a surplus that could have been "lockboxed" after all.

8. http://www.msnbc.msn.com/id/6853606/.

9. http://en.wikisource.org/wiki/Executive_Order_13210.

10. Some critics might say that there was a mutual exclusivity between the reform ideas of political opponents and the president's reform principles. In the vast majority of instances, this was untrue because of the wide policy flexibility permitted by the wording of the principles.

11. Cynics might say that this is a low standard. The U.S. Senate, however, has featured countless individuals of impressive intellect and Senator Moynihan would have stood out in virtually any crowd.

12. More recently, Parsons demonstrated his political independence by joining President Obama's economic advisory team.

13. http://www.accessmylibrary.com/coms2/summary_0286-7367261_ITM is but one example.

14. Statement of Horace Deets, May 2, 2001. Deets's statement said that the commission "lacks the balance of opinion that is essential for public credibility" and that the commission's underpinnings "show a fundamental misunderstanding of the Social Security system." Deets's statement was released before the commission had made any public statements or had begun to develop its own policy views and recommendations.

15. http://govinfo.library.unt.edu/csss/reports/Report-Interim.pdf.

16. Andrew Biggs's comprehensive paper, "Perspectives on the President's Commission to Strengthen Social Security" contains an illuminating analysis of how public discussions of the Social Security Trust Fund changed in 2001. The Commission's Interim Report contained an explanation, buttressed by lengthy quotations from CBO, GAO, CRS, and the Public Social Security Trustees, that the Trust Fund was not a net asset of the government and thus did not reduce the size of future shortfalls facing taxpayers. Several individuals who criticized the commission on this point had previously written essentially to the same effect. See pp. 10-15 of http://www.cato.org/pubs/ssps/html/ssp27/ssp27index.html. Only in 2001 when the Commission's Interim Report repeated these standard explanations did several critics change course to argue that the Trust Fund embodied real saving. For one example of the analytical reversal, see http://www.cbpp.org/archiveSite/7-23-01socsec.pdf. To fully detail the issues surrounding the criticisms in this paper would require more space than is available here and would divert from the main purpose of this narrative. To briefly summarize, the critics later justified their changed stance by pointing to the existence of the congressional "lockbox" that would supposedly ensure the Trust Fund would henceforth be saved. We now know based on subsequent revisions to economic data that the government was not on course to save future Social Security surpluses in any event, invalidating the central premise of the lockbox and further supporting the commission's view of the Trust Fund. Moreover, the commission's point regarding the lack of saving would still have been valid as it pertained to the many years of surpluses that financed government consumption after the 1983 reforms. In another episode, a draft report of the interim report was the subject of a petty attack by AARP Executive Director William Novelli, disparaging the interim report's "staff draft" for referring to Social Security as a "novelty" and portraying the program "in the worst possible light." See http://bulk.resource.org/gpo.gov/record/2001/2001_E01390.pdf. The word "novelty" appeared only in Moynihan's first draft of the co-chairs' introduction to the interim report and was actually in the context of praise for the establishment of Social Security and its creators in the 1930s. In response to these attacks, co-chairs Moynihan and Parsons changed the introduction's sentence, which had always been innocuous, to "For our forebears, Social Security was a transforming innovation." The Center on Budget and Policy Priorities paper cited here similarly attempted to make an issue of some of Moynihan's phrasings in the first draft of the co-chairs' introduction.

17. http://www.economagic.com/em-cgi/data.exe/var/rgdp-qtrchg.

18. http://www.gpoaccess.gov/usbudget/fy09/hist.html, Table 1.2.

19. SSAC Chairman Ned Gramlich had proposed a plan that took this approach in 1996, but in 2001 no support was expressed within Congress for any specific plan along these lines.

20. The precise interest rate varied from plan to plan—3.5 percent above inflation for Model 1, 2 percent for Model 2, and 2.5 percent for Model 3. These different interest rates reflected different judgments about the value, to workers and to the government, of allowing workers to shift their contributions from one part of the system to another. Some critics charged that applying any interest rate less than 3 percent—the ongoing actuarial projection for the Trust Fund interest rate—meant that the traditional system would be weakened by "subsidizing" the personal accounts. This would be true if otherwise the money would have been saved by the government through the Trust Fund mechanism, thus either earning interest or reducing debt costs at a 3 percent interest rate. Under the empirical assumption that the government would otherwise spend the money, then each of the offset rates above would have considerably improved the government's ability to finance future Social Security benefits. The appropriate assumption to make is a subject of continuing debate among analysts, but it is important to understand that the initial assumption drives the ultimate conclusion as to whether such personal accounts would help or hurt system finances. It is also worth noting that under the actuarial methodology employed by the 1983 Greenspan Commission, as opposed to the post-1988 methodology, the accounts in each of the three models would have been seen as improving Social Security finances in the aggregate.

21. The precision of this statement depends on a couple of factors: discount rates assumed, political economy considerations, administrative costs, and "leakage" through inheritances by families that would not otherwise receive benefits under current law. The fiscal neutrality could be less than exact, as a result of these various factors, but they do not change the qualitative truth of the statement.

22. Whether the personal accounts would worsen the solvency picture in the aggregate was a point of some confusion in the public Social Security discussion. In total, they would not have, at least to the extent that each model's offset interest rate reflected an appropriate discount rate. But, as we have seen, pre-funding does affect the *timing* of financing. Accordingly, a personal account might, in the seventieth year of the valuation period, partially pre-fund a benefit that is only paid out in the eightieth year. A valuation period that cuts off at seventy-five years will thus misinterpret a change in the timing of financing as being a change in the overall level of financing requirements. This accounting artifact was occasionally exploited by personal account opponents to cause the phenomenon of *pre-funding* to be misconstrued as an *addition* to the financing problem. A paper by Diamond-Orszag that predominantly criticized the commission proposals, http://www.tcf .org/Publications/RetirementSecurity/Diamond_Orszag.pdf, implicitly acknowledged this reality in a text box deep into the paper: ". . . (Commission) Model 2 would leave the Social Security system with more assets at the end of the seventy-five-year period. Under Model 2, but not the alternative, the Social Security system

would remain in balance after 2076." The "alternative" referred to here is an alternative baseline developed by Diamond-Orszag that purported to require an equal amount of general revenue transfers over seventy-five years while continuing pay-as-you-go financing. As this text acknowledged, the alternative baseline would not adequately finance nor pre-fund any benefits beyond seventy-five years, whereas a partially pre-funded system would. Although this acknowledgment was contained deep in the Diamond-Orszag paper, the overall tenor of the paper implied that the commission's proposed personal accounts would unnecessarily *increase* costs or pay lower benefits for the same cost, as opposed to simply shifting the timing of costs. This clearly confused many readers, including the *New York Times*'s Paul Krugman, who in a June 21, 2002, column wrote, "The Diamond-Orszag report is informative; even I was surprised by a couple of revelations. For example, the mystery money infusions that the commission assumes will somehow be forthcoming are almost enough to preserve Social Security exactly as it is, with no benefit cuts, forever." Krugman got it exactly backward; as Diamond-Orszag had noted, it was the commission's partially pre-funded plan with personal accounts that would be sustainably solvent, whereas the alternative baseline assuming an equal amount of general revenues for the pay-as-you-go system would not be.

23. John Cogan and Olivia Mitchell, "Perspectives from the President's Commission on Social Security Reform," *Journal of Economic Perspectives*, Volume 17, Number 2 (Spring 2003): 149-172. http://papers.ssrn.com/sol3/papers.cfm?abstract_id=331020.

24. Andrew Biggs "Perspectives on the President's Commission to Strengthen Social Security," Cato Institute (2002). http://www.cato.org/pubs/ssps/ssp27.pdf,

25. http://www.ssa.gov/OACT/solvency/index.html.

26. http://www.concordcoalition.org/press-releases/1998/0209/president-announces-first-concord-aarp-conference-social-security-reform-be.

27. AARP draws substantial income from health insurance sales.

28. http://www.oaklandnews.com/archives/000147.html.

29. For typical examples, see the president's remarks on Social Security at Gainesville Florida, http://georgewbush-whitehouse.archives.gov/news/releases/2004/10/20041031-5.html; in Tampa, http://georgewbush-whitehouse.archives.gov/news/releases/2004/10/20041031-3.html; in Miami, http://georgewbush-whitehouse.archives.gov/news/releases/2004/10/20041031-1.html; and in Orlando, http://georgewbush-whitehouse.archives.gov/news/releases/2004/10/20041030-12.html. The language was virtually identical in the upper Midwest, in Minneapolis, http://georgewbush-whitehouse.archives.gov/news/releases/2004/10/20041030-8.html; in Grand Rapids, http://georgewbush-whitehouse.archives.gov/news/releases/2004/10/20041030-3.html, and in many other places around the country.

30. http://www.nytimes.com/2004/11/04/politics/04BUSHTRANS.html ?pagewanted=4&_r=1. The full quote was as follows: "I made Social Security an issue for those of you who had to suffer through my speeches on a daily basis, for those of you who actually listened to my speeches on a daily basis, you might remember every speech I talked about the duty of an American president to lead. And we must lead on Social Security because the system is not going to be whole for our children or our grandchildren. And so to answer your second question is, we'll start on Social Security now. We'll start bringing together those in Congress who agree with my assessment that we need to work together. We've got a good blueprint, a good go-by. You mentioned Senator Moynihan, I had asked him prior to his passing to chair a committee of notable Americans to come up with some ideas on Social Security. And they did so. And it's a good place for members of Congress to start. The president must have the will to take on the issue, not only in the campaign but now that I'm elected. And this, reforming Social Security, will be a priority of my administration. Obviously, if it were easy it would have already been done. And this is going to be hard work to bring people together and to make, to convince the Congress to move forward. And there are going to be costs. But the cost of doing nothing is [not] insignificant—is much greater than the cost of reforming the system today. That was the case I made on the campaign trail. And I was earnest about getting something done. And as a matter of fact I talked to members of my staff today as we're beginning to plan the strategy to move agendas forward about how to do this and do it effectively."

31. ABC News/Washington Post Poll, March 10-13, 2005, CNN/USA Today/Gallup Poll, April 29-May 1, 2005, Associated Press/Ipsos Poll, May 2-4, 2005, NBC News/Wall Street Journal Poll, May 12-16, 2005, CBS/New York Times Poll, June 10-15, 2005.

32. http://www.americanrhetoric.com/speeches/stateoftheunion2005.htm.

33. See questions on the accounts' effect on finances during the press briefing at http://www.nytimes.com/2005/02/03/politics/03social-txt.html?pagewanted= 1&_r=1.

34. Some estimates range as low as 6-8 basis points, though the actuary's estimate for President Bush's proposed accounts in Social Security was 30 basis points. TSP is able to have somewhat lower costs in part because all TSP participants are employees of the federal government.

35. The neutrality would be inexact, affected by such factors as administrative costs, pre-retirement-age inheritances, and the assumed discount rate. These factors are relatively small, however, preserving qualitative neutrality. For example, under the post-1988 assumption that Social Security assets are entirely saved and earn interest, the net fiscal effect of the accounts would be slightly negative, owing

primarily to administrative costs. Under the 1983 actuarial methods, by contrast, the net fiscal effect of the accounts would be slightly positive.

36. Individuals who declined to specify an investment choice would be invested automatically in this fund. Also, individuals not previously so invested would be placed anew into this fund fifteen years before retirement, unless they affirmatively opted out and certified that they were aware of the risks of stock investments.

37. http://www.brookings.edu/papers/2002/0618communitydevelopment_diamond.aspx.

38. http://papers.ssrn.com/sol3/papers.cfm?abstract_id=703221. One expert was also quoted in multiple places including http://www.washingtonpost.com/wp-dyn/articles/A60749-2005Feb3.html and http://www.retiredamericans.org/ht/display/ArticleDetails/i/1003/pid/473 as saying "It's not a nest egg. It's a loan."

39. Jonathan Weisman, "Participants Would Forfeit Part of Accounts' Profits," *Washington Post*, February 3, 2005. http://www.washingtonpost.com/wp-dyn/articles/A60749-2005Feb3.html.

40. http://www.washingtonpost.com/wp-dyn/articles/A60749-2005Feb3.html.

41. http://www.washingtonpost.com/wp-dyn/articles/A60749-2005Feb3.html.

42. http://www.retiredamericans.org/ht/display/ArticleDetails/i/1003/pid/473.

43. http://www.nationalreview.com/nrof_luskin/kts200502040954.asp "Real economists . . . call such a thing not a loan, but an 'opportunity cost'."

44. http://www.ssa.gov/OACT/solvency/RPozen_20050210.pdf.

45. http://georgewbush-whitehouse.archives.gov/news/releases/2005/02/20050204-7.html. The full quote was: "(As) a result of living longer, you've got people who have been made promises by the government, receiving checks for a longer period of time than was initially envisioned under Social Security. Secondly, the benefits that had been promised are increasing, so you've got more—and thirdly, baby boomers like me and (Senator) Hagel and a bunch of others are getting ready to retire. So you've got *more people retiring, living longer, with the promise of greater benefits.* The problem is, is that the number of people putting money into the system (per beneficiary) is declining. So you can see the mathematical problem, right? Greater promises to more people who are living longer, with fewer payers. That's a problem—particularly when you start doing the math. And it's summed up by this chart, that says, in 2018—the facts are, in 2018, that the amount of money going out of Social Security is greater than the amount of money coming into Social Security. And as you can see from the chart, it gets worse every year. That's what that red means. So . . . for example, in 2027, the amount of money

required for the government to come up with to meet the promises is $200 billion above the payroll taxes collected."

46. http://georgewbush-whitehouse.archives.gov/news/releases/2005/02/20050204-7.html. The full quote follows: "Let me just say right off the bat, I'm open for any idea except raising payroll taxes to solve the problem. If anybody—(applause)—anybody has got an idea, bring it forth. I don't care if it's a Democrat idea, or a Republican idea, or an independent idea, I'm interested in working with the people who end up writing the law to come up with a good idea. And so all options are on the table, as I said in the State of the Union the other night. Bring them on, and we'll sit down and we'll have a good discussion about how to get something done. I think it's really important that the Congress understand that's how I feel. And we're not going to play political 'gotcha.' Dealing with our—dealing with the security of our youngsters is vital. And now is not the time to make this issue a highly partisan issue. I really mean that when I say that."

47. http://www.nytimes.com/2005/01/16/magazine/16SOCIAL.html, http://money.cnn.com/2004/12/15/retirement/what_crisis/; http://usliberals.about.com/b/2005/03/03/there-is-no-crisis-in-social-security.htm; http://www.talkingpointsmemo.com/archives/week_2005_01_30.php, http://www.cbpp.org/cms/index.cfm?fa=view&id=1453.

48. http://www.cbpp.org/cms/?fa=view&id=67.

49. CBS News/New York Times Poll, June 10-15, 2005. NBC News/Wall Street Journal Poll conducted by the polling organizations of Peter Hart (D) and Bill McInturff (R), May 12-16, 2005. Associated Press/Ipsos poll conducted by Ipsos-Public Affairs, May 2-4, 2005. FOX News/Opinion Dynamics Poll, March 29-30, 2005. ABC News/Washington Post Poll, March 10-13, 2005.

50. http://www.pbs.org/newshour/bb/congress/jan-june05/reid_2-17.html.

51. http://schumer.senate.gov/new_website/record.cfm?id=260923&; http://www.housedems.com/news/article/democrats-assail-social-security-reform-plan.

52. http://www.ssa.gov/OACT/solvency/index.html. The Bennett plan lacks personal accounts, but was not introduced until 2006 (Bennett has orally expressed support for personal accounts as well). The Diamond-Orszag proposal lacks personal accounts and would be sustainably solvent, but was not introduced in Congress. The DeFazio proposal lacked personal accounts but was not sustainably solvent. All other congressional proposals that would achieve sustainable solvency include a personal account.

53. http://archive.democracycorps.com/reports/analyses/Democracy_Corps_February_2005_Analysis.pdf.

54. Examples included Finance Committee Chairman Chuck Grassley, Senator Lindsey Graham, and Congressman Jim Kolbe.

55. http://waysandmeans.house.gov/hearings.asp?formmode=view&id=2520.

56. In addition to the February 3, 2005, *Washington Post* story described earlier, there were several other notable examples. After the State of the Union (SOTU), *Newsweek* published a piece indicating that the White House's SOTU briefing showed support for Social Security Commission Model 2, in which the basic Social Security benefit formula would be price-indexed. This was neither said in the briefing nor implied, nor did it represent the behind-the-scenes thinking of the Bush administration. No correction was issued.

57. http://www.washingtonpost.com/wp-dyn/articles/A19257-2005Jan18.html, http://query.nytimes.com/gst/fullpage.html?res=9C02E5DD133DF931A3 5750C0A9639C8B63&sec=&spon=, http://www.washingtonpost.com/wp-dyn/articles/A12913-2005Mar30.html.

58. There were exceptions that bridged these perspectives, such as Sebastian Mallaby's http://www.washingtonpost.com/wp-dyn/articles/A32587-2005Mar13 .html?nav, in which Mallaby made the proper substantive case that "Social Security's deficit does need to be fixed, and the fix will be harder if we miss the current opportunity," while also arguing a political case that "the Democrats have no proposal of their own. They sound negative and irresponsible."

59. ". . . (A)nd the Democrats' Reply: Cynicism That Needs to Stop" *Washington Post* editorial, August 4, 2006.

60. http://www.generationstogether.net/about_generations.aspx.

61. http://americansunitedforchange.org/about/.

62. http://www.factcheck.org/aarp_claims_bushs_plan_is_a_homewrecker.html.

63. http://faculty.chicagobooth.edu/austan.goolsbee/research/ssecfees.pdf.

64. "An Assessment of the Proposals of the President's Commission to Strengthen Social Security," Diamond-Orszag, August 2002.

65. Robert J. Shiller, "The Life-Cycle Personal Accounts Proposal for Social Security: A Review," Working Paper 11,300, National Bureau of Economic Research, Cambridge, Massachusetts, May 2005.

66. These are well explained in Andrew Biggs's paper, "Social Insecurity," http://www.aei.org/outlook/28971. This paper concludes that the vast majority of account holders would have received an increase in total benefits. "These findings, which appear to support personal accounts invested in stocks and bonds, are contrary to Shiller's. This seems odd at first glance because the results here are built upon his data and methods. Shiller's paper was widely perceived to show that accounts would not be a good deal for a large number of participants. Specifically, Shiller concluded that almost one-third of cohorts would fail to break even if accounts were simulated relative to historical returns. If future stock returns were below the historical average, Shiller projects, more than 70 percent of cohorts might lose money. How could such similar simulations offer such contrary conclu-

sions? . . . Shiller's approach accurately represents the Bush proposal. Problems arise, however, because Shiller applies this interest rate not prospectively but retrospectively. His modeling mixes a 3 percent offset interest rate based on projections of *future* bond rates with a data set of *historical* bond returns that may be quite different. . . . The key factor is the *placement* of bond returns throughout the historical sample . . . the model first simulates a cohort investing from 1871 through 1915, then a second cohort investing from 1872 through 1916, and so on. This technique implies that returns at the beginning and end of the sample period will have less influence on the overall results than those toward the middle . . . As it happens, however, actual government bond returns at the beginning and end of the 1871-2008 period are significantly higher than those toward the middle."

67. http://www.foxnews.com/projects/pdf/033105_poll2.pdf.

68. http://www.cbsnews.com/stories/2005/03/02/opinion/polls/main677680.shtml.

69. http://georgewbush-whitehouse.archives.gov/news/releases/2005/04/20050428-7.html.

70. http://www.opinionjournal.com/extra/?id=110006627.

71. This effect, obviously, could be avoided by turning off progressive indexing by a certain date.

72. As noted earlier, the correctness of this argument depends on the discount rate applied to future federal spending.

73. http://www.cbpp.org/cms/?fa=view&id=348.

74. http://www.cbpp.org/cms/?fa=view&id=234.

75. http://www.cbpp.org/cms/?fa=view&id=48.

76. http://www.factcheck.org/social-security/a_rigged_calculator.html; Factcheck.org, "A Rigged Calculator."

77. CBS New York Times Poll, June 10-15, 2005.

78. http://www.nationalreview.com/beltway/062069.html.

79. CNN/USA Today/Gallup Poll. April 29-May 1, 2005.

80. CBS News Poll. May 20-24, 2005.

81. http://www.ssa.gov/OACT/NOTES/ran5/index.html, See Table A.

82. http://www.house.gov/pelosi/press/releases/May05/sswomen.html.

83. http://www.house.gov/pelosi/press/releases/May05/sswomen.html.

84. http://www.retiredamericans.org/skins/ara1/pdf/ssvideo/SS_Primer_videokit.pdf.

85. Even the harshest critics among serious opposition analysts conceded in the fine print of their articles that even the president's incomplete proposals would have improved system solvency in the aggregate.

86. CBS New York Times Poll. June 10-15, 2005.

11. *The Certainty and Severity of the Social Security Shortfall*

1. http://www.ssa.gov/history/gwbushstmts5.html. The link reproduces the text of President Bush's speeches throughout early 2005, which can be readily searched for words such as "crisis" and "problem."

2. http://www.ssa.gov/history/clntstmts.html.

3. http://dccc.org/newsroom/entry/20050217_shays/, http://www.democrats .org/a/2005/05/bankrupt_social.php. http://www.washingtonpost.com/wp-dyn/ articles/A866-2005Jan11.html.

4. http://www.ssa.gov/OACT/TR/2009/lr5b1.html.

5. The most relevant historical period for comparisons is a subject of constant evaluation by analysts supporting both the Social Security trustees and the Congressional Budget Office. But whether one compares with the last three, four, or five business cycles, the trustees' future productivity projections are generally consistent with past experience.

6. http://www.ssa.gov/OACT/TR/2009/lr5b2.html.

7. http://www.bea.gov/regional/gsp/.

8. http://www.ssab.gov/Publications/Financing/tech99.pdf; http://www.ssab .gov/documents/2003TechnicalPanelRept_000.pdf,

9. http://robertreich.blogspot.com/2009/05/truth-behind-social-security -and.html.

10. Saul Friedman, "Emboldening Social Security," *Newsday,* May 12, 2007.

11. http://www.csmonitor.com/2006/0508/p17s01-cogn.html.

12. Jonathan Weisman, "Post Politics Hour," April 27, 2007, http://www .washingtonpost.com/wp-dyn/discussion/2007/04/23/DI2007042301225_pf.html.

13. In the neighborhood of 2.4 percent annually. There exists no time period from 1951 through the present (i.e., 1951-2008, 1952-2008, 1953-2008) over which average annual productivity growth has remained this high.

14. http://www.ssa.gov/OACT/TR/2009/lr5b1.html.

15. One could argue that wage growth will increase somewhat as labor force growth decelerates, and the trustees' projections do posit a future increase in the rate of real wage growth. As the subsequent section documents, however, even a doubling of real wage growth rates doesn't come close to eliminating the shortfall.

16. http://www.ssa.gov/OACT/TR/2009/VI_stochastic.html#105337.

17. http://www.ssa.gov/OACT/TR/2009/VI_stochastic.html#105337.

18. http://www.ssa.gov/OACT/TR/2009/lr5a4.html.

19. http://www.ssa.gov/OACT/TR/2009/lr5a1.html.

20. http://www.ssa.gov/OACT/TR/2009/lr5b1.html.

21. http://www.marketwatch.com/story/why-social-security-isnt-going -broke.

22. http://robertreich.blogspot.com/2009/05/truth-behind-social-security-and.html.

23. http://www.prospect.org/cs/articles?article=there_is_no_social_security _crisis, Paul Waldman, "There Is No Social Security Crisis," *The American Prospect,* February 24, 2009.

24. "Wage Growth and the Measurement of Social Security's Financial Condition," Andrew Biggs and Jagadeesh Gokhale, Cato Institute, June 2006.

25. http://www.ssa.gov/OACT/TR/2009/VI_LRsensitivity.html#93098.

26. http://budget.senate.gov/democratic/statements/2005/hrngstmt_socsec-finankc042605.pdf.

27. http://www.washingtonmonthly.com/archives/individual/2005_01/ 005467.php.

28. Charles Blahous, "Have the Social Security Trustees Been Too Conservative?" Presentation to the American Enterprise Institute, September 7, 2007.

29. http://www.ssa.gov/history/reports/trust/1996/appendices.htm.

30. http://www.ssa.gov/history/reports/trust/1983/1983c.pdf. See p. 74.

31. http://www.ssa.gov/history/reports/trust/1983/1983d.pdf. See p. 96.

32. http://www.ssa.gov/OACT/TR/2009/V_economic.html#133682.

33. http://www.cbo.gov/ftpdocs/96xx/doc9649/AppendixB.5.1.shtml.

34. http://www.washingtonmonthly.com/archives/individual/2004_12/ 005316.php.

35. http://robertreich.blogspot.com/2009/05/truth-behind-social-security -and.html.

12. President Bush's Reform Initiative

1. Again, progressive indexation would have resolved the majority but not the entire Social Security shortfall, and thus it was left open whether a complete proposal to attain Social Security solvency would do the rest of the job by raising taxes or further constraining costs. Congress never indicated how the rest of the shortfall should be made up, and philosophically the president clearly favored cost containment over tax increases.

2. http://www.epi.org/publications/entry/ib211/; http://ncpssm.altruistmedia. com/progressive-price-indexing-and-social-security-benefits; http://www.cbpp.org/ cms/?fa=view&id=48.

3. http://www.house.gov/pelosi/press/releases/May05/sswomen.html.

4. http://www.ssa.gov/OACT/TR/TR05/lr6F2-2.html.

5. http://www.ssa.gov/history/pdf/tr05summary.pdf.

6. http://www.ssa.gov/OACT/solvency/RPozen_20050210.pdf.

7. http://www.ssa.gov/OACT/solvency/provisions_tr2005/charts/chart_run184.html.

8. http://www.ssa.gov/OACT/solvency/provisions_tr2005/charts/chart_run218.html.

9. http://www.ssa.gov/OACT/solvency/provisions_tr2005/charts/chart_run219.html.

10. http://www.ssa.gov/OACT/solvency/provisions_tr2005/charts/chart_run220.html.

11. http://www.ssa.gov/OACT/solvency/provisions_tr2005/charts/chart_run143.html.

12. http://www.ssa.gov/OACT/solvency/provisions_tr2005/tables/table_run143.html. To perform the calculation, one must account for the fact that the proposal would change the definition of "taxable payroll." See the rightmost column in the actuary's chart. In its 2009 estimates, the SSA Actuary has helpfully performed this adjustment for the reader in the primary figures that it reports. Also, as explained in chapter 4, under the program's current structure, raising the cap would actually increase outgoing benefit costs by obligating additional benefit payments to affected participants.

13. http://aging.senate.gov/events/hr211ab.pdf.

14. http://query.nytimes.com/gst/fullpage.html?res=950DE0DE1F31F931A35756C0A9639C8B63&sec=&spon=&pagewanted=1.

15. http://www.house.gov/pelosi/press/releases/May05/sswomen.html.

16. All figures in this paragraph are 2005 figures. In 2010, the tax cap is $106,800 and the upper fifteenth percentile of the wage distribution is in the $60,000s.

17. Sometimes critics of progressive indexing made favorable references to the Diamond-Orszag proposal as a preferable alternative. See http://www.cbpp.org/cms/?fa=view&id=48 in which it is noted that the Diamond-Orszag proposal would affect scheduled benefits less than would progressive indexing. This is true, but only because the Diamond-Orszag proposal would impose its "pain" primarily on the tax side. Workers at all wage levels (including the poorest) would be hit with the plan's increase in the payroll tax rate, which would climb from 12.4 percent to 15.36 percent within the valuation period and continue to rise thereafter. The plan would also increase the cap on taxable wages, affecting another 22 percent of workers. Many of these would be assessed a further "legacy charge," a tax on income above the cap. The plan also contains changes to the rate of growth of benefits as well, though these would be largely offset by other benefit increases for

the poorest workers. Overall, however, the Diamond-Orszag proposal is *less* progressive than President Bush's, meaning that it would require middle- and lower-income workers to shoulder a higher share of the burden in attaining sustainable solvency. The chief difference is that the Diamond-Orszag proposal would impose these costs primarily in the form of higher taxes.

18. "Making Social Security's benefit formula this progressive could risk undermining some of the broad-based political support that Social Security enjoys." See http://www.cbpp.org/cms/?fa=view&id=48.

19. "Indeed, it may be argued that the President's plan is not progressive enough. As noted, his plan would apply the *same* magnitude of benefit reductions to a worker whose annual earnings average $90,000 as to one whose annual earnings average $9 million. Someone making $60,000 annually would get about 85 percent as large a percentage benefit reduction as the individual who makes $9 million." See http://www.cbpp.org/cms/?fa=view&id=234 It should be noted in response to this criticism that historically Social Security has always based benefits on taxable earnings, meaning that the Social Security system has always paid the same benefits to someone who earns $90,000 as someone who earns $9 million. Thus, any changes to the benefit formula would apply to the same degree to each such worker. This feature of Social Security has nothing to do with progressive indexing but results from the historic design of the program in which benefits are tied only to earnings below the cap on taxable wages. Because this is a feature of the *current* Social Security system, the criticism could be applied just as readily to virtually *any* slowing of the growth of future benefits, even highly progressive changes.

20. The statement is attributed to Senator Trent Lott (R-MS).

21. http://www.cbpp.org/cms/?fa=view&id=48.

22. http://www.ssa.gov/OACT/TR/2009/lr6f10.html.

23. http://www.ssa.gov/OACT/TR/2009/lr6f2.html.

24. http://www.ssa.gov/OACT/solvency/provisions/charts/chart_run204.html, with adjustments for the changes in the projections after the 2008 trustees' report.

25. http://www.cbpp.org/cms/?fa=view&id=234, see the appendix.

26. http://www.ssa.gov/OACT/solvency/RPozen_20050210.pdf, Table 1b.c, see column for changes in annual unified budget cash flow.

27. Calculations based on Pozen memo, http://www.ssa.gov/OACT/solvency/RPozen_20050210.pdf, but updated for the Bush administration's lower benefit offset rate and 2009 benefit projections.

28. http://georgewbush-whitehouse.archives.gov/stateoftheunion/2005/index.html.

29. This is slightly different from President Bush's proposal insofar as the treatment of the disabled is concerned.

30. http://www.cbpp.org/files/2-2-05socsec4.pdf.

31. http://cbo.gov/ftpdocs/70xx/doc7069/03-14-PresidentsBudget.pdf.

32. http://www.gpoaccess.gov/usbudget/fy06/pdf/budget/overview.pdf, see page 4.

33. Minus administrative costs and the effects of pre-retirement inheritances.

34. http://www.cbpp.org/cms/?fa=view&id=261. This paper, for example, finds that President Bush's proposals would close 24 percent of the shortfall. Advocates for his proposals would argue that they would close far more of the shortfall, but both sides agreed that the net effect was *positive.*

35. "Gross debt" and "debt subject to limit" are not exactly the same, but the differences are not significant enough to treat here.

36. http://www.ipi.org/ipi/IPIPressReleases.nsf/0/54104fea4414f1a485256f9d0080594d?OpenDocument.

37. In the last section, we reviewed how personal accounts might be seen as either lessening or worsening the traditional system's shortfall depending on the scorekeeping, the design of the accounts, and assumptions about discount rates, political economy, and other factors. This is a separate question from how personal accounts affect the net benefit losses that current and future generations must expect in the course of repairing the system's financial shortfall. Personal accounts could, for example, be designed so as to either lessen or increase the net shortfall of the traditional part of the Social Security system. This doesn't change the fact that the personal accounts don't change the *total* fiscal shortfall that current and future generations inevitably face.

38. "Guaranteed" is in quotation marks here because no Social Security benefit is "guaranteed" in that it can be changed at any time under law. The point is that, to the extent that a benefit is being represented as free of investment risk, it cannot be funded less expensively by investing in risk-bearing investments.

39. Zvi Bodie, Harvard Business School Working Paper no. 95-013 (December 1994): "For guarantors of money-fixed annuities, the proposition that stocks in their portfolio are a better hedge the longer the maturity of their obligations is unambiguously wrong." See http://papers.ssrn.com/sol3/papers.cfm?abstract_id=5771.

40. http://article.nationalreview.com/?q=MTE0YjlhNjYwYjQwNjk4MmQ0ZTc2NmQ3MzM3MMjVlNGQ=.

41. http://www.ssa.gov/OACT/solvency/CShaw_20050512.pdf, and http://www.ssa.gov/OACT/solvency/PFerrara_20031201.html, among others.

42. It's unclear whether a posture of embracing a Social Security solution requiring trillions in additional tax revenue infusions can fairly be called a "conservative" position.

43. http://www.ssa.gov/history/ssa/ssa2000chapter3.html.

44. http://www.ssa.gov/OACT/solvency/AARP_20080619.pdf. This proposal refers only to "options" and represents two particular members of the AARP Public Policy Institute, but AARP has sporadically expressed support for the concept of investing the Trust Fund in the stock market. Interestingly, the same memorandum discusses a provision to impose a "legacy tax" on earnings above the taxable maximum, which would sever the contribution-benefit connection by not counting toward benefits. At various times AARP has expressed vigorous opposition to severing the contribution-benefit link, but has curiously entertained occasional proposals to do so at other times.

45. See http://www.ssa.gov/OACT/solvency/DeFazio_20011130.html and http://www.ssa.gov/OACT/solvency/RBall_20050414.html, among others.

46. Nor has the search for "free lunch" solutions been confined to advocates of stock investments. In 2007, for example, some attempted to assert that closing the "tax gap" (the gap between all taxes owed and collected) could be a meaningful start to the Social Security solvency discussion and a way of avoiding other tough choices. See http://www.ncpssm.org/pdf/senate_ss_funding.pdf. In reality, closing the "tax gap" is probably more likely to increase Social Security's deficit than to reduce it, because it involves payment failures by many low-income self-employed who would receive very high returns in Social Security benefits if their taxes were paid.

13. Seizing the Common Ground

1. Of the proposals listed in the table at the close of chapter 9, all would attain sustainable annual cash surpluses by the end of the seventy-five-year valuation period except for the Diamond-Orszag and Hagel proposals. Each of these two plans comes extremely close and could be tweaked slightly (roughly 0.3 percent of taxable payroll in the seventy-fifth year) to attain the standard.

2. The Kolbe-Boyd proposal envisions a change in CPI. In the OACT memo on Kolbe-Boyd, the provision is implemented by subtracting 0.4 percent from CPI, but the authors have stated that the intention is to reflect an actual reform of the CPI calculation. http://www.ssa.gov/OACT/solvency/Kolbe_20051104.pdf.

3. This section glosses over whether increasing the taxation of Social Security benefits should be on the table. Though technically not a "benefit change," a near-term change in this policy would change the dollar amount of benefits seniors receive after taxation. As a practical matter, congressional authors have tended to shy away from increasing benefit taxes. Republicans' aversion to raising taxes as well as both parties' aversion to adversely affecting current seniors make it unlikely that benefit taxes would be increased for those now receiving benefits.

4. The same caveat applies with respect to CPI reform that applied in the previous section on current beneficiaries.

5. http://www.cbo.gov/ftpdocs/56xx/doc5665/07-21-KolbeLongTermLetter .pdf.

6. http://www.ssa.gov/OACT/solvency/Liebman_20051117.pdf.

7. http://www.ssa.gov/OACT/solvency/RBennett_20090212.pdf.

8. http://www.cbo.gov/ftpdocs/60xx/doc6044/12-22-Diamond-Orszag.pdf.

9. For the majority, however, we can only afford considerably less than the full rate of wage-indexed growth under the current benefit formula.

10. The intention would be to finance the general revenue transfers through the implementation of the recommendations of a commission to reduce corporate welfare.

11. Through the end of the valuation period, the payroll tax rate would exceed 15 percent and would be applied to a base roughly 12 percent larger than under current law.

12. http://www.ssa.gov/OACT/solvency/RBennett_20090212.pdf.

13. The Gramlich proposal was developed for the 1994-96 Advisory Council under the contemporaneous assumptions of the Social Security Trustees. It is mentioned here because it has a philosophical kinship with other more recent proposals. It is not analyzed at greater length, as too much time has passed for the Gramlich proposal itself to be implemented.

14. For all actuarial analyses of these proposals, see http://www.ssa.gov/ OACT/solvency/index.html. The Ball proposal would collect significant additional tax revenues up front but is not sustainable on an annual cash basis, and in any case found no congressional support.

15. This is the glaring flaw in options lists compiled by groups such as AARP. Individual provisions on these lists might stand a chance of garnering congressional support, but listing provisions' effects separately in no way implies that they would add up to a sensible whole. One option list compiled by AARP, for example, is nearly certain to produce a combined result that congressional negotiators would reject for its implausible net effect on annual spending trends, even as the separate provisions appear to add up to seventy-five-year actuarial balance. See http://www.ssa.gov/OACT/solvency/AARP_20080619.html.

16. Congressional opponents of personal accounts have on occasion authored proposals, but these would not achieve sustainable solvency.

17. The Clinton administration released a Universal Savings Account proposal toward this end. The Obama administration supports auto-IRA legislation essentially similar to the proposal developed by David John of the Heritage Foundation and Mark Iwry of the Brookings Institution, which is not technically "universal" but would be extended to workers in firms with ten or more employees.

18. These are not mutually exclusive camps; some support both.

19. This is an important caveat to reflect the ethic of the leading bipartisan plans, such as the LMS plan and Kolbe-Boyd.

20. As one example, see http://keithhennessey.com/2009/07/17/hennessey health-plan/. Congress did not implement this reform as part of the 2010 health care legislation. The 2010 health care bill did include a tax on "Cadillac" employer-provided plans, but the vast majority of the differential tax treatment of health care compensation remains.

21. Hypothesize a personal account in which X percent of worker wages are contributed to the personal accounts starting today. These accounts pre-fund an equal amount of future Social Security benefits, in present-value dollars. Determine which level of X percent produces the least variation in the ratio of benefit replacement rates to lifetime cost burdens, each expressed as a percentage of taxable worker wages.

22. Thanks to Jonathan Swanson and Andrew Biggs for the calculations. The answer is imprecise and depends on many assumptions, including projected returns from personal accounts. The optimal size, from a generational equity perspective, for accounts earning only a Treasury bond return would be in excess of 3 percentage points of worker wages; 2.5 percent is closer to the answer generated if it is assumed that the accounts earn the returns associated with SSA's higher intermediate portfolio assumptions. This author believes that the analysis based on Treasury bond returns is analytically more meaningful but nevertheless would favor the conservative choice of the smaller account size, given other near-term fiscal pressures and the resulting uncertainty that the full amount of a larger account would increase national saving.

23. Andrew Biggs, "Will Your Social Insurance Pay Off?" American Enterprise Institute (January 2009), http://www.aei.org/outlook/29198.

24. http://www.ssa.gov/OACT/NOTES/ran5/index.html. See Table A in the April 2009 report on internal rates of return.

25. The calculations assume that the exclusion would be set at $13,000 and would ultimately be indexed to the growth of health inflation.

26. The proposal by Rep. Nick Smith (R-MI) was introduced in various forms before his retirement from Congress. It is worth mentioning here because its fiscal achievements would have been comparable to the most tightly constructed plans introduced over the last decade. It is not analyzed here at greater length, as our text focuses on plans that have remained more prominent in the current Social Security debate.

ABOUT THE AUTHOR

One of the nation's foremost Social Security experts, Chuck Blahous serves as one of two public trustees for the Social Security and Medicare programs. Blahous served as deputy director of President George W. Bush's National Economic Council, and before that as executive director of the president's bipartisan Social Security Commission and as Special Assistant for Economic Policy. Blahous previously served as legislative and policy director for U.S. Senators Alan Simpson and Judd Gregg. Blahous's career in public service began when he was named the American Physical Society's 1989–90 Congressional Science Fellow. He lives in Rockville, Maryland, with his wife and daughter.

INDEX

Aaron, Henry J., 37, 54–55

AARP. *See* American Association of Retired Persons

ABC/Washington Post poll, 254

academia, 379–80

accounting, xiv; analysis of, 287; federal debt and, 99; interpreting, xvi; personal accounts and, 174; post-1988, 75–79; transparency, 95–96

actuarial balance, 9; annual imbalances and, 350; average cost method, 69; effects of progressive indexing and personal accounts on, 315; level financing method, 68–69; transition costs and, 286

actuarial method, 30, 190

administrative costs, 183–84, 187, 234

advance funding. *See* pre-funding

AEI. *See* American Enterprise Institute

aggregate payments, growth of, 48

AIME. *See* average indexed monthly earnings

American Association of Retired Persons (AARP): free lunch solution and, 334; Greenspan Commission and, 43; investment risk and, 182; lobbying efforts of, 70; Medicare prescription drug bill and, 226; NAM and, 225–27; personal accounts and, 207; reform initiative of 2005 and, 214–15, 251–53; reforms and, 43–44; seventy-five-year balance and, 18; Social Security Trust Fund investing and, 95; Treasury bonds and, 52–53

American Enterprise Institute (AEI), 80, 277

American Prospect, 276

annual operations, 71, 92, 312

annuitization: over, 175, 186; of personal accounts, 185

AOL-Time-Warner, 212

Archer, Bill, 95

Asner, Ed, 207

average cost method, 69

average earnings profile, 6

average indexed monthly earnings (AIME), 6, 21; calculating, 163; reformulating, 370

average-lifetime-indexed-taxable-wage income, 21

baby boomers, 9–10; Bush references to, 242–43; labor force growth and, 269–70; pre-funding and, 60–61, 133; surge in costs for, 290; surge of, 48; surpluses for, 82

Baker, Dean, 49

Baker, Howard, 26, 39

Balanced Budget Act of 1997, 96–97

Ball, Robert, 39, 85, 88, 94–95, 225

bankruptcy, 268–69

baselines, shifting, 295

bend points, 365–67, 366f

benefit costs. *See* costs

Breinigsville, PA USA
27 October 2010
248189BV00002B/7/P